ASVAB

ASVAB

Fourth Edition

NEW YORK

Library of Congress Cataloging-in-Publication Data:
ASVAB. —4th ed.
      p. cm.
  ISBN 978-1-57685-741-0
  1. Armed Services Vocational Aptitude Battery—Study guides. I. LearningExpress (Organization) II. Title:
Armed Services Vocational Aptitude Battery.
  U408.5.A83 2010
  355.00973—dc22

                                            2009036754

Printed in the United States of America

9 8 7 6 5 4 3 2

Fourth Edition

ISBN-10 1-57685-741-7
ISBN-13 978-1-57685-741-0

For information or to place an order, contact LearningExpress at:
   2 Rector Street
   26th Floor
   New York, NY 10006

Or visit us at:
   www.learnatest.com

Contents ▶

Contributors

The following individuals contributed to the content of this book.

Pamela Harrell is an editor and writer living in New York City; she has a Master of Science degree in entomology.

Clay McGann is an electrical engineer who designs electrical systems for space launch vehicles.

CDR Bill Paisley is a former F-14 Tomcat radar intercept officer with 25 years active and reserve service. He holds two undergraduate degrees in education and a masters of arts in National Security. He lives in northern Virginia and works as a modeling and simulation professional for the U.S. Navy.

Shirley Tarbell is a test development specialist and writer living in Portland, Maine.

Steven Truitt, P.E., is a civil engineer and technical writer specializing in environmental engineering and pollution control in Golden, Colorado.

ASVAB

CHAPTER 1

ABOUT
THE ASVAB

CHAPTER SUMMARY

This chapter will introduce the Armed Services Vocational Aptitude Battery (ASVAB), describe what is included on the test, and explain how this book can help you prepare and achieve maximum exam success.

The Armed Services Vocational Aptitude Battery (ASVAB) is a multiple-aptitude test taken by over 800,000 Americans every year. It is comprised of timed subtests in different subjects that measure the range of aptitudes necessary for military enlistment and job placement. A breakdown of these subtests—by test version—is shown in the table on pages 2–3, and a more detailed description of each subtest test appears later in this chapter.

The ASVAB, which was created by the United States Department of Defense in 1968 and adopted by all armed services by 1976, is used for two main purposes:

- **As a military recruiting tool.** The United States Department of Defense uses the ASVAB to determine the abilities of potential recruits, to gauge what they already know about certain subjects, to measure their general learning and vocational aptitude; and to predict performance in certain academic areas.
- **As a guide for high school and post-secondary school students.** The ASVAB helps students make decisions about their career paths, whether in the military or in some other field.

ASVAB: Paper and Pencil vs. CAT

Individuals can expect to take a paper and pencil version of the ASVAB at their local high school or a neighboring school offering the test. The student version of the exam (offered to high school juniors and seniors) is often referred to as the *institutional* version; candidates for military enlistment take the *production* version.

Depending on where an enlistee takes the ASVAB, he or she will take either the computer version of the ASVAB, called the CAT-ASVAB, or the paper-and-pencil version. Candidates taking the ASVAB at a Military Entrance Processing Station (MEPS) will take the computer version, while candidates for enlistment taking the ASVAB at a reserve center or Mobile Examination Team (MET) site will take the paper-and-pencil version.

The paper and pencil version of the ASVAB consists of either eight subtests (if you're a student) or nine subtests (if you're a candidate for enlistment). The majority of military applicants, approximately 70%, take the CAT-ASVAB. The CAT-ASVAB is a computer-adaptive test, which means that the test adapts to your ability level. The computer will give you the first question, and, if you answer correctly, it gives you another question on the same subject—but one that is a bit harder than the first. The questions get harder as you progress, and after you answer a certain number of questions correctly the computer skips to the next subtest.

The following is additional information about the CAT-ASVAB:

- It consists of ten subtests—the Auto Information and Shop Information subtests are administered separately. However, the results are combined into one score (labeled AS).
- The test takes about $1\frac{1}{2}$ hours to complete.
- Each subtest must be completed within a certain timeframe. Most individuals complete the subtests within the time alloted.
- Once you have completed a subtest, you do not have to wait for everyone else to finish—you can move on to the next subtest.
- As you complete each subtest, the computer displays the number of items and amount of time remaining for that subtest in the lower right-hand corner of the screen.
- Once an answer has been submitted, you cannot review or change it.
- Test scores are available as soon as you complete the test.
- If you choose to take the CAT-ASVAB, you will be trained on answering test questions, using the computer keyboard and mouse, and getting help before starting the exam.
- The number of subtests, number of questions, and time limits for the CAT-ASVAB differ from the paper-and-pencil version in the following ways:

NUMBERS OF ITEMS AND TESTING TIME FOR THE PAPER & PENCIL ASVAB		
Subtest	Number of Questions	Time (Minutes)
General Science (GS)	25	11
Arithmetic Reasoning (AR)	30	36
Word Knowledge (WK)	35	11
Paragraph Comprehension (PC)	15	13
Mathematics Knowledge (MK)	25	24

NUMBERS OF ITEMS AND TESTING TIME FOR THE PAPER & PENCIL ASVAB (continued)

Subtest	Number of Questions	Time (Minutes)
Electronics Information (EI)	20	9
Auto and Shop Information (AS)	25	11
Mechanical Comprehension (MC)	25	19
Assembling Objects* (AO)	25	15
Institutional Version Totals	**200 Items**	**134 Minutes**
Production Version Totals	**225 Items**	**149 Minutes**

*The Assembling Objects (AO) subtest is not included in the institutional version of the ASVAB taken by high school students as part of the ASVAB Career Exploration Program.

NUMBER OF ITEMS AND TESTING TIME FOR THE CAT-ASVAB

Subtest	Number of Questions	Time (Minutes)
General Science (GS)	16	8
Arithmetic Reasoning (AR)	16	39
Word Knowledge (WK)	16	8
Paragraph Comprehension (PC)	11	22
Mathematics Knowledge (MK)	16	20
Electronics Information (EI)	16	8
Auto Information (AI)	11	7
Shop Information (SI)	11	6
Mechanical Comprehension (MC)	16	20
Assembling Objects (AO)	16	16
Totals	**145 Items**	**154 Minutes**

The ASVAB Subtests

The following is a detailed description of each of the subtests on the ASVAB. Most sections of the ASVAB depend on your knowledge of the subject as covered in high school courses or other related reading. The two sections that do not depend on knowledge of the subjects in advance are the Paragraph Comprehension and Assembling Objects sections. For the Paragraph Comprehension questions, you will be able to find the answers using the information given in the paragraph provided. The Assembling Objects section tests your natural spatial aptitude skills.

Subtest 1: General Science

The General Science subtest consists of questions that are designed to measure your ability to recognize, apply, and analyze basic scientific principles in the areas of:

- **life science:** botany, zoology, anatomy and physiology, ecology
- **physical science:** force and motion, energy, fluids and gases, atomic structure, chemistry
- **earth and space science:** astronomy, geology, meteorology, oceanography

General Science questions are covered in Chapter 6 of this book.

Subtest 2: Arithmetic Reasoning

The Arithmetic Reasoning subtest consists of word problems describing everyday life situations, and is designed to measure your reasoning skills and understanding of:

- operations with whole numbers
- operations with fractions, decimals, and money
- ratio and proportion
- calculating interest and percentage
- measurement of perimeter, area, volume, time, and temperature

Arithmetic Reasoning questions are covered in Chapter 7 of this book.

Subtest 3: Word Knowledge

The Word Knowledge subtest consists of questions that ask you to choose the correct definitions of verbs, nouns, adjectives, and adverbs. These questions come in two forms:

- words presented alone, with no context
- words presented in the context of a short sentence

Word Knowledge questions are covered in Chapter 8 of this book.

Subtest 4: Paragraph Comprehension

The Paragraph Comprehension subtest consists of questions that are based on several short passages, written on a variety of topics. No prior knowledge of the subject is required—all the information you need to answer the questions will be found in the passage. The questions in this subtest are designed to test the following abilities:

- **literal comprehension:** ability to identify stated facts, reworded facts, and determine sequence of events
- **implicit, inferential, or critical comprehension:** ability to draw conclusions, identify the main idea of a paragraph, determine the author's purpose, mood, or tone, and identify style and technique
- **comprehension of main idea or words in context:** ability to condense a paragraph into a single main idea, and determine the meaning of an unfamiliar word based on its context or usage

Paragraph Comprehension questions are covered in Chapter 9 of this book.

Subtest 5: Mathematics Knowledge

The Mathematics Knowledge subtest contains questions designed to measure your understanding and ability to recognize and apply mathematical concepts, principles, and procedures. The questions cover:

- **number theory:** factors, multiples, reciprocals, number properties, primes, and integers
- **numeration:** fractions, decimals, percentages, conversions, order of operations, exponents, rounding, roots, radicals, and signed numbers
- **algebraic operations and equations:** solving or determining equations, factoring, simplifying algebraic expressions, and converting sentences to equations

- **geometry and measurement:** coordinates, slope, Pythagorean theorem, angle measurement, properties of polygons and circles, perimeter, area, volume, and unit conversion
- **probability:** analyzing and determining probability

Mathematics Knowledge questions are covered in Chapter 7 of this book.

Subtest 6: Electronics Information

The Electronics Information subtest consists of 20 questions that are designed to measure basic knowledge of principles of electrical and electronics systems:

- electrical tools, symbols, devices, and materials
- electrical circuits
- electricity and electronic systems
- electrical current, voltage, conductivity, resistance, and grounding

Electronics Information questions are covered in Chapter 12.

Subtest 7: Auto and Shop Information

The Auto and Shop Information subtest includes questions on automotive repair and building construction. General shop practices are also included. The CAT-ASVAB splits these two subtests into separate subtests, but combines results into one score. The questions cover the following topics:

- automotive components
- automotive systems
- automotive tools
- automotive troubleshooting and repair
- shop tools
- building materials
- building and construction procedures

Auto and Shop Information questions are covered in Chapter 10 of this book.

Subtest 8: Mechanical Comprehension

The Mechanical Comprehension subtest consists of problems—many of them illustrated—covering general mechanics, physical principles, and principles of simple machines such as gears, pulleys, levers, force, and fluid dynamics. Problems involving basic properties of materials are also included. The questions may test knowledge, application, and analysis of:

- **basic compound machines:** gears, cams, pistons, cranks, linkages, belts, and chains
- **simple machines:** levers, planes, pulleys, screws, wedges, wheels, and axles
- **mechanical motion:** friction, velocity, direction, acceleration, and centrifugal force
- **fluid dynamics:** hydraulic forces and compression
- **properties of materials:** weight, strength, expansion/contraction, absorption, and center of gravity
- **structural support**

Mechanical Comprehension questions are covered in Chapter 11.

Subtest 9: Assembling Objects

The Assembling Objects subtest consists of illustrated questions that test your ability to determine how an object should look when its parts are put together. These questions measure:

- general mechanics and physical principles
- aptitude for discerning spatial relations
- problem-solving abilities

Assembling Objects questions are covered in Chapter 13 of this book.

Arranging to Take the ASVAB

Over 14,000 high schools across the United States offer the ASVAB. If you are in high school, ask your guidance counselor about taking the ASVAB. Many high schools offer the ASVAB at a specific time during the school year. If you missed your school's offering of the ASVAB, chances are a neighboring school will be offering it at another time during the school year.

If you're out of high school, go to the nearest recruiter of the branch of the armed services that you're interested in. There is no charge to take the ASVAB. Taking the exam doesn't obligate you to join the military, although you can probably expect a persuasive sales pitch about the opportunities available in the Army, Air Force, Navy, Marine Corps, and U.S. Coast Guard. The military service in charge of maintaining the administrative elements of the ASVAB is the Army, but all armed services use the information provided by taking the test. For more details about the ASVAB, visit the ASVAB website at www.goarmy.com.

What the ASVAB Means for You

If you're taking the ASVAB as a high school student with no intention of entering the military, the test can help you find out what things you're good at and what areas might be good career paths. Your ASVAB results can also help you decide whether or not to go to college or get training for a specialized career in an area such as electronics. Your scores may also show you areas that you have less aptitude for. Your guidance counselor can explain your score report and how best to use it.

Approximately 500,000 people each year take the ASVAB in order to enlist in the military. Your scores on certain subtests of the ASVAB help determine your eligibility. Furthermore, once you're enlisted your scores on various subtests help determine which jobs, or Military Occupational Specialties, you'll be allowed to

train in. For example, if you want to learn how to be a computer operator, you need good scores in the Paragraph Comprehension, Word Knowledge, Mathematics Knowledge, General Science, and Mechanical Comprehension subtests. See Chapter 3 for more details on what your score means to your choice of military careers.

The bottom line is that you want to score well on the ASVAB if you're looking forward to a career in the armed forces, and this book is here to help.

Advice For Parents

As your son or daughter prepares for the transition to their next phase of life, there are a number of things you can do to help pave the way for a successful ASVAB experience and score. Chapter 4 of this book, "The LearningExpress Test Preparation System," provides valuable guidelines and suggestions for ways your child can prepare for this test. The nine-step process includes sections (such as Straight Talk about the ASVAB and Conquer Test Anxiety) that will address concerns you or your child may have about this exam, while the section titled Reach Your Performance Peak will provide valuable tips on how to do your best on test day.

The Internet can be a great source of ASVAB information and assistance as well. The ASVAB Career Exploration Program webpage, sponsored by the Department of Defense, is aimed at high school students and their parents and can be viewed at www.asvabprogram.com.

It's also important to remember that the ASVAB is not only for military recruits. It is offered at no cost to high school students across the nation and is a great tool for helping students determine their aptitude across a wide variety of technical, scientific, and social fields.

As a parent, your knowledge of your son or daughter's efforts and accomplishments over the years, coupled with your own experience, makes you an invaluable resource to your child. Being a positive and encouraging part of your child's ASVAB prep is a great way to help make his or her goals a reality.

How to Use This Book to Increase Your Score

The key to success in almost anything is preparation. One of the very best ways to prepare for the ASVAB is to read this book carefully, take the practice tests, measure how you're doing as you pass each milestone, and review and improve in the areas you're weakest in.

To ensure that you're clear on the basic information, be sure to read Chapter 2, which explains how the ASVAB fits into the recruitment and enlistment process. To learn more about the score you need for the job you want, read Chapter 3. Chapter 4 takes you through the 9-step LearningExpress Test Preparation System, which will help you get into top physical and mental shape for test day.

Armed with the knowledge you have gained in the first four chapters, take the ASVAB diagnostic test in Chapter 5. This test will help you see how you would perform if it were test day. Based on your score, you can determine your strengths and weaknesses and tailor the rest of your preparation accordingly. Chapters 6 through 13 include targeted review and practice for each of the subtests on the ASVAB.

Finally, Chapters 14 through 17 include four additional practice tests. Use these additional tests to track your progress. You can return to the review and practice chapters as needed to ensure that you are focusing on the material that you need the most help in. Remember, practice and preparation are the keys to doing well on this or any exam. This book will give you everything you need to score your best. Good luck!

C H A P T E R

GETTING INTO THE MILITARY

CHAPTER SUMMARY

You may find joining the military an appealing career choice. Once you have made the decision that the military is where you are headed, you will need to be armed with information about the enlistment process. That is what this chapter has to offer.

Your introduction to the military enlistment process usually starts with a visit to your local recruiting office. A search on the Internet for *military recruiter*, along with your geographical location, should provide you with the information you are looking for. Remember, all of the military service branches have a robust online presence through their various web pages, and you can find a great deal of information there:

- **Navy:** www.navy.com
- **Army:** www.goarmy.com
- **Air Force:** www.airforce.com
- **Marine Corp:** www.marines.com
- **United States Coast Guard:** www.gocoastguard.com

Don't narrow your options too soon, though. If you are thinking of a career in the military, visiting a recruiter from each of the five branches—Army, Navy, Air Force, Marines, and Coast Guard. There are lots of similarities, but the subtle differences in what each branch of service has to offer you could make a lot of difference in your career.

Basic Requirements

There are certain requirements you will have to meet in order to enlist in any branch of the military. Some of these requirements vary with each branch, so make sure you ask your recruiter any questions you may have. You must:

- be between 17 and 42 years of age, and have a parent or guardian's permission if you are under 18
- be a U.S. citizen or permanent resident with a green card
- have a high school diploma or GED
- be drug-free
- have a clean arrest record

It is important to be truthful with your recruiter about any trouble you have had in the past with drugs or with the law. Criminal history checks are conducted on applicants. However, some kinds of problems can be overcome, if they are really *in the past,* not current difficulties. Check with your recruiter.

Working with Your Recruiter

The recruiter is there to help you. In speaking with him or her, you will have the opportunity to ask as many questions as you want and to get a detailed picture of what each branch has to offer if you shop around. All recruiters will have brochures, videotapes, pamphlets, and years of personal experience to offer as resources. Don't be afraid to bring along a parent, guardian, or a trusted friend to help you ask questions. In fact, it is highly encouraged—they might ask helpful questions that you had not thought of.

You can ask about the service and its benefits—salaries and fringe benefits, postings, and educational opportunities, including financial aid for college once you get out. (See the table on pages 12–13 for the basic salary for various grades of enlisted personnel in all the services.) The recruiter will also ask about you: your education, your physical and mental health, and all sorts of in-depth questions about your goals, interests, hobbies, and life experience.

Before you take the Armed Services Vocational Aptitude Battery (ASVAB), you will be given a brief test designed to give the recruiter an idea of how well you will perform on the real test. This pretest covers math and vocabulary. Although the ASVAB has other subtests, it's the math and verbal portions that determine whether or not you pass the test. The other sections are designed to discover what your aptitudes are for different jobs. There is no limit to how many times you can take this brief test in the recruiter's office.

The recruiter will talk to you about the benefits of enlisting: the pay, the travel, the experience, the training. You and the recruiter can also start to discuss the kinds of jobs available to you in the military. But before that discussion can go very far, you will have to be tested to see, first, if you can enlist, and second, what specialties you qualify for. That's where your trip to the Military Entrance Processing Station comes in.

Military Entrance Processing Station (MEPS)

The recruiter will schedule you for a trip to a MEPS facility in your area (there are 65 facilities located throughout the United States) for required testing and evaluation. Depending on the service and location, your MEPS visit will take either one or two days. You will travel as a guest by plane, train, bus, or car, depending on how far you live from the nearest facility. MEPS schedules vary from area to area, but they all operate five days a week and are open a few Saturdays during the year.

The MEPS is where all applicants for every branch of the military begin the enlistment process. So, even if the Marine Corps is your future employer, you can expect to see staff wearing Navy blue, Army green, or Air Force blue. When you walk through the door,

Important Documents

Throughout the enlistment process, you will have to present certain documents. Have the following available to ensure you are prepared:

- birth certificate, proof of permanent residency, or other proof of citizenship and date of birth
- valid Social Security card or two other pieces of Social Security identification
- high school diploma or GED certificate
- letter or transcript documenting your midterm graduation from high school, if applicable
- college transcript, if applicable, showing credits earned
- parental or guardian consent form if you are under 18 years old
- doctor's letter if you have, or have a history of, special medical condition(s)
- marriage certificate, if applicable
- divorce papers, if applicable

you will check in at the control desk and be sent to the liaison office for your branch of the service.

Your MEPS Day at a Glance

During your day at MEPS you will go through three phases:

- mental (aptitude) testing
- medical exam
- administrative procedures

Your schedule may vary from the one outlined here, depending on how much of the process you have completed in advance. Some applicants, for example, may have already taken the ASVAB at a Mobile Examining Team (MET) site near their hometown recruiting station.

Mental (Aptitude) Testing

Your day at MEPS will most likely begin with the ASVAB, if you haven't already taken it. (See Chapter 1, "About the ASVAB") Don't underestimate the impact the ASVAB will have on your entry into the military. Results of the ASVAB test and the physical and mental exam you receive during the entrance process are used

to determine whether or not you can join the branch of the military you prefer and which training programs you are qualified to enter.

Some MEPS are now conducting ASVAB testing on computer. The computer version of the test takes one hour and forty minutes to complete, as opposed to over two hours for the paper-and-pencil version. The computer ASVAB works a little differently than the paper versions. The computer will give you the first question, and, if you get this question right, it gives you another question on the same subject—but this question is a bit harder than the first one. The questions get harder as you progress, and, after you answer a certain number correctly, the computer skips to the next subtest. So, you could get eight questions right, for example, and then the computer might go to the next subtest instead of requiring you to answer every question in that one subtest.

Most MEPS do not have enough computers to test everyone. If you notice that some applicants are taken to a room with the computer testing and the others are required to take the ASVAB with pencil and paper, don't worry. Either way, the information and skills you need remain the same.

2009 MILITARY MONTHLY BASE PAY RATES

Commissioned Officers

Pay Grade	Years of Service														
	Under 2	Over 2	Over 3	Over 4	Over 6	Over 8	Over 10	Over 12	Over 14	Over 16	Over 18	Over 20	Over 22	Over 24	Over 26
O–10	–	–	–	–	–	–	–	–	–	–	–	14,688.60	14,688.60	14,688.60	14,688.60
O–9	–	–	–	–	–	–	–	–	–	–	–	12,846.90	13,032.00	13,299.30	13,765.80
O–8	9,090.00	9,387.60	9,585.30	9,640.50	9,887.10	10,299.00	10,395.00	10,786.20	10,898.10	11,235.30	11,722.50	12,172.20	12,472.50	12,472.50	12,472.50
O–7	7,553.10	7,904.10	8,066.40	8,195.40	8,429.10	8,660.10	8,926.80	9,192.90	9,460.20	10,299.00	11,007.30	11,007.30	11,007.30	11,007.30	11,063.10
O–6	5,598.30	6,150.30	6,553.80	6,553.80	6,578.70	6,860.70	6,897.90	6,897.90	7,290.00	7,983.30	8,390.10	8,796.60	9,027.90	9,262.20	9,716.70
O–5	4,666.80	5,257.20	5,621.40	5,689.80	5,916.60	6,052.80	6,570.60	5073.30	6,853.80	7,287.30	7,493.40	7,697.40	7,928.70	7,928.70	7,928.70
O–4	4,026.90	4,661.40	4,972.20	5,041.80	5,330.40	5,640.00	6,325.50	4930.20	6,534.30	6,654.00	6,723.30	6,723.30	6,723.30	6,723.30	6,723.30
O–3	3,540.30	4,013.40	4,332.00	4,722.90	4,948.80	5,197.20	5,622.30	4441.20	5,759.70	5,759.70	5,759.70	5,759.70	5,759.70	5,759.70	5,759.70
O–2	3,058.80	3,483.90	4,012.50	4,148.10	4,233.30	4,233.30	4,233.30	3344.10	4,233.30	4,233.30	4,233.30	4,233.30	4,233.30	4,233.30	4,233.30
O–1	2,655.30	2,763.60	3,340.50	3,340.50	3,340.50	3,340.50	3,340.50	2638.50	3,340.50	3,340.50	3,340.50	3,340.50	3,340.50	3,340.50	3,340.50

Commissioned Officers with More Than Four Years of Active Service as an Enlisted Member or Warrant Officer

Pay Grade	Years of Service														
	Under 2	Over 2	Over 3	Over 4	Over 6	Over 8	Over 10	Over 12	Over 14	Over 16	Over 18	Over 20	Over 22	Over 24	Over 26
O–3E	–	–	–	4,722.90	4,948.80	5,197.20	5,358.00	5,622.30	5,844.90	5,972.70	6,146.70	6,146.70	6,146.70	6,146.70	6,146.70
O–2E	–	–	–	4,148.10	4,233.30	4,368.30	4,595.70	4,771.50	4,902.30	4,902.30	4,902.30	4,902.30	4,902.30	4,902.30	4,902.30
O–1E	–	–	–	3,340.50	3,567.60	3,699.30	3,834.30	3,966.60	4,148.10	4,148.10	4,148.10	4,148.10	4,148.10	4,148.10	4,148.10

Warrant Officers

Pay Grade	Years of Service														
	Under 2	Over 2	Over 3	Over 4	Over 6	Over 8	Over 10	Over 12	Over 14	Over 16	Over 18	Over 20	Over 22	Over 24	Over 26
W–5	–	–	–	–	–	–	–	–	–	–	–	6,505.50	6,835.50	7,081.20	7,353.60
W–4	3,658.50	3,935.70	4,048.80	4,159.80	4,351.20	4,540.50	4,732.20	5,021.10	5,274.00	5,514.60	5,711.40	5,903.40	6,185.70	6,417.30	6,681.90
W–3	3,340.80	3,480.30	3,622.80	3,669.90	3,819.60	4,114.20	4,420.80	4,574.70	4,731.90	4,904.10	5,213.10	5,422.20	5,547.30	5,680.20	5,860.80
W–2	2,956.50	3,236.10	3,322.20	3,381.60	3,573.30	3,871.20	4,018.80	4,164.30	4,341.90	4,480.80	4,606.80	4,757.10	4,856.40	4,935.00	4,935.00
W–1	2,595.30	2,874.00	2,949.60	3,108.30	3,286.50	3,572.70	3,701.70	3,882.30	4,059.90	4,199.40	4,328.10	4,484.40	4,484.40	4,484.40	4,484.40

2009 MILITARY MONTHLY BASE PAY RATES (continued)

Enlisted

Pay Grade	Years of Service														
	Under 2	Over 2	Over 3	Over 4	Over 6	Over 8	Over 10	Over 12	Over 14	Over 16	Over 18	Over 20	Over 22	Over 24	Over 26
E-9	–	–	–	–	–	–	4,420.50	4,520.70	4,646.70	4,795.50	4,944.90	5,185.20	5,388.00	5,601.90	5,928.30
E-8	–	–	–	–	–	3,618.60	3,778.80	3,877.80	3,996.60	4,125.00	4,357.20	4,474.80	4,674.90	4,785.90	5,059.50
E-7	2,515.50	2,745.60	2,850.60	2,990.10	3,098.70	3,285.30	3,390.30	3,577.50	3,732.60	3,838.50	3,951.30	3,995.40	4,142.10	4,221.00	4,521.00
E-6	2,175.60	2,394.00	2,499.60	2,602.20	2,709.30	2,950.80	3,044.70	3,226.20	3,282.00	3,322.50	3,369.90	3,369.90	3,369.90	3,369.90	3,369.90
E-5	1,993.50	2,127.00	2,229.60	2,334.90	2,499.00	2,670.90	2,811.00	2,828.40	2,828.40	2,828.40	2,828.40	2,828.40	2,828.40	2,828.40	2,828.40
E-4	1,827.60	1,920.90	2,025.00	2,127.60	2,218.50	2,218.50	2,218.50	2,218.50	2,218.50	2,218.50	2,218.50	2,218.50	2,218.50	2,218.50	2,218.50
E-3	1,649.70	1,753.50	1,859.70	1,859.70	1,859.70	1,859.70	1,859.70	1,859.70	1,859.70	1,859.70	1,859.70	1,859.70	1,859.70	1,859.70	1,859.70
E-2	1,568.70	1,568.70	1,568.70	1,568.70	1,568.70	1,568.70	1,568.70	1,568.70	1,568.70	1,568.70	1,568.70	1,568.70	1,568.70	1,568.70	1,568.70
E-1 >4	1,399.50	1,399.50	1,399.50	1,399.50	1,399.50	1,399.50	1,399.50	1,399.50	1,399.50	1,399.50	1,399.50	1,399.50	1,399.50	1,399.50	1,399.50
E-1 <4 w/less than 4 months	1,294.50														

Note: Basic Pay for O7–O10 is limited to level III of the executive schedule.
Note: Basic Pay for O6 and below is limited to level V of the executive schedule.

Medical Exam

Next is the medical exam. All of the doctors you will see at this point are civilians. You will see them at least three times during the day. During the first visit, you and the medical staff will thoroughly pore over your medical prescreening form, your medical history form, and all of the medical records you have been told by your recruiter to bring along. This meeting will be one-on-one.

After this meeting, you will move on to the examining room. You'll strip down to your underwear and perform a series of about 20 exercises that will let the medical staff see how your limbs and joints work. You may be with a group of other applicants of the same sex during this examination or you may be alone with the doctor.

Your third meeting with the doctor will be where you receive a routine physical. Among the procedures you can expect are:

- blood pressure evaluation
- pulse rate evaluation
- heart and lung check
- evaluation of blood and urine samples
- eye exam
- hearing exam
- height-proportional-to-weight check
- chest X-ray
- HIV test

Female applicants will be given a pelvic/rectal examination. Another woman will be present during this procedure, but otherwise this exam will be conducted in private.

After these checks, you will find out whether your physical condition is adequate. If the medical staff uncovers a problem that will keep you from joining the service, they will discuss the matter with you. In some cases the doctor may tell you that you are being disqualified at the moment, but that you can come back at a later date to try again. For example, if you are overweight, you could lose a few pounds and then come back to the MEPS for another try.

If the doctor wants to have a medical specialist examine you for some reason, you may have to stay overnight, or the doctor may schedule an appointment for a later date—at the military's expense, of course. Unless you do need to see a specialist, the medical exam should take no more than three hours.

Paper Work

The rest of your day will be taken up with administrative concerns. First you will meet with the guidance counselor for your branch of the service. He or she will take the results of your physical test, your ASVAB scores, and all the other information you have provided and enter this information into a computer system. The computer will show which military jobs are best suited to you. Then you can begin asking questions about your career options. Before you leave the room you will know:

- for which jobs you are qualified
- which jobs suit your personality, abilities, and interests
- which jobs are available
- when that training is available

You will also be able to decide whether you prefer to enter the military on this very day or to go in under the Delayed Entry Program. Some applicants raise their right hand during swearing-in ceremonies at the end of the processing day, while others prefer to go home and decide what they want to do.

Either way, it's critical that you ask as many questions as possible during this visit with the counselor. Take your time, and be sure you know what you want before you go any further in the process. Be aware, though, that the seats in the popular training programs go fast. The earlier you make your decision, the more likely you will have a chance to get what you really want.

Delayed Entry Programs

Delayed Entry Programs allow you to enlist with your chosen branch of the military and report for duty up to 365 days later. This is a popular program for students who are still in high school or for those who have other obligations that prevent them from leaving for Basic Training right away.

Officer

If your desire is to become an officer in the military, all service branches have enlisted-to-officer ascension programs where you can achieve your goal. The manner in which you perform your assignments during your enlisted commitment is one of the major criteria in being accepted to an enlisted-to-officer program, so scoring well on the ASVAB and getting assigned in a field where you have the chance to excel is extremely important.

Basic Training

Everything you have done has been leading up to this moment—the day you leave for Basic Training. You will report back to the MEPS to prepare to leave for Basic Training. If you have been in the Delayed Entry Program, you will get a last-minute mini-physical to make sure your condition is still up to par. You will also be asked about any changes that might affect your eligibility since the last time you were at MEPS. If you have been arrested or had any medical problems, now is the time to speak up.

Your orders and records will be completed at MEPS, and then you are on your way to Basic, by plane, bus, or car—it will all be at military expense. Where you train will depend on the branch of service. The Air Force, Navy, and Coast Guard each have only one training facility. The Marines have two, and the Army has quite a few because where the Army sends you will depend on the specialized training you signed up for at MEPS.

The First Few Days

No matter which branch of service you join, the first few days of Basic Training are pretty much the same. You will spend time at an intake facility, where you will be assigned to a basic training unit and undergo a quick-paced introduction to your branch of the service. Your days will include:

- orientation briefings
- uniform distribution
- records processing
- I.D. card preparation
- barracks upkeep training
- drill and ceremony instruction
- physical training (PT)

You will be assigned to a group of recruits ranging from 35 to 80 people. The Navy calls this training group a "company," the Army and Marine Corps call it a "platoon," and the Air Force calls it a "flight." And let's not forget your "supervisor" for these early days of your military career—the drill instructor. This is your primary instructor throughout your entire stay at basic training.

BASIC TRAINING (BY BRANCH)		
Branch	**Location of Training Facility**	**Length of Training**
Army	Fort Jackson, SC; Fort Knox, Louisville, KY; Fort Leonard Wood, Waynesville, MO; Fort Sill, Lawton OK; Fort Benning, Columbus, GA	9 weeks + 1 week of in-processing
Navy	Great Lakes Naval Training Center, Great Lakes, Illinois	8 weeks
Air Force	Lackland Air Force Base, TX	$8\frac{1}{2}$ weeks
Marine Corps	Parris Island, SC* or San Diego, CA	13 weeks
Coast Guard	Cape May, NJ	$7\frac{1}{2}$ weeks

*All female Marines and male Marines from the East Coast attend basic training at Parris Island. All men from the West Coast attend San Diego.

The Following Weeks

From the intake facility, you will go to your Basic Training site. You can expect your training day to start around 5 A.M. and officially end around 9 P.M. Most Saturdays and Sundays are light training days. You won't have much free time, and your ability to travel away from your unit on weekends will be very limited, if you get this privilege at all. In most cases you will not be eligible to take leave (vacation time) until after Basic Training, although exceptions can sometimes be made in case of family emergency.

The subjects you learn in Basic Training include:

- military courtesy
- military regulations
- military rules of conduct
- hygiene and sanitation
- organization and mission
- handling and care of weapons
- tactics and training related specifically to your service

While you are in Basic Training, you can expect plenty of physical training. Physical fitness is critical for trainees, and your drill instructor will keep tabs on your progress throughout Basic Training by giving you tests periodically. Your best bet is to start a running and weight-lifting program *the instant* you make your decision to join the military. Recruits in all branches of the service run mile after mile, perform hundreds of sit-ups and push-ups, and become closely acquainted with obstacle courses. These courses differ in appearance from facility to facility, but they all require the same things: plenty of upper body strength and overall endurance, as well as the will to succeed.

ENLISTMENT DURATIONS BY BRANCH	
Branch of Service	Terms of Enlistment
Army	2, 3, 4, 5, or 6 years
Navy	4-6 years
Air Force	2, 4, or 6 years
Marine Corps	4-6 years
Coast Guard	4 or 6 years

Lifetime Opportunities

Basic Training, no matter which branch of the service you choose, is a time in your life that you will never forget. No one is promising you it will be pleasant, but during this time you will forge friendships you will keep for the rest of your life. And the opportunities you will have during and after your military service will be unparalleled. You may choose a lifetime career in the military, or you may use it as a springboard to a rewarding career in the private sector. Either way, your future starts now and this book is designed to prepare you for it.

THE SCORE YOU NEED FOR THE JOB YOU WANT

CHAPTER SUMMARY

To get the most out of this book, you need to know the score you need to get into the service branch of your choice, and the score you need to get the specialties that interest you. This chapter walks you step-by-step through the process of converting your scores on the practice tests in this book into the scores the military uses. Reading this chapter, you will also learn what scores you need for selected Military Occupational Specialties.

When you take the five practice tests in this book, you will want to know whether your scores measure up. You will also probably want to know what kinds of jobs or Military Occupational Specialties (MOSs), your score will enable you to select. You will need some patience here. There are several different kinds of composite scores you will need to compute from your raw scores on the individual parts of the ASVAB.

About Your Scores

Your first step is to convert the raw scores you got on your practice exam to the scores the military uses to compute the various composites—the composite score that says whether or not you can enlist, and the composite scores that show which MOSs you qualify for.

In the table on the following page, write your scores on ASVAB Practice Test 1 in the column that says "Raw Score" under Practice Test 1. Your raw score is simply the number you got right on that subtest. For the raw score in the last blank, Verbal Equivalent, add together your raw scores on both the Word Knowledge (WK) and Paragraph Comprehension (PC) subtests.

Note that blanks are also provided for ASVAB Practice Test 2 through 5; you can fill in those blanks when you take those tests. This table will help you keep track of your improvement as you work through the practice tests in this book.

All of the score conversions throughout this chapter are approximate. Different versions of the ASVAB vary in their score conversions, and your scores on the practice tests in this book will not be exactly the same as your score on the real ASVAB. Use the exams in this book to get an *approximate* idea of where you stand and how much you're improving.

Now you need to fill in the column on this page labelled "Scaled Score." On the following page is a table that shows you approximate correlations between raw scores and scaled scores for each subtest. On the left are raw scores. The other columns show the equivalent scaled score for each test. (Make sure you're using the column for the proper subtest! The subtests are labelled with the abbreviations shown in the left-hand column of the table below.*)

Do You Qualify?

Now that you have your scaled score for each subtest filled in on the table on this page, you're ready for the next steps: finding out if your score will get you in to the military and finding out which MOSs your scores may qualify you for. Remember to use only your *scaled scores,* not your raw scores, for these conversions.

The Armed Forces Qualifying Test (AFQT) Score

All five branches of the military compute your AFQT score—the one that determines whether or not you can enlist—in the same way. Only the Verbal Equivalent (which you determined by adding Word Knowledge and Paragraph Comprehension scores and then converting to a scaled score), Arithmetic Reasoning, and Mathematics Knowledge scaled scores count toward your AFQT. The military just wants to know if you have basic reading and arithmetic skills. The score conversion goes like this:

$$2(VE) + AR + MK = AFQT$$

YOUR SCORES										
	Diagnostic Test		Practice Test 1		Practice Test 2		Practice Test 3		Practice Test 4	
Subtest	Raw Score	Scaled Score	Raw Score	Scaled Score	Raw Score	Scaled Score	Raw Score	Scaled Score	Raw Score	Scaled Score
General Science (GS)										
Arithmetic Reasoning (AR)										
Word Knowledge (WK)										
Paragraph Comprehension (PC)										
Mathematics Knowledge (MK)										
Electronics Information (EI)										
Auto and Shop Information (AS)										
Mechanical Comprehension (MC)										
Verbal Equivalent (VE = WK + PC)										

Please note: Assembling Objects (AO) has been omitted from these tables because at the time of publication only the Navy uses the (AO) score.

RAW SCORE TO SCALED SCORE CONVERSION

Raw	GS	AR	WK	PC	MK	EI	AS	MC	VE
0	20	26	20	20	27	26	28	27	20
1	21	26	20	20	27	29	30	28	20
2	23	28	20	20	28	31	31	29	20
3	25	29	22	23	30	33	33	31	20
4	27	31	23	26	32	35	35	32	20
5	28	32	24	30	33	38	36	33	20
6	30	33	25	33	35	40	38	35	20
7	32	35	27	36	37	42	40	37	21
8	34	36	28	39	38	44	41	38	22
9	36	37	29	42	40	47	43	40	23
10	38	39	30	45	42	49	45	42	24
11	40	40	32	48	43	51	47	44	25
12	42	42	33	51	45	53	48	46	26
13	44	43	34	54	47	56	50	48	27
14	46	44	35	58	48	58	52	50	27
15	48	46	36	61	50	60	53	52	28
16	50	47	38		52	63	55	54	29
17	52	48	39		53	65	57	56	30
18	54	50	40		55	67	58	58	31
19	56	51	41		56	69	60	60	32
20	58	53	43		58	72	62	62	33
21	60	54	44		60		63	65	34
22	62	55	45		61		65	67	35
23	64	57	46		63		67	69	26
24	65	58	47		65		68	71	37
25	67	59	49		66		70	72	37
26		61	50						38
27		62	51						39
28		63	52						40
29		65	54						41
30		66	55						42
31			56						43
32			57						44
33			58						45
34			60						46
35			61						47
36									48
37									48
38									49
39									50
40									51
41									52

RAW SCORE TO SCALED SCORE CONVERSION (continued)									
Raw	**GS**	**AR**	**WK**	**PC**	**MK**	**EI**	**AS**	**MC**	**VE**
42									53
43									54
44									55
45									56
46									57
47									58
48									58
49									59
50									60

Find the subtest you want to score in the boxes on the top. Then, on the left column, find your raw score for that subtest. Follow the raw-score row to the right until you get to the proper subtest. That number is your scaled score for this subtest.

In other words, your AFQT (scaled score) is your Verbal Equivalent scaled score, doubled, added to your Arithmetic Reasoning and Mathematics Knowledge scaled scores. Fill in the blanks below to find your AFQT on the ASVAB Diagnostic Test.

VE score   ____   × 2 = ____

AR score   ____

MK score   + ____

AFQT (scaled score)   ____

Now use the table "AFQT Scaled Score to Percentile Conversion" on page 21. Look up the score you wrote in the blank for AFQT scaled score above, and next to it, you'll find your approximate percentile score.

If your AFQT score on the diagnostic isn't up to par, don't despair. You're using this book to help you improve your score, after all, and you've just gotten started. Remember, too, that your score on these practice exams may not be exactly the same as your score on the actual test.

On the other hand, a higher score makes you more attractive to recruiters, and depending on your score on individual subtests, it may qualify you for more of the occupational specialities you want.

Military Occupational Specialty Qualifying Scores

If your AFQT is high enough to get you in, the next thing your scores will be used for is to help determine which Military Occupational Specialities (MOSs) you qualify for. For this purpose, the branches of the military use composite scores—different from the AFQT—made up of scores on various subtests.

Each branch of the military has its own way of computing composites and its own classification system for the MOSs. The tables here use the Army's MOSs and composites. All of the branches offer similar MOSs, and the composite scores required are also similar. So if you're considering another branch of the service, you can still use these tables to get a good idea of where you stand.

Turn to pages 22–25 to find a list of selected MOSs and the requirements for each job. If you're using the ASVAB for career guidance rather than for entrance into the military, pay special attention to the column labelled Equivalent Civilian Occupations.

In the column Minimum ASVAB Composite Score, you'll see which composite is used to determine if you're qualified for a given MOS and the minimum score required on that composite. Go on to the section "Computing Your Composites" on page 26 to find out whether you match that minimum score.

AFQT SCALED SCORE TO PERCENTILE CONVERSION

Standard Score	Percentile	Standard Score	Percentile	Standard Score	Percentile
≤109	1	185	33	218	68
110–118	2	186	34	219	69
119–124	3	187–188	35	220–221	70
125–133	4	189	36	222	71
134–137	5	190	38	223	72
138–141	6	191	39	224	73
142–145	7	192	40	225	74
146–147	8	193	41	226	75
148–151	9	194	42	227	76
152–153	10	195	43	228	77
154–156	11	196	44	229	78
157	12	197	45	230	79
158–159	13	198	46	231	80
160	14	199	47	232	81
161–162	15	200	48	233–234	82
163–164	16	201	49	235	83
165–166	17	202	50	236	84
167	18	203	51	237–238	85
168–169	19	204	52	239	86
170	20	205	53	240	87
171	21	206	54	241–242	88
172–173	22	207	55	243	89
174	23	208	56	244–245	90
175	24	209	57	246	91
176–177	25	210	59	247–248	92
178	26	211	60	249–251	93
179	27	212	61	252–253	94
180	28	213	62	254–256	95
181	29	214	63	257–259	96
182	30	215	64	260–263	97
183	31	216	66	264–268	98
184	32	217	67	≥ 269	99

REQUIREMENTS FOR SELECTED MILITARY OCCUPATIONAL SPECIALITIES

Military Occupational Speciality	Physical Demands	Minimum ASVAB Composite Score	Other Requirements	Equivalent Civilian Occupations
Infantryman*	very heavy	CO 90	red/green color discrimination, vision correctable to 20/20 in one eye and 20/100 in the other	none
Combat Engineer*	very heavy	CO 90	normal color vision	truck driver, construction worker, laborer, blaster, others
PATRIOT Missile Crewmember	moderately heavy	OF 100	red/green color discrimination, SECRET security clearance	none
M1 Armor (tank) Crewman*	very heavy	CO 90	normal color vision, vision correctable to 20/20 in one eye and 20/100 in the other, maximum height of 6' 1"	none
Multimedia Illustrator	moderately heavy	ST 95, EL 95	nomal color vision	illustrator, sign painter
PATRIOT System Repairer	medium	MM 185	normal color vision, SECRET security clearance	radar mechanic, electronics technician
Radio Repairer	heavy	EL 110	normal color vision, SECRET security clearance, one year of high school algebra and science	radio mechanic, electronics mechanic
Single Channel Radio Operator	very heavy	SC 100, EL 100	SECRET security clearance, ability to enunciate English, ability to type 25 WPM	radio operator, communications equipment operator, radio installer
Aviation Systems Repairer	moderately heavy	ST 115	normal color vision, TOP SECRET security clearance, completion of high school algebra course; certain restrictions on foreign ties	automatic equipment technician, radio repairer, teletypewriter installer
Psychological Operations Specialist	medium	ST 105	normal color vision, SECRET security clearance, minimum score on language test	editor, intelligence specialist

REQUIREMENTS FOR SELECTED MILITARY OCCUPATIONAL SPECIALITIES (continued)

Military Occupational Specialty	Physical Demands	Minimum ASVAB Composite Score	Other Requirements	Equivalent Civilian Occupations
Dental Laboratory Specialist	moderately heavy	GM 100, ST 95	normal color vision	dental laboratory technician
Fabric Repair Specialist	very heavy	GM 85	civilian acquired skills (i.e., prior training in fabric repair)	sewing machine operator, automobile upholsterer, tailor, canvas worker
Machinist	heavy	GM 100	normal color vision, visual acuity of 20/30 without correction, minimum score on other visual tests	machinist, welder, drop hammer operator
Broadcast Journalist	light	GT 110	ability to type 20 WPM, completion of at least 2 years of high school English, driver's license	announcer, continuity writer, reader, screen writer
Carpentry and Masonry Specialist	very heavy	GM 90	normal color vision, freedom from vertigo	carpenter, bricklayer, cement mason, stonemason, rigger, structural steel worker
Interior Electrician	heavy	EL 95	normal color vision	electrician
Ammunition Specialist	very heavy	ST 100	normal color vision, CONFIDENTIAL security clearance, not allergic to explosive components, not claustrophobic	accounting clerk, stock control supervisor, supply clerk, explosives operator
Crane Operator	very heavy	GM 90	red/green color discrimination, driver's license	crane operator, power shovel operator
Light-Wheel Vehicle Mechanic	very heavy	MM 90	normal color vision, equipment qualifications	automobile mechanic, diesel mechanic
UH-60 Helicopter Repairer	very heavy	MM 105	normal color vision, no history of alcohol or drug abuse	aircraft mechanic

REQUIREMENTS FOR SELECTED MILITARY OCCUPATIONAL SPECIALITIES (continued)

Military Occupational Speciality	Physical Demands	Minimum ASVAB Composite Score	Other Requirements	Equivalent Civilian Occupations
Executive Administrative Assistant	not applicable	ST 105	SECRET security clearance, ability to type 35 WPM, minimum score on English test	stenographer, administrative assistant, secretary
Legal Specialist	light	CL 110	ability to type 35 WPM, no civil convictions	court clerk, law clerk
Administrative Specialist	medium	CL 95	ability to type 25 WPM	administrative assistant, clerk typist, office helper, mail clerk
Finance Specialist	light	CL 95	no record of dishonesty or moral turpitude	bookkeeper, cashier, payroll clerk
Information Systems Operator	moderately heavy	ST 100	normal color vision, SECRET security clearance	computer operator, data processing technician, coding clerk
Personnel Administration Specialist	medium	CL 95	ability to type 20 WPM	personnel clerk
Cartographer	light	ST 85	normal color vision, other visual tests	drafter, cartographic technician
Watercraft Operator	very heavy	MM 100	normal color vision, vision correctable to 20/20 in one eye and 20/40 in the other, prior training	boat operator, seaman
Motor Transport Operator	very heavy	OF 90	red/green color discrimination, driver's license	chauffeur, truck driver, dispatcher
Medical Specialist	moderately heavy	ST 95	normal color vision	medical assistant, first aid attendant, emergency medical technician, nurse's aide
Practical Nurse	not applicable	ST 95	normal color vision; ability to complete licensure training or already licensed	licensed practical nurse

REQUIREMENTS FOR SELECTED MILITARY OCCUPATIONAL SPECIALITIES (continued)

Military Occupational Speciality	Physical Demands	Minimum ASVAB Composite Score	Other Requirements	Equivalent Civilian Occupations
Behavioral Science Specialist	light	ST 105		caseworker
Radiology Specialist	moderately heavy	ST 110		X-ray technician, radiologic technologist
Animal Care Specialist	moderately heavy	ST 95	normal color vision, completion of high school course in biology	animal health technician
Food Service Specialist	heavy	OF 90	normal color vision, driver's license, possess or be qualified for food handler's license	chef, cook, butcher, baker
Military Police	moderately heavy	ST 95	red/green color discrimination, minimum height 5' 8" for males, 5' 4" for females, CONFIDENTIAL security clearance, driver's license, no record of civilian convictions	police officer, guard
Intelligence Analyst	medium	ST 105	normal color vision, TOP SECRET security clearance, no record, certain restrictions on foreign ties	editor, intelligence specialist

Computing Your Composites

Maybe you looked at the table of MOSs and said, "Wow, I didn't know the Army had Animal Care Specialists!"—or Broadcast Journalists or Legal Specialists or whatever MOSs caught your eye. The Air Force, Navy, Marines, and Coast Guard have all these specialities, too. You might think, "I could go for Animal Care Specialist training, and then when I get out I could use my G.I. Bill money to go to veterinary school and become a vet. I could work as an assistant in a vet's office while I go to school. This is great! But what does this ST 95 score mean? Can I make it?"

This is absolutely the last score computation you'll have to do, but it's a complicated one. Stick with it, and be patient. Your future may depend on your performance on the ASVAB.

ST 95, like the other letter-number combinations in the Minimum ASVAB Composite Score column, is the composite score the Army uses to determine your eligibility for the given MOS. The composite scores used by the other branches of the service are similar, though not identical. Here's a key to the meaning of the composite scores listed in the MOS table:

- FA: Field Artillery
- OF: Operations and Food Handling
- ST: Skilled Technical
- GT: General Technical
- CL: Clerical
- GM: General Maintenance
- EL: Electronics
- MM: Mechanical Maintenance
- SC: Surveillance/Communications
- CO: Combat

So, if you want to be an Animal Care Specialist, you need to know your ST, or Skilled Technical, composite score. (You'll also, of course, have to meet the other requirements listed in the MOS table. Check with your recruiter.)

Here's how to compute the composites. Look for the composite(s) for the MOS(s) you want in the list below. After the name of the composite is a list of the subtest scores you have to add together. Go back to the table on page 18, where you filled in your subtest scores, and get your scores on those subtests. (Remember to use your scaled scores, not your raw scores!) Adding them up gives you a sum called a Subtest Standard Score (SSS). When you have the SSS for the composite you want, turn to the table on pages 28–29. That table lists SSSs in the left column. Find the SSS you computed for the composite you want, and then follow the line to the right until you get to the composite you're looking for. That's your composite for this subtest, and you should write it in the blank next to the appropriate abbreviation. Now you can compare your composite score to the minimum requirement listed in the MOS table. You don't have to compute all the composite scores, just the ones that are required for the jobs you're interested in.

FA: AR _____ + MK _____ + MC _____ = SSS_____ FA composite: _____
OF: VE _____ + AS _____ + MC _____ = SSS_____ OF composite: _____
ST: GS _____ + VE _____ + MC _____ + MK _____ = SSS_____ ST composite: _____
GT: VE _____ + AR _____ = SSS_____ GT composite: _____
CL: VE _____ + AR _____ + MK _____ = SSS_____ CL composite: _____
GM: GS _____ + AS _____ + MK _____ + EI _____ = SSS_____ GM composite: _____
EL: GS _____ + AR _____ + MK _____ + EI _____ = SSS_____ EL composite: _____
MM: AS _____ + MC _____ + EI _____ = SSS_____ MM composite: _____
SC: VE _____ + AR _____ + AS _____ + MC _____ = SSS_____ SC composite: _____
CO: AR _____ + AS _____ + MC _____ = SSS_____ CO composite: _____

Suppose you want to be an Animal Care Specialist. The composite score you need for this MOS is ST 95. So you look at the ST line on the previous page and find you need to add your scores for VE, MK, MC, and GS. You go back to the table on page 16 and find your *scaled scores* (not raw scores) for these subtests. Let's say you did pretty well in Mechanical Comprehension and General Science, and not as well in Paragraph Comprehension and Word Knowledge (your Verbal Equivalent score) or Mathematics Knowledge. So you fill in line ST above like this:

ST: VE _41_ + MK _38_ + MC _61_ + GS _54_ = SSS____   ST composite: _____

Add up your four subtest scores to get the SSS:

ST: VE _41_ + MK _38_ + MC _61_ + GS _54_ = SSS_194_   ST composite: ____

Now go to the table on the next page. Find ST at the top of the table, and follow that column down until you get to the row for 190–194. You find that your ST composite score is in the range of 95–97; in fact, it's probably about 97, since your SSS is near the top of its range.

ST: VE _41_ + MK _38_ + MC _61_ + GS _54_ = SSS_194_   ST composite: _97_

Is your score good enough to get you Animal Care Specialist training? Well, maybe just. Since you're so close to the minimum of 95, you would want some insurance. Remember, your scores on the exams in this book are only an *approximation* of your scores on the real ASVAB. So you would want to study hard on the subtests that make up your chosen composite, in this case, Paragraph Comprehension, Word Knowledge, Mathematics Knowledge, Mechanical Comprehension, and General Science.

You can use this procedure to find the composite score for whatever job you want. If your score is well above the minimum required for the MOS you want, you don't have much to worry about, though you'll probably want to work through this book just to make sure. If your score is below the minimum required, you know where to concentrate your efforts as you study the chapters in this book and take the practice exams.

STANDARD SUBTEST SCORE (SSS) TO COMPOSITE SCORE CONVERSION										
SSS	FA	OF	ST	GT	CL	GM	EL	MM	SC	CO
45–49				41–45						
50–54				46–50						
55–59				52–56						
60–64				57–61	40					
65–69				62–67	41					
70–74				68–72	42–44					
75–79				73–77	45–48					
80–84	40	40	40	78–83	49–52	40	40	40	40	
85–89	40	40	40	84–88	53–55	40	40	40	40	
90–94	40	40	40	89–94	56–59	40	40	40	40	
95–99	40	40	41–42	95–99	60–63	40–41	41–43	40	40	
100–104	41–42	40	43–45	100–104	64–66	42–44	44–46	40–41	41–44	40
105–109	43–45	41–44	46–48	105–110	67–70	45–47	47–49	42–44	45–47	41–43
110–114	46–48	45–47	49–51	111–115	71–74	48–50	50–51	45–48	48–50	44–46
115–119	49–51	48–50	52–54	116–121	75–77	51–53	52–55	49–51	51–52	47–49
120–124	52–54	51–53	55–56	122–126	78–81	54–56	56–57	52–54	53–55	50–52
125–129	55–57	54–56	57–59	127–131	82–85	57–59	58–60	55–57	56–58	53–55
130–134	58–60	57–59	60–62	132–137	86–88	60–61	61–63	58–60	59–61	56–59
135–139	61–63	60–62	63–65	138–142	89–92	62–64	64–66	61–63	62–64	60–62
140–144	64–66	63–65	66–68	143–148	93–96	65–67	67–68	64–66	65–67	63–65
145–149	67–69	66–68	69–71	149–153	96–99	68–70	69–71	67–69	68–70	66–68
150–154	70–72	69–71	72–74	154–158	100–103	71–73	72–74	70–72	71–73	69–71
155–159	73–75	72–75	75–77	159–160	104–107	74–76	75–77	73–75	74–76	72–74
160–164	76–78	76–78	78–79	160	107–110	77–79	78–80	76–78	77–79	75–77
165–169	79–81	79–81	80–82		111–114	80–82	81–83	79–81	80–82	78–81
170–174	82–84	82–84	83–85		115–118	83–85	84–85	82–84	83–85	82–84

SSS TO COMPOSITE SCORE CONVERSION (continued)										
SSS	FA	OF	ST	GT	CL	GM	EL	MM	SC	CO
175–179	85–87	85–87	86–88		119–121	86–88	86–88	85–87	86–88	85–87
180–184	88–90	88–90	89–91		122–125	89–91	89–91	88–90	89–91	88–90
185–189	91–93	91–93	92–94		126–129	92–94	92–94	91–93	92–94	91–93
190–194	94–96	94–96	95–97		130–132	95–97	95–97	94–96	95–97	94–96
195–199	97–99	97–99	98–99		133–136	98–100	98–100	97–99	98–99	97–99
200–204	100–102	100–102	100–102		137–140	101–102	101–102	100–102	100–102	100–103
205–209	103–105	103–106	103–105		141–143	103–105	103–105	103–106	103–105	104–106
210–214	106–108	107–109	106–108		144–147	106–108	106–108	107–109	106–108	107–109
215–219	109–111	110–112	109–111		148–151	109–111	109–111	110–112	109–111	110–112
220–224	112–115	113–115	112–114		152–154	112–114	112–114	113–115	112–114	113–115
225–229	116–118	116–118	115–117		155–158	115–117	115–116	116–118	115–117	116–118
230–234	119–121	119–121	118–120		159–160	118–120	117–119	119–121	118–120	119–121
235–239	122–124	122–124	121–122		160	121–123	120–122	122–124	121–123	122–125
240–244	125–127	125–127	123–125			124–126	123–125	125–127	124–126	126–128
245–249	128–130	128–130	126–128			127–129	126–128	128–130	127–129	129–131
250–254	131–133	131–134	129–131			130–132	129–131	131–133	130–132	132–134
255–259	134–136	135–137	132–134			133–135	132–133	134–136	133–135	135–137
260–264	137–139	138–140	135–137			136–138	134–136	137–139	136–138	138–140
265–269	140–142	141–143	138–140			139–140	137–139	140–142	139–141	141–143
270–274	143–145	144–146	141–143			141–143	140–142	143–145	142–144	144–147
275–279	146–148	147–149	144–145			144–146	143–145	146–148	145–146	148–150
280–284	149–151	150–152	146–148			147–149	146–148	149–151	147–149	151–153
285–289	152–154	153–155	149–151			150–152	149–150	152–154	150–152	154–156
290–294	155–157	156–158	152–154			153–155	151–153	155–157	153–155	157–159
295–299	158–160	159–160	155–157			156–158	154–156	158–160	156–158	160
300–304	160	160	158–160			159–160	157–159	160	159–160	
305–309			160			160	159–160		160	

29

4 ▶ THE LEARNINGEXPRESS TEST PREPARATION SYSTEM

CHAPTER SUMMARY

Taking the ASVAB can be tough. It demands a lot of preparation if you want to achieve a top score. Whether or not you get into the military depends on how well you do on the AFQT portion of the exam. The LearningExpress Test Preparation System, developed exclusively for LearningExpress by leading test experts, gives you the discipline and attitude you need to be a winner.

Fact: Taking the ASVAB isn't easy, and neither is getting ready for it. Your future military career depends on you passing the core section of the ASVAB—Arithmetic Reasoning, Word Knowledge, Paragraph Comprehension, and Mathematics Knowledge. By focusing on these four subtests, you have taken your first step to getting into the military. However, there are all sorts of pitfalls that can prevent you from doing your best on this all-important portion of the exam. Here are some of the obstacles that can stand in the way of your success:

- being unfamiliar with the format of the exam
- being paralyzed by test anxiety
- leaving your preparation to the last minute
- not preparing at all!
- not knowing vital test-taking skills: how to pace yourself through the exam, how to use the process of elimination, and when to guess
- not being in tip-top mental and physical shape
- messing up on test day by arriving late at the test site, having to work on an empty stomach, or shivering through the exam because the room is cold

What is the common denominator in all these test-taking pitfalls? One word: *control.* Who is in control, you or the exam?

Here is some good news: The LearningExpress Test Preparation System puts you in control. In just nine easy-to-follow steps, you will learn everything you need to know to make sure that you are in charge of your preparation and your performance on the exam. Other test-takers may let the test get the better of them; other test-takers may be unprepared or out of shape, but not you. You will have taken all the steps you need to take to get a high score on the ASVAB.

Here's how the LearningExpress Test Preparation System works: Nine easy steps lead you through everything you need to know and do to get ready to master your exam. Each of the steps listed below includes both reading about the step and one or more activities. It's important that you do the activities along with the reading, or you won't be getting the full benefit of the system. Each step tells you approximately how much time that step will take you to complete.

Step 1. Get Information	30 minutes
Step 2. Conquer Test Anxiety	20 minutes
Step 3. Make a Plan	50 minutes
Step 4. Learn to Manage Your Time	10 minutes
Step 5. Learn to Use the Process of Elimination	20 minutes
Step 6. Know When to Guess	20 minutes
Step 7. Reach Your Peak Performance Zone	10 minutes
Step 8. Get Your Act Together	10 minutes
Step 9. Do It!	10 minutes
Total	**3 hours**

We estimate that working through the entire system will take you approximately three hours, though it's perfectly fine if you work faster or slower than the time estimates assume. If you can take a whole afternoon or evening, you can work through the whole LearningExpress Test Preparation System in one sitting. Otherwise, you can break it up, and do just one or two steps a day for the next several days. It's up to you—remember, you are in control.

Step 1: Get Information

Time to complete: 30 minutes
Activity: Read Chapter 1, "About the ASVAB"
Knowledge is power. The first step in the LearningExpress Test Preparation System is finding out everything you can about the ASVAB. Once you have your information, the next steps in the LearningExpress Test Preparation System will show you what to do about it.

Part A: Straight Talk about the ASVAB

Basically, the United States military invented the whole idea of standardized testing, starting around the time of World War I. The Department of Defense wanted to make sure that its recruits were trainable—not that they already knew the skills they needed to serve in the armed forces, but that they could learn them.

The ASVAB started as an intelligence test, but now it is a test of specific aptitudes and abilities. While some of these aptitudes, such as reading and math problem-solving skills, are important in almost any job, others, such as electronics or automotive principles, are quite specialized. These more specialized subtests don't count toward your Armed Forces Qualifying Test (AFQT) score, which determines your eligibility to enlist in the military. Only the four subtests covered in this book count toward the AFQT score.

It's important for you to realize that your score on the ASVAB does not determine what kind of person you are. There are all kinds of things a written exam like this can't test: whether you can follow orders, whether you can become part of a unit that works together to accomplish a task, and so on. Those kinds of things are hard to evaluate, while a test is easy to evaluate.

This is not to say that the exam is not important! Your chances of getting into the military still depend on your getting a good score on the subtests of the ASVAB core. And that's why you're here—using the LearningExpress Test Preparation System to achieve control over the exam.

Part B: What Is on the Test

If you haven't already done so, stop here and read Chapter 1 of this book, which gives you an overview of the ASVAB.

Step 2: Conquer Test Anxiety

Time to complete: 20 minutes
Activity: Take the Test Stress Test

Having complete information about the exam is the first step in getting control of the exam. Next, you have to overcome one of the biggest obstacles to test success: test anxiety. Test anxiety not only impairs your performance on the exam itself; but also keeps you from preparing! In Step 2, you will learn stress management techniques that will help you succeed on your exam. Learn these strategies now, and practice them as you work through the exams in this book, so they will be second nature to you by exam day.

Combating Test Anxiety

The first thing you need to know is that a little test anxiety is a good thing. Everyone gets nervous before a big exam—and if that nervousness motivates you to prepare thoroughly, so much the better. It's said that Sir Laurence Olivier, one of the foremost British actors of last century, felt ill before every performance. His stage fright didn't impair his performance; in fact, it probably gave him a little extra edge—just the kind of edge you need to do well, whether on a stage or in an examination room.

On page 35 is the Test Stress Test. Stop and answer the questions, to find out whether your level of test anxiety is something you should worry about.

Stress Management before the Test

If you feel your level of anxiety getting the best of you in the weeks before the test, here is what you need to do to bring the level down again:

- **Get prepared.** There is nothing like knowing what to expect and being prepared for it to put you in control of test anxiety. That's why you're reading this book. Use it faithfully, and remind yourself that you are better prepared than most of the people taking the test.

- **Practice self-confidence.** A positive attitude is a great way to combat test anxiety. This is no time to be humble or shy. Stand in front of the mirror and say to your reflection, "I'm prepared. I'm full of self-confidence. I'm going to ace this test. I know I can do it." Say it into a tape recorder and play it back once a day. If you hear it often enough, you will believe it.

- **Fight negative messages.** Every time someone starts telling you how hard the exam is or how it's almost impossible to get a high score, start telling them your self-confidence messages above. Don't listen to the negative messages. Turn on your tape recorder and listen to your self-confidence messages.

- **Visualize.** Imagine yourself reporting for duty on your first day as a military trainee. Think of yourself wearing your uniform and learning skills you will use for the rest of your life. Visualizing success can help make it happen—and it reminds you of why you are going to all this work in preparing for the exam.

- **Exercise.** Physical activity helps calm your body down and focus your mind. Besides, being in good physical shape can actually help you do well on the exam. Go for a run, lift weights, go swimming—and do it regularly.

Stress Management on Test Day

There are several ways you can bring down your level of test anxiety on test day. They will work best if you practice them in the weeks before the test, so you know which ones work best for you.

- **Deep breathing.** Take a deep breath while you count to five. Hold it for a count of one, then let it out on a count of five. Repeat several times.

- **Move your body.** Try rolling your head in a circle. Rotate your shoulders. Shake your hands from the wrist. Many people find these movements very relaxing.

- **Visualize again.** Think of the place where you are most relaxed: lying on a beach in the sun, walking through the park, or whatever. Now close your eyes and imagine you are actually there. If you practice in advance, you will find that you only need a few seconds of this exercise to experience a significant increase in your sense of well-being.

When anxiety threatens to overwhelm you right there during the exam, there are still things you can do to manage the stress level:

- **Repeat your self-confidence messages.** You should have them memorized by now. Say them silently to yourself, and believe them!

- **Visualize one more time.** This time, visualize yourself moving smoothly and quickly through the test answering every question right and finishing just before time is up. Like most visualization techniques, this one works best if you have practiced it ahead of time.

- **Find an easy question.** Skim over the test until you find an easy question, and answer it. Getting even one question finished gets you into the test-taking groove.

- **Take a mental break.** Everyone loses concentration once in a while during a long test. It's normal, so you shouldn't worry about it. Instead, accept what has happened. Say to yourself, "Hey, I lost it there for a minute. My brain is taking a break." Put down your pencil, close your eyes, and do some deep breathing for a few seconds. Then you're ready to go back to work.

Try these techniques ahead of time, and see if they work for you!

Test Stress Test

You only need to worry about test anxiety if it is extreme enough to impair your performance. The following questionnaire will provide a diagnosis of your level of test anxiety. In the blank before each statement, write the number that most accurately describes your experience.

0 = Never   1 = Once or twice   2 = Sometimes   3 = Often

_____ I have gotten so nervous before an exam that I simply put down the books and didn't study for it.

_____ I have experienced disabling physical symptoms such as vomiting and severe headaches because I was nervous about an exam.

_____ I have simply not showed up for an exam because I was scared to take it.

_____ I have experienced dizziness and disorientation while taking an exam.

_____ I have had trouble filling in the little circles because my hands were shaking too hard.

_____ I have failed an exam because I was too nervous to complete it.

_____ **Total: Add up the numbers in the blanks above.**

Your Test Stress Score

Here are the steps you should take, depending on your score:

- **Below 3:** your level of test anxiety is nothing to worry about; it's probably just enough to give you that little extra edge.

- **Between 3 and 6:** your test anxiety may be enough to impair your performance, and you should practice the stress management techniques listed in this section to try to bring your test anxiety down to manageable levels.

- **Above 6:** your level of test anxiety is a serious concern. In addition to practicing the stress management techniques listed in this section, you may want to seek additional, personal help. Call your community college and ask for the academic counselor. Tell the counselor that you have a level of test anxiety that sometimes keeps you from being able to take an exam. The counselor may be willing to help you or may suggest someone else you should talk to.

Step 3: Make a Plan

Time to complete: 50 minutes
Activity: Construct a study plan

Maybe the most important thing you can do to get control of yourself and your exam is to make a study plan. Too many people fail to prepare simply because they fail to plan. Spending hours on the day before the exam poring over sample test questions not only raises your level of test anxiety, it also is simply no substitute for careful preparation and practice over time.

On the following pages are three sample schedules, based on the amount of time you have before you take the ASVAB. If you are the kind of person who needs deadlines and assignments to motivate you for a project, here they are. If you are the kind of person who doesn't like to follow other people's plans, you can use the suggested schedules here to construct your own.

Even more important than making a plan is making a commitment. You can't improve your skills in the four areas tested on the ASVAB core overnight. You have to set aside some time every day for study and practice. Try for at least 30 minutes a day. Thirty minutes daily will do you much more good than two hours on Saturday.

Don't put off your study until the day before the exam. Start now. A few minutes a day, with half an hour or more on weekends, can make a big difference in your score.

Step 4: Learn to Manage Your Time

Time to complete: 10 minutes to read, many hours of practice!

Activities: Practice these strategies as you take the sample tests in this book

Steps 4, 5, and 6 of the LearningExpress Test Preparation System put you in charge of your exam by showing you test-taking strategies that work. Practice these strategies as you take the sample tests in this book, and then you will be ready to use them on test day.

First, you will take control of your time on the exam. Each of the four subtests of the ASVAB core is timed separately. Most allow you enough time to complete the section, though none allows a lot of extra time. You should use your time wisely to avoid making errors. Here are some general tips for the whole exam.

- **Listen carefully to directions.** By the time you get to the exam, you should know how all the subtests work, but listen just in case something has changed.
- **Pace yourself.** Glance at your watch every few minutes, and compare the time to how far you have gotten in the subtest. When one-quarter of the time has elapsed, you should be a quarter of the way through the subtest, and so on. If you're falling behind, pick up the pace a bit.
- **Keep moving.** Don't waste time on one question. If you don't know the answer, skip the question and move on. Circle the number of the question in your test booklet in case you have time to come back to it later.
- **Keep track of your place on the answer sheet.** If you skip a question, make sure you skip on the answer sheet too. Check yourself every 5–10 questions to make sure the question number and the answer sheet number are still the same.
- **Don't rush.** Though you should keep moving, rushing won't help. Try to keep calm and work methodically and quickly.

Schedule A: 30 Days to Get the Score You Need

If you have at least a month to prepare before you take the ASVAB, you have plenty of time—as long as you don't waste it! This schedule will help you achieve the score you need.

TIME	PREPARATION
Day 1	Take the Diagnostic Test in Chapter 5. Score the exam and identify the areas that you need to concentrate on before you take the practice tests.
Days 2–5	Focus on the areas you identify as your weaknesses. Study the review lessons in Chapters 6-13. Review these chapters in detail.
Day 6	Study Chapter 6, General Science Review.
Day 7	Study Chapter 7, Math Review.
Day 8	Study Chapter 8, Word Knowledge Review.

Day 9	Study Chapter 9, Paragraph Comprehension Review.
Day 10	Study Chapter 10, Auto and Shop Information Review.
Day 11	Study Chapter 11, Mechanical Comprehension Review.
Day 12	Study Chapter 12, Electronics Information.
Day 13	Study Chapter 13, Assembling Objects Review.
Day 14	Take a day off, or if you feel up to it, go back and review a chapter that you found especially difficult.
Days 15	Take Practice Test 1 in Chapter 14 and calculate your score. Identify areas to concentrate on before you take the next practice exam.
Days 16–19	Study the areas that gave you the most trouble on Practice Test 1.
Days 20	Take Practice Test 2 in Chapter 15 and calculate your score.
Day 21–23	Study the areas that gave you the most trouble on Practice Test 2.
Day 24	Take Practice Test 3 in Chapter 16 and calculate your score.
Day 25–27	Study the areas that gave you the most trouble on Practice Test 3.
Day 28	Take Practice Test 4 in Chapter 17 and calculate your score. Note how much you have improved.
Day 29	Take an overview of all your study materials, and analyze your strengths and weaknesses.
Day before the exam	Relax. Do something unrelated to the exam and go to bed at a reasonable hour.

Schedule B: 14 Days to Get the Score You Need

If you have two weeks or less before you take the exam, use this schedule to help you get the AFQT score you need.

TIME	PREPARATION
Day 1	Take the Diagnostic Test in Chapter 5. Score the exam and identify the areas that you need to concentrate on before you take the first practice exam.
Days 2–3	Study the areas you identified as your weaknesses. Review the lessons and practice Math, Vocabulary, and Reading questions in Chapters 7-9.
Day 4	Take Practice Test 1 in Chapter 14 and calculate your score. Study the areas that gave you the most trouble.

Days 5–6	Review the lessons and practice questions on Science, Auto and Shop Information, Mechanical Comprehension, Electronics Information, and Assembling Objects in Chapters 6, 10, 11, 12, and 13.
Day 7	Take Practice Test 2 in Chapter 15 and calculate your score. Study the areas that gave you the most trouble.
Day 8	Take Practice Test 3 in Chapter 16 and calculate your score. Study the areas that gave you the most trouble.
Days 9–12	Take an overview of all your study materials, and analyze your strengths and weaknesses.
Day 13	Take Practice Test 4 in Chapter 17 and calculate your score. Note how much you have improved.
Day before the exam	Relax. Do something unrelated to the exam and go to bed at a reasonable hour.

Schedule C: 7 Days to Get the Score You Need

If you have a week or less before test day, use this schedule to help you get the AFQT score you need.

TIME	PREPARATION
Day 1	Take the Diagnostic Test in Chapter 5. Score the exam and identify two areas that you need to concentrate on before you take the first practice exam.
Days 2–3	Study the areas you have identified as your weaknesses. Use the review lessons in Math, Vocabulary, and Reading in Chapters 7-9.
Day 4	Take Practice Test 1 in Chapter 14 and calculate your score. Identify the main area you need to concentrate on.
Day 5	Study the main concentration area you identified, using the Math, Vocabulary, and Reading chapters for help. Take Practice Test 2 in Chapter 15 and calculate your score.
Day 6	Analyze your strengths and weaknesses thus far. Take Practice Test 3 in Chapter 16 and calculate your score.
Day before the exam	Take an overview of all your study materials, and analyze your strengths and weaknesses. If you'd like to take Practice Test 4 in Chapter 17, do so. Also consider spending a couple of hours reviewing key topics. Otherwise, relax.

Step 5: Learn to Use the Process of Elimination

Time to complete: 20 minutes
Activity: Complete worksheet on Using the Process of Elimination

After time management, your next most important tool for taking control of your exam is using the process of elimination wisely. It's standard test-taking wisdom that you should always read all the answer choices before choosing your answer. This helps you find the right answer by eliminating wrong answer choices. And, sure enough, that standard wisdom applies to your exam, too.

You should always use the process of elimination on tough questions, even if the right answer jumps out at you. Sometimes the answer that jumps out isn't right after all. You should always proceed through the answer choices in order. You can start with answer choice **a** and eliminate any choices that are clearly incorrect.

Let's say you're facing a vocabulary question that goes like this:

"Biology uses a *binomial* system of classification." In this sentence, the word *binomial* most nearly means
a. understanding the law.
b. having two names.
c. scientifically sound.
d. having a double meaning.

If you happen to know what *binomial* means, of course, you don't need to use the process of elimination, but let's assume you don't. So, you look at the answer choices. "Understanding the law" sure doesn't sound very likely for something having to do with biology. So you eliminate choice **a**—and now you only have three answer choices to deal with. Mark an X next to choice a so you never have to read it again.

Now, move on to the other answer choices. If you know that the prefix *bi-* means *two*, as in *bicycle*, you will flag answer **b** as a possible answer. Mark a check mark beside it, meaning "good answer, I might use this one."

Choice **c**, "scientifically sound," is a possibility. At least it's about science, not law. It could work here, though, when you think about it, having a "scientifically sound" classification system in a scientific field is kind of redundant. You remember the *bi-* in *binomial*, and probably continue to like answer **b** better. But you're not sure, so you put a question mark next to **c**, meaning "well, maybe."

Now, choice **d**, "having a double meaning." You're still keeping in mind that *bi-* means *two*, so this one looks possible at first. But then you look again at the sentence the word belongs in, and you think, "Why would biology want a system of classification that has two meanings? That wouldn't work very well!" If you're really taken with the idea that *bi-* means *two*, you might put a question mark here. But if you're feeling a little more confident, you'll put an X. You have already got a better answer picked out.

Now your question looks like this:

"Biology uses a *binomial* system of classification." In this sentence, the word *binomial* most nearly means
X **a.** understanding the law.
✓ **b.** having two names.
? **c.** scientifically sound.
? **d.** having a double meaning.

You've got just one checkmark for a good answer. If you're pressed for time, you should simply mark answer **b** on your answer sheet. If you have the time to be extra careful, you could compare your check-mark answer to your question-mark answers to make sure that it's better. (It is: the *binomial* system in biology is the one that gives a two-part genus and species name like *homo sapiens*.)

It's good to have a system for marking good, bad, and maybe answers. Here's one recommendation:

X = bad
✓ = good
? = maybe

If you don't like these marks, devise your own system. Just make sure you do it long before test day—while you're working through the practice exams in this book—so you won't have to worry about it during the test.

Even when you think you are absolutely clueless about a question, you can often use the process of elimination to get rid of one answer choice. If so, you are better prepared to make an educated guess, as you will see in Step 6. More often, the process of elimination allows you to get down to only *two* possibly right answers. Then, you're in a strong position to guess. And sometimes, even though you don't know the right answer, you find it simply by getting rid of the wrong ones, as you did in the example above.

Try using your powers of elimination on the questions in the worksheet Using the Process of Elimination beginning on this page. The answer explanations show one possible way you might use the process to arrive at the right answer.

The process of elimination is your tool for the next step, which is knowing when to guess.

Using the Process of Elimination

Use the process of elimination to answer the following questions.

1. Ilsa is as old as Meghan will be in five years. The difference between Ed's age and Meghan's age is twice the difference between Ilsa's age and Meghan's age. Ed is 29. How old is Ilsa?
   a. 4
   b. 10
   c. 19
   d. 24

2. "All drivers of commercial vehicles must carry a valid commercial driver's license whenever operating a commercial vehicle." According to this sentence, which of the following people need NOT carry a commercial driver's license?
   a. a truck driver idling his engine while waiting to be directed to a loading dock
   b. a bus operator backing her bus out of the way of another bus in the bus lot
   c. a taxi driver driving his personal car to the grocery store
   d. a limousine driver taking the limousine to her home after dropping off her last passenger of the evening

3. Smoking tobacco has been linked to
   a. increased risk of stroke and heart attack.
   b. all forms of respiratory disease.
   c. increasing mortality rates over the past ten years.
   d. juvenile delinquency.

4. Which of the following words is spelled correctly?
   a. incorrigible
   b. outragous
   c. domestickated
   d. understandible

Answers

Here are the answers, as well as some suggestions as to how you might have used the process of elimination to find them.

1. d. You should have eliminated answer **a** off the bat. Ilsa can't be four years old if Meghan is going to be Ilsa's age in five years. The best way to eliminate other answer choices is to try plugging them in to the information given in the problem. For instance, for answer **b**, if Ilsa is 10, then Meghan must be 5. The difference in their ages is 5. The difference between Ed's age, 29, and Meghan's age, 5, is 24. Is 24 two times 5? No. Then answer **b** is wrong. You could eliminate answer **c** in the same way and be left with answer **d**.

2. c. Note the word *not* in the question, and go through the answers one by one. Is the truck driver in choice **a** "operating a commercial vehicle"? Yes, idling counts as "operating," so he needs to have a commercial driver's license. Likewise, the bus operator in answer **b** is operating a commercial vehicle; the question doesn't say the operator has to be on the street. The limo driver in **d** is operating a commercial vehicle, even if it doesn't have passenger in it. However, the cabbie in answer **c** is *not* operating a commercial vehicle, but his own private car.

3. a. You could eliminate answer **b** simply because of the presence of the word *all*. Such absolutes hardly ever appear in correct answer choices. Choice **c** looks attractive until you think a little about what you know—aren't fewer people smoking these days, rather than more? So how could smoking be responsible for a higher mortality rate? (If you didn't know that *mortality rate* means the rate at which people die, you might keep this choice as a possibility, but you'd still be able to eliminate two answers and have only two to choose from.) Choice **d** is plain silly, so you could eliminate that one, too. You're left with the correct choice, **a**.

4. a. How you used the process of elimination here depends on which words you recognized as being spelled incorrectly. If you knew that the correct spellings were *outrageous*, *domesticated*, and *understandable*, then you were home free. You probably knew that at least one of those words was wrong.

Step 6: Know When to Guess

Time to complete: 20 minutes
Activity: Complete worksheet on Your Guessing Ability

Armed with the process of elimination, you are ready to take control of one of the big questions in test-taking: Should I guess? The first and main answer is Yes. Some exams have what is called a "guessing penalty," in which a fraction of your wrong answers is subtracted from your right answers—but the ASVAB isn't one of them. The number of questions you answer correctly yields your raw score. So you have nothing to lose and everything to gain by guessing.

The more complicated answer to the question "Should I guess?" depends on you—your personality and your "guessing intuition." There are two things you need to know about yourself before you go into the exam:

- Are you a risk-taker?
- Are you a good guesser?

You will have to decide about your risk-taking quotient on your own. To find out if you're a good guesser, complete the worksheet "Your Guessing Ability" that begins on this page. Frankly, even if you're a play-it-safe person with lousy intuition, you are still safe in guessing every time. The best thing would be if you could overcome your anxieties and go ahead and mark an answer. But you may want to have a sense of how good your intuition is before you go into the exam.

Your Guessing Ability

The following are ten really hard questions. You are not supposed to know the answers. Rather, this is an assessment of your ability to guess when you don't have a clue. Read each question carefully, just as if you did expect to answer it. If you have any knowledge at all about the subject of the question, use that knowledge to help you eliminate wrong answer choices.

ANSWER GRID

1. ⓐ ⓑ ⓒ ⓓ   5. ⓐ ⓑ ⓒ ⓓ   9. ⓐ ⓑ ⓒ ⓓ
2. ⓐ ⓑ ⓒ ⓓ   6. ⓐ ⓑ ⓒ ⓓ   10. ⓐ ⓑ ⓒ ⓓ
3. ⓐ ⓑ ⓒ ⓓ   7. ⓐ ⓑ ⓒ ⓓ
4. ⓐ ⓑ ⓒ ⓓ   8. ⓐ ⓑ ⓒ ⓓ

1. September 7 is Independence Day in
   a. India.
   b. Costa Rica.
   c. Brazil.
   d. Australia.

2. Which of the following is the formula for determining the momentum of an object?
   a. $p = mv$
   b. $F = ma$
   c. $P = IV$
   d. $E = mc^2$

3. Because of the expansion of the universe, the stars and other celestial bodies are all moving away from each other. This phenomenon is known as
   a. Newton's first law.
   b. the big bang.
   c. gravitational collapse.
   d. Hubble flow.

4. American author Gertrude Stein was born in
   a. 1713.
   b. 1830.
   c. 1874.
   d. 1901.

5. Which of the following is NOT one of the Five Classics attributed to Confucius?
   a. *I Ching*
   b. *Book of Holiness*
   c. *Spring and Autumn Annals*
   d. *Book of History*

6. The religious and philosophical doctrine that holds that the universe is constantly in a struggle between good and evil is known as
   a. Pelagianism.
   b. Manichaeanism.
   c. neo-Hegelianism.
   d. Epicureanism.

7. The third Chief Justice of the U.S. Supreme Court was
- **a.** John Blair.
- **b.** William Cushing.
- **c.** James Wilson.
- **d.** John Jay.

8. Which of the following is the poisonous portion of a daffodil?
- **a.** the bulb
- **b.** the leaves
- **c.** the stem
- **d.** the flowers

9. The winner of the Masters golf tournament in 1953 was
- **a.** Sam Snead.
- **b.** Cary Middlecoff.
- **c.** Arnold Palmer.
- **d.** Ben Hogan.

10. The state with the highest per capita personal income in 1980 was
- **a.** Alaska.
- **b.** Connecticut.
- **c.** New York.
- **d.** Texas.

Answers

Check your answers against the correct answers below.

1. c.
2. a.
3. d.
4. c.
5. b.
6. b.
7. b.
8. a.
9. d.
10. a.

How Did You Do?

You may have simply gotten lucky and actually known the answer to one or two questions. In addition, your guessing was more successful if you were able to use the process of elimination on any of the questions. Maybe you didn't know who the third Chief Justice was (question 7), but you knew that John Jay was the first. In that case, you would have eliminated choice **d** and therefore improved your odds of guessing correctly from one in four to one in three.

According to probability, you should get $2\frac{1}{2}$ answers correct, so getting either two or three right would be average. If you got four or more right, you may be a really terrific guesser. If you got one or none right, you may be a really bad guesser.

Keep in mind, though, that this is only a small sample. You should continue to keep track of your guessing ability as you work through the sample questions in this book. Circle the numbers of questions you guess on as you make your guess; or, if you don't have time while you take the practice exams, go back afterward and try to remember which questions you guessed at. Remember, on an exam with four answer choices, your chances of getting a right answer is one in four. So keep a separate "guessing" score for each exam. How many questions did you guess on? How many did you get right? If the number you got right is at least one-fourth of the number of questions you guessed on, you are at least an average guesser, maybe better—and you should always go ahead and guess on a real exam. If the number you got right is significantly lower than one-fourth of the number you guessed on, you would, frankly, be safe in guessing anyway, but maybe you would feel more comfortable if you guessed only selectively, when you can eliminate a wrong answer or at least have a good feeling about one of the answer choices.

Step 7: Reach Your Peak Performance Zone

**Time to complete: 10 minutes to read;
weeks to complete
Activity: Complete the Physical Preparation
Checklist**

To get ready for a challenge like a big exam, you have to take control of your physical, as well as your mental, state. Exercise, proper diet, and rest will ensure that your body works with, rather than against, your mind on test day, as well as during your preparation.

Exercise

If you don't already have a regular exercise program going, the time during which you are preparing for an exam is actually an excellent time to start one. You will have to be pretty fit to make it through the first weeks of Basic Training anyway. And if you're already keeping fit—or trying to get that way—don't let the pressure of preparing for an exam fool you into quitting now. Exercise helps reduce stress by pumping wonderful good-feeling hormones called endorphins into your system. It also increases the oxygen supply throughout your body, including your brain, so you will be at peak performance on test day.

A half hour of vigorous activity—enough to raise a sweat—every day should be your aim. If you are really pressed for time, every other day is OK. Choose an activity you like and get out there and do it. Jogging with a friend always makes the time go faster, or take a radio.

But don't overdo it. You don't want to exhaust yourself. Moderation is the key.

Diet

First of all, cut out the junk. Go easy on caffeine and nicotine, and eliminate alcohol and any other drugs from your system at least two weeks before the exam. Promise yourself a treat the night after the exam, if need be.

What your body needs for peak performance is simply a balanced diet. Eat plenty of fruits and vegetables, along with protein and carbohydrates. Foods that are high in lecithin (an amino acid), such as fish and beans, are especially good brain foods.

The night before the exam, you might "carbo-load" the way athletes do before a contest. Eat a big plate of spaghetti, rice and beans, or whatever your favorite carbohydrate is.

Rest

You probably know how much sleep you need every night to be at your best, even if you don't always get it. Make sure you do get that much sleep, though, for at least a week before the exam. Moderation is important here, too. Extra sleep will just make you groggy.

If you are not a morning person and your exam will be given in the morning, you should reset your internal clock so that your body doesn't think you're taking an exam at 3:00 A.M. You have to start this process well before the exam. The way it works is to get up half an hour earlier each morning, and then go to bed half an hour earlier that night. Don't try it the other way around: You will just toss and turn if you go to bed early without having gotten up early. The next morning, get up another half an hour earlier, and so on. How long you will have to do this depends on how late you're used to getting up. Use the Physical Preparation Checklist on page 45 to make sure you are in tip-top form.

Step 8: Get Your Act Together

**Time to complete: 10 minutes to read;
time to complete will vary
Activity: Complete Final Preparations worksheet**

You are in control of your mind and body; you are in charge of test anxiety, your preparation, and your test-taking strategies. Now it's time to take charge of external factors, like the testing site and the materials you need to take the exam.

Getting to the MEPS

You will be the guest of the Department of Defense in your trip to the Military Entrance Processing Station (MEPS). Expect to spend up to two days at the MEPS. Most MEPS centers schedule one day for travel and testing and one day for medical/physical tests and administration requirements. Your recruiter will tell you when and where you will be picked up for your trip to the MEPS. Make sure you know how to get to that location, if it's not your recruiting station, and how long it will take to get there. Figure out how early you will have to get up that morning, and get up that early every day for a week before your MEPS day.

Physical Preparation Checklist

For the week before the test, write down 1) what physical exercise you engaged in and for how long and 2) what you ate for each meal. Remember, you're trying for at least half an hour of exercise every other day (preferably every day) and a balanced diet that's light on junk food.

Exam minus 7 days

Exercise: _____ for _____ minutes

Breakfast: _____

Lunch: _____

Dinner: _____

Snacks: _____

Exam minus 6 days

Exercise: _____ for _____ minutes

Breakfast: _____

Lunch: _____

Dinner: _____

Snacks: _____

Exam minus 5 days

Exercise: _____ for _____ minutes

Breakfast: _____

Lunch: _____

Dinner: _____

Snacks: _____

Exam minus 4 days

Exercise: _____ for _____ minutes

Breakfast: _____

Lunch: _____

Dinner: _____

Snacks: _____

Exam minus 3 days

Exercise: _____ for _____ minutes

Breakfast: _____

Lunch: _____

Dinner: _____

Snacks: _____

Exam minus 2 days

Exercise: _____ for _____ minutes

Breakfast: _____

Lunch: _____

Dinner: _____

Snacks: _____

Exam minus 1 day

Exercise: _____ for _____ minutes

Breakfast: _____

Lunch: _____

Dinner: _____

Snacks: _____

Gather Your Materials

The night before the exam, lay out the clothes you will wear and the materials you have to bring with you to the MEPS. Plan on dressing in layers; you won't have any control over the temperature of the examination room. Have a sweater or jacket you can take off if it's warm. Use the checklist on the Final Preparations worksheet on this page to help you pull together what you will need.

Don't Skip Breakfast

Even if you don't usually eat breakfast, do so on exam morning. A cup of coffee doesn't count. Don't do doughnuts or other sweet foods, either. A sugar high will leave you with a sugar low in the middle of the exam. A mix of protein and carbohydrates is best: cereal with milk and just a little sugar, or eggs with toast, will do your body a world of good.

Step 9: Do It!

Time to complete: 10 minutes, plus test-taking time
Activity: Ace the ASVAB!

Fast forward to exam day. You are ready. You made a study plan and followed through. You practiced your test-taking strategies while working through this book. You are in control of your physical, mental, and emotional state. You know when and where to show up and what to bring with you. In other words, you are better prepared than most of the other people taking the ASVAB with you. You are psyched.

Just one more thing. When you're done with your day at the MEPS, you will have earned a reward. Plan a celebration. Call up your friends and plan a party, or have a nice dinner for two—whatever your heart desires. Give yourself something to look forward to.

And then do it. Take the ASVAB, full of confidence, armed with the test-taking strategies you have practiced until they are second nature. You are in control of yourself, your environment, and your performance on the exam. You are ready to succeed. So do it. Go in there and ace the exam. And look forward to your future military career!

Final Preparations

Getting to the MEPS Pickup Site

Location of pickup site: _____

Date: _____

Departure time: _____

Do I know how to get to the pickup site?   Yes ___   No ___

If no, make a trial run.

Time it will take to get to the pickup site: _____

Things to lay out the night before

Clothes I will wear   ___

Sweater/jacket   ___

Watch   ___

Photo ID   ___

4 No. 2 pencils   ___

5 ▶ ASVAB DIAGNOSTIC TEST

CHAPTER SUMMARY

This is the first of five practice test batteries in this book. This diagnostic is based on the actual ASVAB—use it to see how you would do if you took the exam today and to determine your strengths and weaknesses as you plan your study schedule.

T he ASVAB consists of the following timed subtests: General Science, Arithmetic Reasoning, Word Knowledge, Paragraph Comprehension, Mathematics Knowledge, Electronics Information, Auto and Shop Information, Mechanical Comprehension, and Assembling Objects. The amount of time allowed for completing each subtest will be found at the beginning of that subtest. All the subtests here, except the Assembling Objects (AO) subtest, have the same number of questions found in the paper and pencil version of the ASVAB; the number of AO questions matches the CAT-ASVAB.

It is recommended that you take the tests in as relaxed a manner as you can, using the answer sheet on pages 49–51. After you take the test, use the detailed answer explanations that follow to review each question.

Part 1: General Science

	a	b	c	d			a	b	c	d			a	b	c	d
1.	ⓐ	ⓑ	ⓒ	ⓓ		10.	ⓐ	ⓑ	ⓒ	ⓓ		19.	ⓐ	ⓑ	ⓒ	ⓓ
2.	ⓐ	ⓑ	ⓒ	ⓓ		11.	ⓐ	ⓑ	ⓒ	ⓓ		20.	ⓐ	ⓑ	ⓒ	ⓓ
3.	ⓐ	ⓑ	ⓒ	ⓓ		12.	ⓐ	ⓑ	ⓒ	ⓓ		21.	ⓐ	ⓑ	ⓒ	ⓓ
4.	ⓐ	ⓑ	ⓒ	ⓓ		13.	ⓐ	ⓑ	ⓒ	ⓓ		22.	ⓐ	ⓑ	ⓒ	ⓓ
5.	ⓐ	ⓑ	ⓒ	ⓓ		14.	ⓐ	ⓑ	ⓒ	ⓓ		23.	ⓐ	ⓑ	ⓒ	ⓓ
6.	ⓐ	ⓑ	ⓒ	ⓓ		15.	ⓐ	ⓑ	ⓒ	ⓓ		24.	ⓐ	ⓑ	ⓒ	ⓓ
7.	ⓐ	ⓑ	ⓒ	ⓓ		16.	ⓐ	ⓑ	ⓒ	ⓓ		25.	ⓐ	ⓑ	ⓒ	ⓓ
8.	ⓐ	ⓑ	ⓒ	ⓓ		17.	ⓐ	ⓑ	ⓒ	ⓓ						
9.	ⓐ	ⓑ	ⓒ	ⓓ		18.	ⓐ	ⓑ	ⓒ	ⓓ						

Part 2: Arithmetic Reasoning

	a	b	c	d			a	b	c	d			a	b	c	d
1.	ⓐ	ⓑ	ⓒ	ⓓ		11.	ⓐ	ⓑ	ⓒ	ⓓ		21.	ⓐ	ⓑ	ⓒ	ⓓ
2.	ⓐ	ⓑ	ⓒ	ⓓ		12.	ⓐ	ⓑ	ⓒ	ⓓ		22.	ⓐ	ⓑ	ⓒ	ⓓ
3.	ⓐ	ⓑ	ⓒ	ⓓ		13.	ⓐ	ⓑ	ⓒ	ⓓ		23.	ⓐ	ⓑ	ⓒ	ⓓ
4.	ⓐ	ⓑ	ⓒ	ⓓ		14.	ⓐ	ⓑ	ⓒ	ⓓ		24.	ⓐ	ⓑ	ⓒ	ⓓ
5.	ⓐ	ⓑ	ⓒ	ⓓ		15.	ⓐ	ⓑ	ⓒ	ⓓ		25.	ⓐ	ⓑ	ⓒ	ⓓ
6.	ⓐ	ⓑ	ⓒ	ⓓ		16.	ⓐ	ⓑ	ⓒ	ⓓ		26.	ⓐ	ⓑ	ⓒ	ⓓ
7.	ⓐ	ⓑ	ⓒ	ⓓ		17.	ⓐ	ⓑ	ⓒ	ⓓ		27.	ⓐ	ⓑ	ⓒ	ⓓ
8.	ⓐ	ⓑ	ⓒ	ⓓ		18.	ⓐ	ⓑ	ⓒ	ⓓ		28.	ⓐ	ⓑ	ⓒ	ⓓ
9.	ⓐ	ⓑ	ⓒ	ⓓ		19.	ⓐ	ⓑ	ⓒ	ⓓ		29.	ⓐ	ⓑ	ⓒ	ⓓ
10.	ⓐ	ⓑ	ⓒ	ⓓ		20.	ⓐ	ⓑ	ⓒ	ⓓ		30.	ⓐ	ⓑ	ⓒ	ⓓ

Part 3: Word Knowledge

	a	b	c	d			a	b	c	d			a	b	c	d
1.	ⓐ	ⓑ	ⓒ	ⓓ		13.	ⓐ	ⓑ	ⓒ	ⓓ		25.	ⓐ	ⓑ	ⓒ	ⓓ
2.	ⓐ	ⓑ	ⓒ	ⓓ		14.	ⓐ	ⓑ	ⓒ	ⓓ		26.	ⓐ	ⓑ	ⓒ	ⓓ
3.	ⓐ	ⓑ	ⓒ	ⓓ		15.	ⓐ	ⓑ	ⓒ	ⓓ		27.	ⓐ	ⓑ	ⓒ	ⓓ
4.	ⓐ	ⓑ	ⓒ	ⓓ		16.	ⓐ	ⓑ	ⓒ	ⓓ		28.	ⓐ	ⓑ	ⓒ	ⓓ
5.	ⓐ	ⓑ	ⓒ	ⓓ		17.	ⓐ	ⓑ	ⓒ	ⓓ		29.	ⓐ	ⓑ	ⓒ	ⓓ
6.	ⓐ	ⓑ	ⓒ	ⓓ		18.	ⓐ	ⓑ	ⓒ	ⓓ		30.	ⓐ	ⓑ	ⓒ	ⓓ
7.	ⓐ	ⓑ	ⓒ	ⓓ		19.	ⓐ	ⓑ	ⓒ	ⓓ		31.	ⓐ	ⓑ	ⓒ	ⓓ
8.	ⓐ	ⓑ	ⓒ	ⓓ		20.	ⓐ	ⓑ	ⓒ	ⓓ		32.	ⓐ	ⓑ	ⓒ	ⓓ
9.	ⓐ	ⓑ	ⓒ	ⓓ		21.	ⓐ	ⓑ	ⓒ	ⓓ		33.	ⓐ	ⓑ	ⓒ	ⓓ
10.	ⓐ	ⓑ	ⓒ	ⓓ		22.	ⓐ	ⓑ	ⓒ	ⓓ		34.	ⓐ	ⓑ	ⓒ	ⓓ
11.	ⓐ	ⓑ	ⓒ	ⓓ		23.	ⓐ	ⓑ	ⓒ	ⓓ		35.	ⓐ	ⓑ	ⓒ	ⓓ
12.	ⓐ	ⓑ	ⓒ	ⓓ		24.	ⓐ	ⓑ	ⓒ	ⓓ						

Part 4: Paragraph Comprehension

	a	b	c	d			a	b	c	d			a	b	c	d
1.	ⓐ	ⓑ	ⓒ	ⓓ		6.	ⓐ	ⓑ	ⓒ	ⓓ		11.	ⓐ	ⓑ	ⓒ	ⓓ
2.	ⓐ	ⓑ	ⓒ	ⓓ		7.	ⓐ	ⓑ	ⓒ	ⓓ		12.	ⓐ	ⓑ	ⓒ	ⓓ
3.	ⓐ	ⓑ	ⓒ	ⓓ		8.	ⓐ	ⓑ	ⓒ	ⓓ		13.	ⓐ	ⓑ	ⓒ	ⓓ
4.	ⓐ	ⓑ	ⓒ	ⓓ		9.	ⓐ	ⓑ	ⓒ	ⓓ		14.	ⓐ	ⓑ	ⓒ	ⓓ
5.	ⓐ	ⓑ	ⓒ	ⓓ		10.	ⓐ	ⓑ	ⓒ	ⓓ		15.	ⓐ	ⓑ	ⓒ	ⓓ

Part 5: Mathematics Knowledge

1.	ⓐ	ⓑ	ⓒ	ⓓ	10.	ⓐ	ⓑ	ⓒ	ⓓ	19.	ⓐ	ⓑ	ⓒ	ⓓ
2.	ⓐ	ⓑ	ⓒ	ⓓ	11.	ⓐ	ⓑ	ⓒ	ⓓ	20.	ⓐ	ⓑ	ⓒ	ⓓ
3.	ⓐ	ⓑ	ⓒ	ⓓ	12.	ⓐ	ⓑ	ⓒ	ⓓ	21.	ⓐ	ⓑ	ⓒ	ⓓ
4.	ⓐ	ⓑ	ⓒ	ⓓ	13.	ⓐ	ⓑ	ⓒ	ⓓ	22.	ⓐ	ⓑ	ⓒ	ⓓ
5.	ⓐ	ⓑ	ⓒ	ⓓ	14.	ⓐ	ⓑ	ⓒ	ⓓ	23.	ⓐ	ⓑ	ⓒ	ⓓ
6.	ⓐ	ⓑ	ⓒ	ⓓ	15.	ⓐ	ⓑ	ⓒ	ⓓ	24.	ⓐ	ⓑ	ⓒ	ⓓ
7.	ⓐ	ⓑ	ⓒ	ⓓ	16.	ⓐ	ⓑ	ⓒ	ⓓ	25.	ⓐ	ⓑ	ⓒ	ⓓ
8.	ⓐ	ⓑ	ⓒ	ⓓ	17.	ⓐ	ⓑ	ⓒ	ⓓ					
9.	ⓐ	ⓑ	ⓒ	ⓓ	18.	ⓐ	ⓑ	ⓒ	ⓓ					

Part 6: Electronics Information

1.	ⓐ	ⓑ	ⓒ	ⓓ	10.	ⓐ	ⓑ	ⓒ	ⓓ	19.	ⓐ	ⓑ	ⓒ	ⓓ
2.	ⓐ	ⓑ	ⓒ	ⓓ	11.	ⓐ	ⓑ	ⓒ	ⓓ	20.	ⓐ	ⓑ	ⓒ	ⓓ
3.	ⓐ	ⓑ	ⓒ	ⓓ	12.	ⓐ	ⓑ	ⓒ	ⓓ					
4.	ⓐ	ⓑ	ⓒ	ⓓ	13.	ⓐ	ⓑ	ⓒ	ⓓ					
5.	ⓐ	ⓑ	ⓒ	ⓓ	14.	ⓐ	ⓑ	ⓒ	ⓓ					
6.	ⓐ	ⓑ	ⓒ	ⓓ	15.	ⓐ	ⓑ	ⓒ	ⓓ					
7.	ⓐ	ⓑ	ⓒ	ⓓ	16.	ⓐ	ⓑ	ⓒ	ⓓ					
8.	ⓐ	ⓑ	ⓒ	ⓓ	17.	ⓐ	ⓑ	ⓒ	ⓓ					
9.	ⓐ	ⓑ	ⓒ	ⓓ	18.	ⓐ	ⓑ	ⓒ	ⓓ					

Part 7: Auto and Shop Information

1.	ⓐ	ⓑ	ⓒ	ⓓ	10.	ⓐ	ⓑ	ⓒ	ⓓ	19.	ⓐ	ⓑ	ⓒ	ⓓ
2.	ⓐ	ⓑ	ⓒ	ⓓ	11.	ⓐ	ⓑ	ⓒ	ⓓ	20.	ⓐ	ⓑ	ⓒ	ⓓ
3.	ⓐ	ⓑ	ⓒ	ⓓ	12.	ⓐ	ⓑ	ⓒ	ⓓ	21.	ⓐ	ⓑ	ⓒ	ⓓ
4.	ⓐ	ⓑ	ⓒ	ⓓ	13.	ⓐ	ⓑ	ⓒ	ⓓ	22.	ⓐ	ⓑ	ⓒ	ⓓ
5.	ⓐ	ⓑ	ⓒ	ⓓ	14.	ⓐ	ⓑ	ⓒ	ⓓ	23.	ⓐ	ⓑ	ⓒ	ⓓ
6.	ⓐ	ⓑ	ⓒ	ⓓ	15.	ⓐ	ⓑ	ⓒ	ⓓ	24.	ⓐ	ⓑ	ⓒ	ⓓ
7.	ⓐ	ⓑ	ⓒ	ⓓ	16.	ⓐ	ⓑ	ⓒ	ⓓ	25.	ⓐ	ⓑ	ⓒ	ⓓ
8.	ⓐ	ⓑ	ⓒ	ⓓ	17.	ⓐ	ⓑ	ⓒ	ⓓ					
9.	ⓐ	ⓑ	ⓒ	ⓓ	18.	ⓐ	ⓑ	ⓒ	ⓓ					

Part 8: Mechanical Comprehension

1.	ⓐ	ⓑ	ⓒ	ⓓ	10.	ⓐ	ⓑ	ⓒ	ⓓ	19.	ⓐ	ⓑ	ⓒ	ⓓ
2.	ⓐ	ⓑ	ⓒ	ⓓ	11.	ⓐ	ⓑ	ⓒ	ⓓ	20.	ⓐ	ⓑ	ⓒ	ⓓ
3.	ⓐ	ⓑ	ⓒ	ⓓ	12.	ⓐ	ⓑ	ⓒ	ⓓ	21.	ⓐ	ⓑ	ⓒ	ⓓ
4.	ⓐ	ⓑ	ⓒ	ⓓ	13.	ⓐ	ⓑ	ⓒ	ⓓ	22.	ⓐ	ⓑ	ⓒ	ⓓ
5.	ⓐ	ⓑ	ⓒ	ⓓ	14.	ⓐ	ⓑ	ⓒ	ⓓ	23.	ⓐ	ⓑ	ⓒ	ⓓ
6.	ⓐ	ⓑ	ⓒ	ⓓ	15.	ⓐ	ⓑ	ⓒ	ⓓ	24.	ⓐ	ⓑ	ⓒ	ⓓ
7.	ⓐ	ⓑ	ⓒ	ⓓ	16.	ⓐ	ⓑ	ⓒ	ⓓ	25.	ⓐ	ⓑ	ⓒ	ⓓ
8.	ⓐ	ⓑ	ⓒ	ⓓ	17.	ⓐ	ⓑ	ⓒ	ⓓ					
9.	ⓐ	ⓑ	ⓒ	ⓓ	18.	ⓐ	ⓑ	ⓒ	ⓓ					

Part 9: Assembling Objects

1.	ⓐ	ⓑ	ⓒ	ⓓ
2.	ⓐ	ⓑ	ⓒ	ⓓ
3.	ⓐ	ⓑ	ⓒ	ⓓ
4.	ⓐ	ⓑ	ⓒ	ⓓ
5.	ⓐ	ⓑ	ⓒ	ⓓ
6.	ⓐ	ⓑ	ⓒ	ⓓ

7.	ⓐ	ⓑ	ⓒ	ⓓ
8.	ⓐ	ⓑ	ⓒ	ⓓ
9.	ⓐ	ⓑ	ⓒ	ⓓ
10.	ⓐ	ⓑ	ⓒ	ⓓ
11.	ⓐ	ⓑ	ⓒ	ⓓ
12.	ⓐ	ⓑ	ⓒ	ⓓ

13.	ⓐ	ⓑ	ⓒ	ⓓ
14.	ⓐ	ⓑ	ⓒ	ⓓ
15.	ⓐ	ⓑ	ⓒ	ⓓ
16.	ⓐ	ⓑ	ⓒ	ⓓ

Part 1: General Science

Time: 11 minutes

1. An element's location on the periodic table is determined by its number of
   a. electrons.
   b. neutrons.
   c. protons.
   d. nuclei.

2. What are atoms of the same element that have different numbers of neutrons called?
   a. alloys
   b. isotopes
   c. alkali metals
   d. ions

3. Marine biology is most closely associated with which field of science?
   a. geography
   b. botany
   c. oceanography
   d. geology

4. Which of the following symbols represents a molecule of carbon dioxide?
   a. C
   b. O
   c. CO
   d. CO_2

5. The driver of a car you are riding in loses control in a snowstorm. The car spins 360 degrees and you are thrown against the car door. Which of the following is the best description of what you are experiencing?
   a. fundamental forces
   b. center of mass
   c. centrifugal force
   d. Coriolis effect

6. If particles of food coloring are dropped into a glass of hot water, they will spread rapidly. This is an example of
   a. osmosis.
   b. diffusion.
   c. evaporation.
   d. active transport.

7. Which of the following represents a chemical change?
   a. tearing a piece of paper
   b. melting an ice cube
   c. cooking a hamburger
   d. dissolving sugar in water

8. Carbohydrates are much better foods for quick energy than fats because they
   a. are digested more easily and absorbed more quickly.
   b. supply essential amino acids, which provide energy.
   c. are high in both protein and iron.
   d. carry oxygen to the blood.

9. Which of the following atmospheric levels is closest to the Earth's surface?
   a. mesosphere
   b. stratosphere
   c. thermosphere
   d. troposphere

10. All of the following are characteristics of reptiles EXCEPT
    a. internal development of eggs.
    b. eggs laid on land.
    c. land-dwelling adults.
    d. scaly skin.

11. Which of the following is a vertebrate?
  a. a sponge
  b. a starfish
  c. an octopus
  d. a snake

12. The process by which an organism adapts physiologically to the rigors of a new environment is known as
  a. natural selection.
  b. acclimatization.
  c. evolution.
  d. mutation.

13. Which of the following is the best description of what an omnivore eats?
  a. animal matter only
  b. vegetable matter only
  c. detritus only
  d. both animal and vegetable matter

14. Which of the following has the shortest wavelength?
  a. ultraviolet
  b. X-rays
  c. microwave
  d. infrared

15. The fundamental force that is the natural force of attraction acting between objects with mass is which of the following?
  a. electromagnetism
  b. strong nuclear force
  c. weak nuclear force
  d. gravity

16. Where is most of the mass of our solar system?
  a. Sun
  b. Earth
  c. Venus
  d. Jupiter

17. Absolute zero is equal to which of the following?
  a. 0 degrees Fahrenheit
  b. 30 degrees Fahrenheit
  c. 30 degrees Kelvin
  d. −273 degrees Celsius

18. Our solar system is made up of the Sun and how many planets?
  a. eight
  b. nine
  c. ten
  d. eleven

19. A cell containing chloroplasts would most likely belong to which organism?
  a. rabbit
  b. fern
  c. roach
  d. lizard

20. In animal cells, what organelle contains the DNA?
  a. nucleus
  b. cytoplasm
  c. Golgi apparatus
  d. ribosomes

21. How many chromosomes do normal human sex cells have?
  a. 8
  b. 16
  c. 23
  d. 46

22. When you separate the elements that make up water, what substances would you have?
  a. hydrogen and nitrogen
  b. hydrogen and oxygen
  c. carbon and helium
  d. nitrogen and oxygen

23. In vertebrates, which of the following is not controlled by the autonomic nervous system?
   a. speech
   b. salivation
   c. digestion
   d. heart rate

24. Which of the following is a defining characteristic of the subphylum vertebrates?
   a. open circulatory system
   b. single-celled
   c. a spinal cord enclosed in a flexible, bony column
   d. a hard, coiled shell that a body can retract into

25. To which class do elephants belong?
   a. Mammalia
   b. Proboscidea
   c. *Palaeomastodon*
   d. Chordata

Part 2: Arithmetic Reasoning

Time: 36 minutes

1. It costs $0.85 to make a single color copy at a copy center. At this price, how many copies can be purchased with $68.00?
   a. 9
   b. 45
   c. 80
   d. 72

2. An aquarium has a base length of 12 inches and a width of 5 inches. If the aquarium is 10 inches tall, what is the total volume?
   a. 480 cubic inches
   b. 540 cubic inches
   c. 600 cubic inches
   d. 720 cubic inches

3. A man turns in a woman's handbag to the Lost and Found Department of a large downtown store. The man informs the clerk in charge that he found the handbag on the floor beside an entranceway. The clerk estimates that the handbag is worth approximately $150. Inside, the clerk finds the following items:
   - 1 leather makeup case valued at $65
   - 1 vial of perfume, unopened, valued at $75
   - 1 pair of earrings valued at $150
   - cash $178

The clerk is writing a report to be submitted along with the found property. What should he write as the total value of the found cash and property?
   a. $468
   b. $608
   c. $618
   d. $718

Use the following information to answer questions 4–6.

The cost of movie theater tickets is $7.50 for adults and $5 for children ages 12 and under. On Saturday and Sunday afternoons until 4:00 P.M., there is a matinee price: $5.50 for adults and $3 for children ages 12 and under. Special group discounts are available for groups of 30 or more people.

4. Which of these can be determined from the information given in the above passage?
   a. how much it will cost a family of four to buy movie theater tickets on Saturday afternoon
   b. the difference between the cost of two movie theater tickets on Tuesday night and the cost of one ticket on Sunday at 3:00 P.M.
   c. how much movie theater tickets will cost each person if he or she is part of a group of 40 people
   d. the difference between the cost of a movie theater ticket for an adult on Friday night and a movie theater ticket for a 13-year-old on Saturday afternoon at 1:00 P.M.

5. Based on the passage, how much will movie theater tickets cost for two adults, one 15-year-old child and one 10-year-old child at 7:00 P.M. on a Sunday night?
   a. $17.00
   b. $19.50
   c. $25.00
   d. $27.50

6. Using the passage, how can you find the difference in price between a movie theater ticket for an adult and a movie theater ticket for a child under the age of 12 if the tickets are for a show at 3:00 P.M. on a Saturday afternoon?
   a. subtract $3.00 from $5.50
   b. subtract $5.00 from $7.50
   c. subtract $7.50 from $5.50
   d. add $5.50 and $3.00 and divide by 2

7. It takes a typist 0.50 seconds to type one word. At this rate, how many words can be typed in 60 seconds?
   a. 2.25
   b. 50
   c. 90
   d. 120

8. If the average woman burns 8.2 calories per minute while riding a bicycle, how many calories will she burn if she rides for 35 minutes?
   a. 286
   b. 287
   c. 387
   d. 980

9. Dr. Drake charges $36.00 for an office visit, which is $\frac{3}{4}$ of what Dr. Jean charges. How much does Dr. Jean charge?
   a. $48.00
   b. $27.00
   c. $38.00
   d. $57.00

10. Thirty percent of the students at a middle school are involved in the vocal and instrumental music programs. If 15% of the musicians are in the choir, what percentage of the whole school is in the choir?
   a. 4.5%
   b. 9.0%
   c. 15%
   d. 30%

Use the information below to answer questions 11 and 12.

Basic cable television service, which includes 16 channels, costs $15 a month. The initial labor fee to install the service is $25. A $65 deposit is required but will be refunded within two years if the customer's bills are paid in full. Other cable services may be added to the basic service: the movie channel service is $9.40 a month; the news channels are $7.50 a month; the arts channels are $5.00 a month; the sports channels are $4.80 a month.

11. A customer's cable television bill totaled $20 a month. Using the passage above, what portion of the bill was for basic cable service?
   a. 25%
   b. 33%
   c. 50%
   d. 75%

12. A customer's first bill after having cable television installed totaled $112.50. This customer chose basic cable and one additional cable service. Which additional service was chosen?
   a. the news channels
   b. the movie channels
   c. the arts channels
   d. the sports channels

13. Out of every 200 shoppers polled, 60 said they buy fresh vegetables every week. How many shoppers out of 40,000 could be expected to buy fresh vegetables every week?
   a. 3,600
   b. 9,000
   c. 12,000
   d. 24,000

Use the following chart to answer questions 14 and 15.

Compact Discs Sold

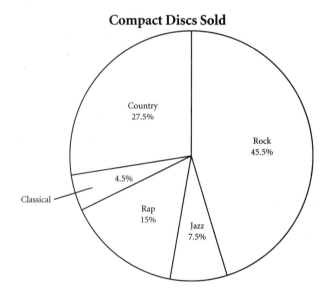

14. If 400 compact discs were sold altogether, how many of the compact discs sold were country music?
   a. 11
   b. 28
   c. 55
   d. 110

15. Based on the graph, which types of music represent exactly half of the compact discs sold?
   a. rock and jazz
   b. classical and rock
   c. rap, classical, and country
   d. jazz, classical, and rap

16. Last year, 220 people bought cars from a certain dealer. Of those, 60 percent reported that they were completely satisfied with their new cars. How many people reported being unsatisfied with their new car?
   a. 36
   b. 55
   c. 88
   d. 132

17. Of 1,125 university students, 135 speak fluent Spanish. What percentage of the student body speaks fluent Spanish?
   a. 7.3%
   b. 8.3%
   c. 12%
   d. 14%

18. The perimeter of a rectangle is 268 feet. Its two longest sides add up to 156 feet. What is the length of each of its two shortest sides?
   a. 43 feet
   b. 56 feet
   c. 72 feet
   d. 80 feet

19. A piece of ribbon 3 feet 4 inches long was divided in 5 equal parts. How long was each part?
   a. 1 foot 2 inches
   b. 10 inches
   c. 8 inches
   d. 6 inches

20. A middle school cafeteria has three different options for lunch.

    For $2, a student can get either a sandwich or two cookies.

    For $3, a student can get a sandwich and one cookie.

    For $4, a student can get either two sandwiches, or a sandwich and two cookies.

    If Jimae has $6 to pay for lunch for her and her brother, which of the following is not a possible combination?

a. three sandwiches and one cookie

b. two sandwiches and two cookies

c. one sandwich and four cookies

d. three sandwiches and no cookies

21. A bed is 4 feet wide and 6 feet long. What is the area of the bed?

a. 24 square feet

b. 20 square feet

c. 10 square feet

d. 36 square feet

22. Mr. Beard's temperature is 98 degrees Fahrenheit. Using the formula $C = \frac{5}{9}(F - 32)$, what is his temperature in degrees Celsius?

a. 35.8

b. 36.7

c. 37.6

d. 31.1

23. All of the rooms on the main floor of an office building are rectangular, with 8-foot high ceilings. Keira's office is 9 feet wide by 11 feet long. What is the combined surface area of the four walls of her office, including any windows and doors?

a. 99 square feet

b. 160 square feet

c. 320 square feet

d. 792 square feet

24. A recipe serves four people and calls for $1\frac{1}{2}$ cups of broth. If you want to serve six people, how much broth do you need?

a. 2 cups

b. $2\frac{1}{4}$ cups

c. $2\frac{1}{3}$ cups

d. $2\frac{1}{2}$ cups

25. Greenville is 1,200 miles west and 90 miles north of Johnson City. How long is a direct straight line route from Greenville to Johnson City?

a. 100 miles

b. 125 miles

c. 150 miles

d. 180 miles

26. A builder has 27 cubic feet of concrete to pave a sidewalk whose length is 6 times its width. The concrete must be poured 6 inches deep. How long is the sidewalk?

a. 9 feet

b. 12 feet

c. 15 feet

d. 18 feet

27. Which of the following brands is the least expensive?

Brand	W	X	Y	Z
Price	0.21	0.48	0.56	0.96
Weight in ounces	6	15	20	32

a. W

b. X

c. Y

d. Z

28. A salesman drives 2,052 miles in 6 days, stopping at 2 towns each day. How many miles does he average between stops?
   a. 171
   b. 342
   c. 684
   d. 1,026

29. A cook spends $540 on silverware. If a place setting includes 1 knife, 1 fork, and 2 spoons, and if knives cost twice as much as forks or spoons, how many place settings did the cook buy?
   a. 90
   b. 108
   c. 135
   d. 180

30. An office uses 2 dozen pencils and $3\frac{1}{2}$ reams of paper each week. If pencils cost 5 cents each and a ream of paper costs $7.50, how much does it cost to supply the office for a week?
   a. $7.55
   b. $12.20
   c. $27.45
   d. $38.25

Part 3: Word Knowledge

Time: 11 minutes

1. Mediate most nearly means
   a. ponder.
   b. interfere.
   c. reconcile.
   d. dissolve.

2. The attorney wanted to expedite the process.
   a. accelerate
   b. evaluate
   c. reverse
   d. justify

3. The student gave a plausible explanation for his lateness so it was excused by the teacher.
   a. unbelievable
   b. credible
   c. insufficient
   d. apologetic

4. Concurrent most nearly means
   a. incidental.
   b. simultaneous.
   c. apprehensive.
   d. substantial.

5. Impromptu most nearly means
   a. tactless.
   b. passive.
   c. rehearsed.
   d. spontaneous.

6. Induce most nearly means
   a. prompt.
   b. withdraw.
   c. presume.
   d. represent.

7. He based his conclusion on what he inferred from the evidence, not on what he actually observed.
   a. intuited
   b. imagined
   c. surmised
   d. implied

8. Saturate most nearly means
   a. deprive.
   b. construe.
   c. soak.
   d. verify.

9. Synopsis most nearly means
 a. summary.
 b. abundance.
 c. stereotype.
 d. verify.

10. Hyperbole most nearly means
 a. sincerity.
 b. exaggeration.
 c. understatement.
 d. indignation.

11. Proscribe most nearly means
 a. measure.
 b. recommend.
 c. detect.
 d. forbid.

12. Proponent most nearly means
 a. advocate.
 b. delinquent.
 c. idealist.
 d. critic.

13. Intrepid most nearly means
 a. belligerent.
 b. consistent.
 c. timid.
 d. fearless.

14. Statute most nearly means
 a. replica.
 b. ordinance.
 c. collection.
 d. hypothesis.

15. The general public was apathetic about the verdict.
 a. enraged
 b. indifferent
 c. suspicious
 d. saddened

16. The theories of some astronomers were fortified by the new research.
 a. reinforced
 b. altered
 c. disputed
 d. developed

17. Refrain most nearly means
 a. desist.
 b. secure.
 c. glimpse.
 d. persevere.

18. One of the duties of a captain is to delegate responsibility.
 a. analyze
 b. respect
 c. criticize
 d. assign

19. Spurious most nearly means
 a. prevalent.
 b. false.
 c. melancholy.
 d. actual.

20. The spokesperson must articulate the philosophy of an entire department.
 a. trust
 b. refine
 c. verify
 d. express

21. Disparage most nearly means
 a. endorse.
 b. finalize.
 c. restrict.
 d. criticize.

22. The hospital was an <u>expansive</u> facility.
   a. obsolete
   b. meager
   c. spacious
   d. costly

23. <u>Urbane</u> most nearly means
   a. foolish.
   b. vulgar.
   c. sophisticated.
   d. sentimental.

24. <u>Rationale</u> most nearly means
   a. explanation.
   b. regret.
   c. denial.
   d. anticipation.

25. The ruling proved to be <u>detrimental</u> to the investigation.
   a. decisive
   b. harmful
   c. worthless
   d. advantageous

26. <u>Brevity</u> most nearly means
   a. speed.
   b. idleness.
   c. thickness.
   d. shortness.

27. <u>Fiasco</u> most nearly means
   a. car.
   b. humiliating failure.
   c. revolution.
   d. threat.

28. <u>Nomad</u> most nearly means
   a. settler.
   b. immigrant.
   c. wanderer.
   d. visitor.

29. There was a <u>paucity</u> of qualified firefighters.
   a. abundance.
   b. absence.
   c. scarcity.
   d. just enough

30. <u>Obstrusive</u> most nearly means
   a. heavy.
   b. forward.
   c. slow.
   d. reluctant.

31. <u>Impede</u> most nearly means
   a. obstruct.
   b. to pedal.
   c. decide.
   d. to think.

32. <u>Demure</u> most nearly means
   a. modest.
   b. excitable.
   c. mute.
   d. delay.

33. <u>Abeyance</u> most nearly means
   a. obedience.
   b. reluctance.
   c. suspension.
   d. relief.

34. <u>Accolade</u> most nearly means
   a. praise.
   b. disbelief.
   c. impression.
   d. happiness.

35. <u>Accretion</u> most nearly means
   a. deletion
   b. agreement
   c. suspense
   d. accumulation

Part 4: Paragraph Comprehension

Time: 13 minutes

Hearsay evidence, which is the secondhand reporting of a statement, is allowed in court only when the truth of the statement is irrelevant. Hearsay that depends on the statement's truthfulness is inadmissible because the witness does not appear in court and swear an oath to tell the truth. Because his or her demeanor when making the statement is not visible to the jury, the accuracy of the statement cannot be tested under cross-examination, and to introduce it would be to deprive the accused of the constitutional right to confront the accuser. Hearsay is admissible, however, when the truth of the statement is unimportant. If, for example, a defendant claims to have been unconscious at a certain time, and a witness claims that the defendant actually spoke to her at that time, this evidence would be admissible because the truth of what the defendant actually said is irrelevant.

1. The main purpose of the passage is to
   a. explain why hearsay evidence abridges the rights of the accused.
   b. question the probable truthfulness of hearsay evidence.
   c. argue that rules about the admissibility of hearsay evidence should be changed.
   d. specify which use of hearsay evidence is inadmissible and why.

2. Which of the following is NOT a reason given in the passage for the inadmissibility of hearsay evidence?
   a. Rumors are not necessarily credible.
   b. The person making the original statement was not under oath.
   c. The jury should be able to watch the gestures and facial expressions of the person making the statement.
   d. The person making the statement cannot be cross-examined.

3. How does the passage explain the proper use of hearsay evidence?
   a. by listing a set of criteria
   b. by providing a hypothetical example
   c. by referring to the Constitution
   d. by citing case law

4. The passage suggests that the criterion used for deciding that most hearsay evidence is inadmissible was most likely
   a. the unreliability of most hearsay witnesses.
   b. the importance of physical evidence to corroborate witness testimony.
   c. concern for discerning the truth in a fair manner.
   d. doubt about the relevance of hearsay testimony.

During the next year, every licensed taxi driver with more than five years of service must complete a defensive driving course taught by the police department in order to keep his or her license. The police have found that drivers who have completed this class have fewer accidents and are better able to pay attention to what is happening around them. They also have safer driving habits and better hand-eye coordination.

5. All licensed taxi drivers with more than five years of service are required to do which of the following?
   a. finish a defensive driving obstacle course
   b. complete a driving course from any school within the next five years
   c. complete a course on defensive driving from the police department
   d. none of the above

6. The main purpose of the defensive driving course is to
   a. make sure that taxi drivers have fewer accidents.
   b. give experienced taxi drivers a chance to learn new skills.
   c. test a driver's comprehension of driving laws.
   d. reduce the taxi insurance rates.

The city has distributed standardized recycling containers to all households with directions that read: "We would prefer that you use this new container as your primary recycling container. Additional recycling containers may be purchased from the city."

7. According to the directions, each household
   a. may only use one recycling container.
   b. must use the new recycling container.
   c. should use the new recycling container.
   d. must buy a new recycling container.

8. According to the directions, which of the following is true about the new containers?
   a. The new containers are better than other containers.
   b. Households may use only the new containers for recyclable items.
   c. The new containers hold more than the old containers did.
   d. Households may use other containers besides the new ones if they wish.

After a snow or ice fall, the city streets are treated with ordinary rock salt. In some areas, the salt is combined with calcium chloride, which is more effective in below-zero temperatures and which melts ice better. This combination of salt and calcium chloride is also less damaging to foliage along the roadways.

9. In deciding whether to use ordinary rock salt or the salt and calcium chloride on a particular street, which of the following is NOT a consideration?
   a. the temperature at the time of treatment
   b. the plants and trees along the street
   c. whether there is ice on the street
   d. whether the street is a main or secondary road

10. According to the snow treatment directions, which of the following is true?
   a. If the temperature is below zero, salt and calcium chloride is effective in treating snow- and ice-covered streets.
   b. Crews must wait until the snow or ice stops falling before salting streets.
   c. The city always salts major roads first.
   d. If the snowfall is light, the city will not salt the streets as this would be a waste of the salt supply.

On February 3, 1956, Autherine Lucy became the first African-American student to attend the University of Alabama, although the dean of women refused to allow Autherine to live in a university dormitory. White students rioted in protest of her admission, and the federal government had to assume command of the Alabama National Guard in order to protect her. Nonetheless, on her first day in class, Autherine bravely took a seat in the front row. She remembers being surprised that the professor of the class appeared not to notice she was even in class. Later she would appreciate his seeming indifference, as he was one of only a few professors to speak out in favor of her right to attend the university.

11. This passage is most likely from a book called
   a. *20th Century United States History.*
   b. *A Collection of Favorite Children's Stories.*
   c. *A History of the Civil War.*
   d. *How to Choose the College That Is Right for You.*

12. According to the passage, Autherine Lucy
   a. lived in a dormitory.
   b. sat in the front row of her class.
   c. became a lawyer.
   d. majored in history.

Some people may act deceptively by telling the truth but omitting important information rather than outright lying. This is often called a half-truth. Although a half-truth is not technically a lie, it is still dishonest. Some politicians use the tactic during campaigning in an attempt to discredit their opponent. Advertisers will also use this tactic in order to convince you to purchase their products. Unfortunately, some people do not see anything wrong with telling half-truths because what they say is true— but the understanding of the situation is inaccurate due to the omission of key facts.

13. What is the main idea of the passage?
   a. the truth can be used in dishonest ways
   b. you cannot trust advertisers
   c. there is nothing wrong with omitting facts
   d. all politicians are corrupt

14. According to the passage, the author wants you to do what?
   a. never trust advertising
   b. think about everything you hear and read
   c. learn to lie by omission
   d. don't believe anyone

15. Which of the following is the most appropriate title for the passage?
   a. Everyone Lies
   b. The Bold Lie
   c. Lying with the Truth
   d. The Deal of the Century

Part 5: Mathematics Knowledge

Time: 24 minutes

1. In the figure below, angle *POS* measures 90 degrees. What is the measure of angle *ROQ*?

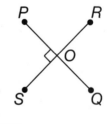

   a. 45 degrees
   b. 90 degrees
   c. 180 degrees
   d. 270 degrees

2. $4\frac{1}{5} + 1\frac{2}{5} + 3\frac{3}{10} =$
   a. $8\frac{9}{10}$
   b. $9\frac{1}{10}$
   c. $8\frac{4}{5}$
   d. $8\frac{6}{15}$

3. $\frac{3}{4}$ is equal to
   a. 0.50
   b. 0.25
   c. 0.75
   d. 0.30

4. $76\frac{1}{2} + 11\frac{5}{6} =$
   a. $87\frac{1}{2}$
   b. $88\frac{1}{3}$
   c. $88\frac{2}{3}$
   d. $88\frac{5}{6}$

5. What is the decimal equivalent of $\frac{1}{6}$ rounded to the nearest thousandth?
   a. 0.165
   b. 0.666
   c. 0.123
   d. 0.167

6. $\frac{1}{6} + \frac{7}{12} + \frac{2}{3} =$
   a. $\frac{10}{24}$
   b. $2\frac{1}{6}$
   c. $1\frac{5}{6}$
   d. $1\frac{5}{12}$

7. Which of the following is equivalent to 202,436?
   a. $20,000 + 2,000 + 400 + 30 + 6$
   b. $2,000 + 40 + 300 + 6$
   c. $200,000 + 2,000 + 400 + 30 + 6$
   d. $200,000 + 2,000 + 4,000 + 300 + 6$

8. What are the missing integers on this number line?

   a. −4 and 1
   b. −6 and 1
   c. −6 and −1
   d. 4 and 9

9. $1\frac{1}{2}$ is equal to
   a. 0.50
   b. 1.25
   c. 2.50
   d. 1.50

10. If $\frac{x}{54} = \frac{2}{9}$, then x is
   a. 12
   b. 14
   c. 18
   d. 108

11. Which of the following is divisible by 7 and 8?
   a. 63
   b. 106
   c. 114
   d. 112

12. What is $\frac{3}{8}$ equal to?
   a. 0.25
   b. 0.333
   c. 0.60
   d. 0.375

13. What is another way to write $4 \times 4 \times 4$?
   a. 3×4
   b. 8×4
   c. 4^3
   d. 3^4

14. Which of the following choices completes this number sentence? $5\underline{\quad} = (10 \times 2) + (5 \times 3)$
    a. $\times (5 + 2)$
    b. $+ (5 + 2)$
    c. $\times (5 \times 2)$
    d. $+ (5 \times 2)$

15. . Which of these is equivalent to 20° C?
    $(F = \frac{9}{5}C + 32)$
    a. 68° F
    b. 95° F
    c. 45° F
    d. 19° F

16. What is the volume of a pyramid that has a rectangular base 5 feet by 3 feet and a height of 8 feet? $(V = \frac{1}{3}lwh)$
    a. 16 feet³
    b. 30 feet³
    c. 40 feet³
    d. 120 feet³

17. What is another way to write 7.25×10^3?
    a. 72.5
    b. 725
    c. 7,250
    d. 72,500

18. How many inches are there in $3\frac{1}{3}$ yards?
    a. 126
    b. 120
    c. 160
    d. 168

19. $\frac{3}{5} =$
    a. 0.60
    b. 0.20
    c. 0.50
    d. 0.80

20. 0.97 is equal to
    a. 97%
    b. 9.7%
    c. 0.97%
    d. 0.097%

21. In a triangle, angle A is 70 degrees and angle B is 30 degrees. What is the measure of angle C?
    a. 90 degrees
    b. 70 degrees
    c. 80 degrees
    d. 100 degrees

22. Which value of x will make the following number sentence true?
    $x + 32 \leq 14$
    a. -16
    b. -21
    c. 12
    d. 38

23. What is the length of a rectangle if its width is 6 feet and its area is 108 square feet?
    a. 1.8 feet
    b. 10.5 feet
    c. 18 feet
    d. 16 feet

24. 37.5 percent is equal to
    a. $\frac{3}{8}$
    b. $\frac{5}{8}$
    c. $4\frac{3}{4}$
    d. $6\frac{3}{4}$

25. 0.15 is equal to
    a. $\frac{2}{5}$
    b. $\frac{3}{20}$
    c. $\frac{2}{10}$
    d. $\frac{1}{20}$

Part 6: Electronics Information

Time: 9 minutes

1. A power plant that generates two hundred kilo-watts generates how many watts?
   a. 2,000 watts
   b. 20,000 watts
   c. 200,000 watts
   d. 2,000,000 watts

2. A static charge
   a. moves from one terminal of a battery to the other.
   b. does not move.
   c. does work.
   d. is the force between an electron and a proton.

3. Increasing the voltage in a circuit will cause which of the following?
   a. the current will decrease
   b. the resistance will increase
   c. the current will increase
   d. the resistance will decrease

4. Which of the following is the current when 300 coulombs of charge move through a light bulb in one minute?
   a. 5 A
   b. 20 A
   c. 100 A
   d. 300 A

5. Which of the following is NOT a good insulator?
   a. a car tire
   b. a wooden dowel
   c. glass
   d. gold

6. Resistance in an electric circuit
   a. forces current to flow.
   b. opposes the flow of current.
   c. is usually harmful.
   d. is usually beneficial.

7. Which of the following is NOT needed to make an electric circuit?
   a. a closed path
   b. resistance
   c. a switch
   d. a potential voltage source

8. In Ohm's Law, E is measured in what unit?
   a. watts
   b. amperes
   c. volts
   d. ohms

9. Electric charge in motion is
   a. current.
   b. power.
   c. energy.
   d. voltage.

10. Most computer memory chips are made from silicon. Silicon is an example of
    a. an insulator.
    b. a resistor.
    c. a conductor.
    d. a semiconductor.

11. Metals are very good conductors of electricity because they
    a. are high in resistance.
    b. have electrons that are able to move freely.
    c. are inexpensive.
    d. are easily formed into wires.

12. A material with a very large resistance is classified as
  a. an insulator.
  b. a conductor.
  c. a semiconductor.
  d. a transformer.

13. A voltmeter is connected to a circuit as shown. What will the meter read?

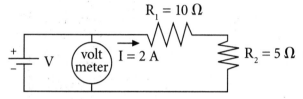

  a. 5 volts
  b. 10 volts
  c. 15 volts
  d. 30 volts

14. Two light bulbs are connected to a parallel circuit. If another bulb is added in parallel, what will happen?
  a. the circuit resistance will increase
  b. the current draw will increase
  c. choices **a** and **b** are correct
  d. neither choice **a** nor **b** is correct

15. What is the total resistance when two five-ohm light bulbs are connected in series?
  a. 2.5 Ω
  b. 5.0 Ω
  c. 10.0 Ω
  d. 0.2 Ω

16. A voltmeter is connected to a circuit as shown. What will the meter read?

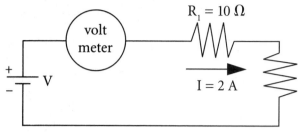

  a. 0 volts
  b. 10 volts
  c. 20 volts
  d. 30 volts

17. Two 8-ohm speakers are connected in series to an amplifier with a 24-volt output. What is the voltage across each speaker?
  a. 3 volts
  b. 6 volts
  c. 12 volts
  d. 24 volts

18. What does a semiconductor do?
  a. it conducts electricity better than a conductor
  b. it inhibits the flow of electrons around the outer shell
  c. it insulates the electrical current from contact with other material
  d. it is useful for controlling the flow of electricity

19. Which electronic component can be used to change the value of an alternating voltage?
  a. a diode
  b. a capacitor
  c. a transformer
  d. an inductor

20. When two parallel resistances are combined, the equivalent resistance is
   a. less than either of the two parallel resistances.
   b. equal to the sum of the two parallel resistances.
   c. greater than either of the two parallel resistances.
   d. less than the sum of the two parallel resistances.

Part 7: Auto and Shop Information

Time: 11 minutes

1. The purpose of a crankshaft in an internal combustion engine is to
   a. provide ignition of the fuel.
   b. provide cooling of the engine.
   c. provide lubrication of the engine.
   d. transfer energy to the drive train.

2. All of the following are types of screwdrivers except
   a. star.
   b. dual hasp.
   c. phillips.
   d. Robertson.

3. Which of the following items is used to gain a mechanical advantage?
   a. a lever
   b. a protractor
   c. a spring
   d. a gear

4. A tachometer measures what?
   a. resale value
   b. miles per hour (MPH)
   c. revolutions per minute (RPM)
   d. miles per gallon (MPG)

5. What type of gauge would be read in units of mph (miles per hour)?
   a. a speed gauge
   b. a depth gauge
   c. a pressure gauge
   d. a temperature gauge

6. The main purpose of a muffler on a car is to
   a. cool the engine.
   b. conserve fuel.
   c. reduce engine noise.
   d. increase horsepower.

7. A vehicle's differential is found in the
   a. engine
   b. drive axle
   c. suspension system
   d. instrument panel

8. Of the definitions below, which one best describes "preventative maintenance"?
   a. fixing a device after it fails for the first time
   b. periodically making small adjustments to a device to prevent failure
   c. purchasing a new device in anticipation of the old one's wearing out
   d. purchasing a new device after an old one wears out

9. Which tool listed below is the best for cutting metal?
   a. a handsaw
   b. a circular saw
   c. a hacksaw
   d. a back saw

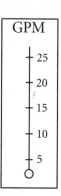

10. Which of the following is the type of gauge shown above? (Note: GPM = gallons per minute.)
  a. pressure gauge
  b. altitude gauge
  c. temperature gauge
  d. flow meter gauge

11. An internal combustion engine requires what three basic items in order to operate properly?
  a. fire, oxygen, and a fixed timing sequence
  b. fire, fuel, and heat
  c. fire, fuel, and oxygen
  d. fire, fuel, and hydraulic fluid

12. In the United States, most speedometers on automobiles have two different scales: mph, which stands for miles per hour, and kph, which stands for
  a. kilometers per mile.
  b. kilometers per hour.
  c. kilograms per hour.
  d. kilobytes per hour.

13. The tool shown above would most likely be used to
  a. drive nails.
  b. weld metal.
  c. tighten bolts.
  d. carve wood.

14. Which of the following items is typically part of the suspension of a car?
  a. the carburetor
  b. the wheels
  c. the rods
  d. the pistons

15. "Stilson," "strap," "torque," and "spanner" all denote types of
  a. saws.
  b. hammers.
  c. pliers.
  d. wrenches.

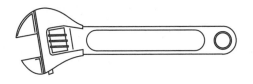

16. The hand tool shown above is a(n)
   a. crescent wrench.
   b. offset wrench.
   c. box wrench.
   d. socket wrench.

17. Which of the following portions of a building must be constructed before all the others listed?
   a. flooring
   b. framing
   c. foundation
   d. walls

18. Which would be the best tool to use to cut a piece of 4 × 8 plywood?
   a. table saw
   b. hand saw
   c. circular saw
   d. coping saw

19. Which construction procedure listed below is most likely to require the use of a saw for cutting wood?
   a. building a foundation for a bridge
   b. building a wall for an apartment building
   c. building a deck for a house
   d. all of the above

20. What is the name of the building procedure that is used to pinpoint the exact location of a corner of a building or the exact elevation of a bridge deck?
   a. forming
   b. surveying
   c. masonry
   d. all of the above

21. The sub-flooring of a typical residential house in the United States is normally made of which of the following materials?
   a. plastic
   b. wood
   c. fiberglass
   d. resin

22. Which of the following are types of screwdrivers?
   a. Phillips
   b. Allen
   c. socket
   d. all of the above

23. Which automotive system uses the following components: water pump, radiator, and thermostat?
   a. the interior heating system
   b. the engine cooling system
   c. the exhaust system
   d. the braking system

24. Which of the following refers to a kind of chisel?
   a. diamond point
   b. dovetail
   c. coping
   d. duck bill

25. If your car will not start due to a dead battery, which of the following measures should be taken to get the car started?
   a. install a new starter
   b. check the fuel level
   c. use jumper cables
   d. replace all of the fuses

Part 8: Mechanical Comprehension

Time: 19 minutes

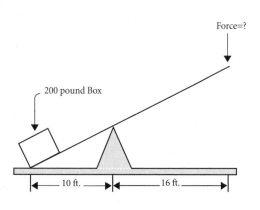

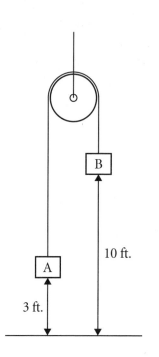

1. In the diagram shown above, Frank must lift a 200-pound box using a lever. How many pounds of force must Frank apply to the right side of the lever to lift the box? $w \times d_1 = f \times d_2$
   a. 100 pounds
   b. 125 pounds
   c. 200 pounds
   d. 320 pounds

2. If there are 5 gears, with each gear turning the one next to it, and the first gear is turning clockwise at a constant speed of 10 rpm, what direction and speed would the last gear be turning?
   a. clockwise at 5 rpm
   b. counterclockwise at 10 rpm
   c. clockwise at 10 rpm
   d. counterclockwise at 20 rpm

3. In the diagram above, how much must block A be raised to allow block B to rest on the floor beneath it?
   a. 3 feet
   b. 10 feet
   c. 13 feet
   d. 7 feet

4. A spring is most likely to be used on which of the following?
   a. a cabinet door
   b. a table
   c. an electric cord
   d. a pogo stick

5. If there are two connected pulleys and one is smaller than the other, which one turns faster?
   a. the smaller one
   b. the larger one
   c. they turn at the same speed
   d. not enough information is provided to answer the question

6. An elevator uses which of the following mechanical devices?
   a. a cable
   b. a pulley
   c. a motor
   d. all of the above

7. The Earth is a sphere that rotates about an axis that passes through the north pole and the south pole. If one person is standing at the north pole, another at the south pole, and a third at the equator of the Earth, which one will be traveling at a higher tangential velocity? (Tangential velocity means the speed parallel to the surface of the Earth.)
   a. the person at the south pole
   b. the person at the north pole
   c. the person at the equator
   d. all will be traveling at the same tangential velocity

8. Lori and Steve are sitting in separate cars at a stop sign. Lori accelerates at twice the rate that Steve accelerates. After five minutes of constant acceleration, who has traveled a longer distance?
   a. Steve
   b. Lori
   c. they have traveled the same distance
   d. not enough information to answer the question

9. You are in Denver and it is 1:00 P.M. You need to be in Moab, Utah, by 8:00 P.M. Moab is 350 miles from Denver. Assuming you drive straight through with no stops, what must your average speed be in order to arrive in Moab by 8:00 P.M.?
   a. 50 mile per hour
   b. 56 miles per hour
   c. 42 miles per hour
   d. 65 miles per hour

10. A metal plate is hanging from the ceiling by a chain in each of its corners. If one chain breaks, how is the weight distributed?
   a. the weight is evenly distributed to the remaining three chains
   b. the two chains diagonally from each other carry all the weight
   c. the two chains on the opposite side from the one that broke carry most of the weight, with the third carrying a small portion
   d. the plate will fall because the remaining three chains cannot hold it

11. A block of wood rests on a level surface. What mechanical principle makes it more difficult to push this block sideways if the surface is made of sandpaper than if it is made of glass?
   a. centrifugal force
   b. gravity
   c. wind resistance
   d. friction

12. Water is flowing through a piping system. Eventually, due to friction losses and a rise in elevation of the piping, the flow rate of the water becomes very slow. What mechanical device can best be used to increase the flow of the water?
   a. a gear
   b. a winch
   c. a pump
   d. a compressor

Chain traveling clockwise around gears

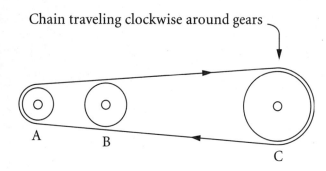

A   B   C

13. In the diagram above, gears A, B, and C are connected by a chain. The diameters of the gears are 1 inch, 2 inches, and 4 inches respectively. If gear A is turning at 20 revolutions per minute (RPM), what is the turning rate of gear C?
a. 5 RPM
b. 20 RPM
c. 40 RPM
d. 80 RPM

14. Water has a density of 62.4 pounds per cubic foot. Mercury has a density of 848.6 pounds per cubic foot. If mercury is poured into a glass of water, what will happen?
a. The mercury will sink.
b. The mercury will float.
c. The weight of the glass of water will decrease.
d. None of the above is true.

15. A steel bar is transferred from a freezer at 30 degrees Fahrenheit to a room at 70 degrees Fahrenheit. The bar will
a. get shorter.
b. break.
c. stay the same length.
d. get longer.

16. A bridge spans 100 feet. It is supported by Pier A on the right and Pier B on the left and has no center or intermediate supports. If a truck is at the center of the bridge, which statement best describes the structural support system of the bridge?
a. The truck is supported more by Pier A than by Pier B.
b. The truck is supported more by Pier B than by Pier A.
c. The truck is supported equally by Pier A and Pier B.
d. There is not enough information to answer the question.

17. As an object is submerged deeper and deeper in a body of water, what happens to the pressure exerted by the water on the object?
a. it increases
b. it decreases
c. it becomes zero
d. it stays the same

18. Why do large steel ships float?
a. Steel is lighter than water.
b. The propellers keep the ships afloat.
c. The ships displace more water than their weight.
d. Steel is heavier than water.

19. If a car is traveling at a constant speed of 70 miles per hour and it traveled 105 miles, how long has it been traveling?
(Distance = rate × time)
a. 45 minutes
b. 1 hour
c. 30 minutes
d. 1 hour 30 minutes

20. What common mechanical device is typically used on a push button, such as on a push-button telephone, a computer keyboard, and an electric garage door opener, in order to return the button to its original position?

a. a wheel
b. a pulley
c. a spring
d. a gear

21. Which of the following types of wire cutters would allow a worker to cut a heavy piece of wire using the least force?

a. a wire cutter with very thick handles
b. a wire cutter whose handles are longer than its blades
c. a wire cutter with finger groves on the grip
d. a wire cutter whose blades are longer than its handles

22. What are usually found between a wheel and an axle to reduce friction?

a. levers
b. springs
c. bearings
d. hinges

23. What type of gauge is read in units of psi (pounds per square inch)?

a. a pressure gauge
b. a depth gauge
c. a speed gauge
d. an RPM gauge

24. Newton's First Law of physics says, "A body [such as a car] that is in motion along a straight line will remain in motion, at the same speed, along the same straight line, unless acted upon by an outside force." A car is traveling down a straight, flat road at 30 miles per hour. The operation of all but one of the items listed below can help demonstrate Newton's Second Law. Which item CANNOT be used to demonstrate this Law?

a. the brakes
b. the gas pedal
c. the steering wheel
d. the radiator

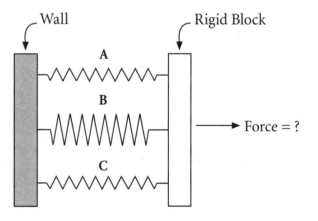

25. Three springs are arranged in parallel between a wall and a rigid block, as shown above. The spring constants are 5 pounds per inch, 12 pounds per inch, and 5 pounds per inch respectively. What force is required to move the block 2 inches to the right?

a. 12 pounds
b. 44 pounds
c. 22 pounds
d. 10 pounds

Part 9: Assembling Objects

Time: 16 minutes

Each question is comprised of five separate drawings. The problem is presented in the first drawing and the remaining four drawings are possible solutions. Determine which of the choices best solves the problem shown in the first picture. Note: images are not drawn to scale.

1.

2.

3.

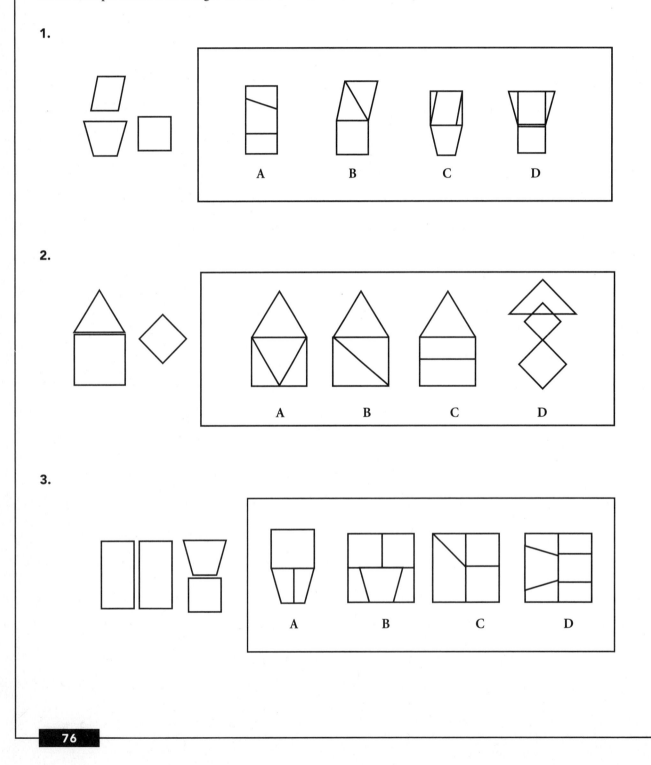

4.

5.

6.

7.

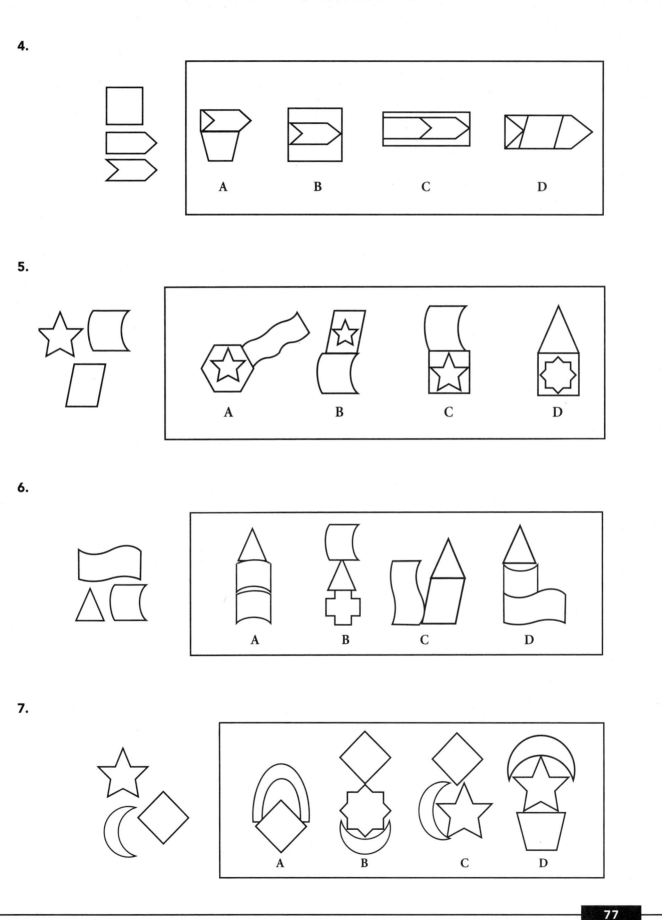

8.

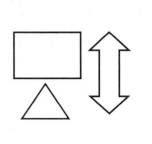

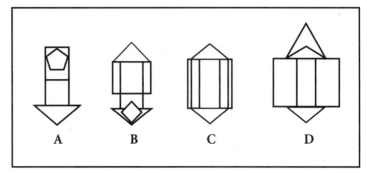

9.

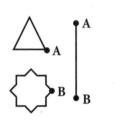

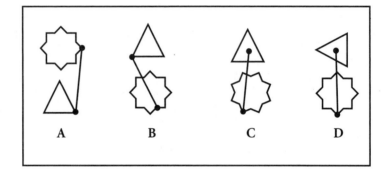

10.

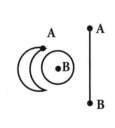

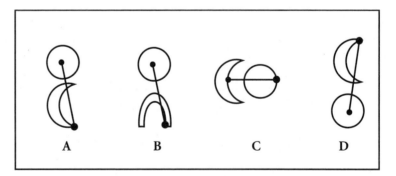

11.

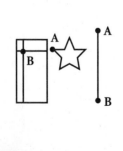

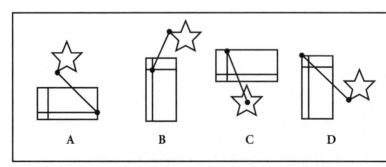

12.

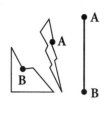

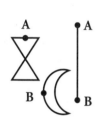

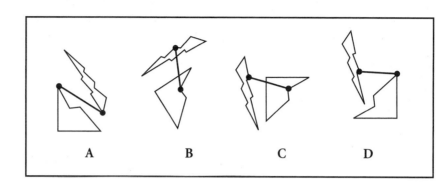

A   B   C   D

13.

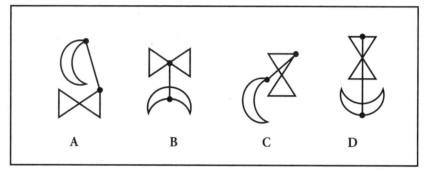

A   B   C   D

14.

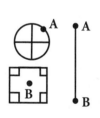

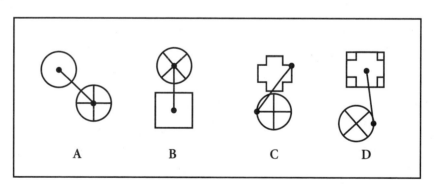

A   B   C   D

15.

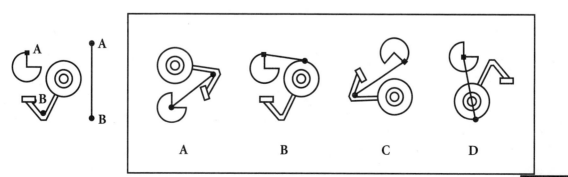

A   B   C   D

16.

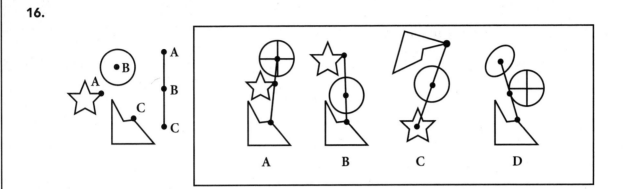

Answers
Part 1: General Science

1. c. An element's number of protons determines its location on the periodic table. For instance, hydrogen (H) has one proton, helium (He) has two protons, and lithium (Li) has three protons, so H, He, Li are numbers 1, 2, and 3 on the periodic table.

2. b. Isotopes are atoms of the same element with varying atomic masses depending how many neutrons are in the nucleus.

3. c. Marine biology is the study of the plants, animals, and microbes found under water and is a branch of the larger encompassing field of oceanography.

4. d. A single molecule of any substance must contain the same elements in the same proportions as a larger amount of that substance. Therefore, a molecule of carbon dioxide (CO_2) must have 1 carbon atom and 2 oxygen atoms.

5. c. The concept of centrifugal force suggests that the mass of an object will be pushed in an outward direction when it is spinning in a circular motion. Fundamental forces usually refer to forces between elementary particles such as electromagnetism or gravity. The Coriolis effect is caused by the rotation of the Earth on its axis.

6. b. The food coloring spreading out into the water is an example of diffusion, which is the spreading out of the molecules of a substance from places of greater molecular concentration to places of lower concentration.

7. c. Cooking a hamburger involves a chemical change. The other choices involve physical changes.

8. a. Carbohydrates are digested more easily and absorbed more quickly than fats. Choice **b** is incorrect because amino acids are the building blocks of proteins. Choices **c** and **d** are not true of carbohydrates.

9. d. The troposphere is closest to the Earth's surface, then the stratosphere, mesosphere and, furthermost out from the surface, is the thermosphere.

10. a. Reptiles lay their eggs on land, so they do not have internal development of eggs.

11. d. The snake is the only vertebrate—that is, it is the only one of the four animals that has a backbone.

12. b. One organism may acclimate itself to the stresses associated with a new environment. Evolution and the process of natural selection occur over several generations.

13. d. Omnivores eat many types of food, including plants and flesh.

14. b. The electromagnetic spectrum contains these wavelengths, from shortest to longest: gamma rays, X-rays, ultraviolet, visible, infrared, microwave, radio.

15. d. Gravity is the weakest of the four fundamental forces. Gravity controls the movement of planets, stars, and galaxies, as well as holding objects on Earth.

16. a. The Sun is a star in the center of the solar system, and it is almost 110 times the diameter of the Earth. Venus is slightly smaller than the Earth. Jupiter is the largest planet in the Solar System (with a diameter 11 times that of the Earth), but it only contains 0.1 percent of a solar mass.

17. d. Absolute zero, when all atoms in solid matter stop vibrating, is –273 degrees Celsius or 0 degrees Kelvin.

18. a. Our solar system contains eight planets: Mercury, Venus, Earth, Mars, Jupiter, Saturn, Uranus, and Neptune.

19. b. Only a plant or algae cell contains chloroplasts, the site of photosynthesis in plants and algae. Therefore, fern (a plant) is the only possible answer.

20. a. Deoxyribonucleic acid (DNA), the genetic blueprint of cells, is located in the nucleus of animal cells.

21. c. Human sex cells (gametes) have 23 chromosomes. All other human cells have 46 chromosomes—23 from the mother and 23 from the father.

22. b. Breaking a water molecule up into its specific elements would yield hydrogen and oxygen.

23. a. Speech is not controlled by the autonomic nervous system (ANS). The ANS stimulates involuntary muscles and glands in the body.

24. c. Vertebrates have a spinal cord enclosed in a flexible, bony column.

25. a. Elephants are in the phylum Chordata, class Mammalia, and order Proboscidae. Genus and species names are always underlined or italicized, as in the species name *Palaeomastodon*.

Part 2: Arithmetic Reasoning

1. c. Since the price per copy is $0.85, divide 68 by .85 to find the total number that can be purchased with $68; $68 ÷ .85 = 80 copies that can be purchased.

2. c. The volume of the aquarium can be found by using the formula $V = l \times w \times h$. Since the length is 12 inches, the width is 5 inches and the height is 10 inches, multiply $V = 12 \times 5 \times 10$ to get a volume of 600 cubic inches.

3. c. The value of the handbag ($150) must be included in the total.

4. d. Both choices **a** and **b** can be ruled out because there is no way to determine how many tickets are for adults or for children. Choice **c** can be ruled out because the price of group tickets is not given.

5. d. Because the 15-year-old requires an adult ticket, there are 3 adult tickets at $7.50 each and one child's ticket at $5.

6. a. The adult price on Saturday afternoon is $5.50; the child's price is $3.00.

7. d. This problem is solved by dividing 60 by 0.50. $60 ÷ .50 = 120$.

8. b. This is a multiplication problem, which is solved by multiplying 35 times 8.2.

9. a. You know the ratio of Drake's charge to Jean's charge is 3 to 4, or $\frac{3}{4}$. To find what Jean charges, you use the equation $\frac{3}{4} = \frac{36}{x}$, or $3x = 4(36)$; $(4)(36) = 144$, which is then divided by 3 to arrive at $x = 48$.

10. a. In this question, you need to find 15% of the 30% of students that are in the music program. To find 15% of 30%, change the percents to decimal form and multiply. Since 30% = 0.30 and 15% = 0.15, multiply $(0.30)(0.15) = 0.045$. As a decimal, this is equivalent to 4.5% which is choice **a**.

11. d. The basic cable service fee of $15 is 75% of $20.

12. a. The labor fee ($25) plus the deposit ($65) plus the basic service ($15) equals $105. The difference between the total bill, $112.50, and $105 is $7.50, the cost of the news channels.

13. c. 60 out of 200 is 30%. Thirty percent of 40,000 is 12,000.

14. d. 27.5% of 400 is 110.

15. b. Rock is 45.5%; when we add 4.5% for classical we arrive at 50%.

16. c. If 60% of the people were satisfied with their new car, 40% were unsatisfied; 40% of 220 is 88.

17. c. Divide 135 Spanish-speaking students by 1,125 total number of students to arrive at .12 or 12%.

18. b. The first step in solving the problem is to subtract 156 from 268. $268 - 156 = 112$. The remainder, 112, is then divided by 2. $112 ÷ 2 = 56$.

19. c. Three feet 4 inches equals 40 inches; 40 divided by 5 is 8.

20. a. It will cost $3 for a sandwich and a cookie. To get two additional sandwiches, it would cost another $4. Therefore, it would cost $7 to get three sandwiches and a cookie. Since she only has $6 to spend, this combination is not possible.

21. a. Area = width × length. In this case, 4 × 6 = 24 square feet.

22. b. Use the formula beginning with the operation in parentheses: 98 − 32 = 66. Then multiply 66 by $\frac{5}{9}$, first multiplying 66 by 5 to get 330; 330 divided by 9 is 36.66667, which is rounded up to 36.7.

23. c. Each 9-foot wall has an area of 9 × 8 or 72 square feet. There are two such walls, so those two walls combined have an area of 72 × 2 or 144 square feet. Each 11-foot wall has an area of 11 × 8 or 88 square feet, and again there are two such walls: 88 × 2 = 176. To find the total surface area, add 144 and 176 to get 320 square feet.

24. b. $1\frac{1}{2}$ cups equals $\frac{3}{2}$ cups. The ratio is 6 people to 4 people, which is equal to the ratio of x to $\frac{3}{2}$. By cross multiplying, we get $6(\frac{3}{2})$ equals $4x$, or 9 equals $4x$. Dividing both sides by 4, we get $\frac{9}{4}$, or $2\frac{1}{4}$ cups.

25. a. The distance between Greenville and Johnson City is the hypotenuse of a right triangle with sides of length 90 and 120. The length of the hypotenuse equals the square root of the sum of the other two sides squared. $90^2 + 120^2 = 22{,}500$. $\sqrt{22{,}500} = 150$ miles.

26. d. The volume of concrete is 27 cubic feet. Volume is length times width times depth, or $(L)(W)(D)$, so $(L)(W)(D) = 27$. We're told that the length L is 6 times the width W, so L equals $6W$. We're also told that the depth is 6 inches, or 0.5 feet. Substituting what we know about the length and depth into the original equation and solving for W, we get $(L)(W)(D) = (6W)(W)(0.5) = 27$. $3W^2 = 27$; $W^2 = 9$, so $W = 3$. To get the length, we remember that L equals $6W$, so L equals $(6)(3)$, or 18 feet.

27. c. Find the price per ounce of each brand, as follows: Brand W is $\frac{21}{6}$ or 3.5 cents per ounce; Brand X is $\frac{48}{15}$ or 3.2 cents per ounce; Brand Y is $\frac{56}{20}$ or 2.8 cents per ounce; Brand Z is $\frac{96}{32}$ or 3.0 cents per ounce. It is then easy to see that Brand Y, at 2.8 cents per ounce, is the least expensive.

28. a. 2,052 miles divided by 6 days is 342 miles per day; 342 miles divided by 2 stops is 171 miles.

29. b. K + F + 2S = 540. Also, K = 2F and S = F, which changes the original equation to 2F + F + 2F = 540, so 5F = 540 and F = 108. Since there is one fork per place setting, the cook can buy 108 place settings.

30. c. First find the total price of the pencils: (24 pencils)($0.05) = $1.20. Then find the total price of the paper: (3.5 reams)($7.50 per ream) = $26.25. Next, add the two totals together: $1.20 + 26.25 = $27.45.

Part 3: Word Knowledge

1. c. To *mediate* is to settle disputes; to *reconcile* is to bring into agreement.

2. a. To *expedite* a process is to hurry it up or *accelerate* it.

3. b. If something is *plausible*, it is believable or *credible*.

4. b. *Concurrent* means happening at the same time; *simultaneous* means the same thing.

5. d. *Impromptu* means without preparation; *spontaneous* means unpremeditated.

6. a. To *induce* is to bring about; to *prompt* is to provoke or induce to action.

7. c. To *infer* something is to *surmise* it or deduce it from the evidence.

8. c. To *saturate* is to fill or to load to capacity; to *soak* is to penetrate or permeate.

9. a. A *synopsis* is an abbreviated version; a *summary* is a brief statement of facts or points.

10. b. A *hyperbole* is an extravagant statement; an *exaggeration* is an overstatement.

11. d. One of the meanings of to *proscribe* is to prohibit; to *forbid* is to command (someone) not to do something. *Proscribe* should not be confused with *prescribe*, which is what a doctor does with a medication.

12. a. A *proponent* is a supporter of something; an *advocate* is someone who supports something—for instance, a cause.

13. d. An *intrepid* person approaches a challenge without fear; a *fearless* person behaves the same way.

14. b. A *statute* is a law; an *ordinance* is a rule or law.

15. b. To be *apathetic* is to show little or no interest or to be *indifferent*.

16. a. To be *fortified* is to be strengthened or *reinforced*.

17. a. To *refrain* is to hold back from doing something; to *desist* is to cease doing something.

18. d. To *delegate* a task is to *assign* it or to appoint another to do it.

19. b. Something that is *spurious* is not genuine; something that is *false* is also not genuine.

20. d. To *articulate* something is to give words to it or *express* it.

21. d. To *disparage* is to talk about something or someone in a negative manner; to *criticize* is to find fault with something.

22. c. If something is *expansive,* it is broad, open, or *spacious.*

23. c. To be *urbane* is to show the refined manners of high society; to be *sophisticated* is to show worldly knowledge or refinement.

24. a. A *rationale* is a reason for something; an *explanation* is a clarification or definition or something.

25. b. If a thing is *detrimental,* it is injurious or *harmful.*

26. d. *Brevity* means *shortness* or briefness.

27. b. A *fiasco* is a complete and *humiliating failure.*

28. c. A *nomad* is one who wanders.

29. c. *Paucity* denotes a *scarcity* or smallness of required numbers.

30. b. *Obstrusive* means to be *forward* in manner or conduct.

31. a. To *impede* is to retard in movement or progress by means of obstacles or hindrances or *obstruct.*

32. a. *Demure* means someone or something is characterized by shyness and modesty.

33. c. *Abeyance* means *suspension* or being temporarily suspended or set aside.

34. a. *Accolade* means praise or approval. It also means a ceremonial embrace in greeting or a ceremonial tap on the shoulder to confer knighthood.

35. d. *Accretion* is growth or increase by gradual, successive addition; building up.

Part 4: Paragraph Comprehension

1. d. Although the last sentence expands on the main point, the rest of the passage explains why hearsay evidence is only admissible when it doesn't matter whether or not the statement is true.

2. a. This statement may be true, but it isn't in the passage.

3. b. See the last sentence of the passage.

4. c. The passage mentions the truthfulness of testimony several times.

5. d. According to the passage, all taxi drivers are not required to take the course—only drivers that have been working more than 5 years.

6. a. The last sentence indicates the purpose.

7. c. The directions indicate that the city prefers, but does not require, use of the new container. In addition, it appears the city only charges residents for additional containers.

8. d. The directions state the city would like households to use the new containers as their primary containers; this means other containers are allowed.

9. d. The directions mention nothing about main or secondary roads.

10. a. The other choices are not mentioned in the directions.

11. a. The passage states that the events it described happened in 1956; this rules out choice **c.** The purpose of the passage is to explain a historical event, so choices **b** and **d** are clearly wrong.

12. b. See the first paragraph. Choice **a** is contradicted in the first paragraph, and the passage does not discuss Lucy's later profession (choice **c**) or major (choice **d**).

13. a. The first sentence provides the main idea of the passage. It makes a statement and expounds upon it throughout the rest of the passage.

14. b. Choices **a**, **c**, and **d** are never implied in the passage. Choice **b** is the only choice that can be inferred from the passage.

15. c. The passage builds on the premise introduced in the first sentence.

Part 5: Mathematics Knowledge

1. b. *PQ* and *RS* are intersecting lines. The fact that angle *POS* is a 90-degree angle means that *PQ* and *RS* are perpendicular, indicating that all the angles formed by their intersection, including *ROQ*, measure 90 degrees.

2. a. Incorrect answers include adding both the numerator and the denominator and not converting fifths to tenths properly.

3. c. To convert a fraction to a decimal, divide the numerator, 3, by the denominator, 4. $3.00 \div 4 = 0.75$

4. b. The correct answer is $88\frac{1}{3}$.

5. b. Divide the numerator by the denominator: $1.000 \div 3 = 0.166667$. Round the answer to the thousandths place (three decimal places) to get the answer 0.167.

6. d. You have to convert all three fractions to twelfths before adding them.

7. c. Choice **a** reads 22,436; choice **b** reads 2,346; choice **d** reads 206,306.

8. a. The first box is one greater than –5; the second is one greater than 0.

9. d. $1\frac{1}{2}$ is a mixed number. To convert this into a decimal, first take the whole number (in this case, 1) and place it to the left of the decimal point. Then, take the fraction (in this case, $\frac{1}{2}$) and convert it to a decimal by dividing the numerator by the denominator. Putting these two steps together gives the answer, 1.50.

10. a. Raise the fraction $\frac{2}{9}$ to 54ths by multiplying both numerator and denominator by 6.

11. d. $7(8)(2) = 112$.

12. d. Divide 3 by 8 in order to convert the fraction into a decimal. $3 \div 8 = 0.375$.

13. c. The meaning of 4^3 is 4 times itself 3 times.

14. a. The total on the right is 35. On the left, you need an operation you can do on 5 to get 35. Multiplying by $(5 + 2)$ does the trick.

15. a. Using 20 for C: $F = (\frac{9}{5} \times 20) + 32$. Therefore $F = 36 + 32$, or 68.

16. c. $5(3)(8) = 120; 120 \div 3 = 40$

17. c. $10(10)(10) = 1,000; 1,000(7.25) = 7,250$

18. b. To solve this problem, you must first convert yards to inches. There are 36 inches in a yard; $36(3\frac{1}{3}) = 120$.

19. a. Divide 3 by 5 to convert from a fraction into a decimal; $3 \div 5 = 0.60$.

20. a. 0.97 multiplied by 100 is 97; therefore, the correct answer is 97%.

21. c. The sum of the measure of the angles in a triangle is 180 degrees; 70 degrees + 30 degrees = 100 degrees; 180 degrees – 100 degrees = 80 degrees. Therefore, angle *C* is 80 degrees.

22. b. Since the solution to the problem $x + 32 = 14$, $x = -18$. Choices **a**, **c**, and **d** are all too large to be correct.

23. c. To solve this problem you should use the formula $A = lw$ or $108 = l \times 6$. Next, you must divide 108 by 6 to find the answer. $108 \div 6 = 18$.

24. a. 37.5% is the same as $\frac{37.5}{100}$. You should multiply both the numerator and denominator by 10 to move the decimal point, resulting in $\frac{375}{1,000}$. Next, factor both the numerator and denominator to find out how far you can reduce the fraction: $\frac{5 \times 5 \times 5 \times 3}{5 \times 5 \times 5 \times 8}$. If you cancel the three 5s that are in both the numerator and the denominator, you get $\frac{3}{8}$.

25. b. In the decimal, 0.15, the 5 falls in the hundredths place (two places to the right of the decimal). To convert this to a fraction, the 15 is placed over 100. Reduce, which gives you $\frac{3}{20}$.

Part 6: Electronics Information

1. c. The prefix "kilo" is a multiplier of 1,000; $200 \times 1,000 = 200,000$.

2. b. A static charge does not move. It has the potential to do work; it does not do work. It is not a force.

3. c. Whenever the voltage is increased, the current flow will also increase.

4. a. $I = \frac{Q}{T} = \frac{300\ C}{60\ seconds} = 5\ A$.

5. d. Gold is a metal and a good conductor.

6. b. Resistance is defined as the opposition to the flow of current.

7. c. The three elements of an electric circuit are a potential voltage source, resistance, and a closed path for current to flow.

8. c. E stands for electromotive force, which is the same as voltage. Voltage is measured in volts.

9. a. Current is defined as electric charge in motion.

10. d. Silicon is a semiconductor material.

11. b. A good conductor has electrons which are free to move, and metal is a good conductor. Metals are low in resistance. Metals can be expensive and easily formed into wires; however, that is not why they are good conductors.

12. a. An insulator has very large resistance. A conductor has a small resistance. A semiconductor has a medium resistance. A transformer is a coil of wire and has a small resistance.

13. d. The voltage across the meter will equal the sum of the voltages across the series resistors R1 and R2. So: $V = (I \times R_1) + (I \times R_2) = (2\ A \times 10\ \Omega) + (2\ A \times 5\ \Omega) = 20\ V + 10\ V = 30\ V$.

14. b. In a parallel circuit, the current will increase and the resistance will decrease.

15. c. The total resistance of series resistors is the sum of the resistance. $RT = R1 + R2 = 5\ \Omega + 5\ \Omega = 10\ \Omega$.

16. a. The meter will read zero because the meter is not connected across a resistance.

17. c. Because the resistances are equal, they will each have one-half of the applied voltage across them.

18. d. The semi-conductor allows current to pass through but will add some resistance.

19. c. Transformers are used to scale the value of an AC voltage. The ratio of the number of coils determines the voltage.

20. a. The resistance that results from combining two parallel resistances is always less than either of the original resistances.

Part 7: Auto and Shop Information

1. d. The crankshaft is rotated by the up and down movement of the piston and transfers the energy from the internal combustion engine to the drive train (transmission). The spark plugs provide fuel ignition. The radiator provides engine cooling. The oil provides lubrication.

2. b. There is no such thing as a dual hasp screwdriver.

3. a. A lever is the correct choice. A protractor is used to measure angles. A spring is used for many purposes but not to gain a mechanical advantage. A gear is used to change rotational speeds of shafts.

4. c. A tachometer measures revolutions per minute (rpm).

5. a. A speed gauge is the correct answer. A depth gauge would use units of length such as feet or meters. A pressure gauge would use units of pressure such as psi (pounds per square inch) or bar. A temperature gauge would use units of temperature such as degrees Celsius or degrees Fahrenheit.

6. c. The muffler is placed at the end of the exhaust system of an automobile to reduce engine noise. It is a chamber that dampens the noise coming from the internal combustion engine.

7. b. The differential is part of the drive axle; it allows the left and right wheels to turn at different speeds as the vehicle goes around corners.

8. b. Preventive maintenance is periodically making small changes and adjustments on a device to prevent failure. Examples include changing the oil in a car engine, adjusting the brakes on a car, lubricating the moving parts on a pump, and changing the fan belts and hoses on a truck.

9. c. A hacksaw is the correct answer. This type of saw is similar to a saw for cutting wood except that the teeth are very small and close together.

10. d. The flow meter gauge measures liquid flow rate, which is typically measured in units of volume per unit time, such as gallons per minute or cubic meters per second.

11. c. An internal combustion engine needs fire (in the form of a spark from a spark plug usually), fuel (in the form of gasoline), and oxygen to ignite the fuel and run the mechanical elements of the engine.

12. b. Kilometers per hour is the correct answer. A kilometer is a unit of distance in the metric system that is roughly equivalent to 0.6 miles.

13. d. This tool carves wood. Hammers are used to drive nails; welders or torches are used to weld metal; wrenches are used to tighten bolts.

14. b. The suspension of an automobile is typically composed of springs, shocks, wheels, and tires.

15. d. All these are names applied to various kinds of wrenches.

16. a. The correct answer is a crescent wrench.

17. c. The foundation is the base upon which the building is constructed. Therefore, it must be constructed before the framing, the walls, or the flooring.

18. a. A table saw would give you the best control to cut a 4 × 8 piece of plywood.

19. d. The saw could be used to cut the wood used for the forms for a concrete bridge foundation. It could be used for cutting the studs for the apart-

ment building wall. It could also be used for cutting the wood for a cedar deck railing.

20. b. Surveying is the practice of determining locations and elevations of structures and roadways. This is accomplished through the use of many instruments and tools, including levels for measuring elevations or heights, tape measures for measuring distances, and transits for measuring angles.

21. b. The sub-floor of a residential house consists of joists to support the structural load and decking for the surface. The joists are usually made of 2-inch by 10-inch lumber, and the decking is usually made of $\frac{3}{4}$-inch plywood.

22. a. A Phillips screwdriver is a very common type used on screws that have an indented cross on the head. You may find this type of screw on objects such as door hinges, television sets, and bicycles.

23. b. The internal combustion engine in an automobile generates heat and must be cooled. The typical cooling system is based on pumping water around the hot engine block. The heated water is then pumped into the radiator, where it is cooled and then re-circulated back to the engine block. The thermostat is used to regulate the flow of water to keep the engine warm but not let it overheat.

24. a. *Diamond point* is a kind of chisel. *Dovetail* and *coping* describe kinds of saws. *Duck bill* describes a kind of pliers.

25. c. Use jumper cables to get a charge from another battery. Installing a new starter will not help; the battery will still be dead. Adding fuel and changing fuses also will not recharge the battery. Jumper cables can be used to connect your dead battery to another live car battery to start the car.

Part 8: Mechanical Comprehension

1. b. (200 pounds)(10 feet) = f(16 feet). Solving for f gives 125 pounds.

2. c. All the gears would be turning at the same rate with every other one turning clockwise.

3. b. The blocks are tied together with a cable, which keeps the distance between the blocks constant. Therefore, if block B is to be lowered 10 feet to the floor, then block A must be raised the same amount.

4. d. Of all the items, only a pogo stick uses springs.

5. a. The smaller pulley has to go faster to keep up with the larger one.

6. d. All of the choices are correct. A motor is used to wind a cable around a pulley in order to raise and lower the car.

7. c. The two people at the poles will just spin around the axis of rotation and have no tangential velocity. The person at the equator will travel much faster since he or she is rotating at the same rate as the people at the poles and is located far away—half the diameter of the Earth—from the axis of rotation.

8. b. Lori's acceleration rate is twice Steve's rate. Since they both started at the same time and accelerated for the same amount of time, Lori will travel twice as far as Steve.

9. a. The equation used to solve this problem is: distance equals rate multiplied by time ($d = r \times t$). The distance is 350 miles; the time is 7 hours (from 1:00 P.M. to 8:00 P.M.). Solving for the rate gives 50.

10. b. If one chain breaks, the two chains diagonally from each other carry all the weight.

11. d. Friction is the force that must be overcome in order to slide one object across another.

12. c. Pumps are used to move liquids through piping systems.

13. a. Gear C is 4 times the diameter of gear A. Since the gears are all connected by a chain, the tip velocity of all the gears must be the same; otherwise, the chain would come off the gears.

Therefore, if the tip velocity is to be the same for all gears and gear C is 4 times larger than gear A, then gear C must be turning 4 times slower than gear A. 20 RPM divided by 4 equals 5 RPM.

14. a. Since mercury is more dense (one cubic foot of mercury weighs more than one cubic foot of water), it will sink to the bottom of the glass.

15. d. The bar will get longer. Metallic objects such as this steel bar have a positive coefficient of thermal expansion, which means that, as their temperature increases, their volume or length will increase. Moving the bar from the freezer to the room causes the bar's temperature to increase.

16. c. The truck is supported equally by Pier A and Pier B. Since the truck is exactly in the center of the bridge, half of its weight is transferred to each pier.

17. a. As the object goes deeper, there is more weight of water pressing on it; therefore, the pressure increases.

18. c. This is the Archimedes Principle. If you fill a glass to the top with water and then place a ball in the glass, some water will spill over the top. If the weight of this displaced water is more than the weight of the ball, it will float. If not, it will sink. The same is true for the ship.

19. d. The formula can be rearranged by dividing both sides by the rate. This will give you the distance divided by the rate, or 105 miles divided by 70 mph. 105 ÷ 70 = 1.5 hours.

20. c. A compression coil spring is typically placed behind the button. When the button is pressed, the spring is compressed and then springs back to return the button to its original position.

21. b. A wire cutter whose handles are longer than its blades provides the mechanical advantage of a lever.

22. c. The bearings are a set of small metal balls, often lubricated with grease or oil, and are located in a groove between the wheel and axle.

23. a. A pressure gauge is measured in psi. The other gauges are read in the following units: A depth gauge uses a unit of length such as feet or meters; a speed gauge uses a unit of velocity such as miles per hour (mph) or kilometers per hour (kph); the RPM gauge measures revolutions per minute.

24. d. Newton's First Law mandates that a vehicle will move "at the same speed" unless an outside force is applied. Both the brakes and the gas pedal could be used to apply such a force. Newton's Second Law also mandates that the vehicle will travel "along the same straight line" unless an outside force—the action of the steering wheel, for instance—is applied. The radiator has nothing to do with the speed or direction of the vehicle.

25. b. All three springs must be stretched 2 inches. The question tells you that it takes 5 pounds to stretch spring A one inch. Therefore, it takes 10 pounds to stretch it 2 inches. Apply this to the other two springs and add up the total to get 44 pounds.

Part 9: Assembling Objects

1. c.
2. d.
3. d.
4. b.
5. b.
6. d.
7. c.
8. d.
9. a.
10. d.
11. b.
12. c.
13. d.
14. d.
15. c.
16. b.

Scoring

Write your raw score (the number you got right) for each test in the blanks below. Then turn to Chapter 3 to find out how to convert these raw scores into the scores the armed services use.

1. General Science: _____ right out of 25
2. Arithmetic Reasoning: _____ right out of 30
3. Word Knowledge: _____ right out of 25
4. Paragraph Comprehension: _____ right out of 15
5. Mathematics Knowledge: _____ right out of 35
6. Electronics Information: _____ right out of 20
7. Auto and Shop Information: _____ right out of 25
8. Mechanical Comprehension: _____ right out of 25
9. Assembling Objects: _____ right out of 16

6 ▶ GENERAL SCIENCE REVIEW

CHAPTER SUMMARY

This chapter presents an outline and review of the important general science concepts that are tested by the ASVAB.

This chapter helps you prepare for the ASVAB's General Science subtest by reviewing some of the important science topics you're likely to encounter on the test. Use it as an aid to help you recall what you learned in high school and to identify what you have forgotten and need to review further.

The General Science subtest of the ASVAB deals with basic concepts and terms covered in most high school science curricula. It is a survey of important topics in life science, physical science, and earth science, with the first two being the most important.

Each of these three major areas covers more specific fields:

- **Life science** includes biology, ecology, human anatomy, and nutrition
- **Physical science** includes chemistry, measurements, and physics
- **Earth science** includes astronomy, geology, and meteorology

Life Science

Biology is the study of living things. We share the planet with over a million plants and animals. A Swedish scientist named Carl Linné, also known as Linnaeus, devised the classification system used in modern biological science. Every organism is grouped according to seven basic levels of classification, which are, from broadest to most specific: kingdom, phylum, class, order, family, genus, species.

Classification

Linnaeus's system describes organisms that have shared physical traits with a two-word, or **binomial**, name. The scientific name of an organism consists of a **genus** name and a **species** name. A genus name, always capitalized, precedes the species name, which is in lowercase. Both genus and species names are underlined or italicized.

- A human belongs to genus *Homo*, species *sapiens*, so it is *Homo sapiens.*
- A common frog belongs to genus *Rana*, species *temporaria*, so it is *Rana temporaria.*
- An African violet belongs to genus *Saintpaulia*, species *ionantha*, so it is *Saintpaulia ionantha.*

Most biologists divide all living things into five major types, each forming a kingdom: animals, plants, fungi, protists, and monerans. This chapter focuses on animals and plants because those kingdoms contain the majority of life. It is useful, however, to know a little about the other three kingdoms.

Monerans, such as blue-green algae and bacteria, are single-celled organisms containing no nuclei. Blue-green algae produce their own food through photosynthesis (defined later in this chapter). Many bacteria are parasites that cause diseases, or they are decomposers, meaning that they absorb food from decaying material.

Protists, such as protozoa and algae, are single-celled organisms that contain cell nuclei. **Fungi,** such as molds and mushrooms, are multiple-celled organisms that form spores and decompose other organic matter. Yeasts are unicellular fungi that form colonies.

Kingdom	Number of Cells	Type
Monera	one-celled organisms	"simple," no cell nucleus
Protista	one-celled organisms	"complex," contain cell nucleus
Fungi	multiple-celled organisms	"complex," contain organized cell nucleus, decomposers, form spores

Plants

Plants contain many cells and make their own food through photosynthesis. The two phyla, or large groupings within the plant kingdom, are the **Bryophyta,** such as mosses and hornworts, and the **Tracheophyta,** including flowering plants and pine trees. Bryophytes are tiny, grow on surfaces, and reproduce by spores. They are simply organized and lack the structural support of true roots, stems and woody tissue. Tracheophytes, or vascular plants, are the plants that we encounter every day. Almost all have roots, stems of woody tissue—which allow them to grow to great heights and in soil with a dry surface—and leaves.

The largest class of the Tracheophyta is composed of the following divisions:

- **Filicophytes,** or ferns
- **Angiosperms (Magnoliophyta),** flowering plants that produce seeds with protective coverings
- **Gymnosperms (encompassing four divisions),** which produce seeds without protective covering, though some produce seed cones, such as the pine cone

Angiosperms are further divided into monocots and dicots. **Monocots** bear seeds with only one **cotyledon**, a leaf within the embryo. Monocots, such as onions, tulips, and palms, are characterized by parallel leaf veins and flowers in groups of threes. **Dicots** bear two cotyledons. Dicots, such as potatoes, roses, and oaks, are characterized by net-like leaf veins and flower parts in fours, fives, or multiples of either four or five.

Animals

Animals are many-celled, mobile organisms that cannot produce their own food. The animal kingdom is divided into approximately 26 phyla. Some of the major animal phyla are shown in the table on this page.

Vertebrates

The vertebrates are a subphlylum in the chordate phylum and include birds, fish, mammals, and reptiles. (All other animals are invertebrates.) Vertebrates have a spinal cord enclosed in a flexible, bony column that extends down the long axis of the body, providing skeletal support. There are eight classes of vertebrates. Four of the vertebrate classes are fish: agnatha (lamprey), chondrichthyes (shark), osteichthyes (trout), and the extinct placodermi. The other four classes of vertebrates and some of their characteristics are listed in the table on the next page.

ANIMAL PHYLA		
Phylum	**Characteristics**	**Example**
Porifera	aquatic; pores in body allow flow of water to bring in nutrients and take out waste products	sponges
Coelenterata	aquatic; have stinging cells to capture prey; may be free-swimming or sedentary	jellyfish, coral
Platyhelminthes	flat body; one opening to digestive system; often live as parasites in humans	flukes, tapeworms
Aschelminthes	smooth, round body tapered at both ends; two openings to digestive system; often parasitic	nematodes
Annelida	segmented worms; closed circulatory system	earthworms
Mollusca	most have unsegmented bodies, hard shells	clams, snails
Echinodermata	marine; usually having five radial arms	starfish
Arthropoda	jointed exoskeletons and at least three pairs of jointed legs	insects, crabs, spiders
Chordata	inner skeleton; gills at some point in development; hollow, dorsal nerve cord	humans, horses, geckos, trout

VERTEBRATES		
Class	**Characteristics**	**Example**
Amphibia	aquatic as both eggs and larvae; land-dwelling as adults	frogs
Aves	have feathers; external development of eggs	birds
Mammalia	have fur and are milk-producing; internal development of eggs	humans
Reptilia	eggs laid on land, land-dwelling adults, scaly skin	turtles

Only the aves and mammalia are **warm-blooded**. Birds and humans generate and regulate their own body heat. Feathers on birds and fur on mammals help them retain body heat, and sweating (yes, birds sweat) helps them cool down. All of the other vertebrates are **cold-blooded**. This means that their body temperature is determined by the temperature of their surrounding environment.

Mammals

All mammals share certain characteristics. They are warm-blooded, have a hair or fur covering for insulation, have a four-chambered heart, and breathe with lungs. In addition, females produce milk for their young. Mammals are divided further by body structures into 17 orders containing a total of only approximately 4,250 species. Some of the more important mammal orders are shown on the table at the bottom of this page.

Viruses

Viruses are difficult to classify because scientists do not agree on the definition of a virus. Some scientists believe that a virus is nonliving because, alone, a virus is incapable of reproducing. However, viruses consist of a DNA or RNA core encapsulated in a protein coat (a capsid), which causes many to argure for its status as a life form. A virus has no true cell structure, and it is incapable of independent metabolism and reproduction without the aid of a host cell. Once inside another cell, a virus takes over and uses the host cell's resources to replicate viral DNA. Eventually the host cell dies and the (many) replicated viruses are released to infect new cells. Viral diseases in animals include the common cold, influenza, herpes, measles, polio, and rabies.

Basic Life Principles

All living organisms perform certain biochemical and biophysical activities to achieve homeostasis—

MAMMALS		
Order	**Characteristics**	**Example**
Cetaceans	marine; forelimbs are flippers	whales, dolphins
Marsupials	carry young in a pouch	kangaroos, possums
Primates	highly developed brain; stand erect	humans, apes
Rodents	teeth specialized for gnawing	mice, beavers
Ungulates	hoofed, teeth specialized for grinding	horses, deer

a balanced internal environment. The life functions are as follows:

- **Circulation:** the transport of materials such as oxygen and nutrients throughout an organism
- **Excretion:** the elimination of metabolic waste products from an organism
- **Growth:** cell division and/or enlargement
- **Nutrition:** getting nutrients, or food molecules, from the environment via eating, absorption, or photosynthesis
- **Regulation:** the chemical control and coordination of life activities
- **Reproduction:** the production of new individuals
- **Respiration:** organic substances are broken down to simpler products with the release of energy, which is used to fuel other metabolic processes (in animals and plants)

The Cell

Cells are the basic structural and functional unit of living things. One cell, alone, is the smallest unit of matter that is considered living. In general, plant and animal cells are similar, except that plant cells contain chloroplasts and cell walls. Chloroplasts contain chlorophyll, a food-generating substance. Cell walls, containing cellulose and other compounds, give plant cells a rigid structure and prevent desiccation, or drying out.

The size of cells varies, but most are microscopic (an average of 0.01–0.1 mm in diameter). They may exist independently, or they may form colonies or tissues—like those in plants and animals. Each cell contains a mass of protein, called protoplasm, that consists of jelly-like cytoplasm and a nucleus. The nucleus, in turn, contains deoxyribonucleic acid, or DNA, which is the genetic material of most organisms. The protoplasm is bound by a cell or plasma membrane, which controls the materials that pass in and out of the cell.

There are two types of cells, distinguished from one another by a number of characteristics, one being the way in which they reproduce. Bacteria are one example of **prokaryotic cells.** The nuclear material in prokaryotic cells is not bound by a membrane, and cell reproduction occurs by fission—asexual cell cleavage—the cell breaks apart to form another, identical cell. The other type of cell, found in most plants and animals, is a **eukaryotic cell**, in which the nucleus is separated from the cytoplasm by the nuclear membrane and there are separate organelles. In

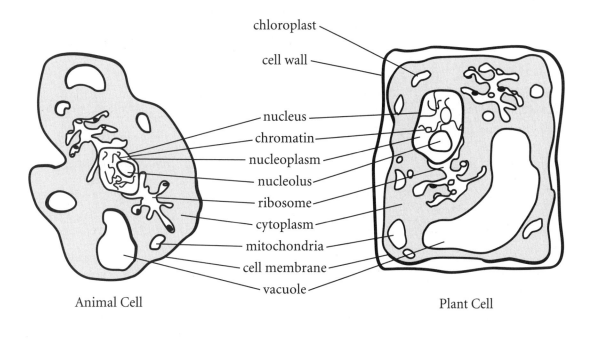

chloroplast

cell wall

nucleus

chromatin

nucleoplasm

nucleolus

ribosome

cytoplasm

mitochondria

cell membrane

vacuole

Animal Cell

Plant Cell

eukaryotic plant and animal cells, the major cell organelles are as follows:

- **Cell membrane:** partially permeable membrane that regulates flow of materials in and out of the cell and holds the structure of the cell together
- **Cytoplasm:** jelly-like material that encompasses the other cell structures
- **Endoplasmic reticulum:** a network of membranes extending from the nucleus into the cytoplasm, responsible for making lipids, proteins (in association with ribosomes), and transporting these products throughout the cell
- **Golgi body/apparatus:** stores and transports secretory products within the cell
- **Lysosome:** contains and releases enzymes within the cell
- **Mitochondrion:** the largest organelle and site of energy production, known as cellular respiration, in the cell (there are several mitochondria in each cell)
- **Nucleus:** contains genetic material and functions as the control center of the cell
- **Ribosome:** site of protein synthesis (there are many ribosomes in each cell)

Plant cells additionally have chloropoasts, where photosynthesis takes place, and a cell wall.

Genetics

Genetics is the study of heredity and variation. **Heredity** is the transmission of characteristics from parents to offspring via chromosomes. Gregor Mendel, a European monk in the late 18th century, developed some of the basic laws of heredity which have been updated, but are still applicable today:

- **Law of Segregation:** each hereditary characteristic is controlled by alleles that separate in the reproductive cells
- **Law of Independent Assortment:** each characteristic is inherited independent of other characteristics

- **Law of Dominance:** when two different alleles for the same characteristic are present in one cell, only one allele will be expressed, or **dominant**, and the other will be masked, or **recessive**.

The structure and function of every cell in the human body is predetermined by units of heredity called **genes**, located in specific positions on the chromosomes in a cell nucleus. Genes are made up of DNA. Genes give the cell instructions about how to function, when to reproduce, and even when to die. The process of cell reproduction through cell division is called *mitosis*. During mitosis, the genes of the parent cell are copied. Then, when the parent cell divides, it becomes two identical daughter cells.

Most cells in the human body have 46 chromosomes—23 chromosomes from the mother (female, egg cell) and 23 chromosomes from the father (male, sperm cell). However, human sex cells (egg or sperm) have 23 chromosomes each. When the sex cells, or **gametes**, undergo the process of **fertilization**—the union of female and male sex cells—the resulting fertilized cell has 46 chromosomes. This fertilized cell will multiply to form a new individual consisting of a combination of chromosomes from the mother and the father. This fusion of two gametes during fertilization to produce offspring is referred to as sexual reproduction.

The sex of a human embryo is determined by the 23rd chromosome in the sperm. Human females have the chromosome pair XX. Males have the pair XY. Females, therefore, always give offspring an X chromosome, whereas males give either an X or a Y chromosome to the offspring.

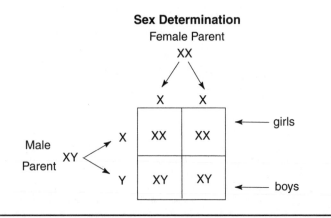

Sex Determination

Structure and Function of Human Systems

The human body can be divided into 11 systems, each of which is discussed below.

Integumentary System

The integument—the skin—is the outermost covering of the body. It consists of the epidermis (the thinner outermost layer) and the dermis (the thicker innermost layer). It also includes the hair and nails. Beneath the skin is the subcutaneous tissue.

The integumentary system has the following functions:

- protecting the body from injury, dehydration, and invasion by harmful agents such as bacteria
- providing sensitivity to pain, temperature, and pressure
- regulating body temperature

Skeletal System

The skeleton provides the structure of the body. Comprised of 206 bones, along with cartilage and ligament, the skeletal system is rigid yet flexible. Joints are points where bones meet and may or may not move against each other. The cartilage is the flexible but strong substance found in joints, nose, and ears. The ligaments, made of softer, flexible tissue, attach bones to each other.

The skeletal system has the following functions:

- providing mechanical support
- protecting body organs
- making body movement possible (along with the muscles)
- storing calcium in the bones, which contain marrow for production of red and white blood cells and platelets

Muscular System

Muscles are made of sheets or bundles of cells. Muscles can do work only by contracting; expansion is passive. Therefore, skeletal muscles are usually attached to a bone in opposing pairs—one to contract while the other expands. There are three major types of muscles:

- **Voluntary** (or striated) muscles can be controlled by conscious thought.
- **Involuntary** (or smooth) muscles cannot be controlled by the will.
- **Cardiac** (or heart) muscles exist only in the heart. They contract spontaneously without needing nervous stimulation.

Tendons attach muscles to the skeleton.

Circulatory System

The circulatory system consists of the cardiovascular and lymphatic systems, including:

- the heart
- blood components such as red blood cells and platelets
- blood vessels, including arteries, veins, and capillaries
- lymphatic vessels and nodes
- lymph

The circulatory system circulates blood throughout the body, making the body's other functions possible by bringing oxygen and other materials to the cells and carrying away waste products and other secretions.

Immune System

The immune system is the body's protective mechanism. It consists of the lymphatic system; the white cells of the blood and bone marrow; antibodies; the thymus gland; and the skin.

The basic characteristics of the immune system include the concepts of:

- **Specificity:** the capacity to recognize and get rid of **antigens** by producing lymphocytes and antibodies. An antigen (literally meaning "antibody-generating") can include anything "foreign" to the body, such as viruses, bacteria, pollen, and, unfortunately, tissue that has been transplanted.
- **Diversity:** the capacity to respond to millions of kinds of invaders.
- **Self/nonself recognition:** the ability to distinguish the body's own molecules ("self") from antigens ("nonself").
- **Memory:** the capacity to "remember" previously encountered antigens and react more quickly when exposed again. This process is called acquired immunity.

The immune system's basic function is to protect the body from disease and injury.

Respiratory System

The respiratory system is responsible for taking oxygen into the body and eliminating carbon dioxide. It includes the lungs, nose, pharynx, larynx, trachea, bronchi, and diaphragm.

Digestive (or Gastrointestinal) System (GI)

The digestive system includes the gastrointestinal (GI) tract (also called the alimentary canal). This is basically a tube with two openings—the mouth and anus—for intake of food and elimination of waste. The parts of the GI tract are the mouth, the esophagus, the stomach, the small intestine, and the large intestine. Also included in this system are structures such as teeth, tongue, liver, pancreas, and gallbladder.

The digestive system breaks down food for energy, reabsorbs water and nutrients, and eliminates waste.

Urinary or Excretory System

The urinary system consists of:

- **Kidneys:** two compact, bean-shaped organs through which blood is cycled for removal of waste
- **Nephrons:** excretory tubes in the kidneys
- **Blood vessels** that serve the kidneys
- **Urinary structures** that carry waste out of the body—the ureters, bladder, and urethra

The kidneys remove waste or toxic byproducts from the blood and maintain homeostasis of blood and body fluids.

Nervous System

The nervous system is made up of the nerves, brain, spinal cord, and sense organs for sight, sound, smell, and taste. The brain is the nervous system's main control center and consists of three parts:

- The **cerebral hemispheres** are responsible for the higher functions, such as speech and hearing.
- The **cerebellum** is responsible for subconscious activities and some balance functions.
- The **brain stem** is responsible for basic functions such as breathing and circulation

The nervous system controls the flow of information between the sensory and motor cells and organs.

Endocrine System

The endocrine system controls communication between systems in the body. It consists of:

- **Hormones** are substances that regulate the growth or function of a specific tissue or organ. Hormones include insulin, sex hormones, adrenaline, and serotonin.
- **Glands** that secrete hormones include the pituitary, adrenal gland, thyroid, ovary, testis, and part of the pancreas.

VITAMINS		
Vitamin	Sources	Results of Deficiency
A	green and yellow vegetables	night blindness, skin problems
B$_1$ (thiamine)	cereals and yeast	beriberi
B$_2$ (riboflavin)	green vegetables, yeast, liver, milk	sores on tongue, lips, mouth
B$_{12}$	liver and meat (strictly from animals)	anemia—iron-poor blood
C (ascorbic acid)	green vegetables and citrus fruits	scurvy
D	fortified milk, fish-liver oils	rickets—deformed, weakened bones
E	cereal grains, green vegetables	muscular dystrophy, liver damage, infertility

Together with the nervous system, the endocrine system regulates and balances bodily fluids and chemicals. Hormones affect the body's growth, the development and functioning of reproductive organs and sexual characteristics, the development of higher nervous functions such as personality, and the ability of the body to handle stress and resist disease.

Reproductive System

Reproduction in humans involves two sets of organs, the internal reproductive organs and the external genitalia. In reproduction, the female ovum and the male spermatozoon fuse to form a zygote, which eventually develops into a fetus.

The reproductive system functions to create new individuals from existing ones and propagate the species.

Nutrition

The process by which organisms obtain energy from food for growth, maintenance, and repair is called **nutrition**. Food provides nutrients, such as carbohydrates, proteins, and fats. In humans, energy in the form of calories is gleaned chiefly from carbohydrates. A calorie is actually a unit of heat. It is the unit of heat necessary to raise the temperature of one gram of water one degree Celsius.

Carbohydrates are starches or sugars that fuel all of the cells in the body. Common sources of carbohydrates are potatoes, beans, cereals, fruit, and milk. Both starches and sugars ultimately yield glucose. Cells convert glucose to energy or store excess glucose, called glycogen, in the liver and muscles. If the excess glucose exceeds a certain point, the excess glucose is converted to fat and stored.

Proteins are abundant in all living organisms. Structural proteins make up the fingernails, skin, bones, and teeth in humans. Other proteins regulate metabolism, produce movement, and transport oxygen and other substances in and out of body cells. Common sources of protein are meat, cheese, beans, nuts, and fish.

Fats are also essential for human nutrition. Fats function in cellular structure, composition, and transport. Containing approximately twice the caloric value of carbohydrates, fats are found in butter, cream, eggs, and most cheese.

Vitamins are other organic substances required in small amounts to maintain normal health. Most animals cannot manufacture many vitamins themselves and must have adequate amounts in the diet. The table above shows the major vitamins.

Ecology

Ecology is the study of interrelationships between organisms and their physical environment. Ecologists consider animals and plants in terms of an ecosystem—the interaction of different populations of the same species in a shared environment. The sun fuels all of the energy in an ecosystem.

Ecosystems vary in size. Each contains air, soil, Producers, Consumers, and Decomposers; the latter three transfer energy in a process called the food chain. A food chain can be visualized as follows:

sunlight ➡ green plants (Producers) ➡ herbivores (Consumers) ➡ carnivores (Consumers) ➡ bacteria (Decomposers) ➡ soil ➡ green plants, etc.

Producers, such as green plants, use sunlight in the photosynthesis process to create their own food. The Producers are the food for Consumers, such as animals, which can't make their own food. The two main types of Consumers are herbivores and carnivores. **Herbivores** are animals that eat only vegetation. They have teeth and digestive systems adapted for processing plants. Examples of herbivores include rabbits, cows, and squirrels. **Carnivores** are animals that feed only on the flesh of other animals. They have powerful jaws and teeth. Examples of carnivores are tigers, wolves, and hyenas. Human beings are **omnivores**. Our bodies are capable of meeting nutritional needs using both plants and animal matter. All Consumers eat either Producers or other Consumers and use the energy to do work or radiate the energy back into the atmosphere.

When animals die, the dead organic matter is broken down by Decomposers, such as fungi. During this process of decay, Decomposers reintroduce minerals back into the soil in the ecosystem. Producers then recycle the minerals as they grow, and the process begins again.

Biomes are established ecological systems that extend over a large geographical area and are characterized by a dominant type of vegetation or climatic condition. Organisms in a biome are adapted to the climate associated with the region. The seven major biomes on Earth are:

- **Arctic Tundra:** treeless plains surrounding the Arctic Ocean, with permanently frozen subsoil
- **Deciduous:** leaf-shedding forests in mild climates
- **Desert:** environment with irregular or infrequent rainfall and high temperatures
- **Grassland:** areas with rainfall insufficient to support many trees; grass species dominate
- **Marine:** oceans and seas
- **Taiga:** evergreen forests that survive long winters
- **Tropical rainforest:** constant precipitation and high temperatures, with many plant species

Earth Science

Earth scientists study the Earth or its parts including astronomy, meteorology, geology, and oceanography.

Astronomy

Astronomy, also considered a subdiscipline of physics, is the study of the universe beyond Earth's atmosphere. A solar system consists of a star and its natural satellites: asteroids, comets, meteoroids, and planets. The Sun is at the center of our solar system, which consists of the following planets (listed in order moving away from the sun, with the planet's rank in diameter in parentheses): Mercury (8), Venus (6), Earth (5), Mars (7), Jupiter (1), Saturn (2), Uranus (3), and Neptune (4).

The Sun consists of approximately 75 percent hydrogen and 25 percent helium. With a diameter of 1,392,000 km, the Sun dwarfs everything in our solar system (compare: the Earth has a diameter of 12,756 km).

Other minor bodies in the solar system include:

- **Asteroids:** minor planets sometimes called planetoids
- **Comets:** small bodies of gas and dust consisting of a nucleus of ice and dust, a coma of gas and dust, and the tail (also gas and dust) that is only visible when the comet approaches the Sun
- **Meteors:** any matter that collides with the Earth

The moon orbits the Earth approximately every 27 days. Its gravitational pull on the Earth causes the tides in the ocean. Moonlight is simply reflected sunlight. A lunar eclipse is caused when the Earth comes between the Sun and the Moon. A solar eclipse is caused by the moon blocking sunlight from the Earth.

The Earth orbits the Sun while rotating on its axis, an imaginary line that bisects the Earth from the North to the South Pole. This rotation causes night and day. Only twice a year, on the autumnal and vernal equinoxes, are night and day of exactly equal length. The revolution of the Earth around the Sun causes the seasons. One revolution around the Sun is approximately 365 days, one year.

Meteorology

Meteorology is the study of Earth's atmosphere and its changes and interaction with the ground. The atmosphere consists of several layers:

- The **troposphere** (0–10 km)—where weather occurs
- The **stratosphere** (10–40 km)—contains the jet stream and the ozone layer
- The **mesosphere** (40–70 km)
- The **thermosphere** (70–400 km)
- The **exosphere** (400 km and higher)

Weather refers to the state of the atmosphere, including humidity, precipitation, temperature, cloud cover, visibility, and wind. Most sunlight is reflected by the Earth's atmosphere. Some sunlight penetrates the atmosphere and is absorbed by the Earth's crust. Wind, the motion of air relative to Earth's surface, can be measured with an anemometer and is caused (in part) by the difference in the amount of radiation received at different points on Earth.

Water on Earth is constantly turning to vapor in a process called **evaporation**. When warm air becomes saturated, or full of moisture, the water forms droplets in a process called **condensation**. Then it falls back down to Earth as precipitation: rain, sleet, snow, or hail. Humidity is the amount of moisture in the air at any time. It is measured using a hygrometer. A barometer measures air pressure, which is dependent on both temperature and humidity.

Geology

Geology is the study of the origin, structure, and composition of the Earth. Scientists calculate the age of Earth to be approximately 4,600 million years old. This time has been divided into four geologic eras:

- **Precambrian:** oldest era; a time of massive volcanic activity
- **Paleozoic:** 570 million years ago; the emergence of continents and mountains
- **Mesozoic:** 225 million years ago; more volcanic eruptions; also known as "The Age of Reptiles" (time of dinosaurs)
- **Cenozoic:** began about 65 million years ago. Giant glaciers (slow-moving sheets of ice) retreated from land masses allowing mammals and flowering plants the opportunity to diversify. We are still in the Cenozoic era today.

The Earth is a composed of three layers: the 7,000 km thick central core of solid iron and nickel, the 3,000 km thick semi-molten mantle, and the outer layer of crust. **Plate tectonics** is the study of the movement of large chunks or plates of the Earth's crust. **Faults** are cracks in the Earth's crust. Earthquakes, the sudden movement of plates, are measured according to seismic waves on the Richter Scale.

Rocks, the most familiar and tangible geologic objects, are made of one or more minerals on or just below the surface of the Earth. There are three main types of rocks:

- **Igneous:** formed by the crystallization of magma, or molten lava. An example is granite.
- **Sedimentary:** formed by the accumulation of silt or other rock fragments. Limestone is an example.
- **Metamorphic:** formed when pre-existing rock is subjected to chemical or physical alteration by high heat and pressure. An example is marble.

Oceanography

Oceanography, also known as marine science, is the study of the ocean and all phenomena that occur within. The oceans cover about 70% of the Earth's surface and contain approximately 97% of the Earth's water supply. There are five major oceans on Earth—the Pacific, Atlantic, Indian, Arctic, and Southern Ocean.

The oceans of Earth serve many functions and affect the weather and temperature of the planet in various ways. Nearly every aspect of the oceanic environment can be tied to one of the other scientific disciplines. For example, astronomy is affected by the oceans absorption of incoming solar radiation (stored as heat energy), which also helps moderate global temperatures. Currents throughout the oceans take stored heat energy and distribute it around the globe, which affects global weather patterns.

The oceans are home to more than 1 million known species of plants and animals. However, it is believed there may be as many as 10 times that number waiting to be discovered.

Like the atmosphere, the ocean depths are divided into different zones. The two main zones are:

- **pelagic:** the vast majority of oceanic water. This zone is further divided up into additional zones, based on the amount of surface sunlight that penetrates.

- **hadopelagic:** the deepest water of the oceans, found in trenches nearly 5 miles deep.

There are a number of subspecialty fields of oceanography, all of which are tied to our understanding of the effects of the oceans on our environment. All of these subspecialties are related to the other basic sciences, which is an indication of how important the oceans are to our planet. These subspecialties are:

- **biological oceanography:** also known as marine biology, is the study of the plants, animals, and microbes of the oceans
- **chemical oceanography:** also known as marine chemistry, is the study of the chemistry of the ocean
- **geological oceanography:** also known as marine geology, is the study of the geology of the ocean
- **physical oceanography:** also known as marine physics, is the study of the ocean's physical properties

Physical Science

Chemistry

Chemistry is the study of elements and the compounds they form. Matter can take the form of an element, a compound, or a mixture.

An **element** is the basic form of matter, incapable of being decomposed by chemical means into simpler substances. Each element has distinct chemical and physical characteristics. Hydrogen (H), oxygen (O), and carbon (C) are elements.

A **compound** is a combination of two or more elements chemically combined in a specific proportion. Compounds can be separated by chemical means, and are represented by chemical formulas that include the symbols of all the elements present. Examples of familiar compounds are water (H_2O) and table salt (NaCl). In order to be considered organic, a compound must contain carbon.

A **mixture** is a combination of two or more substances that are not chemically combined. Dissolving salt in water results in a mixture. The two compounds don't react with each other and can be separated by physical means—in this case, heating the water so it evaporates, leaving the salt behind.

All matter is made up of atoms. The following terms are used to define atomic structure:

- **Atom:** the smallest unit of an element that retains all of the element's chemical properties. An atom is composed of three primary particles: electrons, protons, and neutrons.
- **Electron:** found outside the nucleus (the center of an atom), it has a negligible mass and a charge of –1.
- **Proton:** found in the nucleus, it has a mass of 1 amu (atomic mass unit) and a charge of +1.
- **Neutron:** found in the nucleus, it has a mass of 1 amu and no charge.

An atom contains an identical number of protons and electrons, making it electrically neutral.

Atoms of the same element generally have the same properties, unless they are **isotopes**, which can behave differently. Atoms of different elements have different properties and different masses. Atoms of elements combine in simple whole number ratios.

Periodic Table

The periodic table (next page) lists all of the known elements according to their atomic numbers.

Atomic number is the number of protons in the atom. The atomic number determines the element.

$$_{11}Na$$

atomic number

Mass number is the total number of protons and neutrons in one atom of an element. Mass number can vary because the number of neutrons in an atom can change.

$$^{23}Na$$

mass number

The horizontal rows of elements in the periodic table are called **periods**. There are seven periods in all. Moving from left to right across a period, the atomic number increases by one from one element to the next. Each successive element has one more electron in its outer shell. All elements in the same period have the same number of shells.

The vertical columns of elements in the periodic table are **groups**. Elements in the same group have the same number of electrons in their outer shell. They therefore have similar chemical properties.

Electronic Structure of Atoms

According to the periodic table, the atomic number of hydrogen (H) is 1, because it has one proton in its nucleus. The number of protons in an atom determines its atomic nucleus. The atomic number of nitrogen (N) is 7; nitrogen has seven protons in its nucleus.

Niels Bohr, a Danish physicist, proposed a model of the atom that had a nucleus surrounded by concentric orbits

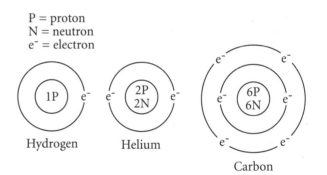

P = proton
N = neutron
e⁻ = electron

Hydrogen   Helium

Carbon

Electrons are found in the orbits. When electrons become excited, they absorb energy and move to an orbit farther from the nucleus. When they release energy, they fall to an orbit with lower energy closer to the nucleus. The energy level (also called electron **shell**) is a region of space in which electrons move around the nucleus.

PERIODIC TABLE OF THE ELEMENTS

IA																	VIIIA
1 H 1.0	IIA											IIIA	IVA	VA	VIA	VIIA	2 He 4.0
3 Li 6.9	4 Be 9.0											5 B 10.8	6 C 12.0	7 N 14.0	8 O 16.0	9 F 19.0	10 Ne 20.2
11 Na 23.0	12 Mg 24.3	IIIB	IVB	VB	VIB	VIIB		VIIIB		IB	IIB	13 Al 27.0	14 Si 28.1	15 P 31.0	16 S 32.1	17 Gl 35.5	18 Ar 39.9
19 K 139.1	20 Ca 40.1	21 Sc 45.0	22 Ti 47.9	23 V 50.9	24 Cr 52.0	25 Mn 54.9	26 Fe 55.8	27 Co 58.9	28 Ni 58.7	29 Cu 63.5	30 Zn 65.4	31 Ga 69.7	32 Ge 72.6	33 As 74.9	34 Se 79.0	35 Br 79.9	36 Kr 83.8
37 Rb 85.5	38 Sr 87.6	39 Y 88.9	40 Zr 91.2	41 Nb 92.9	42 Mo 95.9	43 Tc (97)	44 Ru 101.1	45 Rh 102.9	46 Pd 106.7	47 Ag 107.9	48 Cd 112.4	49 In 114.8	50 Sn 118.7	51 Sb 121.8	52 Te 127.6	53 I 126.9	54 Xe 131.3
55 Cs 132.9	56 Ba 137.3	see below 57-71	72 Hf 178.5	73 Ta 180.9	74 W 183.9	75 Re 186.2	76 Os 190.2	77 Ir 192.2	78 Pt 195.1	79 Au 197.0	80 Hg 200.6	81 7i 204.4	82 Pb 207.2	83 Bi 209.0	84 Po 210	85 At (210)	86 Rn (222)
87 Fr (223)	88 Ra (226)	see below 89-103	104 Rf (267)	105 Db (268)	106 Sg (271)	107 Bh (272)	108 Hs (270)	109 Mt (276)	110 Ds (281)	111 Rg (280)	112 Cn (285)	113 Uut (284)	114 Uuq (289)	115 Uup (288)	116 Uuh (293)	(117) (Uus)	118 Uuo (294)

57 La 138.9	58 Ce 140.1	59 Pr 140.9	60 Nd 144.2	61 Pm (145)	62 Sm 150.4	63 Eu 152.0	64 Gd 157.3	65 Tb 158.9	66 Dy 162.5	67 Ho 164.9	68 Er 167.3	69 Tm 168.9	70 Yb 173.0	71 Lu 175.0
89 Ac (227)	90 Th 232.0	91 Pa 231	92 U 238.0	93 Np (237)	94 Pu (244)	95 Am (243)	96 Cm (247)	97 Bk (247)	98 Cf (251)	99 Es (252)	100 Fm (257)	101 Md (258)	102 No (259)	103 Lw (262)

Chemical Equations

Chemical equations are used to show the result of a physical or chemical change in matter. A physical change is when the shape or size of matter is changed, but the molecules remain unchanged. Steam from a boiling pot of water is an example of a physical change. A chemical change is one in which two or more molecules interact to form new molecules. Paper burning is an example of a chemical change—the paper changes to carbon.

The sum of the atomic weights of all the atoms in a formula is called the formula weight. A mole is the amount of substance containing Avogadro's number of particles, 6.02×10^{23} atoms of an element. The abbreviation is mol.

Use the following rules in balancing equations:

1. All reactants (starting materials) and products must be known, and their formulas must be correctly written.
2. The formulas are never changed in order to balance an equation.
3. The number of atoms of each element in the reactants must be equal to the number of atoms of the element in the products.
4. The numbers to the left of each formula (coefficients) must be reduced to the smallest possible whole numbers.

Types of chemical reactions include:

- **Combination or synthesis reactions:** two chemicals combine to form a new substance
- **Decomposition reactions:** one substance breaks down to create two or more substances

Concentration, Acids, Bases, and pH

Concentration is a measure of how much solute is in a solution. A **solute** is a substance that is dissolved in a medium, and a **solvent** is a medium in which a solute is dissolved. For instance: salt water is a solution—a homogenous mixture consisting of the solute (salt) and the solvent (water).

Acids are proton donors; they release hydrogen ions (protons). Acids have a sour taste. Bases are proton acceptors; they take up hydrogen ions. Bases have a bitter taste and feel slippery. Strong bases take up more hydrogen ions than weak bases.

The relative concentration of hydrogen ions is measured in concentration units called pH units. The pH scale runs from 0 to 14. A substance with a pH of 7 is neutral. Substances such as vinegar and orange juice, with a pH of less than 7, are considered acidic. Substances such as soaps and ammonia, with a pH of more than 7, are considered alkaline.

Measurement

Although you may be more familiar with the English system of measurement (inches, pounds, and so on), the metric system is the standard system of measurement in science. The metric system is a decimal system based on multiples and fractions of ten. The meter (m) is the standard unit of length in the decimal system:

1 meter = 100 centimeters (cm)
1 kilometer (km) = 1,000 meters

The gram (g) is the metric system unit of mass:

1 gram = 1,000 milligrams (mg)
1 kilogram (kg) = 1,000 grams

Volume, the amount of space occupied by a fluid or body, is usually measured using the liter. The cubic meter (cm^3) is actually the standard metric unit of volume, but it is infrequently used.

1 liter (L) = 1,000 milliliters (ml)
1 cm^3 = 1 ml

In science, temperature is most often measured using degrees Celsius (°C). On the Celsius scale, the freezing point for water is 0° and the boiling point for water is 100°. This makes it much easier to use than the Fahrenheit scale, which has a freezing point of 32° and a boiling point of 212°. The two equations below show how to convert a temperature measurement from one scale to the other.

$$°C = \frac{5}{9}(°F - 32)$$
$$°F = \frac{9}{5}(°C + 32)$$

Other important equations are as follows:

- **Speed** is the distance covered or traveled by an object per a certain unit or amount of time:
  Speed = distance/time
- **Momentum** is the tendency of an object to continue moving in the same direction:
  Momentum = mass × speed
- **Work** is a force applied to an object which, in turn, results in movement:
  Work = force × distance
- **Power** is the rate at which work is done. It is measured in joules (J):
  Power = work/time

Note: **Mass** should not be confused with **weight**. Mass is the measurement of the amount of matter in an object. Weight is the force by which gravity attracts a body to Earth.

Energy

Energy, the capacity to do work, is never created or destroyed—it may only be changed in form. There are many forms of energy, including light, sound, heat, chemical, mechanical, and electrical. Energy, like power, is measured in joules.

The two forms of energy are potential and kinetic energy. **Potential energy** is the energy stored in a body or system as a consequence of its position, shape, or state. **Kinetic energy** is the energy of motion, and is usually defined as the work that will be done by the body possessing the energy when it is brought to rest.

Sound and light are measured by their wavelength. A wave is a periodic disturbance in a medium or space. **Sound** is a vibration at a frequency and intensity audible to the normal human ear (20–20,000 Hertz). Vibrations that have a lower frequency are called **infrasounds**, and those with a higher frequency are called **ultrasounds**. **Light** is a form of electromagnetic radiation. Light can pass through a vacuum, but sound cannot. The electromagnetic spectrum is displayed in the following diagram.

low frequency					high frequency	
long wavelength					short wavelength	
radio waves	micro waves	infrared light	visible light	ultraviolet light	X-rays	gamma rays

Refraction is the bending of light, especially when it moves from one material to another. The refraction of sunlight results in a spectrum of colors, such as a rainbow. The colors in a spectrum are red, orange, yellow, green, blue, indigo, and violet.

Another form of energy—heat—may be transferred via conduction, convection, or radiation. **Conduction** is the transmission of heat from a region of high temperature to a region of lower temperature. Putting a cool kettle of water on a stove to boil is a good example. **Convection** is the process by which parts of a fluid or gas change density due to the uneven application of heat. For instance, as a stove heats a cool room, the warmer (less dense) air rises and the cold air remains lower. **Radiation** is heat transmitted via electromagnetic waves. The sun's heat warming the petals of a flower is an example of radiation.

MATH REVIEW

CHAPTER SUMMARY
This chapter gives you some important tips for dealing with math questions and reviews some of the most commonly tested concepts. If you need to learn or review important math skills, this chapter is for you.

Two subtests of the ASVAB—Arithmetic Reasoning and Mathematics Knowledge—cover math skills. Arithmetic Reasoning is basically math word problems. Mathematics Knowledge tests your knowledge of math concepts, principles, and procedures. You don't have to do a lot of calculation in the Mathematics Knowledge subtest; you need to know basic terminology (like *sum* and *perimeter),* formulas (such as the area of a square), and computation rules. Both subtests cover the subjects you probably studied in school. This chapter reviews concepts you will need for both Arithmetic Reasoning and Mathematics Knowledge.

Math Strategies

- **Don't work in your head!** Use your test book or scratch paper to take notes, draw pictures, and calculate. Although you might think that you can solve math questions more quickly in your head, that's a good way to make mistakes. Write out each step.
- **Read a math question in *chunks* rather than straight through from beginning to end.** As you read each *chunk,* stop to think about what it means and make notes or draw a picture to represent that *chunk.*

- **When you get to the actual question, circle it.** This will keep you more focused as you solve the problem.
- **Glance at the answer choices for clues.** If they are fractions, you probably should do your work in fractions; if they are decimals, you should probably work in decimals; etc.
- **Make a plan of attack to help you solve the problem.**
- **If a question stumps you, try one of the *backdoor* approaches explained in the next section.** These are particularly useful for solving word problems.
- **When you get your answer, reread the circled question to make sure you have answered it.** This helps avoid the careless mistake of answering the wrong question.
- **Check your work after you get an answer.** Test takers get a false sense of security when they get an answer that matches one of the multiple-choice answers. Here are some good ways to check your work *if you have time:*
  - Ask yourself if your answer is reasonable, if it makes sense.
  - Plug your answer back into the problem to make sure the problem holds together.
  - Do the question a second time, but use a different method.
- **Approximate when appropriate.** For example:
  - $5.98 + $8.97 is a little less than $15. (Add: $6 + $9)
  - .9876 × 5.0342 is close to 5. (Multiply: 1 × 5)
- **Skip hard questions and come back to them later.** Mark them in your test book so you can find them quickly.

Backdoor Approaches for Answering Tough Questions

Many word problems are actually easier to solve by backdoor approaches. The two techniques that follow are time-saving ways to solve multiple-choice word problems that you don't know how to solve with a straightforward approach. The first technique, *nice numbers*, is useful when there are unknowns (like *x*) in the text of the word problem, making the problem too abstract for you. The second technique, *working backward*, presents a quick way to substitute numeric answer choices back into the problem to see which one works.

Nice Numbers

1. When a question contains unknowns, like *x*, plug nice numbers in for the unknowns. A nice number is easy to calculate with and makes sense in the problem.
2. Read the question with the nice numbers in place. Then solve it.
3. If the answer choices are all numbers, the choice that matches your answer is the right one.
4. If the answer choices contain unknowns, substitute the same nice numbers into all the answer choices. The choice that matches your answer is the right one. If more than one answer matches, do the problem again with different nice numbers. You will only have to check the answer choices that have already matched.

Example: Judi went shopping with *p* dollars in her pocket. If the price of shirts was *s* shirts for *d* dollars, what is the maximum number of shirts Judi could buy with the money in her pocket?

   a. psd
   b. $\frac{ps}{d}$
   c. $\frac{pd}{s}$
   d. $\frac{ds}{p}$

To solve this problem, let's try these nice numbers: $p = \$100$, $s = 2$; $d = \$25$. Now reread it with the numbers in place:

Judi went shopping with *$100* in her pocket. If the price of shirts was *2* shirts for *$25*, what is the maximum number of shirts Judi could buy with the money in her pocket?

Since 2 shirts cost $25, that means that 4 shirts cost $50, and 8 shirts cost $100. So our answer is 8. Let's substitute the nice numbers into all 4 answers:

a. $100 \times 2 \times 25 = 5,000$

b. $\frac{100 \times 2}{25} = 8$

c. $\frac{100 \times 25}{2} = 1,250$

d. $\frac{25 \times 2}{100} = \frac{1}{2}$

The answer is **b** because it is the only one that matches our answer of 8.

Working Backward

You can frequently solve a word problem by plugging the answer choices back into the text of the problem to see which one fits all the facts stated in the problem. The process is faster than you think because you will probably only have to substitute one or two answers to find the right one.

This approach works only when:

- All of the answer choices are numbers.
- You are asked to find a simple number, not a sum, product, difference, or ratio.

Here's what to do:

1. Look at all the answer choices and begin with the one in the middle of the range. For example, if the answers are 14, 8, 2, 20, and 25, begin by plugging 14 into the problem.
2. If your choice doesn't work, eliminate it. Determine if you need a larger or smaller answer.
3. Plug in one of the remaining choices.
4. If none of the answers works, you may have made a careless error. Begin again or look for your mistake.

Example: Juan ate $\frac{1}{3}$ of the jellybeans. Maria then ate $\frac{3}{4}$ of the remaining jellybeans, which left 10 jellybeans. How many jellybeans were there to begin with?

a. 60
b. 90
c. 120
d. 140

Starting with the middle answer, let's assume there were 90 jellybeans to begin with:

Since Juan ate $\frac{1}{3}$ of the jellybeans, that means he ate 30 ($\frac{1}{3} \times 90 = 30$), leaving 60 of them ($90 - 30 = 60$).
Maria then ate $\frac{3}{4}$ of the 60 jellybeans, or 45 of them ($\frac{3}{4} \times 60 = 45$). That leaves 15 jellybeans ($60 - 45 = 15$).

The problem states that there were 10 jellybeans left, and we wound up with 15 of them. That indicates that we started with too big a number. Thus, 90, 120, and 140 are all incorrect! With only two choices left, let's use common sense to decide which one to try. The next lower answer is only a little smaller than 90 and may not be small enough. So, let's try 60:

Since Juan ate $\frac{1}{3}$ of the jellybeans, that means he ate 20 ($\frac{1}{3} \times 60 = 20$), leaving 40 of them ($60 - 20 = 40$). Maria then ate $\frac{3}{4}$ of the 40 jellybeans, or 30 of them ($\frac{3}{4} \times 40 = 30$). That leaves 10 jellybeans ($40 - 30 = 10$).

Because this result of 10 jellybeans remaining agrees with the problem, the right answer is **a**.

Math Glossary

Denominator	The bottom number in a fraction. *Example:* 2 is the denominator in $\frac{1}{2}$.
Difference	Subtract. The difference of two numbers means subtract one number from the other.
Divisible by	A number is divisible by a second number if that second number divides *evenly* into the original number. *Example:* 10 is divisible by 5 ($10 \div 5 = 2$, with no remainder). However, 10 is not divisible by 3. (See *Multiple of*.)
Even Integer	Integers that are divisible by 2, like . . . –4, –2, 0, 2, 4. . . . (See *Integer*.)
Integer	Numbers along the number line, like . . . –3, –2, –1, 0, 1, 2, 3. . . . Integers include the whole numbers and their opposites. (See *Whole Number*.)
Multiple of	A number is a multiple of a second number if that second number can be multiplied by an integer to get the original number. *Example:* 10 is a multiple of 5 ($10 = 5 \times 2$); however, 10 is not a multiple of 3. (See *Divisible by*.)
Negative Number	A number that is less than zero, like . . . –1, –18.6, $-\frac{3}{4}$. . . .
Numerator	The top part of a fraction. *Example:* 1 is the numerator of $\frac{1}{2}$.
Odd Integer	Integers that aren't divisible by 2, like . . . –5, –3, –1, 1, 3. . . .
Positive Number	A number that is greater than zero, like . . . 2, 42, $\frac{1}{2}$, 4.63. . . .
Prime Number	Integers that are divisible only by 1 and themselves, like . . . 2, 3, 5, 7, 11. . . . All prime numbers are odd, except for number 2. The number 1 is not considered prime.
Product	Multiply. The product of two numbers means the numbers are multiplied together.
Quotient	The answer you get when you divide. *Example:* 10 divided by 5 is 2; the quotient is 2.
Real Number	All the numbers you can think of, like . . . 17, –5, $\frac{1}{2}$, –23.6, 3.4329, 0. . . . Real numbers include the integers, fractions, and decimals. (See *Integer*.)
Remainder	The number left over after division. *Example:* 11 divided by 2 is 5, with a remainder of 1.
Sum	Add. The sum of 2 numbers means the numbers are added together.
Whole Number	Numbers you can count on your fingers, like . . . 1, 2, 3. . . . All whole numbers are positive.

Word Problems

Many of the math problems on tests are word problems. A word problem can include any kind of math, including simple arithmetic, fractions, decimals, percentages, even algebra and geometry.

The hardest part of any word problem is translating English into math. When you read a problem, you can frequently translate it *word for word* from English statements into mathematical statements. At other times, however, a key word in the word problem hints at the mathematical operation to be performed. Here are the translation rules:

EQUALS   key words: *is, are, has*

English	Math
Bob is 18 years old.	$b = 18$
There are seven hats.	$h = 7$
Judi has five books.	$j = 5$

ADDITION   key words: *sum; more, greater, or older than; total; altogether*

English	Math
The sum of two numbers is 10.	$x + y = 10$
Karen has $5 more than Sam.	$k = 5 + s$
The base is 3" greater than the height.	$b = 3 + h$
Judi is two years older than Tony.	$j = 2 + t$
The total of three numbers is 25.	$a + b + c = 25$
How much do Joan and Tom have altogether?	$j + t = ?$

SUBTRACTION   key words: *difference, less or younger than, remain, left over*

English	Math
The difference between two numbers is 17.	$x - y = 17$
Mike has five less cats than twice the number Jan has.	$m = 2j - 5$
Jay is two years younger than Brett.	$j = b - 2$
After Carol ate three apples, r apples remained.	$r = a - 3$

MULTIPLICATION   key words: *of, product, times*

English	Math
Twenty percent of Matthew's baseball caps	$.20 \times m$
Half of the boys	$\frac{1}{2} \times b$
The product of two numbers is 12.	$a \times b = 12$

DIVISION   key word: *per*

English	Math
15 drops per teaspoon	$\frac{15 \text{ drops}}{\text{teaspoon}}$
22 miles per gallon	$\frac{22 \text{ miles}}{\text{gallon}}$

Distance Formula: Distance = Rate x Time

The key words are movement words like: plane, train, boat, car, walk, run, climb, swim.

- How far did the plane travel in 4 hours if it averaged 300 miles per hour?

    $d = 300 \times 4$

    $d = 1,200$ miles

- Ben walked 20 miles in four hours. What was his average speed?

    $20 = r \times 4$

    5 miles per hour $= r$

Solving a Word Problem Using the Translation Table

Remember the problem at the beginning of this chapter about the jellybeans?

Example: Juan ate $\frac{1}{3}$ of the jellybeans. Maria then ate $\frac{3}{4}$ of the remaining jellybeans, which left 10 jelly-beans. How many jellybeans were there to begin with?

a. 60

b. 90

c. 120

d. 140

We solved it by *working backward.* Now let's solve it using our translation rules.

Assume Juan started with J jellybeans. Eating $\frac{1}{3}$ of them means eating $\frac{1}{3} \times J$ jellybeans. Maria ate a fraction of the remaining jellybeans, which means we must subtract to find out how many are left: $J - \frac{1}{3} \times J = \frac{2}{3} \times J$. Maria then ate $\frac{3}{4}$, leaving $\frac{1}{4}$ of the $\frac{2}{3} \times J$ jellybeans, or $\frac{1}{4} \times \frac{2}{3} \times J$ jellybeans. Multiplying out $\frac{1}{4} \times \frac{2}{3} \times J$ gives $\frac{1}{6}J$ as the number of jellybeans left. The problem states that there were 10 jellybeans left, meaning that we set $\frac{1}{6} \times J$ equal to 10:

$$\frac{1}{6} \times J = 10.$$

Solving this equation for J gives $J = 60$. Thus, the right answer is **a** (the same answer we got when we *worked backward).* As you can see, both methods—working backward and translating from English to math—work. You should use whichever method is more comfortable for you.

Practice Word Problems

You will find word problems using fractions, decimals, and percentages in those sections of this chapter. For now, practice using the translation table on problems that just require you to work with basic arithmetic. Answers are found on page 135.

_____ **1.** Amir went shopping with $250 and returned home with only $33.56. How much money did he spend?
  a. $208.44
  b. $210.54
  c. $212.44
  d. $216.44
  e. $218.54

_____ **2.** Mark invited ten friends to a party. Each friend brought three guests. How many people came to the party, excluding Mark?
  a. 3
  b. 10
  c. 30
  d. 40
  e. 41

_____ **3.** The office secretary can type 75 words per minute. How many minutes will it take him to type a report containing 1,200 words?
  a. 16
  b. $16\frac{1}{2}$
  c. 17
  d. $17\frac{1}{2}$
  e. 18

_____ **4.** Mr. Wallace is writing a budget request to upgrade his personal computer system. He wants to purchase a cable modem, which will cost $100, two new software programs at $350 each, a color printer for $249, and an additional color cartridge for $25. What is the total amount Mr. Wallace should write on his budget request?
  a. $724
  b. $974
  c. $1,049
  d. $1,064
  e. $1,074

Fraction Review

Problems involving fractions may be straightforward calculation questions, or they may be word problems. Typically, they ask you to add, subtract, multiply, divide, or compare fractions.

Working with Fractions

A fraction is a part of something.

> *Example:* Let's say that a pizza was cut into eight equal slices and you ate three of them. The fraction $\frac{3}{8}$ tells you what part of the pizza you ate. The pizza below shows this: 3 of the 8 pieces (the ones you ate) are shaded.

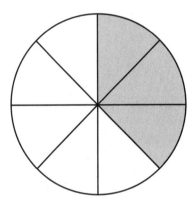

Three Kinds of Fractions

Proper fraction: The top number is less than the bottom number:

$$\frac{1}{2}; \frac{2}{3}; \frac{4}{9}; \frac{8}{13}$$

The value of a proper fraction is less than 1.

Improper fraction: The top number is greater than or equal to the bottom number:

$$\frac{3}{2}; \frac{5}{3}; \frac{14}{9}; \frac{12}{12}$$

The value of an improper fraction is 1 or more.

Mixed number: A fraction written to the right of a whole number:

$$3\frac{1}{2}; 4\frac{2}{3}; 12\frac{3}{4}; 24\frac{3}{4}$$

The value of a mixed number is more than 1; it is the sum of the whole number plus the fraction.

Changing Improper Fractions into Mixed or Whole Numbers

It's easier to add and subtract fractions that are mixed numbers rather than improper fractions. To change an improper fraction, say $\frac{13}{2}$, into a mixed number, follow these steps:

1. Divide the bottom number (2) into the top number (13) to get the whole number portion (6) of the mixed number:

$$\begin{array}{r} 6 \\ 2\overline{)13} \\ \underline{12} \\ 1 \end{array}$$

2. Write the remainder of the division (1) over the old bottom number (2): $\quad 6\frac{1}{2}$
3. Check: Change the mixed number back into an improper fraction (see steps below).

Changing Mixed Numbers into Improper Fractions

It's easier multiply and divide fractions when you're working with improper fractions rather than mixed numbers. To change a mixed number, say $2\frac{3}{4}$, into an improper fraction, follow these steps:

1. Multiply the whole number (2) by the bottom number (4): $\qquad 2 \times 4 = 8$
2. Add the result (8) to the top number (3): $\qquad 8 + 3 = 11$
3. Put the total (11) over the bottom number (4): $\qquad \frac{11}{4}$
4. Check: Reverse the process by changing the improper fraction into a mixed number. If you get back the number you started with, your answer is right.

Reducing Fractions

Reducing a fraction means writing it in *lowest terms*, that is, with smaller numbers. For instance, 50¢ is $\frac{50}{100}$ of a dollar, or $\frac{1}{2}$ of a dollar. In fact, if you have 50¢ in your pocket, you say that you have half a dollar. Reducing a fraction does not change its value.

Follow these steps to reduce a fraction:

1. Find a whole number that divides *evenly* into both numbers that make up the fraction.
2. Divide that number into the top of the fraction, and replace the top of the fraction with the quotient (the answer you got when you divided).
3. Do the same thing to the bottom number.
4. Repeat the first 3 steps until you can't find a number that divides evenly into both numbers of the fraction.

For example, let's reduce $\frac{8}{24}$. We could do it in two steps $\frac{8 \div 4}{24 \div 4} = \frac{2}{6}$; then $\frac{2 \div 2}{6 \div 2} = \frac{1}{3}$. Or we could do it in a single step $\frac{8 \div 8}{24 \div 8} = \frac{1}{3}$.

Shortcut: When the top and bottom numbers both end in zeroes, cross out the same number of zeroes in both numbers to begin the reducing process. For example $\frac{300}{4,000}$ reduces to $\frac{3}{40}$ when you cross out two zeroes in both numbers.

Whenever you do arithmetic with fractions, reduce your answer. On a multiple-choice test, don't panic if your answer isn't listed. Try to reduce it and then compare it to the choices.

Reduce these fractions to lowest terms.

_____ **5.** $\frac{8}{32}$

_____ **6.** $\frac{14}{35}$

_____ **7.** $\frac{27}{72}$

Raising Fractions to Higher Terms

Before you can add and subtract fractions, you have to know how to raise a fraction to higher terms. This is actually the opposite of reducing a fraction.

Follow these steps to raise $\frac{2}{3}$ to 24ths:

1. Divide the old bottom number (3) into the new one (24): $3\overline{)24} = 8$

2. Multiply the answer (8) by the old top number (2): $2 \times 8 = 16$

3. Put the answer (16) over the new bottom number (24): $\frac{16}{24}$

4. Check: Reduce the new fraction to see if you get back the original one: $\frac{16 \div 8}{24 \div 8} = \frac{2}{3}$

Raise these fractions to higher terms.

_____ **8.** $\frac{5}{12} = \frac{}{24}$

_____ **9.** $\frac{3}{4} = \frac{}{36}$

_____ **10.** $\frac{2}{5} = \frac{}{500}$

Adding Fractions

If the fractions have the same bottom numbers, just add the top numbers together and write the total over the bottom number.

Examples: $\frac{2}{9} + \frac{4}{9} = \frac{2+4}{9} = \frac{6}{9}$ Reduce the sum: $\frac{2}{3}$.

$\frac{5}{8} + \frac{7}{8} = \frac{12}{8}$.   Change the sum to a mixed number: $1\frac{4}{8}$; then reduce: $1\frac{1}{2}$.

There are a few extra steps to add mixed numbers with the same bottom numbers, say $2\frac{3}{5} + 1\frac{4}{5}$:

1. Add the fractions: $\frac{3}{5} + \frac{4}{5} = \frac{7}{5}$

2. Change the improper fraction into a mixed number: $\frac{7}{5} = 1\frac{2}{5}$

3. Add the whole numbers: $2 + 1 = 3$

4. Add the results of steps 2 and 3: $1\frac{2}{5} + 3 = 4\frac{2}{5}$

Finding the Least Common Denominator

If the fractions you want to add don't have the same bottom number, you will have to raise some or all of the fractions to higher terms so that they all have the same bottom number, called the common denominator. All of the original bottom numbers divide evenly into the common denominator. If it is the smallest number that they all divide evenly into, it is called the **least common denominator (LCD).**

Here are a few tips for finding the LCD, the smallest number that all the bottom numbers evenly divide into:

- See if all the bottom numbers divide evenly into the largest bottom number.
- Check out the multiplication table of the largest bottom number until you find a number that all the other bottom numbers evenly divide into.
- When all else fails, multiply all the bottom numbers together.

Example: $\frac{2}{3} + \frac{4}{5}$

1. Find the LCD. Multiply the bottom numbers: $\qquad 3 \times 5 \ = \ 15$

2. Raise each fraction to 15ths:
$$\frac{2}{3} = \frac{10}{15}$$
$$+\frac{4}{5} = \frac{12}{15}$$

3. Add as usual:
$$\frac{22}{15}$$

Try these addition problems:

_____ **11.** $\frac{2}{5} + \frac{3}{7}$

_____ **12.** $\frac{7}{8} + \frac{2}{3} + \frac{3}{4}$

_____ **13.** $4\frac{1}{3} + 2\frac{3}{4} + \frac{1}{6}$

Subtracting Fractions

If the fractions have the same bottom numbers, just subtract the top numbers and write the difference over the bottom number.

Example: $\frac{4}{9} - \frac{3}{9} = \frac{4-3}{9} = \frac{1}{9}$

If the fractions you want to subtract don't have the same bottom number, you will have to raise some or all of the fractions to higher terms so that they all have the same bottom number, or LCD. If you forgot how to find the LCD, just read the section on adding fractions with different bottom numbers.

Example: $\frac{5}{6} - \frac{3}{4}$

1. Raise each fraction to 12ths because 12 is the LCD, the smallest number that 6 and 4 both divide into evenly:

2. Subtract as usual:

$$\frac{5}{6} = \frac{10}{12}$$
$$-\frac{3}{4} = \frac{9}{12}$$
$$\frac{1}{12}$$

Subtracting mixed numbers with the same bottom number is similar to adding mixed numbers.

Example: $4\frac{3}{5} - 1\frac{2}{5}$

1. Subtract the fractions: $\frac{3}{5} - \frac{2}{5} = \frac{1}{5}$

2. Subtract the whole numbers: $4 - 1 = 3$

3. Add the results of steps 1 and 2: $\frac{1}{5} + 3 = 3\frac{1}{5}$

Sometimes there is an extra "borrowing" step when you subtract mixed numbers with the same bottom numbers, say $7\frac{3}{5} - 2\frac{4}{5}$:

1. You can't subtract the fractions the way they are because $\frac{4}{5}$ is bigger than $\frac{3}{5}$. So you borrow 1 from the 7, making it 6, and change that 1 to $\frac{5}{5}$ because 5 is the bottom number: $7\frac{3}{5} = 6\frac{5}{5} + \frac{3}{5}$

2. Add the numbers from step 1: $6\frac{5}{5} + \frac{3}{5} = 6\frac{8}{5}$

3. Now you have a different version of the original problem: $6\frac{8}{5} - 2\frac{4}{5}$

4. Subtract the fractional parts of the two mixed numbers: $\frac{8}{5} - \frac{4}{5} = \frac{4}{5}$

5. Subtract the whole number parts of the two mixed numbers: $6 - 2 = 4$

6. Add the results of the last 2 steps together: $4 + \frac{4}{5} = 4\frac{4}{5}$

Try these subtraction problems:

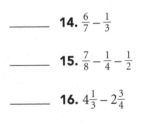

_____ **14.** $\frac{6}{7} - \frac{1}{3}$

_____ **15.** $\frac{7}{8} - \frac{1}{4} - \frac{1}{2}$

_____ **16.** $4\frac{1}{3} - 2\frac{3}{4}$

Now let's put what you have learned about adding and subtracting fractions to work in some real-life problems.

_____ **17.** Manuel drove $3\frac{1}{2}$ miles to work. Then he drove $4\frac{3}{4}$ miles to the store. When he left there, he drove 2 miles to the dry cleaners. Then he drove $3\frac{2}{3}$ miles back to work for a meeting. Finally, he drove $3\frac{1}{2}$ miles home. How many miles did he travel in total?

    a. $17\frac{5}{12}$

    b. $16\frac{5}{12}$

    c. $15\frac{7}{12}$

    d. $15\frac{5}{12}$

    e. $13\frac{11}{12}$

_____ **18.** Before leaving the warehouse, a truck driver noted that the mileage gauge registered $4{,}357\frac{4}{10}$ miles. When he arrived at the delivery site, the mileage gauge then registered $4{,}400\frac{1}{10}$ miles. How many miles did he drive from the warehouse to the delivery site?

    a. $42\frac{3}{10}$

    b. $42\frac{7}{10}$

    c. $43\frac{7}{10}$

    d. $47\frac{2}{10}$

    e. $57\frac{3}{10}$

Multiplying Fractions

Multiplying fractions is actually easier than adding them. All you do is multiply the top numbers and then multiply the bottom numbers.

Examples: $\frac{2}{3} \times \frac{5}{7} = \frac{2 \times 5}{3 \times 7} = \frac{10}{21}$

$\frac{1}{2} \times \frac{3}{5} \times \frac{7}{4} = \frac{1 \times 3 \times 7}{2 \times 5 \times 4} = \frac{21}{40}$

Sometimes you can *cancel* before multiplying. Canceling is a shortcut that makes the multiplication go faster because you're multiplying with smaller numbers. It's very similar to reducing: if there is a number that divides evenly into a top number and bottom number, do that division before multiplying. If you forget to cancel, you will still get the right answer, but you will have to reduce it.

Example: $\frac{5}{6} \times \frac{9}{20}$

1. Cancel the 6 and the 9 by dividing 3 into both of them: $6 \div 3 = 2$ and $9 \div 3 = 3$. Cross out the 6 and the 9.

2. Cancel the 5 and the 20 by dividing 5 into both of them: $5 \div 5 = 1$ and $20 \div 5 = 4$. Cross out the 5 and the 20.

3. Multiply across the new top numbers and the new bottom numbers: $\frac{1 \times 3}{2 \times 4} = \frac{3}{8}$.

Try these multiplication problems.

_____ **19.** $\frac{1}{6} \times \frac{3}{5}$

_____ **20.** $\frac{2}{3} \times \frac{4}{7} \times \frac{3}{5}$

_____ **21.** $\frac{3}{4} \times \frac{8}{9}$

To multiply a fraction by a whole number, first rewrite the whole number as a fraction with a bottom number of 1.

Example: $5 \times \frac{2}{3} = \frac{5}{1} \times \frac{2}{3} = \frac{10}{3}$
(Optional: convert $\frac{10}{3}$ to a mixed number: $3\frac{1}{3}$)

To multiply with mixed numbers, it's easier to change them to improper fractions before multiplying.

Example: $4\frac{2}{3} \times 5\frac{1}{2}$

1. Convert $4\frac{2}{3}$ to an improper fraction: $\qquad 4\frac{2}{3} = \frac{(4 \times 3 + 2)}{3} = \frac{14}{3}$

2. Convert $5\frac{1}{2}$ to an improper fraction: $\qquad 5\frac{1}{2} = \frac{(5 \times 2 + 1)}{2} = \frac{11}{2}$

3. Cancel and multiply the fractions: $\qquad \frac{\cancel{14}^{7}}{3} \times \frac{11}{\cancel{2}_1} = \frac{77}{3}$

4. Optional: convert the improper fraction to a mixed number: $\qquad \frac{77}{3} = 25\frac{2}{3}$

Now try these multiplication problems with mixed numbers and whole numbers:

_____ **22.** $4\frac{1}{3} \times \frac{2}{5}$

_____ **23.** $3\frac{1}{2} \times 73\frac{1}{2} \times 7$

_____ **24.** $3\frac{3}{4} \times 4\frac{4}{5}$

Here are a few more real-life problems to test your skills:

_____ **25.** After driving $\frac{2}{3}$ of the 15 miles to work, Mr. Stone stopped to make a phone call. How many miles had he driven when he made his call?
   a. 5
   b. $7\frac{1}{2}$
   c. 10
   d. 12
   e. $15\frac{2}{3}$

_____ **26.** If Henry worked $\frac{3}{4}$ of a 40-hour week, how many hours did he work?

    a. $7\frac{1}{2}$

    b. 10

    c. 20

    d. 25

    e. 30

_____ **27.** Technician Hamm makes \$13.00 an hour. When she works more than 8 hours a day, she gets overtime pay of $1\frac{1}{4}$ times her regular hourly wage for the extra hours. How much did she earn for working 10 hours in one day?

    a. \$110

    b. \$125.75

    c. \$136.50

    d. \$154.25

    e. \$163.50

Dividing Fractions

To divide one fraction by a second fraction, invert the second fraction (that is, flip the top and bottom numbers) and then multiply.

    Example: $\frac{1}{2} \div \frac{3}{5}$

1. Invert the second fraction ($\frac{3}{5}$): $\frac{5}{3}$

2. Change the division sign ($\div$) to a multiplication sign ($\times$): $\frac{1}{2} \times \frac{5}{3}$

3. Multiply the first fraction by the new second fraction: $\frac{1}{2} \times \frac{5}{3} = \frac{1 \times 5}{2 \times 3} = \frac{5}{6}$

To divide a fraction by a whole number, first change the whole number to a fraction by putting it over 1. Then follow the division steps above.

    Example: $\frac{3}{5} \div 2 = \frac{3}{5} \div \frac{2}{1} = \frac{3}{5} \times \frac{1}{2} = \frac{3 \times 1}{5 \times 2} = \frac{3}{10}$

When the division problem has a mixed number, convert it to an improper fraction and then divide as usual.

    Example: $2\frac{3}{4} \div \frac{1}{6}$

1. Convert $2\frac{3}{4}$ to an improper fraction: $2\frac{3}{4} = \frac{2 \times 4 + 3}{4} = \frac{11}{4}$

2. Divide $\frac{11}{4}$ by $\frac{1}{6}$; flip $\frac{1}{6}$ to $\frac{6}{1}$; change $\div$ to $\times$: $\frac{11}{4} \div \frac{1}{6} = \frac{11}{4} \times \frac{6}{1}$

3. Cancel and multiply: $\frac{11}{\underset{2}{4}} \times \frac{\overset{3}{6}}{1} = \frac{11 \times 3}{2 \times 1} = \frac{33}{2}$

Here are a few division problems to try.

_____ **28.** $\frac{1}{2} \div \frac{1}{3}$

_____ **29.** $2\frac{3}{4} \div \frac{1}{2}$

_____ **30.** $\frac{6}{7} \div 3$

_____ **31.** $3\frac{3}{4} \div 2\frac{1}{3}$

Let's wrap this up with some real-life problems.

_____ **32.** If four friends evenly split $6\frac{1}{2}$ pounds of candy, how many pounds of candy does each friend get?

     a. $\frac{8}{13}$

     b. $1\frac{5}{8}$

     c. $1\frac{1}{2}$

     d. $1\frac{5}{13}$

     e. 4

_____ **33.** How many $2\frac{1}{2}$-pound chunks of cheese can be cut from a single 20-pound piece of cheese?

     a. 2

     b. 4

     c. 6

     d. 8

     e. 10

_____ **34.** Ms. Goldbaum earned \$36.75 for working $3\frac{1}{2}$ hours. What was her hourly wage?

     a. \$10.00

     b. \$10.50

     c. \$10.75

     d. \$12.00

     e. \$12.25

Decimals

A decimal is a special kind of fraction. You use decimals every day when you deal with money—$10.35 is a decimal that represents 10 dollars and 35 cents. The decimal point separates the dollars from the cents. Because there are 100 cents in one dollar, 1¢ is $\frac{1}{100}$ of a dollar, or $.01.

Each decimal digit to the right of the decimal point has a name:

Examples: $.1 = 1$ tenth $= \frac{1}{10}$
$.02 = 2$ hundredths $= \frac{2}{100}$
$.003 = 3$ thousandths $= \frac{3}{1,000}$
$.0004 = 4$ ten-thousandths $= \frac{4}{10,000}$

When you add zeroes after the rightmost decimal place, you don't change the value of the decimal. For example, 6.17 is the same as all of these:

6.170

6.1700

6.17000000000000000

If there are digits on both sides of the decimal point (like 10.35), the number is called a mixed decimal. If there are digits only to the right of the decimal point (like .53), the number is called a decimal. A whole number (like 15) is understood to have a decimal point at its right (15.). Thus, 15 is the same as 15.0, 15.00, 15.000, and so on.

Changing Fractions to Decimals

To change a fraction to a decimal, divide the bottom number into the top number after you put a decimal point and a few zeroes on the right of the top number. When you divide, bring the decimal point up into your answer.

Example: Change $\frac{3}{4}$ to a decimal.

1. Add a decimal point and 2 zeroes to the top number (3):   3.00
2. Divide the bottom number (4) into 3.00:
   Bring the decimal point up into the answer:

$$\begin{array}{r} .75 \\ 4\overline{)3.00} \\ \underline{2\ 8} \\ 20 \\ \underline{20} \\ 0 \end{array}$$

3. The quotient (result of the division) is the answer: .75

Some fractions may require you to add many decimal zeroes in order for the division to come out evenly. In fact, when you convert a fraction like $\frac{2}{3}$ to a decimal, you can keep adding decimal zeroes to the top number forever because the division will never come out evenly. As you divide 3 into 2, you will keep getting 6's:

$$2 \div 3 = .6666666666 \text{ etc.}$$

This is called a *repeating decimal* and it can be written as $.66\overline{6}$ or as $.66\frac{2}{3}$. You can approximate it as .67, .667, .6667, and so on.

Changing Decimals to Fractions

To change a decimal to a fraction, write the digits of the decimal as the top number of a fraction and write the decimal's name as the bottom number of the fraction. Then reduce the fraction, if possible.

Example: .018

1. Write 18 as the top of the fraction: $\underline{18}$
2. Three places to the right of the decimal means *thousandths,* so write 1,000 as the bottom number: $\frac{18}{1,000}$
3. Reduce by dividing 2 into the top and bottom numbers: $\frac{18 \div 2}{1,000 \div 2} = \frac{9}{500}$

Change these decimals or mixed decimals to fractions.

_____ **35.** .008

_____ **36.** 3.48

_____ **37.** 123.456

Comparing Decimals

Because decimals are easier to compare when they have the same number of digits after the decimal point, tack zeroes onto the end of the shorter decimals. Then all you have to do is compare the numbers as if the decimal points weren't there:

Example: Compare .08 and .1

1. Tack one zero at the end of .1: .10
2. To compare .10 to .08, just compare 10 to 8.
3. Since 10 is larger than 8, .1 is larger than .08.

Adding and Subtracting Decimals

To add or subtract decimals, line them up so their decimal points are even. You may want to tack on zeroes at the end of shorter decimals so you can keep all your digits lined up evenly. Remember, if a number doesn't have a decimal point, then put one at the right end of the number.

Example: 1.23 + 57 + .038

1. Line up the numbers like this:
2. Add.

$$\begin{array}{r} 1.230 \\ 57.000 \\ + \ .038 \\ \hline 58.268 \end{array}$$

Example: 1.23 − .038

1. Line up the numbers like this:
2. Subtract.

$$\begin{array}{r} 1.230 \\ - \ .038 \\ \hline 1.192 \end{array}$$

Try these addition and subtraction problems.

_____ **38.** .905 + .02 + 3.075

_____ **39.** .025 + 9 + .4

_____ **40.** 3.48 − 2.573

_____ **41.** 123.456 − 122

_____ **42.** A park ranger drove 3.7 miles to the state park. He then walked 1.6 miles around the park to make sure everything was all right. He got back into the car, drove 2.75 miles to check on a broken light and then drove 2 miles back to the ranger station. How many miles did he drive in total?
  a. 8.05
  b. 8.45
  c. 8.8
  d. 10
  e. 10.05

_____ **43.** The average number of customers at a diner fell from 486.4 per week to 402.5 per week. By how many customers per week did the average fall?
  a. 73.9
  b. 83
  c. 83.1
  d. 83.9
  e. 84.9

Multiplying Decimals

To multiply decimals, ignore the decimal points and just multiply the numbers. Then count the total number of decimal digits (the digits to the *right* of the decimal point) in the numbers you are multiplying. Count off that number of digits in your answer beginning at the right side and put the decimal point to the *left* of those digits.

   Example: 215.7 × 2.4

1. Multiply 2,157 times 24:

$$
\begin{array}{r}
2{,}157 \\
\times\,24 \\
\hline
8{,}628 \\
4{,}314 \\
\hline
51{,}768
\end{array}
$$

2. Because there are a total of two decimal digits in 215.7 and 2.4, count off two places from the right in 51,768, placing the decimal point to the *left* of the last two digits:

   517.68

If your answer doesn't have enough digits, tack zeroes on to the left of the answer.

Example: .03 × .006

1. Multiply 3 times 6: $3 \times 6 = 18$

2. You need five decimal digits in your answer, so tack on three zeroes: 00018

3. Put the decimal point at the front of the number (which is five digits in from the right): .00018

You can practice multiplying decimals with these.

_____ **44.** .05 × .6

_____ **45.** .062 × 7.3

_____ **46.** 38.1 × .0184

_____ **47.** Joe earns $14.50 per hour. Last week he worked 37.5 hours. How much money did he earn that week?
    a. $518.00
    b. $518.50
    c. $525.00
    d. $536.50
    e. $543.75

_____ **48.** Nuts cost $3.50 per pound. Approximately how much will 4.25 pounds of nuts cost?
    a. $12.25
    b. $12.50
    c. $12.88
    d. $14.50
    e. $14.88

Dividing Decimals

To divide a decimal by a whole number, set up the division $(8\overline{).256})$ and immediately bring the decimal point straight up into the answer $(8\overline{)\overset{\cdot}{1}256})$. Then divide as you would normally divide whole numbers:

> *Example:*
>
> $$
> \begin{array}{r}
> .032 \\
> 8\overline{)\overset{\cdot}{1}256} \\
> \underline{0} \\
> 25 \\
> \underline{24} \\
> 16 \\
> \underline{16} \\
> 0
> \end{array}
> $$

To divide any number by a decimal, there is an extra step to perform before you can divide. Move the decimal point to the very right of the number you are dividing by, counting the number of places you are moving it. Then move the decimal point the same number of places to the right in the number you are dividing into. In other words, first change the problem to one in which you are dividing by a whole number.

> *Example:* $.06\overline{).218}$

1. Because there are 2 decimal digits in .06, move the decimal point two places to the right in both numbers and move the decimal point straight up into the answer:

   $.06.\overline{)1.2\overset{\cdot}{1}8}$

2. Divide using the new numbers:

   $$
   \begin{array}{r}
   20.3 \\
   6\overline{)121.8} \\
   \underline{12} \\
   01 \\
   \underline{00} \\
   18 \\
   \underline{18} \\
   0
   \end{array}
   $$

Under certain conditions, you have to tack on zeroes to the right of the last decimal digit in the number you are dividing into:

- if there aren't enough digits for you to move the decimal point to the right
- if the answer doesn't come out evenly when you do the division
- if you are dividing a whole number by a decimal. Then you will have to tack on the decimal point as well as some zeroes.

Try your skills on these division problems:

_____ **49.** $7\overline{)9.8}$

_____ **50.** $.0004\overline{).0512}$

_____ **51.** $.3\overline{)21.9}$

_____ **52.** $.14\overline{)196}$

_____ **53.** If James Worthington drove his truck 92.4 miles in 2.1 hours, what was his average speed in miles per hour?
    a. 41
    b. 44
    c. 90.3
    d. 94.5
    e. 194.04

_____ **54.** Mary Sanders walked a total of 18.6 miles in 4 days. On average, how many miles did she walk each day?
    a. 4.15
    b. 4.60
    c. 4.65
    d. 22.60
    e. 74.40

Percents

A percent is a special kind of fraction or part of something. The bottom number (the *denominator*) is always 100. For example, 17% is the same as $\frac{17}{100}$. Literally, the word *percent* means *per 100 parts*. The root *cent* means 100: a *century* is 100 years; there are 100 *cents* in a dollar, etc. Thus, 17% means 17 parts out of 100. Because fractions can also be expressed as decimals, 17% is also equivalent to .17, which is 17 hundredths.

You come into contact with percents every day. Sales tax, interest, and discounts are just a few common examples.

If you're shaky on fractions, you may want to review the fraction section before reading further.

Changing a Decimal to a Percent and Vice Versa
To change a decimal to a percent, move the decimal point two places to the right and tack on a percent sign (%) at the end. If the decimal point moves to the very right of the number, you don't have to write the decimal point. If there aren't enough places to move the decimal point, add zeroes on the right before moving the decimal point.

To change a percent to a decimal, drop off the percent sign and move the decimal point two places to the left. If there aren't enough places to move the decimal point, add zeroes on the left before moving the decimal point.

Try changing these decimals to percents.

_____ **55.** .67

_____ **56.** .008

_____ **57.** $.16\frac{2}{3}$

Now, change these percents to decimals.

_____ **58.** 12%

_____ **59.** $78\frac{1}{4}\%$

_____ **60.** 250%

Changing a Fraction to a Percent and Vice Versa

To change a fraction to a percent, there are two techniques. Each is illustrated by changing the fraction $\frac{1}{4}$ to a percent:

Technique 1:   Multiply the fraction by 100%.

Multiply $\frac{1}{4}$ by 100%: $\frac{1}{\underset{1}{4}} \times \frac{\overset{25}{\cancel{100}}\%}{1} = 25\%.$

Technique 2:   Divide the fraction's bottom number into the top number; then move the decimal point two places to the right and tack on a percent sign (%).

Divide 4 into 1 and move the decimal point 2 places to the right:

$$4\overline{)1.00}^{\,.25} \qquad\qquad .25 = 25\%$$

To change a percent to a fraction, remove the percent sign and write the number over 100. Then reduce if possible.

Example: Change 4% to a fraction.

1. Remove the % and write the fraction 4 over 100: $\frac{4}{100}$

2. Reduce: $\frac{4 \div 4}{100 \div 4} = \frac{1}{25}$

Here's a more complicated example: Change $16\frac{2}{3}\%$ to a fraction

1. Remove the % and write the fraction $16\frac{2}{3}$ over 100: $\frac{16\frac{2}{3}}{100}$

2. Since a fraction means "top number divided by bottom number," rewrite the fraction as a division problem: $16\frac{2}{3} \div 100$

3. Change the mixed number ($16\frac{2}{3}$) to an improper fraction ($\frac{50}{3}$): $\frac{50}{3} \div \frac{100}{1}$

4. Flip the second fraction ($\frac{100}{1}$) and multiply: $\frac{\overset{1}{\cancel{50}}}{3} \times \frac{1}{\underset{2}{\cancel{100}}} = \frac{1}{6}$

Try changing these fractions to percents.

_____ **61.** $\frac{1}{8}$

_____ **62.** $\frac{16}{25}$

_____ **63.** $\frac{7}{12}$

Now change these percents to fractions.

_____ **64.** 95%

_____ **65.** $37\frac{1}{2}$%

_____ **66.** 150%

Sometimes it is more convenient to work with a percentage as a fraction or a decimal. Rather than have to *calculate* the equivalent fraction or decimal, consider memorizing the equivalence table below. Not only will this increase your efficiency on the math test, but it will also be practical for real life situations.

CONVERSION TABLE		
Decimal	%	Fraction
.25	25%	$\frac{1}{4}$
.50	50%	$\frac{1}{2}$
.75	75%	$\frac{3}{4}$
.10	10%	$\frac{1}{10}$
.20	20%	$\frac{1}{5}$
.40	40%	$\frac{2}{5}$
.60	60%	$\frac{3}{5}$
.80	80%	$\frac{4}{5}$
.33$\overline{3}$	$33\frac{1}{3}$%	$\frac{1}{3}$
.66$\overline{6}$	$66\frac{2}{3}$%	$\frac{2}{3}$

Percent Word Problems

Word problems involving percents come in three main varieties:

■ Find a percent of a whole.
   Example: What is 30% of 40?
■ Find what percent one number is of another number.
   Example: 12 is what percent of 40?
■ Find the whole when the percent of it is given.
   Example: 12 is 30% of what number?

While each variety has its own approach, there is a single shortcut formula you can use to solve each of these:

$$\frac{is}{of} = \frac{\%}{100}$$

The *is* is the number that usually follows or is just before the word *is* in the question.
The *of* is the number that usually follows the word *of* in the question.
The % is the number that is in front of the % or *percent* in the question.

Or you may think of the shortcut formula as:

$$\frac{part}{whole} = \frac{\%}{100}$$
$$part \times 100 = whole \times \%$$

To solve each of the three varieties, let's use the fact that the cross-products are equal. The cross-products are the products of the numbers diagonally across from each other. Remembering that *product* means *multiply,* here's how to create the cross-products for the percent shortcut:

$$\frac{part}{whole} = \frac{\%}{100}$$
$$part \times 100 = whole \times \%$$

Here's how to use the shortcut with cross-products:

■ Find a percent of a whole.
   What is 30% of 40?
   30 is the % and 40 is the *of* number: $\quad \frac{is}{40} = \frac{30}{100}$
   Cross multiply and solve for *is:* $\quad is \times 100 = 40 \times 30$
   $$is \times 100 = 1{,}200$$
   $$12 \times 100 = 1{,}200$$
   Thus, 12 *is* 30% of 40.
■ Find what percent one number is of another number.
   12 is what percent of 40?
   12 is the *is* number and 40 is the *of* number: $\quad \frac{12}{40} = \frac{\%}{100}$
   Cross multiply and solve for %: $\quad 12 \times 100 = 40 \times \%$
   $$1{,}200 = 40 \times \%$$
   $$1{,}200 = 40 \times 30$$
   Thus, 12 is 30% of 40.

■ Find the whole when the percent of it is given.

12 is 30% of what number?

12 is the *is* number and 30 is the %: $\frac{12}{of} = \frac{30}{100}$

Cross-multiply and solve for the *of* number: $12 \times 100 = of \times 30$

$$1,200 = of \times 30$$
$$1,200 = 40 \times 30$$

Thus 12 is 30% of 40.

You can use the same technique to find the percent increase or decrease. The *is* number is the actual increase or decrease, and the *of* number is the original amount.

Example: If a merchant puts his $20 hats on sale for $15, by what percent does he decrease the selling price?

1. Calculate the decrease, the *is* number: $20 – $15 = $5

2. The *of* number is the original amount, $20.

3. Set up the equation and solve for *of* by cross multiplying: $\frac{5}{20} = \frac{\%}{100}$

$$5 \times 100 = 20 \times \%$$
$$500 = 20 \times \%$$
$$500 = 20 \times 25$$

4. Thus, the selling price is decreased by 25%.

If the merchant later raises the price of the hats from $15 back to $20, don't be fooled into thinking that the percent increase is also 25%! It's actually more, because the increase amount of $5 is now based on a lower original price of only $15:

$$\frac{5}{15} = \frac{\%}{100}$$
$$5 \times 100 = 15 \times \%$$
$$500 = 15 \times \%$$
$$500 = 15 \times 33\frac{1}{3}$$

Thus, the selling price is increased by 33%.

Find a percent of a whole:

_____ **67.** 1% of 25

_____ **68.** 18.2% of 50

_____ **69.** $37\frac{1}{2}$% of 100

_____ **70.** 125% of 60

Find what percent one number is of another number.

_____ **71.** 30 is what % of 60?

_____ **72.** 4 is what % of 12?

_____ **73.** 12 is what % of 4?

Find the whole when the percent of it is given.

_____ **74.** 15% of what number is 15?

_____ **75.** $37\frac{1}{2}$% of what number is 3?

_____ **76.** 200% of what number is 20?

Now try your percent skills on some real life problems.

_____ **77.** Last Monday, 20% of 140 staff members was absent. How many employees were absent that day?
   a. 14
   b. 20
   c. 28
   d. 112
   e. 126

_____ **78.** 30% of Vero's postal service employees are women. If there are 90 women in Vero's postal service, how many men are employed there?
   a. 150
   b. 180
   c. 210
   d. 260
   e. 300

_____ **79.** Of the 840 shirts sold at a retail store last month, 42 had short sleeves. What percent of the shirts were short sleeved?
   a. .5%
   b. 2%
   c. 5%
   d. 20%
   e. 50%

_____ **80.** Sam's Shoe Store put all of its merchandise on sale for 20% off. If Jason saved $10 by purchasing one pair of shoes during the sale, what was the original price of the shoes before the sale?

    a. $12

    b. $20

    c. $40

    d. $50

    e. $70

Averages

An average, also called an arithmetic mean, is a number that *typifies* a group of numbers, a measure of central tendency. You come into contact with averages on a regular basis: your bowling average, the average grade on a test, the average number of hours you work per week.

    To calculate an average, add up the number of items being averaged and divide by the number of items.

    Example: What is the average of 6, 10, and 20?

    Solution: Add the three numbers together and divide by 3: $\frac{6 + 10 + 20}{3} = 12$

Shortcut

Here's a shortcut for some average problems.

- Look at the numbers being averaged. If they are equally spaced, like 5, 10, 15, 20, and 25, then the average is the number in the middle, or 15 in this case.
- If there is an even number of such numbers, say 10, 20, 30, and 40, then there is no middle number. In this case, the average is half-way between the two middle numbers. In this case, the average is half-way between 20 and 30, or 25.
- If the numbers are almost evenly spaced, you can probably estimate the average without going to the trouble of actually computing it. For example, the average of 10, 20, and 32 is just a little more than 20, the middle number.

    Try these average questions.

_____ **81.** Bob's bowling scores for the last five games were 180, 182, 184, 186, and 188. What was his average bowling score?

    a. 182

    b. 183

    c. 184

    d. 185

    e. 186

_____ **82.** Jackson averaged 45 miles an hour for the three hours he drove in town and 60 miles an hour for the three hours he drove on the highway. What was his average speed in miles per hour?

    a. 26

    b. $35\frac{1}{2}$

    c. 48

    d. $52\frac{1}{2}$

    e. 105

_____ **83.** There are 10 females and 20 males in a history class. If the females achieved an average score of 85 and the males achieved an average score of 95, what was the class average? (Hint: don't fall for the trap of taking the average of 85 and 95; there are more 95s being averaged than 85s, so the average is closer to 95.)

    a. $90\frac{2}{3}$

    b. $91\frac{2}{3}$

    c. 92

    d. $92\frac{2}{3}$

    e. 95

Geometry

Typically, there are very few geometry problems on the math test. The problems that are included tend to cover the basics: lines, angles, triangles, rectangles, squares, and circles. You may be asked to find the area or perimeter of a particular shape or the size of an angle. The arithmetic involved is pretty simple, so all you really need are a few definitions and formulas.

Glossary of Geometry Terms

Angle   Two rays with a common endpoint called a vertex. There are four types of angles:
        Acute: less than 90°
        Obtuse: more than 90°
        Right: 90°
        Straight: 180°

        acute

Circle   Set of all points that are the same distance from the center.
        Area $= \pi r^2$
        Circumference $= 2\pi r$
        ($\pi = 3.14$; $r =$ radius)

        radius

Circumference   Distance around a circle. (See _Circle._)

Diameter   A line through the center of a circle. The diameter is twice the length of the radius. (See *Circle, Radius.*)

Line   A line extends endlessly in both directions. It is referred to by a letter at the end of it or by two points on it. Thus, the line below may be referred to as line l or as $\overleftrightarrow{AB}$.

Parallel Lines   Two lines in the same plane that do not intersect:
$l \parallel m$

Perimeter   Distance around a figure, such as a triangle or a rectangle. The perimeter of a circle is called its *circumference*.

Perimeter = sum of length of all sides

Perpendicular Lines Two lines in the same plane that intersect to form four right angles. (See *Right Angle.*)

Point   A point has a location but no size or dimension. It is referred to by a letter close to it, like this: • A

Radius   Line segment from the center to any point on a circle. The radius is half the diameter. (See *Circle, Diameter.*)

Rectangle   Four-sided figure with a right angle and both pairs of opposite sides parallel (which implies that all four sides are right angles and that opposite sides are equal in length).

Area = *length* × *width*
Perimeter = 2 × *length* + 2 × *width*

Square   Rectangle with four equal sides (see *Rectangle*):
Area = *(side)*^{2}
Perimeter = 4 × *side*

Triangle   Three-sided figure:
Area = $\frac{1}{2}$(*base* × *height*)
Perimeter = sum of the lengths of all three sides
Angles: The sum of the three angles of a triangle is always 180°.

Practice Problems

Try your hand at these sample problems.

_____ **84.** What is the area in inches of a triangle with base 10" and height 8"?
   a. 80
   b. 40
   c. 20
   d. 10
   e. 8

_____ **85.** Find the perimeter of a triangle with sides of length 4, 6, and 8 units.
   a. 50 units
   b. 18 units
   c. 12 units
   d. 8 units
   e. 7 units

_____ **86.** If the area of a square field measures 256 square feet, how many feet of fencing are needed to completely surround the field?
   a. 256
   b. 128
   c. 64
   d. 32
   e. It cannot be determined.

_____ **87.** The length of a rectangle is twice its width. If the perimeter of the rectangle is 30 units, what is the width of the rectangle?
   a. 30
   b. 20
   c. 15
   d. 10
   e. 5

_____ **88.** A circular opening has a diameter of 12.5 inches. What is the radius in inches of a circular disk that will exactly fit into the opening?
   a. 15
   b. 12.5
   c. 8
   d. 6.25
   e. 4

_____ **89.** The radius of a hoop is 10". If you roll the hoop along a straight path through 6 complete revolutions, approximately how far will it roll, in inches? (Use a value of 3.14 for π.)

    a. 31.4

    b. 62.8

    c. 188.4

    d. 376.8

    e. 1,884

Algebra

There are not many algebra questions on the ASVAB. However, when they do appear, they typically cover the material you learned in pre-algebra or in the first few months of your high school algebra course. Popular topics for algebra questions include:

- solving equations
- positive and negative numbers
- algebraic expressions

What Is Algebra?

Algebra is a way to express and solve problems using numbers and symbols. These symbols, called *unknowns* or *variables,* are letters of the alphabet that are used to represent numbers.

For example, let's say you are asked to find out what number, when added to 3, gives you a total of 5. Using algebra, you could express the problem as $x + 3 = 5$. The variable x represents the number you are trying to find.

Here's another example, but this one uses only variables. To find the distance traveled, multiply the rate of travel (speed) by the amount of time traveled: $d = r \times t$. The variable d stands for *distance,* r stands for *rate,* and t stands for *time.*

In algebra, the variables may take on different values. In other words, they *vary,* and that's why they're called *variables.*

Operations

Algebra uses the same operations as arithmetic: addition, subtraction, multiplication, and division. In arithmetic, we might say $3 + 4 = 7$, while in algebra we would talk about two numbers whose values we don't know that add up to 7, or $x + y = 7$. Here's how each operation translates to algebra:

ALGEBRAIC OPERATIONS	
The sum of two numbers	$x + y$
The difference of two numbers	$x - y$
The product of two numbers	$x \times y$ or $x \bullet y$ or xy
The quotient of two numbers	$\frac{x}{y}$ or $x \div y$

Equations

An equation is a mathematical sentence stating that two quantities are equal. For example:

$$2x = 10$$
$$x + 5 = 8$$

The idea is to find a replacement for the unknown that will make the sentence true. That's called *solving* the equation. Thus, in the first example, $x = 5$ because $2 \times 5 = 10$. In the second example, $x = 3$ because $3 + 5 = 8$.

Sometimes you can solve an equation by inspection, as with the above examples. Other equations may be more complicated and require a step-by-step solution, for example:

$$\frac{n+2}{4} + 1 = 3$$

The general approach is to consider an equation like a balance scale, with both sides equally balanced. Essentially, whatever you do to one side, you must also do to the other side to maintain the balance. Thus, if you were to add 2 to the left side, you would also have to add 2 to the right side.

Let's apply this *balance* concept to our complicated equation above. Remembering that we want to solve it for *n*, we must somehow rearrange it so the *n* is isolated on one side of the equation. Its value will then be on the other side. Looking at the equation, you can see that *n* has been increased by 2 and then divided by 4 and ultimately added to 1. Therefore, we will undo these operations to isolate *n*.

Begin by subtracting 1 from both sides of the equation:

$$\frac{n+2}{4} + 1 = 3$$
$$\underline{-1 \quad -1}$$
$$\frac{n+2}{4} = 2$$

Next, multiply both sides by 4:

$$4 \times \frac{n+2}{4} = 2 \times 4$$
$$n + 2 = 8$$

Finally, subtract 2 from both sides:

$$\underline{-2 \quad -2}$$
$$n = 6$$

Which isolates *n* and solves the equation: $n = 6$.

Notice that each operation in the original equation was undone by using the inverse operation. That is, addition was undone by subtraction, and division was undone by multiplication. In general, each operation can be undone by its *inverse*.

ALGEBRAIC INVERSES	
Operation	**Inverse**
Addition	Subtraction
Subtraction	Addition
Multiplication	Division
Division	Multiplication

After you solve an equation, check your work by plugging the answer back into the original equation to make sure it balances. Let's see what happens when we plug 6 in for *n:*

$$\frac{6+2}{4} + 1 = 3?$$
$$\frac{8}{4} + 1 = 3?$$
$$2 + 1 = 3?$$
$$3 = 3\checkmark$$

Solve each equation:

_____ **90.** $x + 5 = 12$

_____ **91.** $3x + 6 = 18$

_____ **92.** $\frac{1}{4}x = 7$

Positive and Negative Numbers

Positive and negative numbers, also known as *signed* numbers, are best shown as points along the number line:

Numbers to the left of 0 are *negative* and those to the right are *positive*. Zero is neither negative nor positive. If a number is written without a sign, it is assumed to be *positive*. Notice that when you are on the negative side of the number line, numbers with bigger values are actually smaller. For example, –5 is *less than* –2. You come into contact with negative numbers more often than you might think; for example, very cold temperatures are recorded as negative numbers.

As you move to the right along the number line, the numbers get larger. Mathematically, to indicate that one number, say 4, is *greater than* another number, say –2, the *greater than* sign (>) is used:

$$4 > -2$$

On the other hand, to say that –2 is *less than* 4, we use the *less than* sign, (<):

$$-2 < 4$$

Arithmetic with Positive and Negative Numbers

The table below illustrates the rules for doing arithmetic with signed numbers. Notice that when a negative number follows an operation (as it does in the second example below), it is enclosed in parentheses to avoid confusion.

RULE	EXAMPLE
Addition	
If both numbers have the same sign, just add them. The answer has the same sign as the numbers being added. If both numbers have different signs, subtract the smaller number from the larger. The answer has the same sign as the larger number. If both numbers are the same but have opposite signs, the sum is zero.	$3 + 5 = 8$ $-3 + (-5) = -8$ $-3 + 5 = 5 - 3 = 2$ $3 + (-5) = 2$ $3 + (-3) = 0$
Subtraction	
Change the sign of the number to be subtracted and then add as above.	$3 - 5 = 3 + (-5) = -2$ $-3 - 5 = -3 + (-5) = -8$ $-3 - (-5) = -3 + 5 = 2$
Multiplication	
Multiply the numbers together. If both numbers have the same sign, the answer is positive; otherwise, it is negative.	$3 \times 5 = 15$ $-3 \times (-5) = 15$ $-3 \times 5 = -15$ $3 \times (-5) = -15$
If one number is zero, the answer is zero.	$3 \times 0 = 0$
Division	
Divide the numbers. If both numbers have the same sign, the answer is positive; otherwise, it is negative.	$15 \div 3 = 5$ $-15 \div (-3) = 5$ $15 \div (-3) = -5$ $-15 \div 3 = -5$
If the top number is zero, the answer is zero.	$0 \div 3 = 0$

When more than one arithmetic operation appears, you must know the correct sequence in which to perform the operations. For example, do you know what to do first to calculate $2 + 3 \times 4$? You're right if you said, "multiply first." The correct answer is 14. If you add first, you will get the wrong answer of 20. The correct sequence of operations is:

1. parentheses
2. exponents
3. multiplication
4. division
5. addition
6. subtraction

If you remember this saying, you will know the order of operations: **P**lease **e**xcuse **m**y **d**ear Aunt Sally.

Even when signed numbers appear in an equation, the step-by-step solution works exactly as it does for positive numbers. You just have to remember the arithmetic rules for negative numbers. For example, let's solve $14x + 2 = 5$.

1. Subtract 2 from both sides:

$$-14x + 2 = -5$$
$$\underline{ -2 \quad -2}$$
$$-14x = -7$$

2. Divide both sides by -14:

$$-14x \div -14 = -7 \div -14$$
$$x = \frac{1}{2}$$

Now try these problems with signed numbers.

_____ **93.** $1 - 3 \times (-4) = x$

_____ **94.** $-3x + 6 = -18$

_____ **95.** $\frac{x}{-4} + 3 = -7$

Algebraic Expressions

An algebraic expression is a group of numbers, unknowns, and arithmetic operations, like: $3x - 2y$. This one may be translated as, "3 times some number minus 2 times another number." To *evaluate* an algebraic expression, replace each variable with its value. For example, if $x = 5$ and $y = 4$, we would evaluate $3x - 2y$ as follows:

$$3(5) - 2(4) = 15 - 8 = 7$$

Evaluate these expressions.

_____ **96.** $6a + 2b$; $a = 2$ and $b = -1$

_____ **97.** $3mn - 4m + 2n$; $m = 3$ and $n = -3$

_____ **98.** $-2x - \frac{1}{2}y + 4z$; $x = 5$, $y = -4$, and $z = 6$

_____ **99.** The volume of a cylinder is given by the formula $V = \pi r^2 h$, where r is the radius of the base and h is the height of the cylinder. What is the volume of a cylinder with a base radius of 3 and height of 4? (Leave π in your answer.)

_____ **100.** If $x = 3$, what is the value of $3x - x$?

Answers

Word Problems

1. d.
2. d.
3. a.
4. e.

Fractions

5. $\frac{1}{4}$
6. $\frac{2}{5}$
7. $\frac{3}{8}$
8. 10
9. 27
10. 200
11. $\frac{29}{35}$
12. $\frac{55}{24}$ or $2\frac{7}{24}$
13. $7\frac{1}{4}$
14. $\frac{11}{21}$
15. $\frac{1}{8}$
16. $\frac{19}{12}$ or $1\frac{7}{12}$
17. a.
18. b.
19. $\frac{1}{10}$
20. $\frac{8}{35}$
21. $\frac{2}{3}$
22. $\frac{26}{15}$ or $1\frac{11}{15}$
23. $1,800\frac{3}{4}$
24. $\frac{18}{1}$ or 18
25. c.
26. e.
27. c.
28. $\frac{3}{2}$ or $1\frac{1}{2}$
29. $5\frac{1}{2}$
30. $\frac{2}{7}$
31. $\frac{45}{28}$ or $1\frac{17}{28}$

32. b.
33. d.
34. b.

Decimals

35. $\frac{8}{1,000}$ or $\frac{1}{125}$
36. $3\frac{12}{25}$
37. $123\frac{456}{1,000}$ or $123\frac{57}{125}$
38. 4
39. 9.425
40. 0.907
41. 1.456
42. b.
43. d.
44. 0.03
45. 0.4526
46. 0.70104
47. e.
48. e.
49. 1.4
50. 128
51. 73
52. 1,400
53. b.
54. c.

Percents

55. 67%
56. 0.8%
57. 16.67% or $16\frac{2}{3}$%
58. 0.12
59. 0.7825
60. 2.5
61. 12.5% or $12\frac{1}{2}$%
62. 64%
63. 58.33% or $58\frac{1}{3}$%
64. $\frac{19}{20}$
65. $\frac{3}{8}$
66. $\frac{3}{2}$ or $1\frac{1}{2}$

67. $\frac{1}{4}$ or .25
68. 9.1
69. $37\frac{1}{2}$ or 37.5
70. 75
71. 50%
72. $33\frac{1}{3}$%
73. 300%
74. 100
75. 8
76. 10
77. c.
78. c.
79. c.
80. d.

Averages

81. c.
82. d.
83. b.

Geometry

84. b.
85. b.
86. c.
87. e.
88. d.
89. d.

Algebra

90. 7
91. 4
92. 28
93. 13
94. 8
95. 40
96. 10
97. −45
98. 16
99. 36π
100. 6

8 ▶ WORD KNOWLEDGE REVIEW

CHAPTER SUMMARY

This chapter will help you improve your vocabulary skills so that you can score higher on the Word Knowledge section of the ASVAB.

The Word Knowledge subtest of the ASVAB is essentially a vocabulary test. Combined with the Paragraph Comprehension subtest, Word Knowledge helps make up your Verbal Equivalent score—it is also one of the four subtests that determine whether or not you will be allowed to enlist.

Your ability to communicate, whether in the military or working in the private sector, is one of the most important factors in building a successful career. Whether reporting crucial information from the battlefield, or writing a proposal for a key contract, the ability to communicate effectively cannot be understated. Furthermore, your ability to understand military training materials, as well as convey ideas, depends in part on your reading comprehension and vocabulary skill.

There are two different kinds of questions on the Word Knowledge subtest:

- **Synonyms**: identifying words that mean the same as the given words
- **Context**: determining the meaning of a word or phrase by noting how it is used in a sentence or paragraph

Synonyms

A word is a **synonym** of another word if it has the same or nearly the same meaning as the other word. Test questions often ask you to find the synonym or antonym of a word. If you're lucky, the word will be surrounded by a sentence that helps you guess what the word means. If you're less lucky, you will just get the word, and then you have to figure out what the word means without any context.

Questions that ask for synonyms can be tricky because they require you to recognize the meaning of several words that may be unfamiliar—not only the words in the questions but also the answer choices. Usually the best strategy is to *look* at the structure of the word and to *listen* for its sound. See if a part of a word looks familiar. Think of other words you know that have similar key elements. How could those words be related?

Synonym Practice

Try identifying the word parts and related words in these sample synonym questions. Circle the word that means the same or about the same as the italicized word. Answers and explanations appear right after the questions.

1. *incoherent* answer
   a. not understandable
   b. not likely
   c. undeniable
   d. challenging

2. *ambiguous* questions
   a. meaningless
   b. difficult
   c. simple
   d. vague

3. covered with *debris*
   a. good excuses
   b. transparent material
   c. scattered rubble
   d. protective material

4. *inadvertently* left
   a. mistakenly
   b. purposely
   c. cautiously
   d. carefully

5. *exorbitant* prices
   a. expensive
   b. unexpected
   c. reasonable
   d. outrageous

6. *compatible* workers
   a. gifted
   b. competitive
   c. harmonious
   d. experienced

7. *belligerent* attitude
   a. hostile
   b. reasonable
   c. instinctive
   d. friendly

Answers

The explanations are important because they show you how to go about choosing a synonym if you don't know the word.

1. a. *Incoherent* means *not understandable.* To *cohere* means to *connect.* A coherent answer connects or makes sense. The prefix *in-* means *not.*

2. d. *Ambiguous* questions are *vague* or uncertain. The key part of this word is *ambi-*, which means *two* or *both.* An ambiguous question can be taken two ways.

3. c. *Debris* is scattered fragments and trash.

4. a. *Inadvertently* means *by mistake.* The key element in this word is the prefix *in-*, which usually means *not,* or *the opposite of.*

5. d. The key element here is *ex-*, which means *out of* or *away from.* Exorbitant literally means "out of orbit." An *exorbitant* price would be an *outrageous* one.

6. c. *Compatible* means *harmonious.*

7. a. The key element in this word is the root *belli-,* which means *warlike.* The synonym choice, then, is *hostile.*

Context Questions

Context is the surrounding text in which a word is used. Most people use context to help them determine the meaning of an unknown word. A vocabulary question that gives you a sentence around the vocabulary word is usually easier to answer than one with little or no context. The surrounding text can help you as you look for synonyms for the specified words in the sentences.

The best way to take meaning from context is to look for key words in sentences or paragraphs that convey the meaning of the text. If nothing else, the context will give you a means to eliminate wrong answer choices that clearly don't fit. The process of elimination will often leave you with the correct answer.

Context Practice

Try these sample questions. Circle the word that best describes the meaning of the italicized word in the sentence.

8. The maintenance workers were *appalled* by the filthy, cluttered condition of the building.
 a. horrified
 b. amused
 c. surprised
 d. dismayed

9. Even though she seemed rich, the defendant claimed to be *destitute.*
 a. wealthy
 b. ambitious
 c. solvent
 d. poor

10. Though she was *distraught* over losing her keys, the woman was calm enough to remember she had a spare set.
 a. punished
 b. distracted
 c. composed
 d. anguished

11. The evil criminal expressed no *remorse* for his actions.
 a. sympathy
 b. regret
 c. reward
 d. complacency

Answers

Check to see whether you were able to pick out the key words that help you define the target word, as well as whether you got the right answer.

8. a. The key words *filthy* and *cluttered* signify horror rather than the milder emotions described by the other choices.

9. d. The key word here is *rich,* but this is a clue by contrast. The introductory *even though* signals that you should look for the opposite of the idea of having financial resources.

10. d. The key words here are *though* and *losing her keys,* signaling that you are looking for an opposite of *calm* in describing the woman. The only word strong enough to match the situation is *anguish.*

11. b. *Remorse* means *regret* for one's actions. The part of the word here to beware of is the prefix *re-.* It doesn't signify anything in this word, though it often means again or back. Don't be confused by the two choices that also contain the prefix *re-.* The strategy here is to see which word sounds better in the sentence. The key words are *evil* and *no,* indicating that you are looking for something that shows no repentance.

Be very careful not to be confused by the sound of words that may mislead you. Be sure to look at the word carefully, and pay attention to the structure and appearance of the word as well as its sound. You may be used to hearing English words spoken with an accent. The sounds of those words may be misleading in choosing a correct answer.

Word Parts

The best way to improve your vocabulary is to learn word parts: roots, which are the main part of the word; prefixes, which go before the root word; or suffixes, which go after. Any of these elements can carry meaning or change the use of a word in a sentence. For instance, the suffix -s or -es can change the meaning of a noun from singular to plural: *boy, boys*. The prefix *un-* can change the meaning of a root word to its opposite: *necessary, unnecessary*.

In the sections on **prefixes** and **suffixes** are some of the word elements seen most often in vocabulary tests. Simply reading them and their examples for five to ten minutes a day will give you the quick recognition you need to make a good association with the meaning of an unfamiliar word.

Prefixes

In order to be able to unlock the meaning of many words in our language, it is useful for you to understand what a prefix is. A prefix is a word part at the beginning of a word that changes or adds to the meaning of the root word in some way. By learning some common prefixes, you will learn to recognize many unfamiliar words. After you have completed the exercises in this chapter, you will become acquainted with the meanings suggested by some of the more common prefixes, which will improve your reading, speaking, and listening vocabularies.

antecedent   (an·ti·ˈsēd·ənt)
prefix: **ante** means before
(adj.)
going before in time
The event was _____ to the Civil War.

antipathy   (an·ˈtip·ə·thē)
prefix: anti **means against**
(noun)
revulsion; any object of strong dislike
The child had an _____ toward snakes.

circumvent   (sər·kəm·ˈvent)
prefix: **circum and circ** mean around
(verb)
to go around; to catch in a trap; to gain superiority over; to prevent from happening
Police tried to _____ the riot by moving the crowd along.

consensus   (kən·ˈsen·səs)
prefix: **con** means with, together
(noun)
agreement, especially in opinion
The committee reached _____ about gun control.

controversy   (ˈkon·trə·ver·sē)
prefix: **contr** means against
(noun)
a discussion of a question in which opposing views clash
There is a _____ about building nuclear power plants.

decimate   ('des·i·māt)
prefix: **dec** means ten
(*verb*)
to destroy or kill a large portion of something; to
    take or destroy a tenth part of something
Caterpillars can _____ trees.

demote   (di·mōt)
prefix: **de** means down, away from
(*verb*)
to lower in grade or position
Upper ranked officers can _____ a lower ranked
    person.

disinterested   (dis·'in·tər·est·ed)
prefix: **dis** means not, opposite of
(*adj.*)
not motivated by personal interest or selfish motives
A loyal citizen is _____.

euphemism   ('u·fə·mizm)
prefix: **eu** means good, well
(*noun*)
the use of a word or phrase that is considered less
    distasteful or offensive than another
"She is at rest" is a _____ for "she is dead."

exorbitant   (ek·'zor·bi·tənt)
prefix: **ex** means out of, away from
(*adj.*)
going beyond what is reasonable and proper
The colonists rebelled against _____ taxes.

illegible   (i·'lej·ə·bəl)
prefix: **il** means not, opposite
(*adj.*)
not able to be read
The student had to rewrite the _____ paper.

intermittent   (in·tər·'mit·ənt)
prefix: **inter** means between
(*adj.*)
stopping and starting again at intervals
The weather forecaster predicted _____ showers.

malevolent   (mə·'lev·ə·lent)
prefix: **mal** means bad
(*adj.*)
having an evil disposition toward others
A _____ person rejoices in the misfortune of
    others.

precursor   (pre·'kər·sər)
prefix: **pre** means before
(*noun*)
a forerunner, a harbinger; one who or that which
    goes before
Calmness is usually a _____ to a storm.

prognosis   (prog·'nō·sis)
prefix: **pro** means before
(*noun*)
a forecast; especially in medicine
The injured animal's _____ for recovery is good.

retrospect   ('ret·rō·spekt)
prefix: **retro** means back, again
(*verb*)
to think about the past
(*noun*)
looking back on or thinking about things past
In _____, the world leader wished he had acted
    differently.

subordinate (sub·ʹor·din·it)
prefix: **sub** means under
(*adj.*)
inferior to or placed below another in rank, power, or importance
(*noun*)
a person or thing of lesser power or importance than another
(*verb*) (sub·ʹor·din·āt)
to treat as inferior or less important
The wise president treated her _____ with respect.

synthesis (ʹsin·thə·sis)
prefix: **syn**, or **sym** means with or together
(*noun*)
putting of two or more things to together to form a whole
In chemistry, the process of making a compound by joining elements together is called _____.

transcend (tran·ʹsend)
prefix: **trans** means across
(*verb*)
to go beyond the limits of; to overstep; to exceed
A seeing eye dog enables blind people to _____ their disability.

trivial (ʹtriv·ē·əl)
prefix: **tri** means three
(*adj.*)
of little worth or importance
The research scientist did not have time for _____ pursuits because he was so busy conducting important experiments.

Words in Context

The following exercise will help you figure out the meaning of some words from the previous list. Circle any context clues that help you figure out the meaning of the bold words.

In our country, the use of nuclear power as a viable source of energy has been an ongoing **controversy.** During the gas and oil shortages of the 1970s, energy prices were **exorbitant.** The federal government supported nuclear power as a new energy source that would be cost effective. Now, the President's National Energy Policy Report lists nuclear power as a safe and affordable alternative. Today, as in the past, many people have voiced their **antipathy** toward nuclear power plants, especially in the wake of the 1979 partial meltdown of the Three Mile Island nuclear power plant. At that time, scientists scrambled to **circumvent** a total meltdown in a facility that was designed to be fail-safe. There was great fear that the meltdown would be complete and **decimate** the area. Now, the federal government is once again promoting this alternative energy source.

Suffixes

Word endings that are added to the main part or root of words are called **suffixes.** Suffixes are word parts that signal how a word is being used in a sentence. You will note that each word in the list is a particular part of speech (*noun, verb, adjective,* or *adverb*). Suffixes often change the part of speech of a word.

For example, take the word *deferment* from the list below. A *deferment* is a noun that means a postponement. If the suffix (*-ment*) is removed, the word becomes *defer,* and it is used as a verb meaning to postpone.

As a *verb* it appears as *defer*:
I will *defer* the payment until next month.

As a *noun* it appears as it is:
The bank gave him a *deferment.*

As an *adjective* it appears as *deferred*:
The *deferred* payment is due in one month.

The following table shows a list of common suffixes. They are divided into the parts of speech, or the "jobs" they suggest for words. In the last column, add at least one other word that uses the suffix, besides the examples in the word list.

NOUN ENDINGS			
Suffix	Meaning	Examples	Your Word
-tion	act or state of	retraction, contraction	
-ment	quality	deportment, impediment	
-ist	one who	anarchist, feminist	
-ism	state or doctrine of	barbarism, materialism	
-ity	state of being	futility, civility	
-ology	study of	biology	
-esence	state of	adolescence	
-y, -ry	state of	mimicry, trickery	

ADJECTIVE ENDINGS			
Suffix	Meaning	Examples	Your Word
-able	capable	perishable, flammable	
-ic	causing, making	nostalgic, fatalistic	
-ian	one who is or does	tactician, patrician	
-ile	pertaining to	senile, servile	
-ious	having the quality of	religious, glorious	
-ive	having the nature of	sensitive, divisive	
-less	without	guileless, reckless	

VERB ENDINGS			
Suffix	Meaning	Examples	Your Word
-ize	to bring about	colonize, plagiarize	
-ate	to make	decimate, tolerate	
-ify	to make	beautify, electrify	

agrarian   (ə·ˈgrer-ē·ən)
suffix: **-ian** means one who is or does
(*adj.*)
having to do with agriculture or farming
The farmer loved his _____ life.

antagonist   (an·ˈta·gə·nist)
suffix: **-ist** means one who
(*noun*)
one that contends with or opposes another
In the movie *Batman*, the Joker is Batman's _____.

bigotry   (ˈbig·ə·trē)
suffix: **-ry** means state of
(*noun*)
unreasonable zeal in favor of a party, sect, or opinion; excessive prejudice
_____ can lead to malevolent actions.

consummate   ('kon·səm·māt)

suffix: **-ate** means to make

(*verb*)

to complete; to carry to the utmost degree

The business woman needed to _____ the
    deal quickly.

copious   ('cōp·ē·əs)

suffix: **-ious** means having the quality of

(*adj.*)

abundant; plentiful; in great quantities

A _____ amount of sunshine is predicted for
    the summer.

cryptic   ('krip·tik)

suffix: **-ic** means causing

(*adj.*)

hidden; secret; having a hidden or ambiguous
    meaning

The detective uncovered the meaning of the
    _____ message.

deferment   (di·'fər·mənt)

suffix: **-ment** means quality of

(*noun*)

the act of putting off or delaying; postponement

The bank offered the struggling college graduate a
    _____ on his student loan payment.

furtive   ('fər·tiv)

suffix: **-ive** means having the nature of

(*adj.*)

done in a stealthy manner; sly and underhanded

The two criminals who were in cahoots gave
    each other _____ looks behind the
    detective's back.

laudable   ('law·də·bəl)

suffix: **-able** means capable of

(*adj.*)

praiseworthy

Her dedication and ability to rehabilitate the injured
    is _____.

geology   (jē·'ä·lə·jē)

suffix: **-ology** means study of

(*noun*)

the study of the history of the Earth and its life,
    especially as recorded in rocks

The _____ major traveled to Mt. Etna to
    examine the effects of the volcano's most
    recent eruption.

minimize   ('mi·nə·mīz)

suffix: **-ize** means to subject to an action

(*verb*)

to play down; to keep to a minimum

The President tried to _____ his involvement in
    the trial so that he would not be implicated in
    the scandal.

mutation   (mū·'tā·shən)

suffix: **-tion** means action of, state of

(*noun*)

the act or process of changing

Scientists research gene _____ in fruit flies to
    see how genes change from one generation to
    the next.

obsolescence   (äb·sə·'les·ens)

suffix: **-escence** means state of

(*noun*)

the state of being outdated

With the advent of the personal computer, the type-
    writer has been in _____ for many years.

parity   ('par·i·tē)

suffix: **-ity** means state of being

(*noun*)

the state or condition of being the same in power,
    value, or rank; equality

Women and minorities continue to fight for
    _____ in the workplace.

pragmatism ('prag·mə·tizm)

suffix: **-ism** means state or doctrine of

(*noun*)

faith in the practical approach

The man's _____ enabled him to run a
   successful business.

provocative (prō·'vok·ə·tiv)

suffix: **-ive** means having the nature of

(*adj.*)

something that stirs up an action

The _____ words of the environmental activist
   inspired many to go volunteer for the community clean-up day.

puerile ('pyoor·əl)

suffix: **-ile** means pertaining to

(*adj.*)

childish, silly, immature

The teen's _____ actions at the party couldn't
   be ignored.

rectify ('rek·ti·fī)

suffix: **-ify** means to make

(*verb*)

to make right; to correct

The newspaper tried to _____ the mistake by
   correcting the misprint.

relentless (re·'lənt·les)

suffix: **-less** means without

(*adj.*)

harsh; unmoved by pity; unstoppable

She was _____ in her search for knowledge; she
   read everything she could get her hands on.

venerate ('ven·ə·rāt)

suffix: **-ate** means to make

(*verb*)

to look upon with deep respect and reverence

Some cultures _____ their elders.

Words in Context

The following exercise will help you figure out the
meaning of some words from the previous list by looking at context clues. Circle any context clues that help
you figure out the meaning of the bold word.

The latest remake of *Planet of the Apes* develops the
theme of **bigotry** in a world where apes are the
dominant culture and humans are enslaved. **Parity**
between the two species is unthinkable because the
simians regard humans as inferior creatures. Leo,
the central character, is the story's **protagonist**. He
is a human astronaut who lands on a strange
planet where apes **venerate** their own kind by
offering praise and promotions for negative
actions taken against humans. Leo's **antagonist**,
General Thade is the leader of the apes in this
bizarre culture, and encourages the mistreatment
of humans by apes. In General Thade's opinion,
extermination of the humans is a **laudable** cause
and he mounts a full-scale campaign to extermi-
nate humans from the planet.

More Vocabulary Practice

Here is another set of practice exercises with samples
of each kind of question covered in this chapter.
Answers are at the end of the exercise.

Select the word that means the same or nearly the
same as the italicized word.

12. *congenial* company
   a. friendly
   b. dull
   c. tiresome
   d. angry

13. *conspicuous* mess
   a. secret
   b. notable
   c. visible
   d. boorish

How to Answer Vocabulary Questions

- The key to answering vocabulary questions is to **notice and connect** what you do know to what you may not recognize.
- **Know your word parts.** You can recognize or make a good guess at the meanings of words when you see some suggested meaning in a root word, prefix, or suffix.
- **Use process of elimination.** Think of how the word makes sense in the sentence.
- **Don't be confused by words that sound like other words**, but may have no relation to the word you need.

---

14. *meticulous* record-keeping
- **a.** dishonest
- **b.** casual
- **c.** painstaking
- **d.** careless

15. *superficial* wounds
- **a.** life-threatening
- **b.** bloody
- **c.** severe
- **d.** surface

16. *impulsive* actions
- **a.** cautious
- **b.** sudden
- **c.** courageous
- **d.** cowardly

17. *tactful* comments
- **a.** polite
- **b.** rude
- **c.** angry
- **d.** confused

Using the context, choose the word that means the same or nearly the same as the italicized word.

18. Though flexible about homework, the teacher was *adamant* that papers be in on time.
- **a.** liberal
- **b.** casual
- **c.** strict
- **d.** pliable

19. The condition of the room after the party was *deplorable.*
- **a.** regrettable
- **b.** pristine
- **c.** festive
- **d.** tidy

20. Though normally very *gregarious*, Martin was uncharacteristically shy and reserved when he attended the party.
- **a.** generous
- **b.** sociable
- **c.** stingy
- **d.** happy

Answers
- **12.** a.
- **13.** c.
- **14.** c.
- **15.** d.
- **16.** b.
- **17.** a.
- **18.** c.
- **19.** a.
- **20.** b.

CHAPTER

9 ▶ PARAGRAPH COMPREHENSION REVIEW

CHAPTER SUMMARY

Because reading is such a vital skill, the Armed Services Vocational Aptitude Battery includes a reading comprehension section that tests your ability to understand what you read. The tips and exercises in this chapter will help you improve your comprehension of written passages so that you can increase your score in this area.

Memos, policies, procedures, reports—these are all things you will be expected to understand if you enlist in the armed services. Understanding written materials is part of almost any job. That's why the ASVAB attempts to measure how well applicants understand what they read.

The Paragraph Comprehension subtest of the ASVAB is in multiple-choice format and asks questions based on brief passages, much like the standardized tests that are offered in schools. For that matter, almost all standardized test questions test your reading skills. After all, you can't answer the question if you can't read it. Similarly, you can't study your training materials or learn new procedures once you are on the job if you can't read well. So, reading comprehension is vital not only on the test but also for the rest of your career.

Types of Reading Comprehension Questions

You have probably encountered reading comprehension questions before, where you are given a passage to read and then have to answer multiple-choice questions about it. This kind of question has advantages for you as a test taker: You don't have to know anything about the topic of the passage because you are being tested only on the information the passage provides.

But the disadvantage is that you have to know where and how to find that information quickly in an unfamiliar text. This makes it easy to fall for one of the wrong answer choices, especially since they are designed to mislead you.

The best way to do your best on this passage/question format is to be very familiar with the kinds of questions that are typically asked on the test. Questions most frequently ask you to:

1. identify a specific **fact** or **detail** in the passage
2. note the **main idea** of the passage
3. make an **inference** based on the passage
4. define a **vocabulary** word from the passage

In order for you to do well on a reading comprehension test, you need to know exactly what each of these questions is asking. **Facts** and **details** are the specific pieces of information that support the passage's main idea. The **main idea** is the thought, opinion, or attitude that governs the whole passage. Generally speaking, facts and details are indisputable—things that don't need to be proven, like statistics (18 million people) or descriptions (a green overcoat). Let's say, for example, you read a sentence that says *"After the department's reorganization, workers were 50% more productive."* A sentence like this, which gives you the fact that workers were 50% more productive, might support a main idea that says, *"Every department should be reorganized."* Notice that this main idea is not something indisputable; it is an opinion. The writer thinks all departments should be reorganized, and because this is his opinion (and not everyone shares it), he needs to support his opinion with facts and details.

An **inference**, on the other hand, is a conclusion that can be drawn based on fact or evidence. For example, you can infer—based on the fact that workers became 50% more productive after the reorganization, which is a dramatic change—that the department had not been efficiently organized. The fact sentence, *"After the department's reorganization, workers were 50% more productive,"* also implies that the reorganization of the department was the reason

workers became more productive. There may, of course, have been other reasons, but we can infer only one from this sentence.

As you might expect, **vocabulary** questions ask you to determine the meaning of particular words. Often, if you've read carefully, you can determine the meaning of such words from their context, that is, how the word is used in the sentence or paragraph.

Practice Passage 1: Using the Four Question Types

The following is a sample test passage, followed by four questions. Read the passage carefully, and then answer the questions, based on your reading of the text, by selecting your choice. Then refer to the previous list and note under your answer which type of question has been asked. Correct answers appear immediately after the questions.

In the last decade, community policing has been frequently touted as the best way to reform urban law enforcement. The idea of putting more officers on foot patrol in high crime areas, where relations with police have frequently been strained, was initiated in Houston in 1983 under the leadership of then-Commissioner Lee Brown. He believed that officers should be accessible to the community at the street level. If officers were assigned to the same area over a period of time, those officers would eventually build a network of trust with neighborhood residents. That trust would mean that merchants and residents in the community would let officers know about criminal activities in the area and would support police intervention. Since then, many large cities have experimented with Community-Oriented Policing (COP) with mixed results. Some have found that police and citizens are grateful for the opportunity to work together. Others have found that unrealistic expectations by citizens and resistance from officers have combined to hinder the effectiveness of COP. It seems possible, therefore, that a good idea may need improvement before it can truly be considered a reform.

1. Community policing has been used in law enforcement since

   a. the late 1970s.

   b. the early 1980s.

   c. the Carter administration.

   d. Lee Brown was New York City Police Commissioner.

       Question type _____

2. The phrase "a network of trust" in this passage suggests that

   a. police officers can rely only on each other for support.

   b. community members rely on the police to protect them.

   c. police and community members rely on each other.

   d. community members trust only each other.

       Question type _____

3. The best title for this passage would be:

   a. "Community Policing: The Solution to the Drug Problem"

   b. "Houston Sets the Pace in Community Policing"

   c. "Communities and Cops: Partners for Peace"

   d. "Community Policing: An Uncertain Future?"

       Question type _____

4. The word "touted" in the first sentence of the passage most nearly means

   a. praised.

   b. denied.

   c. exposed.

   d. criticized.

       Question type _____

Answers and Explanations

Don't just look at the right answers and move on. The explanations are the most important part, so read them carefully. Use these explanations to help you understand how to tackle each kind of question the next time you come across it.

1. b. Question type: **1**, fact or detail. The passage identifies 1983 as the first large-scale use of community policing in Houston. Don't be misled by trying to figure out when Carter was president. Also, if you happen to know that Lee Brown was New York City's police commissioner, don't let that information lead you away from the information contained in the passage alone. Brown was commissioner in Houston when he initiated community policing.

2. c. Question type: **3**, inference. The "network of trust" referred to in this passage is between the community and the police, as you can see from the sentence where the phrase appears. The key phrase in the question is *in this passage.* You may think that police can rely only on each other, or one of the other answer choices may appear equally plausible to you. But, your choice of answers must be limited to the one suggested *in this passage.* Another tip for questions like this: Beware of absolutes! Be suspicious of any answer containing words like *only, always,* or *never.*

3. d. Question type: **2**, main idea. The title always expresses the main idea. In this passage, the main idea comes at the end. The sum of all the details in the passage suggests that community policing is not without its critics and that therefore its future is uncertain. Another key phrase is *mixed results,* which means that some communities haven't had full success with community policing.

4. a. Question type: **4**, vocabulary. The word *touted* is linked in this passage with the phrase *the best way to reform*. Most people would think that a good way to reform something is praiseworthy. In addition, the next few sentences in the passage describe the benefits of community policing. Criticism or a negative response to the subject doesn't come until later in the passage.

Detail and Main Idea Questions

Main idea questions and fact or detail questions are both asking you for information that's right there in the passage. All you have to do is find it.

Detail or Fact Questions

In detail or fact questions, you have to identify a specific item of information from the text. This is usually the simplest kind of question. You just have to be able to separate important information from less important information. However, the choices may often be very similar, so you must be careful not to get confused.

Be sure you read the passage and questions carefully. In fact, it is usually a good idea to read the questions first, *before* you even read the passage, so you will know what details to look out for.

Main Idea Questions

The main idea of a passage, like that of a paragraph or a book, is what it is *mostly* about. The main idea is like an umbrella that covers all of the ideas and details in the passage, so it is usually something general, not specific. For example, in Practice Passage 1, question 3 asked you what title would be best for the passage, and the correct answer was "Community Policing: An Uncertain Future?" This is the best answer because it's the only one that includes both the positive and negative sides of community policing, both of which are discussed in the passage.

Sometimes the main idea is stated clearly, often in the first or last sentence of the passage. The main idea is expressed in the *last* sentence of Practice Passage 1, for example. The sentence that expresses the main idea is often referred to as the **topic sentence**.

At other times, the main idea is not stated in a topic sentence but is *implied* in the overall passage, and you will need to determine the main idea by inference. Because there may be much information in the passage, the trick is to understand what all that information adds up to—the gist of what the author wants you to know. Often some of the wrong answers on main idea questions are specific facts or details from the passage. A good way to test yourself is to ask, "Can this answer serve as a *net* to hold the whole passage together?" If not, chances are you have chosen a fact or detail, not a main idea.

Practice Passage 2: Detail and Main Idea Questions

Practice answering main idea and detail questions by working on the questions that follow this passage. Circle the answers to the questions, and then check your answers against the key that appears immediately after the questions.

There are three different kinds of burns: first degree, second degree, and third degree. It is important for firefighters to be able to recognize each of these types of burns so that they can be sure burn victims are given proper medical treatment. The least serious burn is the first-degree burn, which causes the skin to turn red but does not cause blistering. A mild sunburn is a good example of a first-degree burn, and, like a mild sunburn, first-degree burns generally do not require medical treatment other than a gentle cooling of the burned skin with ice or cold tap water. Second-degree burns, on the other hand, do cause blistering of the skin and should be treated immediately. These burns should be immersed in warm water and then wrapped in a sterile dressing or bandage. (Do not apply butter or grease to these burns; despite the old wives' tale, butter does *not* help burns heal and actually increases chances of infection.) If second-degree burns cover a large part of the body, then the victim should be taken to the hospital immediately for medical care. Third-degree burns are those that char the skin and turn it black, or burn so deeply that the skin shows white. These burns usually result from direct contact with flames and have a great chance of becoming infected. All third-degree burns should receive immediate hospital care. They should not be immersed in water, and charred clothing should not be removed from the victim. If possible, a sterile dressing or bandage should be applied to burns before the victim is transported to the hospital.

1. Which of the following would be the best title for this passage?
   a. Dealing with Third-Degree Burns
   b. How to Recognize and Treat Different Burns
   c. Burn Categories
   d. Preventing Infection in Burns

2. Second-degree burns should be treated with
   a. butter.
   b. nothing.
   c. cold water.
   d. warm water.

3. First-degree burns turn the skin
   a. red.
   b. blue.
   c. black.
   d. white.

4. Which of the following best expresses the main idea of the passage?
   a. There are three different types of burns.
   b. Firefighters should always have cold compresses on hand.
   c. Different burns require different types of treatment.
   d. Butter is not good for healing burns.

Answers and Explanations

1. **b.** A question that asks you to choose a title for a passage is a main idea question. This main idea is expressed in the second sentence, the topic sentence: *It is important for firefighters to be able to recognize each of these types of burns so that they can be sure burn victims are given proper treatment.* Choice **b** expresses this idea and is the only title that encompasses all of the ideas expressed in the passage. Choice **a** is too limited; it deals only with one of the kinds of burns discussed in the passage. Likewise, choices **c** and **d** are also too limited. Choice **c** covers types of burns but not their treatment, and **d** deals only with preventing infection, which is only a secondary part of the discussion of treatment.

2. **d.** The answer to this fact question is clearly expressed in the sentence, "These burns should be immersed in warm water and then wrapped in a sterile dressing or bandage." The hard part is keeping track of whether "These burns" refers to the kind of burns in the question, which is second-degree burns. It's easy to choose a wrong answer here because all of the answer choices are mentioned in the passage. You need to read carefully to be sure you match the right burn to the right treatment.

3. a. This is another fact or detail question. The passage says that a first-degree burn "causes the skin to turn red." Again, it's important to read carefully because all of the answer choices (except **b**, which can be eliminated immediately) are listed elsewhere in the passage.

4. c. Clearly this is a main idea question, and **c** is the only answer that encompasses the whole passage. Choices **b** and **d** are limited to *particular* burns or treatments, and answer **a** discusses only burns and not their treatment. In addition, the second sentence tells us that "It is important for firefighters to be able to *recognize each of these types of burns so that they can be sure burn victims are given proper medical treatment.*"

Inference and Vocabulary Questions

Questions that ask you about the meaning of vocabulary words in the passage and those that ask what the passage *suggests* or *implies* (inference questions) are different from detail or main idea questions. In vocabulary and inference questions, you usually have to pull ideas from the passage, sometimes from more than one place.

Inference Questions

Inference questions can be the most difficult to answer because they require you to draw meaning from the text when that meaning is implied rather than directly stated. Inferences are conclusions that you draw based on the clues the writer has given you. When you draw inferences, you have to look for such clues as word choice, tone, and specific details that suggest a certain conclusion, attitude, or point of view. You have to read between the lines in order to make a judgment about what an author was implying in the passage.

A good way to test whether you have drawn an acceptable inference is to ask, "What evidence do I have for this inference?" If you can't find any, you probably have the wrong answer. You need to be sure that your inference is logical and that it is based on something that is suggested or implied in the passage itself—not by what you or others might think. You need to base your conclusions on evidence—facts, details, and other information—not on random hunches or guesses.

Vocabulary Questions

Questions designed to test vocabulary are really trying to measure how well you can figure out the meaning of an unfamiliar word from its context. *Context* refers to the words and ideas surrounding a vocabulary word. If the context is clear enough, you should be able to substitute a nonsense word for the one being sought, and you would still make the right choice because you could determine meaning strictly from the sense of the sentence.

For example, you should be able to determine the meaning of the italicized nonsense word below based on its context:

The speaker noted that it gave him great *terivinix* to announce the winner of the Outstanding Leadership Award.

In this sentence, *terivinix* most likely means
a. pain.
b. sympathy.
c. pleasure.
d. anxiety.

Clearly, the context of an award makes **c**, *pleasure*, the best choice. Awards don't usually bring pain, sympathy, or anxiety.

When confronted with an unfamiliar word, try substituting a nonsense word and see if the context gives you the clue. If you are familiar with prefixes, suffixes, and word roots, you can also use this knowledge to help you determine the meaning of an unfamiliar word.

You should be careful not to guess at the answer to vocabulary questions based on how you may have seen the word used before or what you *think* it means. Many words have more than one possible meaning, depending on the context in which they are used, and a word you have seen used one way may mean something else in a test passage. Also, if you don't look at the context carefully, you may make the mistake of confusing the vocabulary word with a similar word. For example, the vocabulary word may be *taut* (meaning *tight),* but if you read too quickly or don't check the context, you might think the word is *tout* (meaning *publicize* or *praise)* or *taunt* (meaning *tease).* Always read carefully and be sure that what you think the word means fits into the context of the passage you are being tested on.

Practice Passage 3: Inference and Vocabulary Questions

The questions that follow this passage are strictly vocabulary and inference questions. Select the answers to the questions, and then check your answers against the key that appears immediately after the questions.

Dealing with irritable patients is a great challenge for healthcare workers on every level. It is critical that you do not lose your patience when confronted by such a patient. When handling irate patients, be sure to remember that they are not angry at you; they are simply projecting their anger at something else *onto* you. Remember that if you respond to these patients as irritably as they act with you, you will only increase their hostility, making it much more difficult to give them proper treatment. The best thing to do is to remain calm and ignore any

imprecations patients may hurl your way. Such patients may be irrational and may not realize what they are saying. Often these patients will purposely try to anger you just to get some reaction out of you. If you react to this behavior with anger, they win by getting your attention, but you both lose because the patient is less likely to get proper care.

1. The word "irate" as it is used in the passage most nearly means
   a. irregular, odd.
   b. happy, cheerful.
   c. ill-tempered, angry.
   d. sloppy, lazy.

2. The passage suggests that healthcare workers
   a. easily lose control of their emotions.
   b. are better off not talking to their patients.
   c. must be careful in dealing with irate patients because the patients may sue the hospital.
   d. may provide inadequate treatment if they become angry at patients.

3. An "imprecation" is most likely
   a. an object.
   b. a curse.
   c. a joke.
   d. a medication.

4. Which of the following best expresses the writer's views about irate patients?
   a. Some irate patients just want attention.
   b. Irate patients are always miserable.
   c. Irate patients should be made to wait for treatment.
   d. Managing irate patients is the key to a successful career.

Answers and Explanations

1. c. This is a vocabulary question. *Irate* means *ill-tempered, angry.* It should be clear that **b**, *happy, cheerful,* is not the answer; dealing with happy patients is normally not *a great challenge.* Patients that are **a**, *irregular, odd,* or **d**, *sloppy, lazy,* may be a challenge in their own way, but they aren't likely to rouse a healthcare worker to anger. In addition, the passage explains that irate patients are not "*angry* at you," and *irate* is used as a synonym for *irritable,* which describes the patients under discussion in the very first sentence.

2. d. This is an inference question, as the phrase "The passage *suggests*" might have told you. The idea that angry healthcare workers might give inadequate treatment is implied by the passage as a whole, which seems to be an attempt to prevent angry reactions to irate patients. Furthermore, the last sentence in particular makes this inference possible: *If you react to this behavior with anger . . . you both lose because the patient is less likely to get proper care.* Choice **c** is not correct, because while it maybe true that some irate patients have sued the hospital in the past, there is no mention of suits anywhere in this passage. Likewise, choice **b** is incorrect; the passage does suggest ignoring patients' insults, but nowhere does it recommend not talking to patients—it simply recommends not talking angrily. And while it may be true that some healthcare workers may lose control of their emotions, the passage does not provide any facts or details to support choice **a**, that they "*easily* lose control." Watch out for key words like *easily* that may distort the intent of the passage.

3. b. If you didn't know what an *imprecation* is, the context should reveal that it's something you can ignore, so neither choice **a**, an *object,* nor choice **d**, a *medication,* is a likely answer. Furthermore, choice **c** is not likely either, since an irate patient is not likely to be making jokes.

4. a. The writer seems to believe that some irate patients just want attention, as is suggested by, "Often these patients will purposely try to anger you just to get some reaction out of you. If you react to this behavior with anger, they win *by getting your attention.*" It should be clear that choice **b** cannot be the answer, because it includes an absolute: "Irate patients are *always* miserable." Perhaps *some* of the patients are *often* miserable, but an absolute like *always* is almost always wrong. Besides, this passage refers to patients who maybe irate in the hospital, but we have no indication of what these patients are like at other times, and *miserable* and *irate* are not exactly the same thing, either. Choice **c** is also incorrect because the purpose of the passage is to ensure that patients receive *proper treatment* and that irate patients are not discriminated against because of their behavior. Thus, *irate patients should be made to wait for treatment* is not a logical answer. Finally, **d** cannot be correct because though it may be true, there is no discussion of career advancement in the passage.

Review: Putting It All Together

A good way to solidify what you have learned about reading comprehension questions is for *you* to write the questions. Here's a passage, followed by space for you to write your own questions. Write one question for each of the four types: fact or detail, main idea, inference, and vocabulary.

The "broken window" theory was originally developed to explain how minor acts of vandalism or disrespect can quickly escalate to crimes and attitudes that break down the entire social fabric of an area. It is a theory that can easily be applied to any situation in society. The theory contends that if a broken window in an abandoned building is not replaced quickly, soon all the windows will be broken. In other words, a small violation, if condoned, leads others to commit similar or greater violations. Thus, after all the windows have been broken, the building is likely to be looted and perhaps even burned down. According to this theory, violations increase exponentially. Thus, if disrespect to a superior is tolerated, others will be tempted to be disrespectful as well. A management crisis could erupt literally overnight. For example, if one firefighter begins to disregard proper housewatch procedure by neglecting to keep up the housewatch administrative journal, and this firefighter is not reprimanded, others will follow suit by committing similar violations of procedure, thinking, "If he can get away with it, why can't I?" So what starts out as a small thing, a violation that may seem not to warrant disciplinary action, may actually ruin the efficiency of the entire firehouse, putting the people the firehouse serves at risk.

1. Detail question: _____

_____

    a.

    b.

    c.

    d.

2. Main idea question: _____

_____

    a.

    b.

    c.

    d.

3. Inference question:_____

_____

    a.

    b.

    c.

    d.

4. Vocabulary question: _____

_____

    a.

    b.

    c.

    d.

Possible Questions

Here is one question of each type based on the passage above. Your questions may be very different, but these will give you an idea of the kinds of questions that could be asked.

1. Detail question: According to the passage, which of the following could happen "overnight"?
    a. The building will be burned down.
    b. The firehouse may become unmanageable.
    c. A management crisis might erupt.
    d. The windows will all be broken.

2. Main idea question: Which of the following best expresses the main idea of the passage?
    a. Even minor infractions warrant disciplinary action.
    b. Broken windows must be repaired immediately.
    c. People shouldn't be disrespectful to their superiors.
    d. Housewatch must be taken seriously.

3. Inference question: The passage suggests that
   a. the broken window theory is inadequate.
   b. managers need to know how to handle a crisis.
   c. firefighters are lazy.
   d. people will get away with as much as they can.

4. Vocabulary question: In this passage, *condoned* most nearly means
   a. punished.
   b. overlooked.
   c. condemned.
   d. applauded.

If English Isn't Your First Language

When non-native speakers of English have trouble with reading comprehension tests, it's often because they lack the cultural, linguistic, and historical frame of reference that native speakers enjoy. People who have not lived in or been educated in the United States often don't have the background information that comes from growing up reading American newspapers, magazines, and textbooks.

A second problem for non-native English speakers is the difficulty in recognizing vocabulary and idioms (expressions like "chewing the fat") that assist comprehension. In order to read with good understanding, it's important to have an immediate grasp of as many words as possible in the text. Test takers need to be able to recognize vocabulary and idioms immediately so that the ideas those words express are clear.

The Long View

Read newspapers, magazines, and other periodicals that deal with current events and matters of local, state, and national importance. Pay special attention to articles related to the career you want to pursue

Be alert to new or unfamiliar vocabulary or terms that occur frequently in the popular press. Use a highlighter pen to mark new or unfamiliar words as you read. Keep a list of those words and their definitions. Review them for 15 minutes each day. Though at first you may find yourself looking up a lot of words, don't be frustrated—you'll look up fewer and fewer as your vocabulary expands.

During the Test

When you are taking the test, make a picture in your mind of the situation being described in the passage. Ask yourself, "What did the writer mostly want me to think about this subject?"

Locate and underline the topic sentence that carries the main idea of the passage. Remember that the topic sentence—if there is one—may not always be the first sentence. If there doesn't seem to be one, try to determine what idea summarizes the whole passage.

Answers
1. c.
2. a.
3. d.
4. b.

Additional Resources

Here are some other ways you can build the vocabulary and knowledge that will help you do well on reading comprehension questions.

- Practice asking the four sample question types about passages you read for information or pleasure.
- Use your library. Many public libraries have sections that contain materials for adult learners. In these sections you can find books with exercises in reading and study skills. It's also a good idea to enlarge your base of information by reading related books and articles. Most libraries have computer systems that allow you to access information quickly and easily. Library personnel will show you how to use the computers and other equipment.

AUTO AND SHOP INFORMATION REVIEW

CHAPTER SUMMARY

This chapter tells you how to prepare for the Auto and Shop Information subtest of the ASVAB. You'll learn about commonly tested concepts, including basic automotive components and systems, shop tools, and basic construction materials and procedures. As a bonus, you'll find sample questions for practice at the end of the chapter.

Repairing a vehicle, constructing a temporary shelter, pouring a foundation for a permanent structure—these are skills that many armed services personnel use regularly. If you choose a Military Occupational Specialty that focuses on automotive or shop concepts, you'll be preparing for a civilian career as well, as skilled workers in these fields are always in demand.

The Auto and Shop Information subtest on the ASVAB is used to help determine whether you can enter a specialty that requires this kind of knowledge. You'll do best on this subtest if you already have a fair amount of background in this area, whether from high school shop classes, jobs you've held, or just puttering around with cars and carpentry.

This chapter can help you review what you already know about how machines work. If you're relatively new to this area, you'll find this chapter makes a good basic introduction to Auto and Shop Information. You'll learn some of the most commonly tested tools, concepts, materials, and procedures. There are suggestions for ways to improve your knowledge by gaining hands-on experience. At the end of the chapter, you can test your knowledge with sample questions similar to those found on the ASVAB.

What Auto and Shop Information Questions Are Like

The Auto and Shop Information subtest covers a wide range of topics. The questions are multiple choice, many of which are accompanied by pictures. Most people find that they can answer all the questions in the time allowed. Though some questions include all the information you need to find the correct answer, most will rely on your previous knowledge of auto and shop concepts.

A typical Auto and Shop Information question will look something like this:

1. Which of the following is NOT part of a typical automotive cooling system?
   a. the radiator
   b. the oil filter
   c. the water pump
   d. the thermostat

The correct answer is **b**, the oil filter. You'll find that a few questions are like this one, using the word NOT to signal the correct answer. The oil filter is the part of the internal combustion engine that cleans the lubrication oil, so it is not part of the cooling system.

Auto Information

Much of the Auto and Shop Information subtest, as you might expect, covers automobiles and other vehicles that use an internal combustion engine. Concepts you can expect to find on the ASVAB include the various systems of an automobile and their functions, as well as how to maintain and repair a vehicle.

Automotive Systems

Cars, trucks, buses, and other vehicles all use literally thousands of **components**, or parts. A combination of several components that work together to perform a specific function is called a **system**. There are several main systems that perform key functions in the automobile: providing power, transferring energy from the engine to the wheels, keeping the engine cool, smoothing out the bumps in the road, and more. You'll learn about the most important systems and components in this section.

The Internal Combustion Engine

Internal combustion engines power many kinds of machines, not just cars and trucks. In general, an internal combustion engine operates by burning fuel to produce kinetic energy. This energy causes the internal workings of the engine to rotate. Ultimately, this energy is transferred to the wheels of the car via gears and other linkages—and the car moves.

> **Kinetic energy:** the energy of motion

Internal combustion engines can be fueled by gasoline, diesel fuel, natural gas, or other combustible fossil fuels. A **fuel pump** moves fuel from the fuel tank into the engine. Inside the engines are typically four, six, or eight **cylinders**, each with one **piston** that moves up and down.

The fuel is injected into the cylinders by the **carburetor** or **fuel injectors.** Each cylinder has one **spark plug** that fires at regular intervals. (The energy for the spark is provided by the electrical system; see page 170.) The spark causes a mini-explosion in the cylinder, driving the piston downward. The **tie rod** to which the piston is fastened is therefore also driven downward. The tie rod is attached to the **crankshaft,** which converts the up-and-down motion of the pistons and tie rod into rotational movement. The gears attached to the crankshaft are connected to other gears on the transmission system (see page 169). Through the transmission, eventually the power is transferred to the wheels of the vehicle, the inner workings of the pump, or whatever machine the engine is driving.

The Transmission System

The **transmission** is the link that transfers power from the engine to the tires and wheels. It typically consists of several shafts, gears, and joints. When the power from the engine rotates the transmission shafts, the car begins to move. The **driveshaft** between the transmission and the axles is typically made of steel so it can withstand the high torque of operation.

Torque: twisting force

As the speed of the car increases, the transmission rotates faster and faster. In order to keep the transmission's rotation speed at acceptable levels, several gears are used. That is why you must shift a car as your speed increases and decreases. Some vehicles have transmissions that shift automatically between the necessary gear sizes. Others, including the heavy vehicles used in the armed forces, have a manual transmission that requires the driver to change the gears using the **clutch** and the **gear shift.** The transmission is disengaged when you press the clutch pedal to the floor. After you move the gear shift into the gear you want, you slowly release the clutch pedal. The transmission gears touch and once again transfer the energy from the engine to the wheels. An automatic transmission does all this work for you.

The Cooling System

An internal combustion engine has many moving parts. As these parts slide past each other, the friction of their movement against each other generates heat. The cooling system dissipates this heat in order to prevent the engine from becoming too hot. The cooling system consists of a **pump** that moves cooling fluid, or **coolant,** from the **radiator** through piping to the engine block. As the coolant passes over the engine block, some of the heat from the engine is transferred into the coolant. The fluid then flows back to the radiator, where it is cooled by the flow of air across the radiator. The reason a vehicle is more likely to overheat on a hot day than on a cold one is that the air moving over the radiator can't cool the fluid effectively.

The Exhaust System

The exhaust system includes a system of piping connected to the engine with welded joints. Several brackets suspend the piping beneath the automobile. The engine's exhaust gases pass from the engine through the piping to the **muffler,** which is an acoustical chamber that reduces the engine noise and removes some of the pollutants created when the fuel burns.

The Suspension System

The suspension is the system that attaches the wheels of the automobile to its body. The wheels cannot be directly attached with a hard connection because the high forces of hitting bumps in the road would cause structural failure—the connections would break. Instead, a combination of **springs** and dampeners are used to "soften" this connection. The springs are typically either leaf springs or coil compression springs. They provide a flexible link between the wheels and the body of the car.

The **shock absorbers** serve to dampen the bumps in the road. Without shock absorbers, when a car hit a bump, it would continue to bounce up and down on the suspension springs for a long time. The shock absorbers are movable but very stiff, so they quickly reduce the movement of the springs. Shock absorbers are typically oil-filled cylinders approximately 12 to 18 inches long. One end is bolted to the body of the automobile, and the other is attached to the axle of the wheels. A vehicle typically has one set of springs and shocks for each wheel.

The Electrical System

The electrical system in an automobile is incredibly complex. It provides the energy for the initial spark from the spark plug that makes the engine run, so without electricity you couldn't go anywhere. It also operates other systems and accessories, including headlights and other lights as well as power windows and door locks. The electrical system is similar to your body's cardiovascular system. The heart of the system is the **battery**. The wiring that runs throughout the automobile is similar to your veins and arteries. The wires transfer energy from the battery to the spark plugs and other devices that use electricity. There are literally hundreds of feet of electrical wiring in modern automobiles.

The battery would quickly lose its charge without a method of recharging. The component of the electrical system that charges the battery is the **alternator**. The alternator rotates to generate electrical energy, which then recharges the battery.

The Braking System

Automobile brakes are activated by pressing the brake pedal. This action compresses a piston to force hydraulic fluid through the **brake line** piping. In disc brakes, the brake fluid presses against a set of mechanical **calipers,** or levers, that squeeze the **brake pads** against the **rotors.** The friction of the pads rubbing against the rotors slows the rotation of the wheels. Springs are used to return the brake pedal and the calipers to their neutral position when the brake pedal is released.

Miscellaneous Components

Many other minor systems and components are used in internal combustion vehicles besides the major systems just listed. Gauges and pumps are used not only on automobiles but also in other kinds of machines you may encounter on the ASVAB.

Gauges

Gauges help operators monitor the condition and performance of machines such as pumps and internal combustion engines, as well as the surrounding atmospheric conditions that can indirectly affect a machine's function.

Gauges are usually marked with the *units* they are measuring. A few examples of different types of units are:

- degrees Celsius or Fahrenheit for temperature gauges (usually called *thermometers*)
- pounds per square inch (psi) for pressure gauges
- gallons or liters for fuel gauges
- amperage for battery gauges

You must be very careful to recognize and understand the units of a gauge that appears in a test question. For instance, a temperature gauge could use either degrees Fahrenheit or degrees Celsius. Mistakes on units can cause major problems, so be careful. The table on this page shows some common automotive types of gauges, what they measure, and the kind of units they use.

AUTOMOTIVE PERFORMANCE GAUGES		
Gauge	**What It Measures**	**Units**
Speedometer	velocity (speed)	miles per hour (mph) or kilometers per hour (kph)
Tachometer	speed of rotation for pumps, engines, fans, etc.	revolutions per minute (rpm)
Pressure gauge	internal pressure, such as oil pressure or water pressure	pounds per square inch (psi) or inches of water
Ammeter	electrical charge	amps
Fuel gauge	remaining volume of fuel	gallons or liters

OTHER GAUGES		
Gauge	**What It Measures**	**Units**
Thermometer	temperature	degrees Fahrenheit or Celsius
Barometer	atmospheric pressure	inches or millimeters of mercury
Hygrometer	relative humidity	percentage of water in air
Flow meter	volume of flow in a piping system	cubic feet per minute (cfm) or gallons per minute (gpm)

Gauges are sometimes marked with warnings about limits of safe operation. For instance, an oil pressure gauge on an internal combustion engine may show a maximum safe working pressure of 15 psi. If you're asked about the safe operation of a device with a gauge on it, you should pay careful attention to any markings that show such a limit.

Gauges are also used for non-automotive machines as well as to monitor conditions of various mechanical and electrical systems. The table "Other Gauges" shows three atmospheric gauges and one kind of gauge used for monitoring mechanical systems not found on an automobile.

Pumps

A pump is a device used to transfer a liquid or a gas from one location, through a piping system, to another location. There are many different types of pumps, including centrifugal pumps, positive displacement pumps, metering pumps, diaphragm pumps, and progressive cavity pumps.

Generally speaking, a working pump consists of the pump itself—case, bearings, impeller, seals, shaft, base, and other components—and an outside energy source. The outside energy source may be an electric motor, an internal combustion engine, or a battery and motor. The energy from this source causes the inner workings of the pump to propel the liquid or gas through the piping system. The flow rate at which the liquid or gas is pushed through the piping system is typically measured by a flow meter in units of gallons per minute (gpm) or cubic feet per minute (cfm).

Some automotive pumps include the fuel pumps used to pump the fuel from a holding tank into your car and the pumps that transfer coolant through the engine's cooling system.

Pumps have many other uses besides automotive ones. They can be used to move drinking water from a reservoir to your house or business. Industrial pumps are also used to move industrial fluids such as chemicals or waste products from one tank to another inside a plant.

Automotive Tools

Car maintenance and repair may require specialized tools as well as some with which you are already familiar. Some of these tools are:

- **Wrenches** to tighten and loosen nuts and bolts. Examples include vice grips and box end wrenches, socket wrenches, crescent wrenches, and pipe wrenches.
- **Screwdrivers** to tighten and loosen the thousands of screws in a car. Both regular head and Phillips head screwdrivers are used. There are also screwdrivers unique to particular vehicles.
- A **spark plug wrench** to change the spark plugs. Typically a spark plug wrench is actually an adapter that connects to a socket wrench.
- A **jack** to lift a car so that you can change a tire.
- A **hoist** to lift heavy objects such as engines and transmission components in order to repair them.

There are lots specialized tools used for repair work, but you're not likely to find them on the ASVAB.

Automotive Maintenance and Troubleshooting

Today's automobiles are such complex machines that explaining how to maintain and repair them can take thousands of pages for each model of car or truck. Most automobiles are sold with a manual for that model, and if you are assigned a specific kind of vehicle in the armed forces, you'll be trained on the specific procedures for that vehicle. Some kinds of maintenance and troubleshooting, however, are common to almost all vehicles.

Preventative Maintenance

Any vehicle requires regular maintenance in order to keep it operating properly and to insure a long, reliable life. Some automotive components wear out and have to be replaced. Also, an automobile has many moving parts that require regular lubrication so they don't wear out before their time.

Obviously tires wear out with use. Tires on a typical car last 30,000 to 80,000 miles, depending on use. Car tires have wear bars that indicate when they should be replaced. Worn tires can be unsafe, so replacing them is a must.

Tires also have to be rotated. The tires in the front will wear more on the outside of the tread because of extra wear from turning. Tires should be rotated, or moved from the front to the back, every 3,000 to 5,000 miles. Tire pressure should also be checked regularly in order to insure proper handling of the car and prevent abnormal wear.

Another part of regular maintenance is keeping the engine and transmission lubricated. The engine uses petroleum-based oil to reduce the friction between moving parts such as the pistons and the cylinder wall. Over time, this oil becomes dirty and must be replaced. Most engine manufacturers recommend three months or 3,000 miles between oil changes. Also, the rotating joints in the transmission have to be lubricated with grease in order to keep operating properly.

Some automotive components that usually need to be replaced during the life of an automobile include the battery, belts and hoses, air filter, shock absorbers, and spark plugs. Also, some automotive systems use fluids that have to be replaced regularly. These include the transmission, brakes, power steering, and cooling system. The replacement intervals vary from vehicle to vehicle. Again, if you are required to do this kind of maintenance as part of your military assignment, you will be trained on the procedures for the vehicles you are responsible for.

Troubleshooting

A few questions on the ASVAB may cover basic troubleshooting—if the vehicle won't start or won't move, what might be the problem? Kinds of repair that only a trained mechanic could attempt will *not* be covered on the exam; only basic diagnosis of a problem is likely to be tested.

An internal combustion engine requires three basic items in order to operate properly: fire, fuel, and oxygen. When an engine will not start, one or more of these items is missing.

Fire—a spark, actually—is provided by the electrical system through the spark plug. If a vehicle won't start, you should check the battery and alternator, the wires connecting the electrical system to the spark plugs, and the plugs themselves.

Fuel is pumped from the fuel tank to the engine by the fuel pump through the fuel line. A lack of fuel in the engine could be caused by a ruptured fuel line or a broken fuel pump. Another possibility is a problem with the carburetor or fuel injectors, which regulate the amount of fuel going to the engine.

Oxygen is necessary for the fuel to burn. If you light a match and then place it under a glass, the match will go out in a few seconds because the oxygen in the glass has been consumed by the burning match. Oxygen—which is provided by the air since air is 21 percent oxygen—comes into the engine through the air filter, controlled by several valves. One possible cause of lack of oxygen is a dirty air filter—a problem you can diagnose simply by looking at the filter.

Another common problem is that the engine runs but the automobile will not move. This problem typically indicates that something is wrong with the transmission. Once you've determined that the transmission is indeed in the correct gear, there wouldn't be much more you could do about this problem. Transmission repair is one of those jobs that only trained mechanics should take on, so you're not likely to find any questions about it on the ASVAB.

Shop Information

Besides automotive concepts, the Auto and Shop Information subtest of the ASVAB also covers shop tools, building materials, and construction procedures.

Hand Tools

Hand tools are defined as tools operated not by motors but by human power. Hand tools likely to be covered on the ASVAB include those used in construction and metalwork, as well as some lawn and garden tools.

Carpenter's Tools

Some of the hand tools used by carpenters and other workers are listed in the table on page 174, along with their most common uses and some examples of each kind.

Gardening and Lawn Care Tools

You may be asking yourself why this chapter would cover gardening hand tools. Well, you might be surprised at how often these tools are used in the armed services: shovels for latrines, trenches, or bunkers; post hole diggers for fences; axes, hoes, and rakes for firefighting. The table on page 175 shows some gardening tools and their uses.

Building Materials

The materials used to construct residential and commercial buildings, bridges, and roads are all commonly used in the armed services and may well appear on the ASVAB. Some materials play structural roles by providing support and load-bearing functions. A few of the most important structural materials include steel, concrete, wood, brick, and cinder block. Other materials are used as decoration or insulation, including glass, fiberglass, and stucco.

Steel

Steel is commonly used in construction because it is relatively inexpensive and is available in many shapes and sizes: I-shapes, channels, circular and square tubing, and rods. Steel comes in several grades, or strengths; the grade used depends on the requirements of the particular application. Structural steel members are typically connected using bolts and/or welds.

One drawback of using steel in outdoor applications, such as bridges, is that it must be painted regularly to prevent corrosion and rust. Common uses for steel include road and pedestrian bridges and large commercial buildings. The use of steel studs in the walls of houses is also gaining popularity.

Concrete

Concrete is a versatile, low-cost building material that can be formed into any shape. Forms are constructed at the project site, and the concrete is poured into the forms. It takes several days or weeks, depending on weather conditions, for the concrete to harden, or **cure**, to full strength. Concrete is very strong for compression loads; that is, it's good at holding up things that are pressing on it. However, it has poor tensile strength; that is, it doesn't hold up well under a pulling force. So concrete is typically used in combination with steel reinforcement bars (commonly called **rebars**) placed inside a concrete beam or column to provide adequate strength.

CARPENTER'S TOOLS		
Tool	**Description/Function**	**Examples**
hammer	used primarily to drive and remove nails, as well as to pound on devices such as chisels	claw hammer, rubber mallet, ball-peen hammer
saw	thin metal blade with a sharp-toothed edge used to cut wood or metal	hand saw, hacksaw, jigsaw
screwdriver	used to tighten and loosen screws and bolts	slotted (regular) head, Phillips head
level	two- to four-foot long piece of metal or plastic that contains calibrated air bubble tubes, used to ensure that things are vertically plumb or horizontally level	hand level, laser level
square	used primarily to aid in drawing a cut line on a board to insure a straight, 90-degree cut	L-square, T-square
plane	metal tool with a handle and an adjustable blade, used to shave off thin strips of wood for the purpose of smoothing or leveling	block plane, various sizes of carpenter's planes
chisel	metal tool with a sharp, beveled edge that is struck with a hammer in order to cut and shape stone, metal, or wood	scoop chisel, beveled chisel, masonry chisel, cold chisel
protractor	half circle with tick marks around the edge spaced at one-degree intervals, used to measure angles	only one type, made of metal or plastic
C-clamp	C-shaped metallic instrument with a threaded stop that can be adjusted to clamp together pieces of material of different thickness	furniture clamps, many types and sizes of metallic C-clamps
compass	V-shaped metallic instrument with a sharp point on the end of one leg and a pencil or pen on the end of the other leg, used to draw circles	only one type

Concrete offers the added benefit of low maintenance since it does not need to be painted. Common structural applications of concrete include road and bridge surfaces, building foundations, and support members on some structures.

Wood

Wood is used for both structural and decorative purposes. Structural applications include use as studs and roof trusses in houses and as beams for light bridges. The decorative uses include moldings, floor coverings, doors, and windows. Wood is also used to cover over steel or concrete beams and columns. Many types of

GARDENING AND LAWN CARE TOOLS		
Tool	**Description/Function**	**Examples**
shovel	a wooden handle with a metallic blade used for digging holes in the earth or for moving material such as rock from one place to another	many types and sizes: snow, flat blade, narrow spade
rake	a wooden handle with metal tines used to uniformly spread material on the ground or to separate two different materials	leaf rake, garden rakes of several sizes
hoe	a wooden handle with a V-shaped or square metallic blade used for digging small trenches and for light excavation	many types and sizes
axe	a wooden handle with a sharp metal blade used to cut wood	double blade or single blade with hammer
post hole digger	two wooden handles with metal blades used to dig small, circular holes a foot or two deep for the placement of fence posts	only one type

wood are used as building material including pine, spruce, oak, walnut, cherry, redwood, and cedar. Wood is not as strong as steel or concrete.

Brick and Block

Brick is a decorative material typically used on the outer surface of walls. Cement mortar is used between bricks to construct a solid wall that is decorative and also protects the inner wall from the elements. Brick is also sometimes used as a paving material for roads and sidewalks.

Cinder blocks are similar to bricks but much larger. The walls of small buildings are often made of cinder block because it is a low-cost material. As with brick, cement mortar is used to connect the blocks together.

Construction Procedures

Constructing a building, road, or bridge requires coordination and planning. Standard construction procedures assure that projects are finished on schedule, within budget, and according to specifications. However, specific procedures vary, depending on what is being built and on local conditions. Some of the common terms and procedures in building construction that may appear on the ASVAB are discussed below.

Foundations

The foundation is the base that supports a building or bridge. Most foundations are made of concrete. Surveyors stake out the locations of the corners and other key areas of the building or bridge pier. Then the earth is excavated so that the forms for the concrete can be built on solid ground. A solid foundation is key to having a long-lasting structure. The design engineer will determine the size and thickness of the foundation based on the anticipated load.

Flooring

There are many kinds of flooring materials and many ways in which floors are constructed, but there are common elements. The **subfloor** is the structural portion of the flooring system; it transfers the loads placed on the floor to the foundation. The design engineer considers the loads that will be placed on the flooring in determining what materials will be used. For instance, a warehouse floor has to be much stronger than the flooring in an office. The warehouse subfloors would be made of concrete while the office subfloor might be consist of wood joists or beams.

The **decking** is the portion of the floor that lies on top of the subfloor beams. Decking usually consists plywood nailed to the beams. The final component of the flooring system is the decorative covering such as tile, vinyl, or carpet.

Framing

The term **framing** refers to the "skeleton" of a structure. In a house, the framing usually consists of wood or steel studs and roof trusses. Larger buildings may use beams and columns made of concrete and/or steel due to the larger loads involved. The framing of a building is typically built right on top of the foundation so that the weight is transferred to the supporting soil.

After it is put up, the framing is covered, on both the inside and the outside of the building, with decorative material. The outside covering might be made of brick, wood, glass, or other weatherproof material. The inside covering might be drywall, brick, or wood. Insulation is normally placed between the inside and outside cover layers in order to keep the building at a constant temperature and to minimize noise from the outside.

Roofing

Many options exist for roofing materials and designs. Roofs can be made flat or with a **pitch**, or slope. This choice affects which materials and construction techniques are used. The structural portion of the roof is typically made of wood or steel trusses, which are simply a collection of beams fastened together using special connectors. Plywood sheeting is then attached to the trusses, and some type of weatherproof covering is placed on the plywood. Options for this covering include asphalt, wood, tile, metal, or concrete shingles.

How to Learn More About Auto and Shop Topics

Auto and shop information is such an integral part of everyday life that there are many real-life sources you can investigate to learn more. A construction site is a great place to visit for a day to learn more about hand tools, cranes, pumps, and other devices. Ask the construction supervisor if you can take a tour.

Another alternative would be to visit an auto repair shop. Internal combustion engines, lifts, levers, and hand tools are only a few of the types of tools and systems you could see in use.

Yet another possibility would be to visit a local manufacturer in your town. Examples include a foundry, a sheet metal fabricator, an automotive manufacturer, or a pump manufacturer. Look in the yellow pages under "manufacturing" for possibilities.

The Internet is another great resource for auto and shop information. There are many websites where you can learn more about the tools and techniques that apply to automobile maintenance and upkeep, and the auto or workshop environment.

Practice Questions

Try some sample Auto and Shop Information questions to get a feel for what this subtest of the ASVAB is like.

1. Of the following mechanical devices on an automobile, which one uses friction to accomplish its purpose?
   a. the steering system
   b. the exhaust system
   c. the braking system
   d. the internal combustion engine

2. What type of mechanical device is used to aid in cooling of an internal combustion engine?
   a. a pump
   b. a lever
   c. a pulley
   d. a hammer

3. What kind of gauge uses kilometers per hour as a unit of measurement?
   a. thermometer
   b. tachometer
   c. speedometer
   d. a pressure gauge

4. Which of the following types of fuel is NOT commonly used in internal combustion engines in vehicles?
   a. natural gas
   b. gasoline
   c. kerosene
   d. diesel fuel

5. The clutch, the gears, and the drive shaft are all parts of which automotive system?
   a. the exhaust system
   b. the transmission
   c. the cooling system
   d. the electrical system

6. Which of the following components reduces the toxicity of the exhaust gases that are generated by an automobile engine?
   a. the radiator
   b. the fuel filter
   c. the distributor
   d. catalytic converter

7. Which automotive system helps to provide a smooth ride?
   a. the suspension system
   b. the internal combustion engine
   c. the exhaust system
   d. the cooling system

8. A compass is used to
   a. measure angles.
   b. tighten and loosen nuts and bolts.
   c. drive and remove nails.
   d. draw circles of various sizes.

9. Which of the following tools would you use to identify an exact point that is vertically beneath a higher point?
   a. a straight edge
   b. a plumb bob
   c. a chalk line
   d. a tape measure

10. A carpenter's square is used to
    a. measure a distance.
    b. cut wood.
    c. draw straight lines.
    d. draw circular arcs.

11. Which of the following building materials can be formed into any shape?
    a. brick
    b. wood
    c. steel
    d. concrete

12. Which of the following is typically used for the construction of a building foundation?
  a. glass
  b. concrete
  c. wood
  d. brick

13. An important characteristic of an Allen wrench is its
  a. ability to adjust to any sized nut.
  b. having interchangeable tips.
  c. hexagonal head.
  d. Phillips-style head.

14. What is the term used to describe the supporting structural portion of a building?
  a. the roof
  b. the framing
  c. the foundation
  d. the atrium

Answers

1. c. The braking system uses friction to slow or stop the rotation of the wheels.

2. a. The water pump moves water through the engine to help dissipate heat and keep the engine cool.

3. c. A speedometer measures the speed of a vehicle. This speed is typically measured in miles per hour or, in this case, kilometers per hour. The unit of measurement for the tachometer is revolutions per minute (rpm), for the thermometer is degrees Fahrenheit or Celsius (F or C), and for the pressure gauge is pounds per square inch (psi).

4. c. Kerosene is not usually used to fuel vehicles. Gasoline and diesel fuel, of course, are the most common fuels, but natural gas is also used.

5. b. The transmission includes the clutch, gears, and driveshaft.

6. d. The construction of the catalytic converter allows it to take the toxic and noxious gas byproducts of an internal combustion engine and, through a series of chemical reactions, renders carbon monoxide to carbon dioxide, and other unburned hydrocarbons (unburned and partially-burned fuel) to carbon dioxide and water.

7. a. The suspension system, including shock absorbers and springs, keeps the bumps the tires experience from being transferred to the body of the vehicle.

8. d. A compass is used to draw circles. The other tasks listed would be accomplished using: a protractor (choice **a**), a wrench (choice **b**), and a hammer (choice **c**).

9. b. A plumb bob is a heavy, pointed weight that can be hung directly below or from a specific higher point to mark a vertical position below.

10. c. A carpenter's square is used to draw a straight cut line on a piece of wood or metal. One leg of the square is placed on the edge of the object to be cut. This places the other leg across the object at a 90-degree angle so that the cut will be straight.

11. d. Liquid concrete is poured into a form and cures, or hardens, into the shape of the form. Almost any shape of form can be used.

12. b. Because of its compression strength, concrete is usually used for foundations.

13. c. A set of Allen wrenches is a graduated-in-size set of hexagonal wrenches designed to fit specific graduated-in-size bolts or screws with the same hexagonal head on them.

14. c. The foundation provides the structural support for a building.

MECHANICAL COMPREHENSION REVIEW

CHAPTER SUMMARY

This chapter will help you prepare for the Mechanical Comprehension subtest of the ASVAB. It presents the most commonly tested concepts: basic and compound mechanical machines and devices, mechanical motion, fluid dynamics, properties of materials, and structural support.

Every day, often without even thinking about it, you use mechanical devices. These could be simple machines such as levers and pulleys, or more complex compound machines such as linkages and gears. The ability to understand and use mechanical concepts is important both for many tasks required in the armed services and in everyday life.

The Mechanical Comprehension subtest of ASVAB may cover topics you are familiar with, as well as some that are new. Understanding the concepts in this chapter will benefit you both for the exam and in your career in the armed services. After an introduction to the Mechanical Comprehension subtest, this chapter summarizes definitions and the most commonly tested mechanical concepts. It also suggests how you can add to your knowledge of mechanical concepts and related scientific and mathematical knowledge. At the end of the chapter, you get an opportunity to review what you've learned by answering sample Mechanical Comprehension questions like those found on the ASVAB.

What Mechanical Comprehension Questions Are Like

The Mechanical Comprehension subtest covers a wide range of topics. It consists of multiple-choice questions, most of which require previous knowledge of the topic. Some questions will provide all of the information you need to figure out the answer.

Some questions require you to identify various mechanical machines or devices. Some of the mechanical devices that may appear on the exam—and are covered in this chapter—include gears, pulleys, levers, fasteners, springs, gauges, hinges, and linkages.

Other questions require knowledge of mechanical motion such as velocity, acceleration, direction, and friction for both solid bodies and fluids. These questions test concepts such as the motion and acceleration of automobiles or the buoyancy and pressure of fluids.

The Mechanical Comprehension subtest also covers the properties of materials and the concept of structural support. The material properties include weight, strength, density, thermal properties, and center of gravity. Structural support includes concepts such as weight distribution.

A typical mechanical comprehension question will look something like this:

1. What is the main function of a pulley?
   a. to increase the strength of a construction crane
   b. to override the power of an electric motor
   c. to add energy to a system
   d. to change the direction of a pulling force

The correct answer is **d**, to change the direction of a pulling force. Pulleys are used to change not the strength of a force but its direction.

Review of Mechanical Comprehension Concepts

As aforementioned, some of the mechanical concepts most likely to appear on the ASVAB include basic and compound machines, mechanical motion, the behavior of fluids, the properties of materials, and structual support.

Basic and Compound Machines

Most mechanical machines and devices were invented in a similar manner: people were looking for easier ways to perform their everyday jobs. Some mechanical devices are thousands of years old, such as the lever, the wheel, and many hand tools. Other more complex devices, such as pumps and valves, were invented more recently. Often the idea of a new mechanical device exists, but the technology to actually make it does not. For example, many years before the pump was invented, people probably discussed the need for an easier way to move water from the river to the town on the hill. However, the technologies of the electric motor and metal casting had not yet been discovered, so the modern pump could not be invented.

In general, a mechanical device is a tool that does physical work and is governed by mechanical forces and movements. In other words, you can usually *see* what a mechanical device does and how it works—as opposed to, say, electrical devices such as light switches or batteries. Some tools are used to directly accomplish a specific task, as when you use a hand saw to cut a piece of wood. Others, such as pulleys and gears, may be used indirectly to accomplish tasks that would be possible without the device but are easier with it. Still others, such as gauges, provide feedback on how well other mechanical devices are working. You see and use mechanical devices many times each day, so there's little reason to be intimidated by an exam question on a mechanical device.

Gears

A gear is a toothed wheel or cylinder that meshes with another gear to transmit motion or to change speed or direction. Gears are usually attached to a rotating shaft that is turned by an energy source such as an electric motor or an internal combustion engine. Mechanical devices that use gears include automotive transmissions, carpenter's hand drills, elevator lifting mechanisms, bicycles, and carnival rides such as Ferris wheels and merry-go-rounds.

Gears are used in different configurations. In an automotive transmission, for instance, two gears may directly touch each other. As one gear spins clockwise, the other rotates counterclockwise. Another possible configuration is to have two gears connected by a loop of chain, as on a bicycle. In this arrangement, the first gear rotates in one direction, causing the chain to move. Since the chain is directly connected to the second gear, the second gear will rotate in the same direction as the first gear.

Often a system will use two gears of different sizes, as on a ten-speed bicycle. This allows changes in speed of the bicycle or machine.

Test questions about gears will always involve rotation, or spinning. The easiest way to approach questions about gears is to use the picture given or to draw one, if it's not already provided. Draw an arrow next to each gear to indicate which direction (clockwise or counterclockwise) it is rotating.

Pulleys

A pulley consists of a wheel with a grooved rim through which a rope or cable is run.

Pulleys are often used to change the direction of a pulling force. For instance, a pulley could be attached to the ceiling of a room. A rope could be run from the floor, up through the pulley, and back down to a box sitting on the floor. The pulley would allow you to pull *down* on the rope and cause the box to go *up*.

Another common use for a pulley is to connect an electric motor to a mechanical device such as a pump. One pulley is placed on the shaft of the motor, and a second pulley is placed on the shaft of the pump. A belt connects the two pulleys. When the motor is turned on, the first pulley rotates and causes the belt to rotate, which in turn causes the second pulley to rotate and turn the pump. This arrangement is very similar to the previous example of a bicycle chain and gears.

You may have seen pulleys used in a warehouse to lift heavy loads. Another use for a pulley is on a large construction crane. The cable extends from the object being lifted up to the top of the crane boom, across a pulley, and back down to the electric winch that is used to pull on the cable. In this situation the pulley again causes a change in direction of the pulling force, from the downward force of the winch that pulls the cable to the upward movement of the object being lifted.

Levers

The lever is a very old mechanical device. A lever typically consists of a metal or wooden bar that pivots on a fixed point. The point of using a lever is to gain a **mechanical advantage**. Mechanical advantage results when you use a mechanical device in order to make a task easier; that is, you gain an advantage by using a mechanical device. A lever allows you to complete a task, typically lifting, that would be more difficult or even impossible without the lever.

The most common example of a lever is a playground seesaw. A force—a person's weight—is applied to one side of the lever and causes the weight on the other side—the other person—to be lifted. However, since the pivot point on a seesaw is in the center, each person must weigh the same or the seesaw won't work well. A seesaw is a lever with no mechanical advantage. If you push down on one side with a weight of ten pounds, you can only lift a maximum of ten pounds on the other side. This is no great advantage.

This brings us to the secret of the lever: in order to lift an object that is heavier than the force you want to apply to the other side of the lever, you must locate the pivot point closer to the object you want to lift. If two 50-pound children sit close to the center of the see-saw, one 50-pound child close to the end of the board on the other side will be able to lift them both.

Test questions about levers may require a bit of math—simple multiplication and division. Lever problems rely on one simple concept: the product of the weight to be lifted times the distance from the weight to the pivot point must be equal to the product of the lifting force times the distance from the force to the pivot point. Stated as an equation, $w \times d_1 = f \times d_2$. Here's an example of a test question using this concept:

2. Bill has a 15-foot long lever and he wants to lift a 100-pound box. If he locates the pivot point 5 feet from the box, leaving 10 feet between the pivot point and the other end of the lever where he will apply the lifting force, how hard must he press on the lever to lift the box?

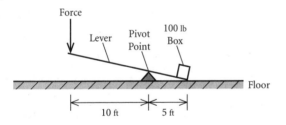

To solve this problem, use the lever formula, $w \times d_1 = f \times d_2$. The weight of 100 pounds times 5 feet must equal 10 feet times the force: $100 \times 5 = 10 \times f$. Multiply 100 by 5 to get 500, and then divide by 10 to get 50 pounds of force, which Bill must apply to the lever to raise the box.

For the ASVAB, it is important to know the three types of levers. They are called first, second, and third class levers. **First class levers** have the fulcrum, or pivot point, in the middle, as in a see-saw. **Second class levers** have the fulcrum at one end, with the effort (force) at the other end and the load in the middle. An ideal example of a second class lever is a wheelbarrow. **Third class levers** have the fulcrum at one end and the load at the other end, with the effort (force) in the middle. A pair of bar-b-que tongs is an example of a third class lever.

Fasteners

A mechanical fastener is any mechanical device or process used to connect two or more items together. Typical examples of fastening **devices** are bolts, screws, nails, and rivets. **Processes** used to join items together mechanically include gluing and welding. The "hook and loop" is a unique mechanical fastener consisting of two tapes of material with many small plastic hooks and loops that stick together. Children's sneakers often use such fastening tape instead of laces.

Springs

A spring is an elastic mechanical device, normally a coil of wire, that returns to its original shape after being compressed or extended. There are many types of springs including the compression coil, spiral coil, flat spiral, extension coil, leaf spring, and torsional spring.

Springs are used for many applications such as car suspensions (compression coil and leaf springs), garage doors (extension coil and torsion springs), wind-up clocks (flat spiral and torsion springs), and some styles of retractable pens (compression coil).

In most questions on the ASVAB, you can assume that springs behave linearly. That is, if an extension spring stretches one inch under a pull of ten pounds, then it will stretch two inches under a pull of twenty pounds. In real life, if you pull too hard on a spring, it will not return to its original shape. This is called exceeding the spring's **elastic limit**.

If several springs are used for one application, they can be arranged in one of two ways: in series or in parallel. The easiest way to remember the difference is that if the springs are all hooked together, end to end, then you have a **series** of springs. The other option is for the springs not to be hooked together but to be lined up side by side, **parallel** to each other. If two springs are arranged in series, they will stretch much farther than the same two springs arranged in parallel under the same pulling force. This is because in series, the total pulling force passes through both springs. If the same springs are arranged in parallel, the pulling force is divided equally with half going through each spring.

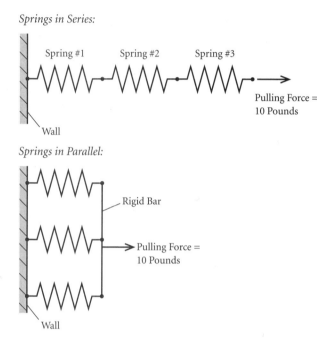

Springs in Series:

Spring #1   Spring #2   Spring #3

Wall

Pulling Force = 10 Pounds

Springs in Parallel:

Rigid Bar

Pulling Force = 10 Pounds

Wall

The key to solving spring problems is to draw a diagram of the arrangement, if one isn't already provided, and follow the pulling force through the system.

Valves

A valve is a mechanical device that controls the flow of liquids, gases, or loose material through piping systems. There are many types of valves including butterfly valves, gate valves, plug valves, ball valves, and check valves.

A valve is basically a gate that can be closed or opened in order to permit a fluid or gas to travel in a particular direction. Exam questions on valves typically require you to follow a piping flow diagram through several sets of valves. The best way to approach these problems is to methodically follow each branch of the piping system from start to finish.

Gauges and Pumps

Gauges and pumps may appear in the Mechanical Comprehension subtest. These devices are discussed in Chapter 10, "Auto and Shop Information."

Linkages

A linkage is a way of connecting objects in order to transfer energy. Belts and chains are commonly used in conjunction with gears and pulleys for this purpose. Chains are typically made of steel or some other metal, while belts are typically made of fiber-reinforced rubber. An example of the use of a belt is the fan belt on the engine of an automobile, which helps transfer the energy from the engine camshaft to the fan. A bicycle uses a chain to transfer the energy from the pedals to the wheel. Another mechanical linkage is the tie rod that connects the piston and crankshaft in an internal combustion engine.

Mechanical Motion

Motion simply means a change of position. The parameters that describe mechanical motion include velocity, direction, acceleration, and friction.

Velocity

Velocity means the rate at which an object is moving in such units as miles per hour or feet per minute. Exam questions on velocity might ask you to use velocity and time to determine the distance traveled. For instance, if a car travels at a constant velocity of 60 miles per hour for two hours, how far does it travel? The answer is velocity multiplied by time, or 60 mph times 2 hours for a total of 120 miles. You might also be asked about relative velocity in a question in which two objects travel at different speeds for different lengths of time.

Direction

If you want to travel quickly from Kansas City to Denver, your velocity is unimportant if you're not traveling in the right direction. When answering mechanical motion questions, always note the direction of travel of the object or objects, if this information is given. Again, drawing a sketch of the situation usually helps.

Acceleration

Acceleration is the rate of change of velocity or, in other words, how much faster you are going from one minute to the next. This is simpler than it sounds. If you are sitting in your car at a stop sign and then you press hard on the gas pedal, you get pushed back into the seat a bit. If you are traveling along the highway at a *constant* 50 mph, you don't have this feeling. However, if you hit the gas and accelerate to 65 mph, you are again pushed back into your seat. You have the same sensation when your airplane takes off on the runway. This sensation is the result of acceleration, an increase in how fast an object is traveling. The opposite of acceleration is **deceleration**, slowing down. Exam questions on acceleration may involve a little simple math.

Friction

Friction is the naturally occurring force that acts to hold back an object in motion. If you slide a block of wood across a floor, the friction between the floor and the block causes a drag on the movement of the block. There are two things you should remember if you encounter an exam question about friction:

- Friction always slows down movement.
- All movement experiences frictional force to some degree.

The drag force of friction varies depending on the materials involved. If you've ever tried to drag a piece of furniture from a room with a carpeted floor to another room with a wood floor, you found that the piece of furniture was much easier to drag on the wood floor than on the carpet. The carpet has a higher **coefficient of friction** than wood. Materials with a high coefficient of friction include such things as sandpaper and brick. Examples of materials with a low coefficient of friction include non-stick cooking surfaces and ice. The differing coefficients of fiction explain why it's more difficult to pull a wooden block across a rough surface such as sandpaper than across a slick surface such as ice.

Fluid Statics and Dynamics

The Mechanical Comprehension subtest includes questions on the behavior of fluids, including questions on pressure, density, and buoyancy.

Pressure

As a solid object is submerged below the surface of a fluid, the fluid exerts a **pressure** on it. Have you ever noticed that when diving in a swimming pool you feel more and more pressure on your ears as you go deeper? This is the effect of the pressure of the fluid, water in this case, on your body. The fluid has weight. As you go deeper, more of this weight presses on your body. All fluids behave this way. The deeper a solid object is submerged, the higher the pressure. This behavior of fluids affects the design of machines such as submarines.

The formula for pressure is:

pressure = density × depth.

Density

Density is a proportion of weight to volume. If you are comparing two fluids, for example, a gallon of the one with the higher density weighs more than the same volume (a gallon) of another liquid. The density of a solid object or other fluid is usually compared to the density of water, 62.4 pounds per cubic foot. Density controls whether an a solid object or another fluid will sink or float in a given fluid. If a solid object sinks when placed in water, then its density is more than that of water. Conversely, if an object floats, then it is less dense than water. Some liquids, such as mercury, are more dense than water. If mercury and water are combined in a jar, the water will float on top of the mercury. Other fluids, such as gasoline or motor oil, are slightly less dense than water. That is why when an oil tanker has a spill, it leaves an oil slick—the oil is floating on the surface of the water.

Density influences the amount of pressure a fluid exerts on an object. The denser the fluid, the faster the pressure increases on an object as it is submerged. Exam questions on density may include simple mathematical calculations, such as computing pressure by multiplying density times depth. Or they may simply ask you to compare the effects of pressure at different depths and densities.

Buoyancy

Buoyancy is the force that acts to push an object submerged in a fluid to the surface. When you force a beach ball under water and then let it go, it springs to the surface. That's the effect of buoyancy.

Here's an example that shows how buoyancy works for an object that is denser than water. Let's say you have a glass that is completely full of water, and the water in the glass weighs one pound. Now put in a eight-pound steel ball, which occupies half of the volume of the glass. When the ball sinks, what happens? Half of the water in the glass, a half-pound worth, spills over the edge of the glass because the ball occupies half the volume of the glass. Now, here's a definition: the uplifting buoyant force acting on this ball is equal to the weight of the water displaced out of the glass by the ball. By definition, therefore, this ball weighs half a pound less when submerged in water than it does just sitting on the table.

The ball weighs less underwater, but it still sinks. Why? Because the ball weighs more than the water it displaces. How, then, is it possible to make a ship that floats in water out of steel, when steel is more dense than water? Simple. Take a thin sheet of steel and form it into a kind of bowl shape. As this thin shell is lowered into the water, it will displace enough water to make it float.

Properties of Materials

Mechanical components and systems can be fabricated using many different materials such as steel, wood, concrete, and plastic. All of these materials react differently to stress, temperature changes, and other external factors. You must understand the properties of materials—weight, strength, density, and thermal properties—in order to answer test questions about them.

Weight

The **weight** of an object is simply a measure of its heaviness.

Strength

The loads and stresses placed on a material must be less than the strength of the material in order to prevent failure. A material's strength can be measured in several ways. A concrete building foundation has lots of weight compressing on it and must have high **compressive** strength. A steel construction girder has a large pulling force acting on it and must therefore have a high **tensile** strength. The materials selected for a given project depend in part on the loads the structure will have to bear.

Density

Think of a one-gallon bottle full of feathers and another full of steel. Which bottle would be heavier? Both bottles have the same volume, but the one full of steel would obviously weigh more, because steel has a higher **density** (weight per unit volume) than feathers. Feathers have a low density; it would take a large volume—a big stack of them—to amount to any significant weight. On the other hand, a small volume of steel, which has a fairly high density, is reasonably heavy. Just remember that a material with a higher density will hurt more if you drop it on your toe!

In the English system of units, density is typically measured in pounds per cubic foot or pounds per cubic inch.

Thermal Properties

The **thermal properties** of materials—how they respond to changes in termperature—affect their suitability for various applications. Most materials expand slightly as the temperature increases and contract as the temperature decreases. This amount of expansion and contraction varies for each material but is typically very small; you could not see it with your eyes.

The effect of even this small amount of expansion or contraction can be significant on some mechanical systems. For instance, the internal combustion engine of a vehicle generates heat as it operates. All of the parts of the engine must be manufactured so that they fit together properly at both high and low temperatures. Likewise, an airplane experiences very low temperatures when flying at high altitudes, so that the metal of its body contracts a bit. The designers of the airplane must take this effect into account.

The strength of some materials is also affected by changes in temperature. Most materials get weaker as the temperature increases because the bonds between the individual molecules that make up the material get weaker as the molecules move more rapidly. This is why some building materials, such as steel, are coated with insulation during construction. If the building catches fire, the insulation will help maintain the strength of the steel girders.

Choosing Materials for a Given Application

In deciding what materials to use for a given application, weight, strength, density, and thermal properties must all be taken into consideration. For instance, if you wanted to build an airplane wing, you might consider using either steel or aluminum. Steel is stronger than aluminum. However, aluminum has a lower density; that is, an aluminum wing would be lighter than a steel wing of the same size. Therefore, you could use more aluminum to provide adequate strength and still have a lighter total weight.

Other factors, such as cost and how easy the materials are to work with, are also taken into account when selecting materials for a project.

Structural Support

Mechanical systems such as buildings and bridges require proper structural support in so they can hold up heavy loads. An object's center of gravity and its weight distribution affect the design of structural support.

Center of Gravity

The **center of gravity** of an object is the point at which all of the object's weight appears to act. For instance, you can balance a pencil on your finger by placing your finger under the pencil at the middle of its length. The center of gravity of that pencil is halfway along its length. Likewise, a round ball has its center of gravity at its center. Other objects that are not so symmetrical also have a center of gravity, which can be located through calculations.

Exam questions on center of gravity usually involve symmetrical objects so that the math does not become complicated. Take your time, draw a sketch of the object, and use common sense.

Weight Distribution

The **distribution of weight** on a structure such as on a bridge is also important to understand. If there are three trucks uniformly spaced across the length of a bridge that is supported only at its ends, then each support bears an equal amount of the load. However, if the trucks are all located close to one end of the bridge, then the support on that end will be holding up a higher load than the support on the opposite end.

Bridges and buildings have highly variable loads. The worst-case weight distribution must be accounted for—for instance, trucks standing nose to tail for the whole length of the bridge—even if that isn't very likely to happen

As with most Mechanical Comprehension questions, using the picture given, or drawing one if it's not provided, will help you see the location and distribution of the objects.

Brushing Up on Related Topics

Some mechanical comprehension questions may require the use of math or science to determine the correct answer. This chapter cannot cover all the possible questions you might be asked on the ASVAB, but here are suggestions for ways to increase your knowledge of math and science and your general mechanical comprehension.

Math

The math you may need for Mechanical Comprehension questions are simple arithmetic (addition, subtraction, multiplication, and division) and geometry (angles and shapes). If you had trouble with arithmetic or geometry in your past schooling, you can brush up by reading the math chapter of this book. If you still want more help, pull out your old high school math book or check out a math book from the library.

Science

Science subjects such as physics, materials science, thermodynamics, and chemistry are confusing for some people, but they needn't be. Science is real, everyday life. You see science in action dozens of times every day. A car is stopped by brakes, which use friction—that's physics. A magnet adheres to the refrigerator door due to the properties of the magnet and carbon steel of which the door is made—that's materials science. A pot of water boils when you set it on the stove and turn on the burner—that's thermodynamics. A cake rises through the release of carbon dioxide from the baking powder or baking soda reacting with heat or an acid—that's chemistry. This chapter has reviewed many of the scientific concepts that are involved in mechanical devices. Again, as with math, you may have science books from previous schooling that you can use to help you solidify your scientific knowledge. If not, the library is full of scientific resources.

General Mechanical Comprehension

Mechanical devices are such an integral part of everyday life that there are many real-life sources you can investigate to gain more knowledge of their design and use. A construction site is a great place to visit for a day to learn more about hand tools, cranes, pumps, and other devices. Ask the construction supervisor if you can take a tour.

Another possibility would be to visit a local manufacturer in your town. Examples include a foundry, a sheet metal fabricator, an automotive manufacturer, or a pump manufacturer. Look in the yellow pages under "manufacturing" for possibilities.

Practice Questions

Try the Mechanical Comprehension questions below. Answers and explanations are at the end of the chapter.

1. In a set of different sized pulleys, which will turn the fastest?
   a. the largest pulley
   b. they will all turn at the same speed, given the same belt speed
   c. the smallest pulley
   d. it depends on the speed of the machine

2. Steve has a lever whose pivot point is 3 feet from the 50-pound box he wants to lift. Steve is standing at the other end of the lever, 6 feet from the pivot point. How much force must he apply to lift the box?

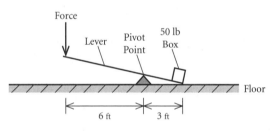

   a. 50 pounds
   b. 25 pounds
   c. 100 pounds
   d. 6 pounds

3. When three identical springs are arranged in series and a pulling force of 10 pounds is applied, the total stretch is 9 inches. If these same three springs are arranged in parallel and the same 10-pound force is applied to the new arrangement, what will be the total distance of stretch?

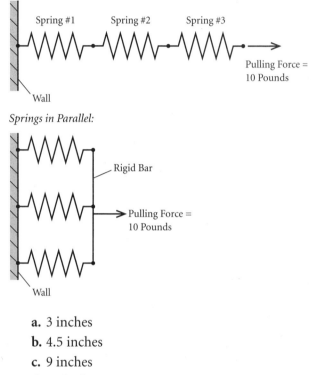

   a. 3 inches
   b. 4.5 inches
   c. 9 inches
   d. 18 inches

4. Jan and Shirley begin traveling from the same point. Jan travels east at 30 mph for half an hour and Shirley travels west at 40 mph for one hour. How far apart are they at the end of their travels?
   a. 25 miles
   b. 55 miles
   c. 70 miles
   d. 120 miles

5. If each of the following objects weighed the same, which would be easiest to drag?

   a. a wood object on a carpeted floor

   b. a wood object on a wood floor

   c. a glass object on a brick floor

   d. a glass object on a tiled floor

6. Which of the following is one of the cycles of a four-stroke engine?

   a. compression

   b. decompression

   c. rotation

   d. ingestion

7. Jar A contains a volume of 2 cubic feet of liquid and weighs 128 pounds. Jar B contains a volume of 3 cubic feet of liquid and weighs 216 pounds. Which liquid has a higher density?

   a. Jar A

   b. Jar B

   c. They have the same density.

   d. There is not enough information to answer the question.

8. Which of the following best explains why wood floats on water?

   a. Wood is less dense than water.

   b. Water is less dense than wood.

   c. Water exerts more pressure than wood.

   d. Water is more buoyant than wood.

How to Answer Mechanical Aptitude Questions

- **Read each problem carefully.** Questions may contain words such as *not*, *all*, or *mostly*, which can be tricky unless you pay attention.
- **Read the entire question once or even a few times before trying to pick an answer.** Decide exactly what the question is asking. Take notes and draw pictures on scratch paper. That way you won't waste time by going in the wrong direction.
- **Use common sense.** Some mechanical concepts can seem intimidating at first but are really a combination of a few more simple ideas. Try to break complicated questions down into smaller, manageable pieces.
- **Answer the questions that are easiest for you first.** You do not have to go in order from start to finish. Read each question and, if you are not sure what to do, move on to the next question. You can go back to harder questions if you have time at the end.
- **Many mechanical concepts are commonly used in everyday life.** You do not have to be a mechanic or an engineer to use these devices. If something seems unfamiliar, try to think of items around your house that might be similar.
- **Don't be intimidated by unfamiliar terms.** In most instances, there are clues in the question that will point you toward the correct answer, and some of the answers can be ruled out by common sense.

9. Which of the following best describes the effect of heating a bar of steel?

    a. The bar will contract.

    b. The bar will expand.

    c. The bar will warp.

    d. The bar will remain unchanged.

10. Given gear B, turning in the direction noted, what direction will gears A and C turn in?

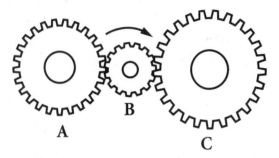

    a. gear A will be clockwise and gear C will be clockwise

    b. gear A will be clockwise and gear C will be counterclockwise

    c. gear A will be counterclockwise and gear C will be counterclockwise

    d. the gears will seize up and not move

Answers

1. c. The smaller pulley will turn faster than those larger than it. It has to turn faster in order to keep up.

2. b. Apply the distance formula, $w \times d_1 = f \times d_2$, to come up with the equation $50 \times 3 = f \times 6$. Solve for the unknown f by multiplying 3 times 50 to get 150 and then dividing by 6 to get 25 pounds.

3. a. The total pulling force will be divided equally, with each spring experiencing one-third of the total force. Since the force is divided by 3, the amount of movement will be divided by 3 also. The original configuration stretched 9 inches, so the new arrangement will stretch only 3 inches.

4. b. Jan has traveled 15 miles to the east of the starting point, and Shirley has traveled 40 miles west of their starting point. Since east and west are in opposite directions, this puts a distance of 55 miles between them. If both had been traveling in the same direction at the given velocity and time, the distance separating them would have been only 25 miles.

5. d. Glass and tile both have relatively low coefficients of friction.

6. a. The four stages of a four-stroke engine are intake, compression, combustion, and exhaust.

7. b. Divide the weight of each jar by its volume. The liquid in Jar A has density of 64 pounds per cubic foot, and the liquid in Jar B has a density of 72 pounds per cubic foot.

8. a. Wood floats because it is less dense than the water it is floating on.

9. b. Most materials expand when heated.

10. c. The center gear is turning clockwise, and will cause the other two gears to turn in the opposite direction, or counterclockwise.

12 ▶ ELECTRONICS INFORMATION REVIEW

CHAPTER SUMMARY

We use electricity every day of our lives. Lightbulbs produce light from electricity. Many ovens use electricity to produce heat. Our televisions and computers use electricity. Our cars use electricity to ignite the fuel in the engine. Batteries produce electricity to power games and calculators. This chapter will add to your knowledge of electronics and review what you already know so that you can get a top score on the Electronics Information subtest of the ASVAB.

The electricity used in the United States is predominately produced from three resources: fossil fuels, such as oil, natural gas, and coal; nuclear materials, primarily uranium; and hydropower from water.

Almost 80 percent of the electrical power used in the United States is produced from the burning of fossil fuels. Fossil fuels are burned to produce heat. The heat is used to produce steam that turns a turbine. The turbine transforms rotational mechanical energy into electric energy which in turn is fed into a power grid.

Nuclear power plants produce about 7 percent of the electricity we consume. A nuclear power plant uses a nuclear reaction (fission) to produce heat that generates steam. The process described above is then used to convert steam into electricity.

About 15 percent of the electricity we use is from hydropower. The kinetic energy of falling water is used to turn turbines that produce the electrical power.

> **Kinetic Energy:** the energy produced by a body in motion.

Basic Electrical Theory

Understanding electricity and electronics is not dependent on understanding the complex structure of the atom—understanding the basics is sufficient. All materials on Earth are made up of atoms. An atom is made up in part of electrons and protons. These two subatomic particles each have an electric charge, or electric polarity. The charge of an electron has a negative polarity while the charge of a proton has a positive polarity. Electricity is essentially the management of positive and negative electric charges.

Charge

Most everyone has experienced the buildup of electric charge when shuffling across a carpet. Your body develops a static charge. It is static because the charge is not moving. When you touch a light switch, the static charge moves, creating a current. You have produced and used electricity.

The symbol for electric charge is **q** or **Q**. Charge is measured in coulombs, **C**. A coulomb of electrons has a negative charge and a coulomb of protons has a positive charge. A coulomb is defined as 6.25×10^{18} electrons or protons:

the charge of 6.25×10^{18} electrons = Q = 1C

Example: What is the charge, in coulombs, of one electron?
You remember that

6.25×10^{18} electrons = 1 Coulomb

To get the charge of one electron, divide both sides by 6.25×10^{18}:

1 electron = $.16 \times 10^{-18}$ C

Voltage

An electric charge has the potential to do work by forcing another charge to move. Opposite charges attract each other and like charges repel each other, just like magnets. Thus, a positive and a negative charge would attract each other, while two negative charges would repel each other. The potential of an electric charge to do work is the **voltage** or the **potential difference**. A battery produces a voltage. This voltage can be thought of as the force that moves electrons from one terminal to the other. This force is called the electromotive force (emf). The accepted symbol for voltage is **V**. The schematic symbol for a DC voltage is:

Voltage: the potential of an electric charge to do work.

Current

All batteries have two terminals, a positive and a negative one. On a flashlight battery, for example, one end (usually marked with a + sign) is the positive terminal, and the other end (usually marked with a − sign) is the negative terminal.

When a battery is connected to a load with wires, the potential difference, or voltage, between the two terminals (the two opposite charges) forces a third charge to move. The charge in motion is called an electric **current**. Current is produced when a potential difference moves an electric charge. Picture a battery connected with wires to a light bulb:

The battery produces a voltage, which forces the free electrons in the wire to move. The mobile free electrons moving in the wire are the current. The current is always a continuous flow of electrons, and at every point in the circuit, the current is the same.

> **Load:** the resistance in an electric circuit.

Electric current is measured in amperes. An **ampere** is defined to be 6.25×10^{18} electrons moving past any given point in one second. This is the same as one coulomb of charge moving past any given point in one second. The symbol for current is **I** or *i*. Mathematically, current is expressed as:

$$I = \frac{Q}{T}$$ where I is current in amperes (A), Q is charge in coulombs (C), and T is time in seconds (s).

Example: What is the current if 10 coulombs of charge flow through a light bulb every 5 seconds?

$$I = \frac{Q}{T}$$
$$I = \frac{10 \text{ C}}{5 \text{ s}}$$
$$I = 2 \text{ A}$$

The charge, or number of electrons, can be determined using the equation above:

$$I = \frac{Q}{T}$$

multiply both sides of the equation by time

$$I \times T = \frac{Q}{T} \times T$$
$$IT = Q \times 1$$
$$IT = Q$$

Therefore, if we solve for charge, or Q, this same equation tells us that charge is equal to current multiplied by time. In other words, charge equals the amount of current during a given time period.

Example: How many electrons are flowing through the light bulb when the current is 2 amperes?

$$Q = I \times T$$
$$Q = 2 \text{ A} \times 1 \text{ s}$$
$$Q = 2 \text{ Coulombs}$$
and
$$2 \text{ C} = 2 \times 6.25 \times 10^{18}$$
$$2 \text{ C} = 12.5 \times 10^{18} \text{ electrons}$$

Alternating Current (AC) and Direct Current (DC)

A battery is an example of a direct voltage source. The terminals of the battery always maintain the same polarity, so the current flow from one terminal to the other is always in the same direction. On the other hand, an alternating voltage source periodically reverses its polarity. The current resulting from an alternating voltage also periodically changes its direction of flow.

The electricity generated in a power plant is by nature an alternating voltage. The magnetic fields developed in a rotating turbine always produce an alternating voltage. The voltage we most often use in our homes is 110 volt 60 Hz. The 60 Hz, or Hertz, refers to the frequency that an alternating voltage changes polarity. In this case the polarity changes from positive to negative and back to positive 60 times a second.

One advantage of producing an alternating voltage is that it is more easily changed to a different value than a direct voltage can be changed. This is very important because power plants produce thousands of volts, while we can safely use just 110 or 220 volts in our homes. Most of our appliances then convert the 110 or 220 volts to even a smaller voltage. Simple transformers are used to step up or down alternating voltages. A direct voltage must first be converted to an alternating voltage before its value can be changed. This adds complexity and cost to using direct voltages.

Another benefit of using alternating voltages and currents is that they can be easily and inexpensively converted into direct voltage and current. A diode is a semiconductor device that allows current to flow in only one direction. When the direction of current flow changes, the diode acts like an insulator and stops the current. Two or four diodes can be used to transform alternating voltages and currents into direct voltages and currents. This process is referred to as **rectifying** an alternating voltage.

Basic electrical theory is most easily understood by studying direct voltages and currents. The study of alternating voltages and currents can become very complex. The rest of this chapter will discuss only direct voltages and currents.

Conductors, Insulators, and Semiconductors

A copper wire is an example of a conductor. A **conductor** is a material that has electrons that can easily move. Metals are very good conductors. Copper is used to make most of the wires we use because it has high conductance and is relatively inexpensive. Aluminum was used in the 1950s to make wires for our homes because it was less expensive than copper; however, it is not as good a conductor.

An **insulator** is a material whose electrons do not move freely. Glass, rubber, wood, and porcelain are all examples of insulators. Insulators are used to prevent the flow of current.

A **semiconductor** is a material that conducts less than a metal conductor but more than an insulator. Silicon is the most recognized semiconductor. Most transistors, diodes, and integrated circuits are produced from semiconductor materials such as silicon or germanium.

Resistance

Resistance is the opposition to current. A copper wire has very little resistance; therefore it is a good conductor. Insulators have a large resistance. The symbol for resistance is **R**. Resistance is measured in **ohms**. The symbol for ohms is the Greek letter omega, Ω. The schematic symbol for resistance is:

A good copper wire has a resistance of about one-hundredth of an ohm, or 0.01 Ω per foot. For comparison, the resistive heating element used in a medium-size hair dryer has a resistance of about 14 Ω.

Resistors are fabricated using many different materials. The most common types of resistors are wire-wound resistors, carbon-composition resistors, and film resistors. Wire-wound resistors are generally used in high-power applications. Carbon resistors are the most common. They are used in most electronic circuits due to their low cost. Carbon resistors can't typically be built with an exact resistance value. Film resistors are used when a more exact resistance is needed. Resistors are easily built with resistance values from 0.01 Ω to many millions of ohms.

Analog Electrical Circuits

All electrical circuits have the three following components:

1. A potential difference or voltage.
2. A closed path for current to flow from one side of the potential difference to the other.
3. Resistance, which is often referred to as a "load."

Ohm's law defines the relationships between voltage, current, and resistance in a simple electrical circuit.

The current flows along the circuit path ...

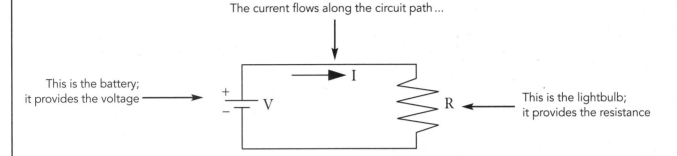

This is the battery; it provides the voltage → V

I

R ← This is the lightbulb; it provides the resistance

Ohm's law states that:

potential difference (or voltage) = current × resistance

or

$$V = I \times R$$

This can be rewritten as:

$$\text{current} = \frac{\text{potential difference}}{\text{resistance}}$$

or

$$I = \frac{V}{R}$$

Example: The battery in the flashlight below supplies 4.5 volts and the light bulb has a resistance of 1.5 Ω. How much current flows in the circuit?

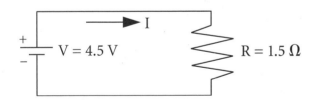

Ohm's law states that current (remember that current is measured in amperes) equals voltage over resistance:

$$I = \frac{V}{R}$$

$$I = \frac{4.5 \text{ V}}{1.5 \text{ }\Omega}$$

$$I = 3\text{A}$$

According to Ohm's law, 3 amperes of current flows through this circuit.

Series Resistance Circuits

Multiple resistance elements may be used in an electric circuit. An example of this type of circuit is the *series resistance circuit*, as represented schematically below:

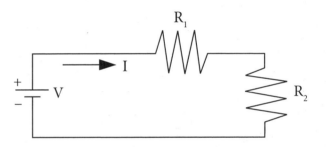

R_1 and R_2 are both in the same current path, providing more total resistance than a single resistance element. It is crucial to remember, however, that in a series resistance circuit, the current is the same everywhere in the circuit. In other words, the current flowing through R_1 is the same as the current through R_2. The total circuit resistance is the sum of the resistance of each individual resistance element.

Example: Christmas tree lights are a good example of a series resistance circuit. The following circuit represents four bulbs in a string connected to a 20-volt source; each bulb provides 5 ohms of resistance. What is the current flowing through the string of lights?

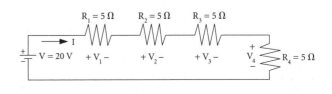

Again, Ohm's law states that the current equals the voltage over the resistance, and in this circuit the total resistance is equal to the sum of the resistance of each of the four bulbs.

$$I = \frac{V}{R_T}$$
$$I = \frac{V}{R_1 + R_2 + R_3 + R_4}$$
$$I = \frac{20\ V}{5\ \Omega + 5\ \Omega + 5\ \Omega + 5\ \Omega}$$
$$I = \frac{20\ V}{20\ \Omega}$$
$$I = 1A$$

The voltage across each of the light bulbs in the example above can also be easily calculated using Ohm's law:

$$V_1 = I \times R_1$$
$$V_1 = 1\ A \times 5\ \Omega$$
$$V_1 = 5\ V$$

Notice that the sum of the voltages across each bulb equals the total voltage. This can be stated:

$$V_T = V_1 + V_2 + V_3 + V_4$$
or
$$V_T = 5\ V + 5\ V + 5\ V + 5\ V$$
$$V_T = 20\ V$$

Parallel Resistance Circuits

A **parallel** resistance circuit has two or more loads connected across a single voltage source. An example of this is plugging your coffee pot and toaster into the same electric outlet. Consider the circuit below, where R_1 is the coffee pot and R_2 is the toaster.

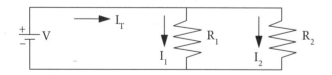

The **voltage** across each resistor of a *parallel* resistance circuit is the same. On the other hand, the **current** through each resistor of a *series* resistance circuit is the same. The current through each resistor in a *parallel* circuit may be different, depending on the resistance of the loads. The total current of the circuit is the sum of the current through each resistor.

$$I_T = I_1 + I_2$$

Again, the voltage across both R_1 and R_2 is the same, it is V. The current through each resistor can still be calculated using Ohm's law.

$$I_1 = \frac{V}{R_1}$$
$$I_2 = \frac{V}{R_2}$$

Example: What is the total current, I_T, that a 120-volt source must supply if a coffee pot with a resistance of 30 ohms and a toaster with a resistance of 20 ohms are plugged into the same outlet?

The total current:
$$I_T = I_1 + I_2$$
$$I_T = \frac{V}{R_1} + \frac{V}{R_2}$$
$$I_T = \frac{120\ V}{30\ \Omega} + \frac{120\ V}{20\ \Omega}$$
$$I_T = 4\ A + 6\ A$$
$$I_T = 10\ A$$

The resultant total resistance of the toaster and coffee pot is the value a single resistor would have if the toaster and coffee pot were combined. Look at the previous example and determine the total resistance. The total resistance is equivalent to the total voltage divided by the total current; therefore, using the coffee pot and toaster:

$$R_T = \frac{V}{I_T}$$

$$R_T = \frac{120 \text{ V}}{10 \text{ A}}$$

$$R_T = 12 \text{ } \Omega$$

We can redraw our circuit now with a single load replacing the coffee pot and toaster. Notice that the equivalent resistance of 12 Ω is indeed less than the resistance of either the toaster or coffee pot.

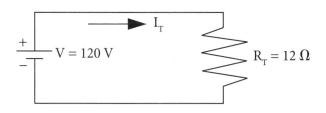

Electrical circuits many times combine series and parallel resistance. Determining the total current depends on first solving for the total resistance. The parallel resistances must first be combined and then added to the series resistance to determine the total resistance.

Ohm's law in a parallel resistance circuit really means that the voltage is constant and the total current is the sum of the currents through each resistor. Ohm's law in a series resistance circuit implies that the current is constant and the total voltage is the sum of the voltages across each resistance.

Electrical Power

The measurement of **power (P)** should be familiar to everyone. Light bulbs are used according to their wattage. Electrical power is measured in **watts (W)**. A watt is defined to be the work done in one second by one volt to move one coulomb of charge. It is written mathematically:

$$P = V \times \frac{Q}{T}$$

or

$$\text{Power} = \text{Voltage} \times \frac{\text{Change}}{\text{Time}}$$

Remember that current is:

$$I = \frac{Q}{T}$$

Substitute I for $\frac{Q}{T}$ into the equation above to give:

$$P = V \times I$$

This is called the power equation; power, or the number of watts, is equal to voltage multiplied by current.

> **Watt:** the work done in one second by one volt to move one coulomb of charge.

Example: Calculate how many watts a light bulb uses when it is connected to a 120-volt circuit with 0.5 A flowing.

$$P = V \times I$$
$$P = 120 \text{ V} \times 0.5 \text{ A}$$
$$P = 60 \text{ watts}$$

One of the most important circuit characteristics an electrical designer must consider is the power dissipated in a resistor when current flows through it. A resistor will heat up when current flows. The heat is equivalent to the power lost in the resistor. We can use the power equation ($P = V \times I$) and Ohm's law ($V = \frac{I}{R}$) to determine the power dissipated in a resistor.

When we substitute Ohm's law into the power equation to calculate power in terms of current:

$$P = V \times I$$

Ohm's law is $V = I \times R$. Substitute ($I \times R$) for V in the power equation giving:

$$P = (I \times R) \times I$$
$$P = I^2 R$$

We can also use Ohm's law to solve the power equation in terms of voltage:

$$P = V \times I$$

Ohm's law is $I = \frac{V}{R}$. Substitute $\frac{V}{R}$ for I in the power equation giving

$$P = V \times \frac{V}{R}$$
$$P = \frac{V^2}{R}$$

The heat generated in a resistor is sometimes harmful and sometimes beneficial. When too much power is lost in a resistor, it can burn up and destroy an appliance. A toaster is an example of using the heat generated in a resistor for benefit. The heating element in a toaster is nothing more than a large resistor.

Example: How much power does the heating element of the toaster use in the following circuit?

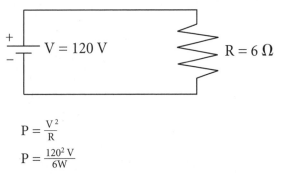

$$P = \frac{V^2}{R}$$
$$P = \frac{120^2 \text{ V}}{6 \text{W}}$$
$$P = 2,400 \text{ watts}$$

Miscellaneous Electrical Components

Capacitors

Most practical circuits contain devices other than voltage sources, resistors, and wires. Capacitors, for instance, are widely used. A **capacitor** is an electrical device that can store electrical charge. A capacitor's function is limited to AC circuits. A common application for capacitors is building filter circuits to protect appliances from voltage spikes. The symbol for a capacitor (C) is similar to a voltage source.

Fuses

Fuses are used to protect almost every electrical item we use. A **fuse** is typically a small piece of wire that will burn up and stop conducting electricity when too much current is forced to flow through it. Fuses are rated to blow at a given current, up to a maximum voltage. For example, a typical fuse in a television may be rated to blow, or open, at 3.0 amperes at any voltage up to 120 volts to protect the television from currents over 3 amperes and voltages over 120 V. An ideal fuse has zero resistance of its own and opens instantly when excess current flows. Some fuses are designed to allow a large current surge to safely flow for a small period of time. This is important because many appliances and motors have what is called an in-rush current surge. A **"slo-blo" fuse** will allow a large current to flow for a few seconds before opening.

Switches

Most circuits wouldn't be practical if we couldn't turn them on and off. **Switches** are used to break a circuit path to stop current flow to a load, such as a lightbulb. There are many types of switches, depending on the application. The most common switches are single-pole-single-throw and double-pole-double-throw switches. The dial used to turn the channel on older televisions is a called a rotary switch. A rotary switch opens and closes contacts when it is turned.

Electronic Manufacturing and Testing

A common workshop will have most of the tools needed to work on electrical equipment. Pliers, screwdrivers, wire cutters, and wrenches are all needed. In addition, a few specialty tools are required. For instance, a wire stripper is a very useful tool. It is used to remove the insulation from a wire in preparation for joining the wire to a circuit element.

Solder

Solder and a soldering iron are used to physically connect most circuit components. **Solder** is a metal alloy usually containing almost equal amounts of tin and lead. Solder is usually specified to be either 40 percent tin and 60 percent lead, 50 percent each, or 60 percent tin and 40 percent lead. The latter mixture does the best soldering job because it melts the easiest, flows the best, and hardens the fastest. However, it is more expensive than the other mixtures. A soldering iron melts solder by heating it to 500 or 600 degrees Fahrenheit; the solder is fused to the metal leads of the electronic components and wires as it cools to permanently bond them together. A joint that has been properly soldered will appear shiny and smooth. A flux must also be used when soldering to remove oxidation from the components to be joined. The flux is typically contained in the solder. One must be careful to not use acid flux when joining electronic components because the acid will eventually corrode the solder joint. A rosin flux is preferred for electronic uses.

Wires and Printed Circuit Boards

Wires have historically been used to connect the components of a circuit. Today's modern technology has

Mastering Zeros

MASTERING ZEROS

The numbers used for circuit analysis are often either very large or very small. Writing out all the zeroes before or after the decimal point can be extremely tedious. Prefixes are used to simplify the writing out of all the zeros. For example a billion words can be written as any of the following:

　　1,000,000,000 words

or

　　1,000 million words

or

　　1×10^9 words

or better yet

　　1G words

The following table lists the prefixes that are typically used to simplify measurement terminology.

prefix	symbol	multiplier
giga	G	10^9
mega	M	10^6
kilo	k	10^3
milli	m	10^{-3}
micro	u	10^{-6}
nano	n	10^{-9}
pico	p	10^{-12}

replaced most wires with **printed circuit boards (PCBs).** Printed circuit boards are thin, typically fiberglass boards with electronic components soldered to them and copper circuit paths, called traces, that replace discrete wires. Complex circuits can be built using multi-layer PCBs. The copper traces can be sandwiched and laminated between more boards. Typical multi-layer circuit boards may have three to seven layers of circuit paths. If you take the top off a computer or television you will see large and small PCBs and relatively few discrete wires. Wires are mostly used today to join PCBs to connectors.

Testing Instruments

The testing of electronic circuits requires a few specialized test instruments. Measuring basic DC circuit parameters can be accomplished with the following instruments:

- ammeter: measures currents
- ohmmeter: measures resistance
- voltmeter: measures voltage

Voltage is the easiest parameter to test. A voltmeter can easily be connected across the device being tested at any point in the current. An ammeter must be connected in series to give a true indication of the current in the circuit. An ohmmeter is typically used on an unpowered device to measure its resistance. Many times the device being measured must be completely removed from the circuit to get an accurate resistance measurement. Power in a circuit is typically calculated after measuring the voltage and current.

Testing AC circuits and digital circuits requires much more complex and expensive test equipment. An oscilloscope is used to display AC and complex voltage waveforms. It is an indispensable tool for analyzing most of the circuits found in today's electronic products. The test equipment needed to test tomorrow's circuits will become more and increasingly specialized with the continued rapid growth of technology.

Radio

The radio was invented by Guglielmo Marconi in the late 1800s.

The theory behind radio is simple; however, the experience needed to fully understand radio may take years of study to develop. The simple drawing below shows how radio communication works.

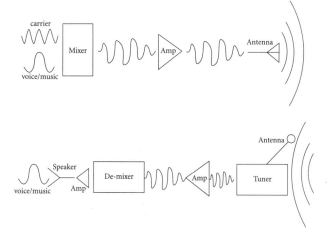

The voice or music signal is combined with a carrier wave and fed into an amplifier and then to an antenna. The antenna transmits the combined signal into the air. The receiving antenna catches the weak signal out of the air and sends it to an amplifier. The signal is amplified, and then the carrier wave is removed, leaving the original voice or music signal intact. The original signal can then be amplified again and listened to through a speaker.

Radio: communication between two or more points using electromagnetic waves as the transmission medium.

Radio communication was first used on ships to communicate at sea. The importance of radio was proven when assistance was requested by the Titanic when it was sinking. Radio communication is not limited to the AM and FM radios we listen to. Television and cellular phones are also examples of radio communication.

Practice Questions

Now use what you've learned to answer the following electronics questions. Answers are at the end of the chapter.

1. An electrical device that can store an electrical charge is called a(n)
   a. fuse.
   b. battery.
   c. capacitor.
   d. ohm.

2. How many electrons are there in four coulombs of charge?
   a. 13.1×10^{18}
   b. 6.25×10^{18}
   c. 6.25×10^{-18}
   d. 2.5×10^{19}

3. Which of the following values would provide the greatest resistance?
   a. $1 \, k \, \Omega$
   b. $1 \, m \, \Omega$
   c. $1 \, u \, \Omega$
   d. $1 \, M \, \Omega$

4. Electrical power is measured in
   a. watts.
   b. volts.
   c. current.
   d. capacitors.

5. Which of the following is a statement of Ohm's law?
   a. $I = \frac{Q}{T}$
   b. $P = V \times I$
   c. $V = I \times R$
   d. $P = I^2 \times R$

6. One of the reasons copper is used to make wires is because it is
   a. grounded.
   b. a very good conductor.
   c. difficult to find, therefore expensive.
   d. easy to shape.

7. Carbon resistors are typically used when
   a. a large resistance is required.
   b. a small resistance is required.
   c. an exact resistance is required.
   d. cost is the most important consideration.

8. A high tension power line has 100 amperes flowing through it. The resistance of the power line is .01 Ω/foot. How much power, in watts, is lost in one foot of wire?
   a. 1 watt
   b. 10 watts
   c. 100 watts
   d. 1,000 watts

9. Electric current is measured in
   a. amperes.
   b. coulombs.
   c. watts.
   d. volts.

10. Special "slo-blo" fuses are required when a circuit exhibits which characteristic?
    a. a short circuit
    b. in-rush current
    c. voltage fluctuations
    d. open circuits

11. Which of the following is NOT an example of radio communication?
    a. AM radio
    b. cellular phones
    c. a tape recorder
    d. television

12. Which electrical component allows current to flow in only one direction?
    a. a capacitor
    b. a resistor
    c. a diode
    d. a wire

Answers

1. c. Since a capacitor can store an electrical charge, a common application for capacitors is protecting appliances from voltage spikes.

2. d. One coulomb is 6.25×10^{18} electrons. Four times $6.25 \times 10^{18} = 25 \times 10^{18} = 2.5 \times 10^{19}$.

3. d. The multipliers are: k $\times$ 1,000
 m $\times$ .001
 u $\times$ .000001
 M $\times$ 1,000,000

4. a. A watt is defined as the work done in one second by one volt to move one coulomb of charge.

5. c. Ohm's law is $V = I \times R$

6. b. Copper is used to make most wires because it is an ideal conductor and it is relatively inexpensive.

7. d. Resistors of all types can be made to have large or small resistances. Carbon resistors are used when cost is the most important consideration.

8. c. $P = I^2 \times R = (100 \text{ A})^2 \times .01 \text{ } \Omega = 100$ watts.

9. a. Electric current is measured in amperes.

10. b. Regular fuses are used to protect against short circuits and voltage fluctuations. Open circuits do not need to be protected by a fuse.

11. c. Tape recorders do not use electromagnetic waves as the transmission medium.

12. c. A diode allows current to flow in one direction only.

13 ▶ ASSEMBLING OBJECTS REVIEW

CHAPTER SUMMARY

This chapter will show you what you can expect on the Assembling Objects subtest. Whether working with engine parts or other types of machinery, perhaps as an engineer in a factory, designing blueprints as an architect, or deployed in the field as a military specialist, your ability to understand and recognize the spatial relationships between different shapes you have to work with is essential.

Understanding how simple and complex objects are put together is a valuable asset for any organization, be it military or civilian. The Assembling Objects (AO) subtest is primarily a spatial awareness and recognition test that examines how well you can put together the parts of an object in your mind. You will be given a picture containing several geometric shapes and you will be asked to find the image that contains either all the parts of the original picture, or else determine which parts are put together in proper sequence.

The AO subtest is currently only administered on the CAT-ASVAB version of the test. Please note that the AO subtest is *not* part of the core battery that is used to determine your enlistment eligibility. The AO portion of the CAT-ASVAB is specifically geared toward determining if you have an aptitude for spatial interpretation/analysis and complex problem solving.

AO Strategies

Use the following AO subtest strategies to help you do your best on this portion of the exam.

- **Be careful.** Examine each possible answer choice completely and carefully. Scrutinize each to ensure that the parts in the original image are all used in the correct answer image.
- **Use process of elimination.** When reviewing the answer choices, eliminate any that contain a shape that is not in the original image.
- **Think spatially.** Don't forget that some shapes may be rotated—they still retain their original

shape, but may look different if their orientation has been changed.

Each question is made up of five separate drawings. The first drawing will be the template showing the shapes that will be used. The remaining four drawings are the possible solutions. Your job is to determine which of the possible solutions represents the correct assembly of the shapes in the first drawing.

Take a look at the following sample question and determine the correct answer.

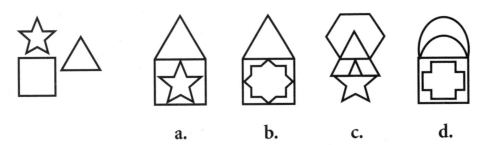

The answer to this sample question is **a**. Choices **b**, **c**, and **d** contain shapes that are not part of the original set.

Another type of Assembling Object question is called a Connector question. In this type, you are first given a number of geometric shapes. These shapes will have a specific spot marked on them, labeled with a letter. A line will be included as well, labeled with corresponding letters at either end. Your job will be to select the answer choice that shows the correct shape assembly, using the line and the labels. Take a look at the following sample question and determine the correct answer.

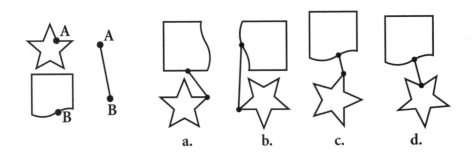

The answer to this question is **d**. Choices **a**, **b**, and **c** all contain a connector line that originates and ends from parts of the shapes which do not correspond to the original set of shapes.

Now that you are familiar with the two types of questions that appear on the Assembling Objects subtest, take the following practice quiz and see how well you do. Answers appear on page 212.

Assembling Objects Practice Quiz

1.

a.   b.   c.   d.

2.

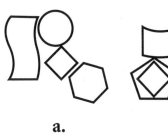

a.   b.   c.   d.

3.

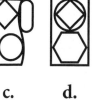

a.   b.   c.   d.

4.

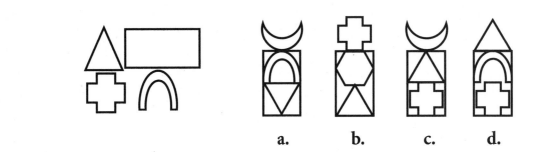

a.   b.   c.   d.

5.

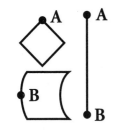   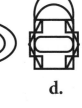   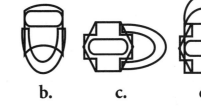

a.   b.   c.   d.

6.

a.   b.   c.   d.

7.

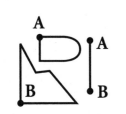   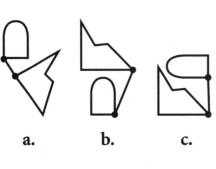   

a.   b.   c.   d.

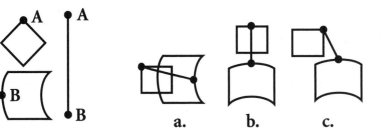

8.

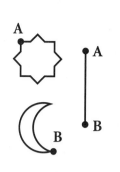    

a.   b.   c.   d.

9.

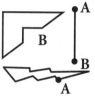 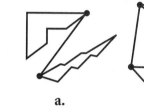 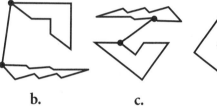 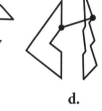

a.   b.   c.   d.

10.

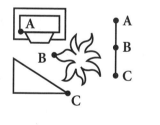  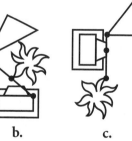 

a.   b.   c.   d.

Answers

How well you perform on this section will help you determine your level of attention to detail and how well your mind processes spatial relationships between different objects.

1. b.
2. d.
3. a.
4. d.
5. c.
6. c.
7. a.
8. d.
9. d.
10. b.

C H A P T E R

14

ASVAB PRACTICE TEST 1

CHAPTER SUMMARY

Here's another sample ASVAB for you to practice with. After working through the review material in the previous chapters, take this test to see how much your score has improved.

For this first practice test, simulate the actual test-taking experience as closely as you can. Find a quiet place to work where you won't be disturbed. If you own this book, tear out the answer sheet on the following pages and find some number 2 pencils to fill in the circles with. Use a timer or stopwatch to time each section. The times are marked at the beginning of each section.

After you take the test, use the detailed answer explanations that follow to review any questions you missed.

Part 1: General Science

	a	b	c	d		a	b	c	d		a	b	c	d
1.	ⓐ	ⓑ	ⓒ	ⓓ	10.	ⓐ	ⓑ	ⓒ	ⓓ	19.	ⓐ	ⓑ	ⓒ	ⓓ
2.	ⓐ	ⓑ	ⓒ	ⓓ	11.	ⓐ	ⓑ	ⓒ	ⓓ	20.	ⓐ	ⓑ	ⓒ	ⓓ
3.	ⓐ	ⓑ	ⓒ	ⓓ	12.	ⓐ	ⓑ	ⓒ	ⓓ	21.	ⓐ	ⓑ	ⓒ	ⓓ
4.	ⓐ	ⓑ	ⓒ	ⓓ	13.	ⓐ	ⓑ	ⓒ	ⓓ	22.	ⓐ	ⓑ	ⓒ	ⓓ
5.	ⓐ	ⓑ	ⓒ	ⓓ	14.	ⓐ	ⓑ	ⓒ	ⓓ	23.	ⓐ	ⓑ	ⓒ	ⓓ
6.	ⓐ	ⓑ	ⓒ	ⓓ	15.	ⓐ	ⓑ	ⓒ	ⓓ	24.	ⓐ	ⓑ	ⓒ	ⓓ
7.	ⓐ	ⓑ	ⓒ	ⓓ	16.	ⓐ	ⓑ	ⓒ	ⓓ	25.	ⓐ	ⓑ	ⓒ	ⓓ
8.	ⓐ	ⓑ	ⓒ	ⓓ	17.	ⓐ	ⓑ	ⓒ	ⓓ					
9.	ⓐ	ⓑ	ⓒ	ⓓ	18.	ⓐ	ⓑ	ⓒ	ⓓ					

Part 2: Arithmetic Reasoning

	a	b	c	d		a	b	c	d		a	b	c	d
1.	ⓐ	ⓑ	ⓒ	ⓓ	11.	ⓐ	ⓑ	ⓒ	ⓓ	21.	ⓐ	ⓑ	ⓒ	ⓓ
2.	ⓐ	ⓑ	ⓒ	ⓓ	12.	ⓐ	ⓑ	ⓒ	ⓓ	22.	ⓐ	ⓑ	ⓒ	ⓓ
3.	ⓐ	ⓑ	ⓒ	ⓓ	13.	ⓐ	ⓑ	ⓒ	ⓓ	23.	ⓐ	ⓑ	ⓒ	ⓓ
4.	ⓐ	ⓑ	ⓒ	ⓓ	14.	ⓐ	ⓑ	ⓒ	ⓓ	24.	ⓐ	ⓑ	ⓒ	ⓓ
5.	ⓐ	ⓑ	ⓒ	ⓓ	15.	ⓐ	ⓑ	ⓒ	ⓓ	25.	ⓐ	ⓑ	ⓒ	ⓓ
6.	ⓐ	ⓑ	ⓒ	ⓓ	16.	ⓐ	ⓑ	ⓒ	ⓓ	26.	ⓐ	ⓑ	ⓒ	ⓓ
7.	ⓐ	ⓑ	ⓒ	ⓓ	17.	ⓐ	ⓑ	ⓒ	ⓓ	27.	ⓐ	ⓑ	ⓒ	ⓓ
8.	ⓐ	ⓑ	ⓒ	ⓓ	18.	ⓐ	ⓑ	ⓒ	ⓓ	28.	ⓐ	ⓑ	ⓒ	ⓓ
9.	ⓐ	ⓑ	ⓒ	ⓓ	19.	ⓐ	ⓑ	ⓒ	ⓓ	29.	ⓐ	ⓑ	ⓒ	ⓓ
10.	ⓐ	ⓑ	ⓒ	ⓓ	20.	ⓐ	ⓑ	ⓒ	ⓓ	30.	ⓐ	ⓑ	ⓒ	ⓓ

Part 3: Word Knowledge

	a	b	c	d		a	b	c	d		a	b	c	d
1.	ⓐ	ⓑ	ⓒ	ⓓ	13.	ⓐ	ⓑ	ⓒ	ⓓ	25.	ⓐ	ⓑ	ⓒ	ⓓ
2.	ⓐ	ⓑ	ⓒ	ⓓ	14.	ⓐ	ⓑ	ⓒ	ⓓ	26.	ⓐ	ⓑ	ⓒ	ⓓ
3.	ⓐ	ⓑ	ⓒ	ⓓ	15.	ⓐ	ⓑ	ⓒ	ⓓ	27.	ⓐ	ⓑ	ⓒ	ⓓ
4.	ⓐ	ⓑ	ⓒ	ⓓ	16.	ⓐ	ⓑ	ⓒ	ⓓ	28.	ⓐ	ⓑ	ⓒ	ⓓ
5.	ⓐ	ⓑ	ⓒ	ⓓ	17.	ⓐ	ⓑ	ⓒ	ⓓ	29.	ⓐ	ⓑ	ⓒ	ⓓ
6.	ⓐ	ⓑ	ⓒ	ⓓ	18.	ⓐ	ⓑ	ⓒ	ⓓ	30.	ⓐ	ⓑ	ⓒ	ⓓ
7.	ⓐ	ⓑ	ⓒ	ⓓ	19.	ⓐ	ⓑ	ⓒ	ⓓ	31.	ⓐ	ⓑ	ⓒ	ⓓ
8.	ⓐ	ⓑ	ⓒ	ⓓ	20.	ⓐ	ⓑ	ⓒ	ⓓ	32.	ⓐ	ⓑ	ⓒ	ⓓ
9.	ⓐ	ⓑ	ⓒ	ⓓ	21.	ⓐ	ⓑ	ⓒ	ⓓ	33.	ⓐ	ⓑ	ⓒ	ⓓ
10.	ⓐ	ⓑ	ⓒ	ⓓ	22.	ⓐ	ⓑ	ⓒ	ⓓ	34.	ⓐ	ⓑ	ⓒ	ⓓ
11.	ⓐ	ⓑ	ⓒ	ⓓ	23.	ⓐ	ⓑ	ⓒ	ⓓ	35.	ⓐ	ⓑ	ⓒ	ⓓ
12.	ⓐ	ⓑ	ⓒ	ⓓ	24.	ⓐ	ⓑ	ⓒ	ⓓ					

Part 4: Paragraph Comprehension

	a	b	c	d		a	b	c	d		a	b	c	d
1.	ⓐ	ⓑ	ⓒ	ⓓ	6.	ⓐ	ⓑ	ⓒ	ⓓ	11.	ⓐ	ⓑ	ⓒ	ⓓ
2.	ⓐ	ⓑ	ⓒ	ⓓ	7.	ⓐ	ⓑ	ⓒ	ⓓ	12.	ⓐ	ⓑ	ⓒ	ⓓ
3.	ⓐ	ⓑ	ⓒ	ⓓ	8.	ⓐ	ⓑ	ⓒ	ⓓ	13.	ⓐ	ⓑ	ⓒ	ⓓ
4.	ⓐ	ⓑ	ⓒ	ⓓ	9.	ⓐ	ⓑ	ⓒ	ⓓ	14.	ⓐ	ⓑ	ⓒ	ⓓ
5.	ⓐ	ⓑ	ⓒ	ⓓ	10.	ⓐ	ⓑ	ⓒ	ⓓ	15.	ⓐ	ⓑ	ⓒ	ⓓ

Part 5: Mathematics Knowledge

1. a b c d
2. a b c d
3. a b c d
4. a b c d
5. a b c d
6. a b c d
7. a b c d
8. a b c d
9. a b c d
10. a b c d
11. a b c d
12. a b c d
13. a b c d
14. a b c d
15. a b c d
16. a b c d
17. a b c d
18. a b c d
19. a b c d
20. a b c d
21. a b c d
22. a b c d
23. a b c d
24. a b c d
25. a b c d

Part 6: Electronics Information

1. a b c d
2. a b c d
3. a b c d
4. a b c d
5. a b c d
6. a b c d
7. a b c d
8. a b c d
9. a b c d
10. a b c d
11. a b c d
12. a b c d
13. a b c d
14. a b c d
15. a b c d
16. a b c d
17. a b c d
18. a b c d
19. a b c d
20. a b c d

Part 7: Auto and Shop Information

1. a b c d
2. a b c d
3. a b c d
4. a b c d
5. a b c d
6. a b c d
7. a b c d
8. a b c d
9. a b c d
10. a b c d
11. a b c d
12. a b c d
13. a b c d
14. a b c d
15. a b c d
16. a b c d
17. a b c d
18. a b c d
19. a b c d
20. a b c d
21. a b c d
22. a b c d
23. a b c d
24. a b c d
25. a b c d

Part 8: Mechanical Comprehension

1. a b c d
2. a b c d
3. a b c d
4. a b c d
5. a b c d
6. a b c d
7. a b c d
8. a b c d
9. a b c d
10. a b c d
11. a b c d
12. a b c d
13. a b c d
14. a b c d
15. a b c d
16. a b c d
17. a b c d
18. a b c d
19. a b c d
20. a b c d
21. a b c d
22. a b c d
23. a b c d
24. a b c d
25. a b c d

Part 9: Assembling Objects

1.	ⓐ	ⓑ	ⓒ	ⓓ
2.	ⓐ	ⓑ	ⓒ	ⓓ
3.	ⓐ	ⓑ	ⓒ	ⓓ
4.	ⓐ	ⓑ	ⓒ	ⓓ
5.	ⓐ	ⓑ	ⓒ	ⓓ
6.	ⓐ	ⓑ	ⓒ	ⓓ

7.	ⓐ	ⓑ	ⓒ	ⓓ
8.	ⓐ	ⓑ	ⓒ	ⓓ
9.	ⓐ	ⓑ	ⓒ	ⓓ
10.	ⓐ	ⓑ	ⓒ	ⓓ
11.	ⓐ	ⓑ	ⓒ	ⓓ
12.	ⓐ	ⓑ	ⓒ	ⓓ

13.	ⓐ	ⓑ	ⓒ	ⓓ
14.	ⓐ	ⓑ	ⓒ	ⓓ
15.	ⓐ	ⓑ	ⓒ	ⓓ
16.	ⓐ	ⓑ	ⓒ	ⓓ

Part 1: General Science

Time: 11 minutes

1. Jonas Salk was responsible for what aspect of the polio virus?
   a. creating the chemical composition
   b. virus identification
   c. antibody elimination
   d. vaccine

2. What is a solution called when it can dissolve no more solutes?
   a. unsaturated
   b. supersaturated
   c. saturated
   d. volatile

3. Which of the following is NOT true of the Sun?
   a. The Sun is almost 110 times the diameter of Earth.
   b. Most of the mass of our solar system can be attributed to the Sun.
   c. The Sun is a typical star that is predicted to shine for approximately nine billion years.
   d. The solid surface of the Sun has a temperature of approximately 15,000,000 K.

4. Gregor Mendel's work with pea plants led to advancements in which field of science?
   a. anatomy
   b. genetics
   c. agriculture
   d. astronomy

5. What is the total number of atoms present in the molecule CH_3NH_2?
   a. 4
   b. 5
   c. 6
   d. 7

6. Which of the following plants lacks a vascular system?
   a. moss
   b. fern
   c. fir tree
   d. peanut plant

7. Saturn's rings are made up of what type of matter?
   a. chemical compounds
   b. gaseous material
   c. small bits of ice and rock
   d. water and acid

8. It is harder to stop a car moving at 60 miles per hour than a car moving at 15 miles per hour because the car moving at 60 miles per hour has more
   a. momentum.
   b. deceleration.
   c. mass.
   d. velocity.

9. The force that opposes the motion of an object is called
   a. gravity.
   b. momentum.
   c. inertia.
   d. friction.

10. The shoulder and hip joints are what types of joints?
    a. hinge joints
    b. pivot joints
    c. ball and socket joints
    d. levered joints

11. In a food chain, which of the following are the Producers?
   a. green plants
   b. bits of dead organic matter
   c. plant-eating animals
   d. meat-eating animals

12. What is the primary purpose of anticoagulants?
   a. to cause amnesia
   b. to paralyze the muscles
   c. to prevent the blood from clotting
   d. to prevent the heart from stopping

13. Which of the following are the blood vessels that carry blood toward the heart?
   a. arteries
   b. veins
   c. capillaries
   d. arterioles

14. When the Moon's orbit carries it across the face of the Sun, and its shadow is cast upon the Earth, this is known as a
   a. lunar eclipse
   b. solar flare
   c. solar eclipse
   d. lunar penumbra

15. Which of the following is the lowest level of Earth's atmosphere?
   a. the stratosphere
   b. the troposphere
   c. the ionsphere
   d. the exosphere

16. What is the latitude of any point on Earth's equator?
   a. 0 degrees
   b. 90 degrees
   c. 180 degrees
   d. 360 degrees

17. The conversion of a vapor to a liquid is called
   a. melting.
   b. condensation.
   c. evaporation.
   d. freezing.

18. What does a barometer measure?
   a. humidity
   b. wind speed
   c. air pressure
   d. temperature

19. The movement of water from a region of high concentration to an area of lower concentration is called
   a. osmosis.
   b. photosynthesis.
   c. respiration.
   d. diffusion.

20. What substance forms the skeletal system of sharks and reduces friction in human joints?
   a. scales
   b. collagen
   c. bone marrow
   d. cartilage

21. Where are the majority of nutrients absorbed in the human digestive system?
   a. in the large intestine
   b. in the mouth
   c. in the small intestine
   d. in the stomach

22. An elevator uses which of the following simple machines?
   a. a pulley
   b. a lever
   c. a wheel and axle
   d. an inclined plane

23. The product of an object's mass and its speed is equal to its
   a. distance.
   b. work.
   c. momentum.
   d. power.

24. What is the process called when a light bulb heats up a lamp shade?
   a. insulation
   b. radiation
   c. convection
   d. conduction

25. Rickets in children, characterized by weak and deformed bones, may be attributed to a deficiency of which vitamin?
   a. A
   b. B
   c. C
   d. D

Part 2: Arithmetic Reasoning

Time: 36 minutes

1. What is the estimated product when 157 and 817 are rounded to the nearest hundred and multiplied?
   a. 160,000
   b. 180,000
   c. 16,000
   d. 80,000

2. A large coffee pot holds 120 cups. It is about two-thirds full. About how many cups are in the pot?
   a. 40 cups
   b. 80 cups
   c. 60 cups
   d. 90 cups

3. If a person's resting heartbeat is 68 beats per minute and she is at rest for eight hours, how many times will her heart beat during that time period?
   a. 4,240
   b. 32,400
   c. 4,080
   d. 32,640

This is a list of ingredients needed to make 16 brownies. Use this list to answer questions 4 and 5.

Deluxe Brownies

$\frac{2}{3}$ cup butter

5 squares (1 ounce each) unsweetened chocolate

$1\frac{1}{2}$ cups sugar

2 teaspoons vanilla

2 eggs

1 cup flour

4. How much sugar is needed to make 8 brownies?
   a. $\frac{3}{4}$ cup
   b. 3 cups
   c. $\frac{2}{3}$ cup
   d. $\frac{5}{8}$ cup

5. What is the greatest number of brownies that can be made if the baker has only 1 cup of butter?
   a. 12
   b. 16
   c. 24
   d. 32

6. One lap on an outdoor track measures a quarter of a mile around. To run a total of three and a half miles, how many laps must a person complete?
   a. 7
   b. 10
   c. 13
   d. 14

7. The state of Connecticut will pay two-fifths of the cost of a new school building. If the city of New Haven is building a school that will cost a total of $15,500,000, what will the state pay?
   a. $3,100,000
   b. $7,750,000
   c. $6,200,000
   d. $4,550,000

8. Body mass index (BMI) is equal to weight in kilograms/(height in meters)^2. A man who weighs 64.8 kilograms has a BMI of 20. How tall is he?
   a. 1.8 meters
   b. 0.9 meters
   c. 2.16 meters
   d. 3.24 meters

9. During exercise, a person's heart rate should be between sixty and ninety percent of the difference between 220 and the person's age. According to this guideline, if a person's minimum heart rate during exercise is approximately 102, what is his age?
   a. 40
   b. 45
   c. 50
   d. 55

10. Newly hired nurses have to buy duty shoes at the full price of $84.50, but nurses who have served at least a year get a 15 percent discount. Nurses who have served at least three years get an additional 10 percent off the discounted price. How much does a nurse who has served at least three years have to pay for shoes?
   a. $63.78
   b. $64.65
   c. $71.83
   d. $72.05

11. There are 176 men and 24 women serving in a particular battalion. What percentage of the battalion's force is women?
   a. 12%
   b. 14%
   c. 16%
   d. 24%

12. The basal metabolic rate (BMR) is the rate at which our body uses calories. The BMR for a man in his twenties is about 1,700 calories per day. If 204 of those calories should come from protein, about what percent of this man's diet should be protein?
   a. 1.2%
   b. 8.3%
   c. 12%
   d. 16%

13. Bob, Bill, Susan, and Tom have each been collecting quarters and putting them in containers that are the same size. Bob's container is $\frac{5}{8}$ full, Bill's container is $\frac{2}{3}$ full, Susan's container is $\frac{3}{4}$ full, and Tom's container is $\frac{2}{5}$ full. Whose container has the most quarters?
   a. Bob
   b. Bill
   c. Susan
   d. Tom

14. If a population of yeast cells grows from 10 to 320 in a period of 5 hours, what is the rate of growth?
   a. It doubles its numbers every hour.
   b. It triples its numbers every hour.
   c. It doubles its numbers every two hours.
   d. It triples its numbers every two hours.

15. A study shows that 750,000 women die each year during childbirth. This is $\frac{1}{4}$ less than what was predicted by doctors. What number did the doctors predict?
   a. 1,000,000
   b. 900,000
   c. 1,200,000
   d. 950,000

16. In the first week of his exercise program, John went on a 15-mile hike. The next week, he increased the length of his hike by 20%. How long was his hike in the second week?
   a. 17 miles
   b. 18 miles
   c. 30 miles
   d. 35 miles

17. All of the rooms in a building are rectangular, with 8-foot ceilings. One room is 9 feet wide by 11 feet long. What is the combined area of the four walls, including doors and windows?
   a. 99 square feet
   b. 160 square feet
   c. 320 square feet
   d. 72 square feet

18. What is the volume of a pyramid that has a rectangular base of 10 inches by 12 inches and a height of 10 inches? ($V = \frac{1}{3} lwh$)
   a. 40 cubic inches
   b. 320 cubic inches
   c. 400 cubic inches
   d. 1,200 cubic inches

19. A child has a temperature of 40 degrees C. What is the child's temperature in degrees Fahrenheit? ($F = \frac{9}{5} C + 32$)
   a. 101 degrees F
   b. 102 degrees F
   c. 103 degrees F
   d. 104 degrees F

20. If jogging for one mile uses 150 calories and brisk walking for one mile uses 100 calories, a jogger has to go how many times as far as a walker to use the same number of calories?
   a. $\frac{1}{2}$
   b. $\frac{2}{3}$
   c. $\frac{3}{2}$
   d. 2

21. A dosage of a certain medication is 12 cc per 100 pounds. What is the dosage for a patient who weighs 175 pounds?
   a. 15 cc
   b. 18 cc
   c. 21 cc
   d. 24 cc

22. During the first week of training, a recruit achieved the following task completion times (in seconds): 53, 68, 56, 49, 59, 55, and 60. Remove the best time and the worst time, and then calculate the recruit's average task completion time for the week.
   a. 57.6 seconds
   b. 56.6 seconds
   c. 55.6 seconds
   d. 58.6 seconds

23. A woman drives west at 45 miles per hour. After half an hour, her husband starts to follow her. How fast must he drive to catch up to her three hours after he starts?
   a. 52.5 miles per hour
   b. 55 miles per hour
   c. 60 miles per hour
   d. 67.5 miles per hour

24. A family's gas and electricity bill averages $80 a month for seven months of the year and $20 a month the rest of the year. If the family's bills were averaged over the entire year, what would the monthly bill be?
   a. $45
   b. $50
   c. $55
   d. $60

25. Jason is six times as old as Kate. In two years, Jason will be twice as old as Kate is then. How old is Jason now?
   a. 3 years old
   b. 6 years old
   c. 9 years old
   d. 12 years old

26. During her first three months at college, a student's long distance phone bills are $103.30, $71.60, and $84.00. Her local phone bill is $18.00 each month. What is her average total monthly phone bill?
   a. $86.30
   b. $92.30
   c. $98.30
   d. $104.30

27. A car uses 16 gallons of gas to travel 448 miles. How many miles per gallon does the car get?
   a. 22 miles per gallon
   b. 24 miles per gallon
   c. 26 miles per gallon
   d. 28 miles per gallon

28. Land in development is selling for $60,000 per acre. If Jack purchases $1\frac{3}{4}$ acres, how much will he pay?
   a. $45,000
   b. $135,000
   c. $105,000
   d. $120,000

29. For every dollar Kyra saves, her employer contributes a dime to her savings, with a maximum employer contribution of $10 per month. If Kyra saves $60 in January, $130 in March, and $70 in April, how much will she have in savings at the end of that time?
   a. $270
   b. $283
   c. $286
   d. $290

30. To lower a fever of 107 degrees, ice packs are applied for 3 minutes and then removed for 15 minutes before being applied again. If each application of the ice pack lowers the fever by $\frac{3}{4}$ of a degree, how long will it take to drop the fever to 98 degrees?
   a. 3 hours
   b. 3 hours and 24 minutes
   c. 3 hours and 36 minutes
   d. 3 hours and 45 minutes

Part 3: Word Knowledge

Time: 11 minutes

1. According to the code of conduct, "Every officer will be <u>accountable</u> for his or her decisions."
   a. applauded
   b. compensated
   c. responsible
   d. approached

2. <u>Scrutinize</u> most nearly means
   a. vanish.
   b. examine.
   c. neglect.
   d. weak.

3. Enumerate most nearly means
   a. pronounce.
   b. count.
   c. explain.
   d. plead.

4. Emulate most nearly means
   a. imitate.
   b. authorize.
   c. fascinate.
   d. punish.

5. The residents of that area were considered to be compliant in regard to the seat belt law.
   a. skeptical
   b. obedient
   c. forgetful
   d. appreciative

6. Following the disturbance, town officials felt the need to augment the laws pertaining to mass demonstrations.
   a. repeal
   b. evaluate
   c. supplement
   d. criticize

7. Aversion most nearly means
   a. harmony.
   b. greed.
   c. weariness.
   d. dislike.

8. Validate most nearly means
   a. confirm.
   b. retrieve.
   c. communicate.
   d. appoint.

9. Antagonist most nearly means
   a. comrade.
   b. opponent.
   c. master.
   d. perfectionist.

10. Perseverance most nearly means
    a. unhappiness.
    b. fame.
    c. persistence.
    d. humility.

11. As soon as the details of the affair were released to the media, the newspaper was inundated with calls from a curious public.
    a. provided
    b. bothered
    c. rewarded
    d. flooded

12. Homogeneous most nearly means
    a. alike.
    b. plain.
    c. native.
    d. dissimilar.

13. Ominous most nearly means
    a. ordinary.
    b. gracious.
    c. quarrelsome.
    d. threatening.

14 When people heard that timid Bob had taken up sky-diving, they were incredulous.
    a. fearful
    b. outraged
    c. disbelieving
    d. inconsolable

15. Recluse most nearly means
a. prophet.
b. fool.
c. intellectual.
d. hermit.

16. The company recruited her because she was proficient in the use of computers.
a. experienced
b. unequaled
c. efficient
d. skilled

17. Defray most nearly means
a. pay.
b. defend.
c. cheat.
d. disobey.

18. Placid most nearly means
a. flabby.
b. peaceful.
c. wise.
d. obedient.

19. The City Council has given tentative approval to the idea of banning smoking from all public buildings.
a. provisional
b. ambiguous
c. wholehearted
d. unnecessary

20. Vast most nearly means
a. attentive.
b. immense.
c. steady.
d. slight.

21. Contemptuous most nearly means
a. respectful.
b. unique.
c. scornful.
d. insecure.

22. Regarding the need for more free coffee and doughnuts, the group's opinion was unanimous.
a. divided
b. uniform
c. adamant
d. clear-cut

23. Distinct most nearly means
a. satisfied.
b. frenzied.
c. recognizable.
d. uneasy.

24. Various methods to alleviate the situation were debated.
a. ease
b. tolerate
c. clarify
d. intensify

25. Enlighten most nearly means
a. relocate.
b. confuse.
c. comply.
d. teach.

26. Ostracize most nearly means
a. shun.
b. accept.
c. neglect.
d. befriend.

27. Everyone wanted to know how George paid for his opulent home.
   a. ugly
   b. destitute
   c. expensive
   d. impoverished

28. Clemency most nearly means
   a. provided.
   b. leniency.
   c. rewarded.
   d. flooded.

29. Defer most nearly means
   a. hasten.
   b. hurry.
   c. deny.
   d. delay.

30. Eschew most nearly means
   a. abandon.
   b. like.
   c. favor.
   d. indulge.

31. Impetuous most nearly means
   a. timed.
   b. impulsive.
   c. planned.
   d. slow.

32. Tom knew the charade was over.
   a. event
   b. statement
   c. demonstration
   d. fake

33. Alacrity most nearly means
   a. sadness.
   b. eagerness.
   c. bitterness.
   d. loneliness.

34. Consternation most nearly means
   a. dismay.
   b. constellation.
   c. reservation.
   d. disbelief.

35. Forbearance most nearly means
   a. poverty.
   b. strength.
   c. patience.
   d. ancestry.

Part 4: Paragraph Comprehension

Time: 13 minutes

The supervisors have received numerous complaints over the last several weeks about buses on several routes running hot. Drivers are reminded that each route has several check points at which drivers should check the time. If the bus is ahead of schedule, drivers should delay at the check point until it is the proper time to leave.

1. In the passage, saying a bus is "running hot" means
   a. the engine is over-heating.
   b. the bus is running ahead of schedule.
   c. the air conditioning is not working.
   d. there is no more room for passengers.

2. According to the passage
  a. every bus stop is also a check point.
  b. it is important to keep customer complaints to a minimum.
  c. drivers tend to rush their routes so they can leave work early.
  d. each bus route has several points at which drivers should check the time.

Beekeeping requires a great deal of work. In the spring, you will be busy getting your colony off to a good start for the season—feeding the bees, adding room or a new queen if needed, starting new colonies from splits, packages, or nucs, taking care of any health issues, and getting your colony up to speed and ready for the summer. During the summer, the work slows down as the colony maintains itself and harvests honey. As late summer or autumn arrives, you need to gather the rest of the honey from your bees, check again for health issues, and prepare the colony for winter. Like gardens, hives need attention after the frosts come—to remove damaged sections or parts that are no longer part of the producing hive, for example.

3. In this passage, the word <u>nucs</u> most likely means
  a. cleaning out the beehive.
  b. closing down the bee hive.
  c. a new colony of bees.
  d. creating additional space in an existing hive.

4. According to the passage, how much work on the beehive should you expect to be doing during the summer months?
  a. little work, as the colony maintains itself
  b. extensive work, to removing damaged sections or parts no longer producing
  c. extensive work on feeding the bees, adding additional room and starting new colonies
  d. no work as it is a hands-off time of year

Hazardous waste is defined as any waste designated by the United States Environmental Protection Agency as hazardous. If a worker is unclear whether a particular item is hazardous, he or she should not handle the item but should instead notify the supervisor and ask for directions.

5. Hazardous waste is
  a. anything too dangerous for workers to handle.
  b. picked up by special trucks.
  c. defined by the United States Environmental Protection Agency.
  d. not allowed with regular residential garbage.

6. A sanitation worker comes upon a container of cleaning solvent along with the regular garbage in front of a residence. The container does not list the contents of the cleaner. He should
  a. assume the solvent is safe and deposit it in the sanitation truck.
  b. leave a note for the residents, asking them to list the contents.
  c. contact the supervisor for directions.
  d. leave the container on the curb.

Why milk a cow instead of a goat? Cows are big and clumsy, and don't they eat a lot? To be quite honest, both cows and goats each have their own distinct advantages and disadvantages. Goats are small, docile, and smart, and they are famous for their ability to escape from most fenced in areas. On the other hand, milk cows are big and docile, and they can usually be kept in a pasture by as little as a few strands of wire, as long as their nutritional needs are met.

Goats produce about a gallon of milk each day, which is often enough for the average family's needs. A milk cow will often produce eight to ten gallons each day. This is often more than adequate for a family's milk supply, as well as an extra amount for cream, butter, yogurt, and cheese—and there may still be enough left over to raise a calf for beef.

Although both the initial and subsequent costs of upkeep for a cow are much higher than for a goat, the returns per annum and final resale value of a cow are much higher.

7. For a small family farm, which animal (goat or cow) do you think the passage is recommending?
   a. goat
   b. cow
   c. there is no difference
   d. neither

8. Which of the following would be the best title for this passage?
   a. How to Manage Your Livestock
   b. Goats or Cows? Pros and Cons for Family Farmers
   c. Milk Products for Your Family
   d. Cost and Upkeep for Your Family Cow

One easy way to plan healthy menus is to shop only in the outer aisles of the grocery store. In most supermarkets, fresh fruit and vegetables, dairy, fresh meat, and frozen foods are in the outer aisles. Grains, like pasta, rice, bread, and cereal, are located on the next aisles, the first inner rows. The inside aisles are where you'll find chips and snacks, cookies and pastries, soda pop and drink mixes—foods that nutritionists say one should eat rarely, if at all. A side benefit of shopping this way is that grocery shopping takes less time.

9. A good title for this article would be
   a. "Why You Should Shop in a Health Food Store"
   b. "How to Complete Your Grocery Shopping in Less Time"
   c. "How to Shop for Healthy Food"
   d. "How to Cook Healthy Food"

10. According to the passage, the best way to shop in the grocery store is to
    a. make a list and stick to it.
    b. stay in the outside aisles.
    c. look for the best prices.
    d. check the newspaper ads each week.

Law enforcement officers often do not like taking time from their regular duties to testify in court, but testimony is an important part of an officer's job. To be good witnesses, officers should keep complete notes detailing any potentially criminal incidents. When on the witness stand, officers may refer to these notes to refresh their memory about particular events. It is also very important for officers to listen carefully to the questions asked by the lawyers and to provide only the information requested.

11. According to the passage, an officer who is testifying in court
    a. will be questioned by the judge.
    b. may refer to his or her notes while on the witness stand.
    c. must do so without pay.
    d. appreciates taking a break from routine assignments.

12. This passage is probably taken from a(n)
    a. memo entitled "Proper Arrest Procedure."
    b. newspaper article.
    c. best-selling novel.
    d. officers' training manual.

13. According to the passage, testifying in court is
    a. an important part of a police officer's job.
    b. difficult, because lawyers try to trick witnesses.
    c. less stressful for police officers than for other witnesses.
    d. a waste of time, because judges usually let criminals off.

In the summer, the northern hemisphere is slanted toward the Sun, making the days longer and warmer than in winter. The first day of summer is called summer solstice and is also the longest day of the year. However, June 21 marks the beginning of winter in the southern hemisphere, when that hemisphere is tilted away from the Sun.

14. According to the passage, when it is summer in the northern hemisphere, in the southern hemisphere it is
  a. spring.
  b. summer.
  c. autumn.
  d. winter.

15. It can be inferred from the passage that, in the southern hemisphere, June 21 is the
  a. autumnal equinox.
  b. winter solstice.
  c. vernal equinox.
  d. summer solstice.

Part 5: Mathematics Knowledge

Time: 24 minutes

1. Which pair of lines is parallel?

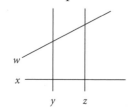

  a. w and x
  b. x and y
  c. x and z
  d. y and z

2. Choose the answer to the following problem:
$3\frac{2}{3} + 6\frac{5}{8} =$
  a. $10\frac{7}{11}$
  b. $9\frac{7}{24}$
  c. $10\frac{7}{24}$
  d. $9\frac{7}{11}$

3. $\frac{4}{5}$ is equal to
  a. 0.80
  b. 0.50
  c. 0.90
  d. 0.45

4. Choose the answer to the following problem:
$x(3x^2 + y) =$
  a. $4x^2 + xy$
  b. $4x^2 + x + y$
  c. $3x^3 + 2xy$
  d. $3x^3 + xy$

5. 35 percent of what number is equal to 14?
  a. 4
  b. 40
  c. 49
  d. 400

6. $\frac{1}{4}$ is equal to
  a. 0.15
  b. 0.25
  c. 0.20
  d. 0.75

7. If $6x + 30 = 90$, then x is
  a. 5
  b. 10
  c. 60
  d. 20

8. What is the reciprocal of $3\frac{7}{8}$?

   a. $\frac{31}{8}$

   b. $\frac{8}{31}$

   c. $\frac{8}{21}$

   d. $-\frac{31}{8}$

9. $3\frac{3}{10}$ is equal to

   a. 3.10

   b. 0.30

   c. 2.30

   d. 3.30

10. Which of these angle measures forms a right triangle?

   a. 45 degrees, 50 degrees, 85 degrees

   b. 40 degrees, 40 degrees, 100 degrees

   c. 40 degrees, 50 degrees, 90 degrees

   d. 20 degrees, 30 degrees, 130 degrees

11. What is another way to write $3\sqrt{12}$?

   a. $12\sqrt{3}$

   b. $6\sqrt{3}$

   c. $2\sqrt{10}$

   d. 18

12. Which is another way to write $\frac{4}{25}$?

   a. 4%

   b. 16%

   c. 40%

   d. 100%

13. Which of the following is equivalent to 2^5?

   a. 12

   b. 32

   c. 24

   d. 8

14. What is the decimal form of $-1\frac{1}{3}$ rounded to the nearest hundredth?

   a. 1.33

   b. −1.33

   c. 3.67

   d. −3.67

15. $1\frac{3}{4} =$

   a. 1.75

   b. 0.75

   c. 1.34

   d. 1.25

16. Triangles *RST* and *MNO* are similar. What is the length of line segment *MO*?

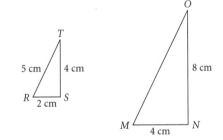

   a. 10 cm

   b. 20 cm

   c. 32 cm

   d. 40 cm

17. Which of the following number sentences is true?

   a. 5.2 > 0.52

   b. 0.52 < 0.052

   c. 0.052 < 0.0052

   d. 0.0052 > 0.52

18. 0.40 =

   a. $\frac{1}{4}$

   b. $\frac{1}{5}$

   c. $\frac{2}{5}$

   d. $\frac{3}{4}$

19. Which of these has a 9 in the thousandths place?

   a. 3.0095

   b. 3.0905

   c. 3.9005

   d. 3.0059

20. $0.75 =$

   a. $\frac{1}{4}$

   b. $\frac{1}{5}$

   c. $\frac{2}{7}$

   d. $\frac{3}{4}$

21. Which of the following is the same as $3x - 8 = 16$?

   a. 3 less than 8 times a number is 16

   b. 8 less than 3 times a number is 16

   c. 8 more than 3 times a number is 16

   d. 11 times a number is 16

22. Lines a, b, and c intersect at point O. Which of these are NOT adjacent angles?

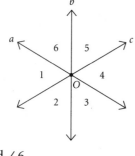

   a. $\angle 1$ and $\angle 6$

   b. $\angle 1$ and $\angle 4$

   c. $\angle 4$ and $\angle 5$

   d. $\angle 2$ and $\angle 3$

23. $2.25 =$

   a. $2\frac{1}{4}$

   b. $2\frac{1}{5}$

   c. $\frac{2}{5}$

   d. $1\frac{3}{4}$

24. Choose the answer to the following equation.

   $(16 \times 4) + 10 =$

   a. 30

   b. 74

   c. 104

   d. 100

25. One side of a square handkerchief is 8 inches long. What is the perimeter of the handkerchief?

   a. 16 inches

   b. 24 inches

   c. 32 inches

   d. 64 inches

Part 6: Electronics Information

Time: 9 minutes

1. A machine has two wires carrying electrical current into it. One of the wires is 6 mm thick and the other is 3 mm thick. What would the relationship be between the two wires if they carried the same current?

   a. the larger wire would need more voltage

   b. the larger wire would need less voltage

   c. they would require the same voltage

   d. none of the above

2. An ammeter reads 287 microamps. Which of the following is equivalent to the meter reading?

   a. 0.00287 A

   b. 0.287 A

   c. 0.0287 A

   d. 0.000287 A

3. A wire stripper is used to
   a. cut a wire.
   b. remove the insulation from a wire.
   c. join two wires together.
   d. add insulation to a wire so that it won't short out.

4. The two most commonly used metals in solder are
   a. gold and lead.
   b. tin and nickel.
   c. gold and silver.
   d. tin and lead.

5. Why shouldn't acid flux be used when soldering electronic components?
   a. It will make the solder joint brittle.
   b. It will corrode the solder joint.
   c. It will soften the solder joint.
   d. It does not flow well.

6. Printed circuit boards are typically made out of
   a. fiberglass.
   b. laminated paper.
   c. glass.
   d. copper.

7. An ideal fuse has what resistance when it is operating normally?
   a. zero Ω
   b. 0.01 Ω
   c. 0.1 Ω
   d. 1.0 Ω

8. A microwave has a rating of 1200 watts. If you have a 120-volt source, how much current is needed?
   a. 1,400 amps
   b. 1 amp
   c. 10 amps
   d. 100 amps

9. Two different wattage light bulbs are connected in series to a voltage source. The first bulb is a 60-watt bulb. The second bulb is a 40-watt bulb. What is the total power the voltage source must supply?
   a. 40 watts
   b. 60 watts
   c. 100 watts
   d. 120 watts

10. An oscilloscope is typically used to analyze
   a. simple circuits.
   b. resistance.
   c. power in a circuit.
   d. complex waveforms.

11. In series circuit A a 10 Ω load dissipates 1 watt. In series circuit B a 10 Ω load dissipates 2 watts. What can be said about the current through the load in circuit A if the voltages in both circuits are equal?
   a. the current through load A is equal to the current through load B
   b. the current through load A is twice the current through load B
   c. the current through load A is half the current through load B
   d. the current through load A is zero

12. Which electronic component can store charge?
   a. a resistor
   b. a capacitor
   c. a transistor
   d. a transformer

13. Silver is a better conductor than copper, but copper is used more often because of
   a. the relative strength of copper.
   b. the relative melting point of copper.
   c. the relative lack of tarnish on copper.
   d. the relative cost of copper.

14. A current meter is connected to a circuit as shown. What does the current meter read?

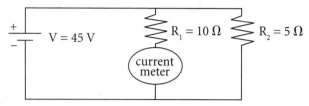

a. 3.0 amperes

b. 4.5 amperes

c. 13.5 amperes

d. 15 amperes

15. The letters AC stand for

a. ampere coil.

b. ampere charge.

c. alternating current.

d. alternating charge.

16. Two 8-ohm speakers are connected in parallel to an amplifier with a 24-volt output. What is the voltage across each speaker?

a. 3 volts

b. 6 volts

c. 12 volts

d. 24 volts

17. Which of the following is NOT a type of switch?

a. single pole-single throw

b. rotary

c. double pole-double throw

d. linear

18. Electrons have a _____ charge while protons have a _____ charge.

a. neutral, positive

b. negative, neutral

c. positive, negative

d. negative, positive

19. Low potential to electricians most closely means

a. 600 watts or lower.

b. circuits that have low chance of overload.

c. a low risk of fire.

d. a low cost of wiring.

20. What is the frequency of the alternating voltage and current typically used in the United States?

a. 20 Hz

b. 40 Hz

c. 60 Hz

d. 110 Hz

Part 7: Auto and Shop Information

Time: 11 minutes

1. Engine overheating can be caused by which of the following?

a. a low fuel level

b. too much motor oil

c. a faulty transmission

d. a faulty thermostat

2. Which of the following automotive systems uses shoes?

a. the transmission system

b. the brake system

c. the suspension system

d. the drive system

3. Which automotive system uses fuses and an alternator?

a. the steering system

b. the cooling system

c. the electrical system

d. the engine

4. What is the function of the spark plugs in the internal combustion engine in a car?
   a. to transfer electricity to the alternator
   b. to increase the cylinder size
   c. to cool the engine
   d. to ignite the fuel

5. Which fluid is contained in a car radiator?
   a. transmission fluid
   b. cooling fluid
   c. brake fluid
   d. steering fluid

6. What is the primary function of the water pump in a car?
   a. to circulate coolant
   b. to evacuate waste water
   c. to remove exhaust
   d. to filter water

7. When is a split lock washer used?
   a. to keep a screw from backing out
   b. to prevent a screw from digging into the surface
   c. to keep screws from skipping
   d. it has no practical use

8. Concrete is typically used in conjunction with which of the following building materials in order to provide a stronger product?
   a. bronze reinforcement
   b. aluminum reinforcement
   c. steel reinforcement
   d. plastic reinforcement

9. Concrete is made up of which of the following components?
   a. cement, water, and steel
   b. gravel and sand
   c. gravel, water, and glass
   d. cement, sand, gravel, and water

10. Which material may be used as the outer material on a roof in order to keep out rain?
    a. tile
    b. wood
    c. asphalt
    d. all of the above

11. The most secure bond between two pieces of wood occurs by joining them with which of the following materials?
    a. nails
    b. white glue
    c. screws
    d. none of the above

12. How often should the oil in a car engine be changed?
    a. after every 300 miles of driving
    b. after every 3,000 miles of driving
    c. after every 30,000 miles of driving
    d. after every 300,000 miles of driving

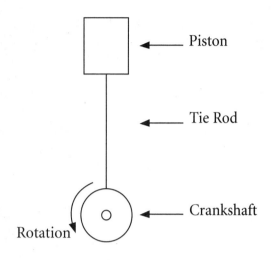

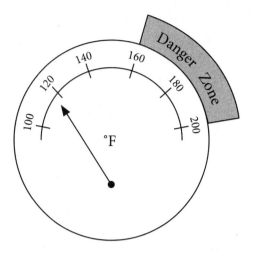

13. The figure above shows a piston that is connected to a crankshaft by a tie rod. The crankshaft has a radius of 1.0 inch. If the crankshaft rotates 180 degrees (one half of a revolution), how far downward will the piston be pulled?
- **a.** 0.5 inches
- **b.** 1.0 inch
- **c.** 1.33 inches
- **d.** 2.0 inches

14. Which system on an automobile uses shock absorbers?
- **a.** the suspension system
- **b.** the exhaust system
- **c.** the electrical system
- **d.** the braking system

15. Which automotive system uses universal joints, a drive shaft, and a clutch?
- **a.** the steering system
- **b.** the cooling system
- **c.** the transmission system
- **d.** the braking system

16. On the temperature gauge above, what is the maximum recommended operating temperature (degrees Fahrenheit) for this gauge in order to remain in a safe zone?
- **a.** 120
- **b.** 140
- **c.** 160
- **d.** 180

17. Of which automotive system does the driver have the most direct control while driving?
- **a.** the exhaust system
- **b.** the cooling system
- **c.** the suspension system
- **d.** the braking system

18. What system in a car should be flushed periodically to allow for optimal performance?
- **a.** the steering system
- **b.** the exhaust system
- **c.** the brake system
- **d.** the cooling system

19. Which of the following systems connects directly to the internal combustion engine in an automobile?
- **a.** the cooling system
- **b.** the suspension system
- **c.** the steering system
- **d.** the braking system

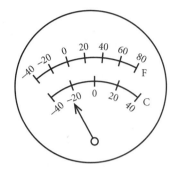

20. The gauge above is
   a. a pressure gauge.
   b. an altitude gauge.
   c. a temperature gauge.
   d. a flow meter gauge.

21. In the typical workshop, a plane is used for what purpose?
   a. welding metal
   b. curing concrete
   c. removing thin strips of wood
   d. loosening bolts

22. The turn signal on an automobile is connected to which of the following automotive systems?
   a. the braking system
   b. the transmission system
   c. the suspension system
   d. the electrical system

23. On which of the following types of material in a workshop would a shear, a brake, a form, and a punch be used?
   a. sheet metal
   b. wood
   c. plastic
   d. angle iron

24. When making a circular cut in a piece of metal, the best chisel to use is a
   a. butt chisel.
   b. round chisel.
   c. framing chisel.
   d. socket chisel.

25. What are scales, calipers, micrometers, and dial indicators all used to measure?
   a. weight
   b. time
   c. length
   d. surface roughness

Part 8: Mechanical Comprehension

Time: 19 minutes

1. A concrete beam has a maximum strength of 3,000 psi (pounds per square inch). In an experiment, a 500-pound weight is placed in the center of the beam, and the stress in the beam is measured to be 1,000 psi. If the stresses in the beam continue to increase at the same rate with added weight, how much additional weight can be added to the same location on the beam before the beam will break?
   a. 500 pounds
   b. 1,000 pounds
   c. 1,500 pounds
   d. 3,000 pounds

2. Two cars have the same weight and the same type of engine and travel at the same speed. One is a boxy minivan and the other a low, sleek sports car. Which factor below best explains why the sports car gets better gas mileage than the minivan?
   a. friction
   b. wind resistance
   c. acceleration
   d. all of the above

3. Which principle of mechanical motion is used in the design of a roller coaster?
   a. momentum
   b. friction
   c. acceleration
   d. all of the above

4. When a rope is stretched so it is taut, it is said to be in a state of
   a. elastic recall.
   b. buoyancy.
   c. tension.
   d. equilibrium.

5. A seesaw works best when both people weigh the same. This demonstrates which principle of mechanical motion?
   a. relative velocity
   b. centrifugal force
   c. acceleration
   d. equilibrium

6. A grandfather clock typically has a long pendulum that swings back and forth to keep time. Which description below best describes the action of this pendulum?
   a. periodic motion
   b. relative velocity
   c. free-falling body
   d. all of the above

7. Which term below best describes the OPPOSITE of "an increase in speed"?
   a. velocity
   b. friction
   c. deceleration
   d. rotation

8. The best and easiest device to use in order to pull a large weight up a hill would be a(n)
   a. block and tackle.
   b. electric winch.
   c. rope.
   d. pulley.

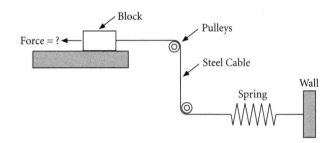

9. In the diagram above, the spring is very stiff and can be stretched 1 inch by a pulling force of 100 pounds. How much force must be applied to the block in order to move the box 3.5 inches to the left?
   a. 100 pounds
   b. 300 pounds
   c. 350 pounds
   d. 3.5 pounds

10. The simple mechanical device used to block the wheels of an airplane to keep it from rolling is best known as a
    a. wedge.
    b. piston.
    c. gear.
    d. pulley.

11. A pump is typically used to accomplish which of the following tasks?
    a. to move liquids downhill
    b. to separate liquids
    c. to clarify liquids
    d. to move liquids uphill

12. Which of the following is a type of lever?
   a. tongs
   b. vice
   c. screw
   d. pulley

13. A valve is used to perform which of the following functions?
   a. increase the temperature of a liquid
   b. control the flow of a liquid
   c. decrease the density of a liquid
   d. aid evaporation of a liquid

14. Which of the following best describes the location of the center of gravity of a steel bar that is four feet long and is the same diameter along its length?
   a. two feet from the left end of the bar
   b. three feet from the right end of the bar
   c. on the right end of the bar
   d. on the left end of the bar

15. Which of the following materials is the LEAST elastic?
   a. silly putty
   b. wax
   c. rubber
   d. paper

16. Block A is twice as big as Block B. Block B is made of a material that is three times as dense as the material in Block A. Which block is heavier?
   a. Block A
   b. Block B
   c. both blocks weigh the same amount
   d. not enough information

17. A block of steel has a density of 0.29 pounds per cubic inch. If the block has dimensions of 1 inch by 1 inch by 2 inches, what is its weight?
   a. 0.29 pounds
   b. 0.58 pounds
   c. 2.0 pounds
   d. 4.0 pounds

18. What is the structural principle behind the use of snowshoes?
   a. to spread the load out on the snow
   b. to increase the weight on the snow
   c. to slow down the person using them
   d. to prevent slippage in the snow

19. The aerodynamic forces that act on an aircraft as it flies are
   a. parasitic drag and augmented thrust.
   b. lift, parasitic drag, and gravity.
   c. lift, weight, thrust, and drag.
   d. atmospheric pressure, lift, and thrust.

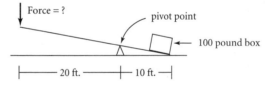

20. In the diagram above, Joe must lift a 100-pound box using a lever. How many pounds of force must Joe apply to the left side of the lever to lift the box? ($w \times d_1 = f \times d_2$)
   a. 100 pounds
   b. 200 pounds
   c. 50 pounds
   d. 33 pounds

21. Because they are nearly 100 percent incompressible, fluids would make an ideal
   a. surface sealant.
   b. hydraulic jack.
   c. engine lubricant.
   d. all the above.

22. Which mechanical device listed below is used to
control the flow of liquids and gases in a piping
system?
   a. a gear
   b. a valve
   c. a piston
   d. a spring

23. A solar panel, a wind mill, an atomic reactor, a
dam on a river, and a steam turbine are all examples of methods that could be used to create
which of the following?
   a. ice
   b. electricity
   c. steel
   d. rain

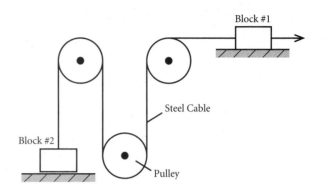

24. In the diagram above, if block #1 is moved
10 feet to the right, how far upward is block #2
lifted?
   a. 3 feet
   b. 5 feet
   c. 10 feet
   d. 20 feet

25. Which of the following groups of items listed
below consists entirely of fasteners—that is, of
devices that are used to connect two items
together?
   a. chairs, tables, and windows
   b. string, scissors, and glue
   c. rivets, levers, and bolts
   d. snaps, buckles, and buttons

Part 9: Assembling Objects

Time: 16 minutes

1.

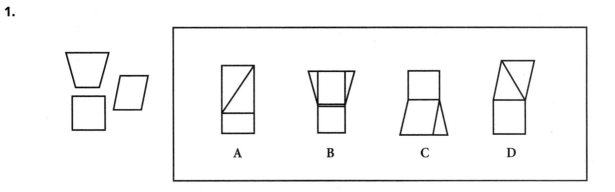

2.

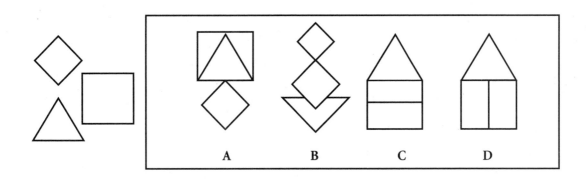

3.

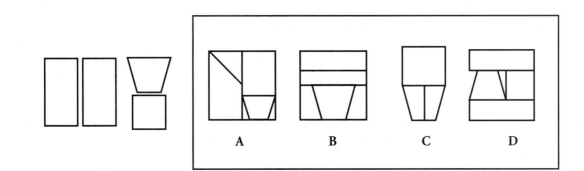

4.

 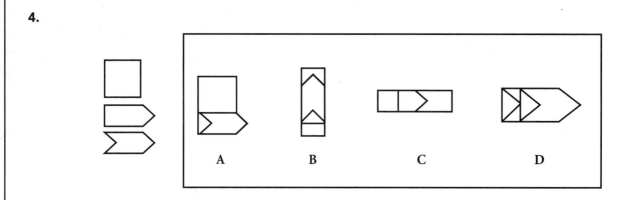

5.

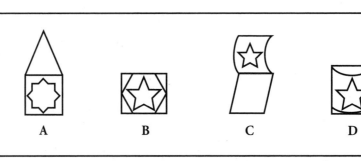

6.

 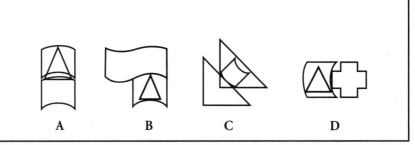

7.

 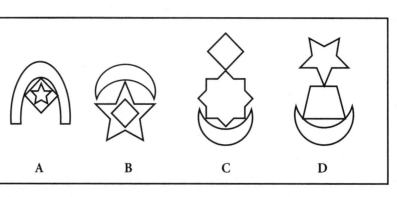

8.

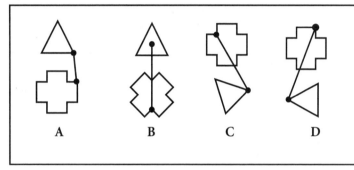

9.

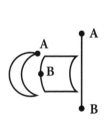

10.

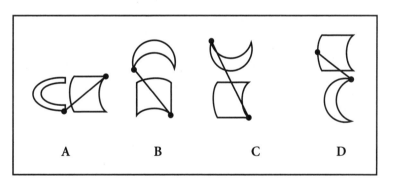

11.

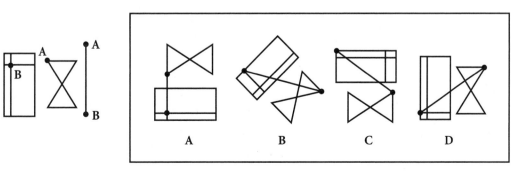

12.

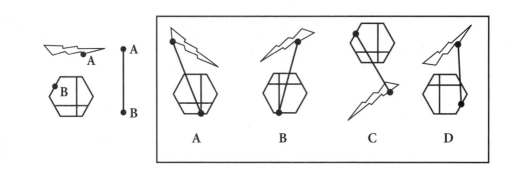

13.

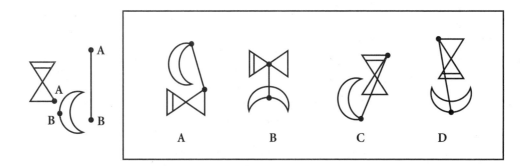

14.

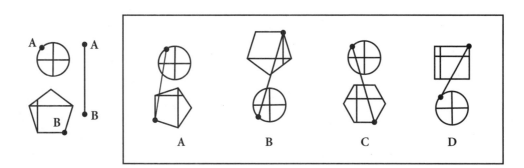

15.

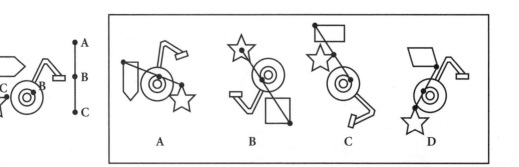

16.

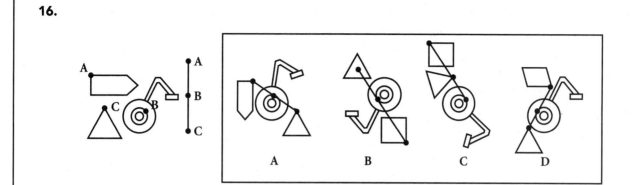

Answers

Part 1: General Science

1. d. Jonas Salk developed the polio vaccine in 1955.

2. c. The dissolved is in equilibrium with the undissolved in saturated solutions.

3. d. The Sun has no solid surface, as it is composed entirely of gas. The core temperature of the Sun is 15,000,000 K, compared to its outer atmosphere temperature of 1,000,000 K.

4. b. Gregor Mendel is sometimes known as the Father of Genetics, due to his work in the field during the mid-19th century.

5. d. The molecule CH_3NH_2 contains 1 atom of carbon, 1 atom of nitrogen, and 5 atoms of hydrogen, for a total of 7 atoms.

6. a. Mosses are bryophytes, which are characterized by their lack of a vascular system.

7. c. Saturn's rings are made of small bits of ice and rock that are captured by the large gas planet's gravitational pull.

8. a. Momentum equals mass (amount of matter in an object) times velocity (speed in a given direction).

9. d. Friction is the force that opposes the motion of an object.

10. c. The shoulder and hip joints are types of ball and socket joints.

11. a. A Producer is a living thing that can make its own food.

12. c. Anticoagulants are defined as any substance that stops the blood from forming clots.

13. b. Veins carry blood in the direction of the heart.

14. c. A solar eclipse occurs when the Moon crosses the face of the Sun and the Moon's shadow crosses the Earth. A lunar eclipse occurs when the Earth passes across the face of the Sun and the Earth's shadow crosses the face of the Moon.

15. b. The troposphere is the lowest level of the atmosphere in which most of the weather occurs. The stratosphere is directly above it.

16. a. All points on the equator have a latitude of 0 degrees. The North Pole has a latitude of 90 degrees north. The South Pole has a latitude of 90 degrees south.

17. b. Condensation is the change of vapor or gas into a liquid. Evaporation is the process by which water changes to a vapor or gas.

18. c. A barometer is a device for measuring atmospheric or air pressure. Humidity is measured by a hygrometer. Wind speed is measured by an anemometer.

19. a. Osmosis is the net movement of water molecules traveling from an area of high concentration to an area of low concentration. Diffusion is the process of any particles moving from higher to lower concentration until uniform concentration is reached.

20. d. Cartilage, a firm, flexible connective tissue, cushions joints and forms the skeleton of cartilaginous fish such as sharks. Bone marrow is a soft tissue in the central internal cavity of a bone.

21. c. The small intestine is the primary site of nutrient absorption in the human digestive system. Saliva breaks down food particles in the mouth, and enzymes and other chemicals break down food in the stomach. The large intestine reabsorbs water and forms the feces.

22. a. An elevator uses a pulley, consisting of a wheel with a flat, crowned, or grooved rim with a belt, rope, or chain that lifts a load. A seesaw or crowbar is an example of a lever.

23. c. Mass × speed = momentum. Force × distance = work.

24. b. Radiation is heat carried by electromagnetic waves from a hot source, such as a light bulb, into surrounding material, such as a lampshade. Conduction is when a hot and cold object come into contact and become an equal temperature.

25. d. Vitamin D aids in the uptake of calcium from the digestive system. Insufficient amounts of vitamin D is characterized by brittle or deformed bones.

Part 2: Arithmetic Reasoning

1. a. Here, 157 is rounded to 200; 817 is rounded to 800. $(200)(800) = 160,000$.

2. b. Multiply 120 by $\frac{2}{3}$. Thus, $\frac{120}{1} \times \frac{2}{3} = \frac{240}{3} = 80$; 120 is written as a fraction with a denominator of 1. The fraction $\frac{240}{3}$ is simplified by dividing 240 by 3 to get 80 cups.

3. d. First, find out how many heart beats there are in an hour by multiplying 68 by 60 minutes. $68 \times 60 = 4,080$. Then multiply 4,080 by the number of hours, 8, to get the total. $4,080 \times 8 = 32,640$.

4. a. The recipe is for 16 brownies. Half of that, 8, would reduce the ingredients by half. Half of $1\frac{1}{2}$ cups of sugar is $\frac{3}{4}$ cup.

5. c. The recipe for 16 brownies calls for $\frac{2}{3}$ cup butter. An additional $\frac{1}{3}$ cup would make 8 more brownies, for a total of 24 brownies.

6. d. To solve this problem, you must convert $3\frac{1}{2}$ to $\frac{7}{2}$ and then divide $\frac{7}{2}$ by $\frac{1}{4}$. The answer, $\frac{28}{2}$, is then reduced to the number 14.

7. c. Multiply $15,500,000 by $\frac{2}{5}$; $\frac{15,500,000}{1} \times \frac{2}{5} = $6,200,000$

8. a. Substituting known quantities into the formula yields $20 = \frac{64.8}{x^2}$. Next, you must multiply through by x^2 to get $20x^2 = 64.8$. Now divide through by 20 to get $x^2 = \frac{64.8}{20} = 3.24$. Now take the square root of both sides to get x equals 1.8.

9. c. The minimum heart rate is 60%. So, set up the equation $.6 \times (220 - x) = 102$, and solve for x. $132 - .6x = 102; -.6x = -30; x = 50$.

10. b. You can't just take 25% off the original price, because the 10% discount after three years of service is taken off the price that has already been reduced by 15%. Figure the problem in two steps: after the 15% discount the price is $71.83; 90% of that—subtracting 10%—is $64.65.

11. a. Add the number of men and women to get the total number: 200. The number of women, 24, is 12 percent of 200.

12. c. The problem is solved by dividing 204 by 1,700. The answer, 0.12, is then converted to a percentage.

13. c. In order to compare the fractions $\frac{5}{8}$, $\frac{2}{3}$, $\frac{3}{4}$, and $\frac{2}{5}$ you must find a common denominator. A common denominator can be found by multiplying 8, 3, and 5, which gives us 120. Therefore, $\frac{5}{8} = \frac{75}{120}$; $\frac{2}{3} = \frac{80}{120}$; $\frac{3}{4} = \frac{90}{120}$; and $\frac{2}{5} = \frac{48}{120}$. Compare the fractions, and you'll see that Susan has the most.

14. a. You can use trial and error to arrive at a solution to this problem. After the first hour, the number would be 20, after the second hour 40, after the third hour 80, after the fourth hour 160, and after the fifth hour 320. The other answer choices do not have the same outcome.

15. a. Let p stand for the prediction. Therefore, $p - \frac{1}{4}p = 750,000$. Simplify to $\frac{3}{4}p = 750,000$ and divide both sides by $\frac{3}{4}$, which gives us $p = 1,000,000$.

16. b. Twenty percent of 15 miles is 3 miles; adding 3 to 15 gives 18 miles.

17. c. Each 9-foot wall has an area of 9(8) or 72 square feet. There are two such walls, so those two walls combined have an area of 144 square feet. Each 11-foot wall has an area of 11(8) or 88 square feet, and again there are two such walls: 88 (2) = 176. Finally, add 144 and 176 to get 320 square feet.

18. c. Using the formula, $V = \frac{1}{3}(10)(12)(10) = 400$.

19. d. Substituting 40 for C in the equation yields $F = (\frac{9}{5})(40) + 32 = 72 + 32 = 104$.

20. b. Here, $150x = (100)(1)$, where x is the part of a mile a jogger has to go to burn the calories a walker burns in 1 mile. If you divide both sides of this equation by 150, you get $x = \frac{100}{150}$. Cancel 50 from both the numerator and denominator to get $\frac{2}{3}$. This means that a jogger has to jog only $\frac{2}{3}$ of a mile to burn the same number of calories a walker burns in a mile of brisk walking.

21. c. The ratio is $\frac{12\,cc}{100\,pounds} = \frac{x}{175\,pounds}$, where x is the number of cc's per 175 pounds. Multiply both sides by 175 to get $(175)(\frac{12}{100})$ equals x, so x equals 21.

22. b. The worst time is 68 seconds and the best is 49 seconds. Remove these two and find the average of the remaining times. $53 + 56 + 59 + 55 + 60 = 283$; $283 \div 5 = 56.6$.

23. a. The woman will have traveled 3.5 hours at 45 miles per hour for a distance of 157.5 miles. To reach her in 3 hours, her husband must travel at 157.5 miles per 3 hours, or 52.5 mph.

24. c. Eighty dollars per month times 7 months is $560. Twenty dollars per month times the remaining 5 months is $100. Add $560 and $100, which equals $660 for the entire year, so $660 divided by 12 months is $55.

25. a. $J = 6K$. $J + 2 = 2(K + 2)$, so $6K + 2 = 2K + 4$, which means K equals $\frac{1}{2}$. J equals 6K, or 3.

26. d. Add each monthly bill plus $54 for total local service to get $312.90 for three months. Dividing by 3 gives an average of $104.30.

27. d. Here, 448 miles divided by 16 gallons is 28 miles per gallon.

28. c. Multiply the cost per acre by the number of acres; $60,000 \times 1\frac{3}{4}$.

29. b. Kyra saves $60 + $130 + $70 = $260. In January, her employer contributes $6 and in April, $7. In March, her employer contributes only $10, the maximum amount. The total in savings is $260 + $6 + $7 + $10 = $283.

30. c. The difference between 107 and 98 is 9 degrees. We are told that the temperature is lowered by $\frac{3}{4}$ of a degree every application of the ice pack, which is a total of $15 + 3 = 18$ minutes, which equals 1 degree every 24 minutes. The total degree difference, 9 degrees, multiplied by 24 minutes gives you 216 minutes or 3 hours and 36 minutes.

Part 3: Word Knowledge

1. c. To be held *accountable* is to be held *responsible*.

2. b. To *scrutinize* is to inspect or *examine* in detail.

3. b. To *enumerate* is to ascertain the number of or *count*.

4. a. To *emulate* a person is to strive to equal that person or to *imitate* that person.

5. b. When one is *compliant*, one is acquiescent or *obedient*.

6. c. To *augment* something is to add to or *supplement* it.

7. d. To have an *aversion* to something is to have a feeling of repugnance for it or to *dislike* it.

8. a. To *validate* something is to *confirm* the authenticity of it.

9. b. To have an *antagonist* is to have an *opponent*, or one who opposes you.

10. c. To have *perseverance* is to be steadfast in your course or to have *persistence*.

11. d. To be *inundated* is to be overwhelmed or *flooded*.

12. a. *Homogeneous* means of the same or a similar kind, *alike*.

13. d. *Ominous* means foreshadowing evil, *threatening*.

14. c. When one is *incredulous*, one is skeptical or *disbelieving*.

15. d. A *recluse* is a person who lives withdrawn or shut up from the world, a *hermit*.

16. d. When one is *proficient* at something, one is expert or *skilled* at it.

17. a. To *defray* is to provide for the payment of something, to *pay*.

18. b. *Placid* means serenely free of disturbance; calm, *peaceful*.

19. a. When something is *tentative* it is of an experimental or *provisional* nature.

20. b. Something that is *vast* is huge or *immense*.

21. c. When one is *contemptuous*, one is disdainful or *scornful*.

22. b. When a group's opinion is *unanimous*, it is in accord or *uniform*.

23. c. When something is *distinct*, it is explicit or *recognizable*.

24. a. To *alleviate* something is to make it more bearable or *ease* it.

25. d. To *enlighten* someone is to impart wisdom to that person or to *teach*.

26. a. To *ostracize* is to *shun* or avoid something or someone.

27. c. Something that is *opulent* is *expensive* or overly ornate.

28. b. To show *clemency* means to show *leniency*.

29. d. To *defer* something means to *delay* it or put it off until later.

30. a. To *eschew* something is to *abandon* or do away with it.

31. b. To be *impetuous* is to be *impulsive* or to act with little or no forethought.

32. d. A *charade* is something that is *fake* or not real.

33. b. *Alacrity* is *eagerness* or cheerful willingness.

34. a. *Consternation* is a feeling of deep, incapacitating horror or *dismay*.

35. c. *Forbearance* means *patience*, willingness to wait, or tolerance.

Part 4: Paragraph Comprehension

1. b. The passage explains the procedure for bus drivers to follow when their bus gets ahead of schedule. Therefore, "running hot" means running ahead of schedule.

2. d. The passage indicates that each route contains several check points at which drivers should check the time to see if they are running on schedule.

3. c. The word *nucs* stands for *nucleus colony* and is used in the passage when discussing starting new colonies from splits or packages.

4. a. The passage talks about what will be required beekeeping work in the summer months. The other choices are tasks that need to be accomplished during other seasons.

5. c. According to the passage, hazardous waste is defined by the United States Environmental Protection Agency.

6. c. According to the passage, he should call his supervisor for directions because he is unclear whether the solvent is unsafe.

7. b. Although the goat is discussed as having certain benefits as a milk source, the passage concludes with a recommendation that the return on investment and resale considerations make the cow a better choice.

8. b. The correct title should include mention that the passage discusses both advantages and disadvantages of goats and cows for family farmers, which is choice **b**.

9. c. This title most nearly captures the main idea of the passage. The other choices either are not mentioned or are secondary ideas in the passage.

10. b. This is the point of the first sentence of the passage.

11. b. The third sentence of the passage states that officers may refer to their notes.

12. d. The passage provides information for law enforcement officers; therefore it is probably not from either a newspaper article or a novel. Choice **a** refers to a memo directed to police officers, but the subject matter is incorrect.

13. a. The first sentence states the importance of officer testimony.

14. d. The first day of summer in the north is the first day of winter in the south.

15. b. The first day of summer is summer solstice; therefore, the first day of winter is winter solstice.

Part 5: Mathematics Knowledge

1. d. The only parallel lines are y and z.

2. c. You must convert both fractions to twenty-fourths before adding. $3\frac{2}{3} + 6\frac{5}{8} = 10\frac{7}{24}$

3. a. Divide 4 by 5 in order to convert the fraction into a decimal. $4 \div 5 = 0.80$.

4. d. x times x^2 is x^3; x times y is xy.

5. b. Divide 14 by 35 and then multiply the answer by 100 to find the percent.

6. b. Divide 1 by 4 in order to convert the fraction into a decimal; $1 \div 4 = 0.25$.

7. b. The first step is to simplify the problem by subtracting 30 from each side, which results in $6x = 60$. Then divide both sides by 6, and $x = 10$.

8. b. Convert the mixed number $3\frac{7}{8}$ to the improper fraction $\frac{31}{8}$ and then invert.

9. d. This is a mixed number so it can be broken down into the whole number plus the fraction; $3\frac{3}{10} = 3.0 + \frac{3}{10}$; divide 3 by 10 in order to convert the fraction into a decimal; $3.00 \div 10 = 0.30$. Therefore, $3.0 + 0.30 = 3.30$.

10. c. This is the only choice that includes a 90-degree angle.

11. b. The square root of 12 is the same as the square root of 4 times 3, which is the same as the square root of 4 times the square root of 3. The square root of 4 is 2. So 3 times the square root of 12 is the same as 3 times 2 times the square root of 3.

12. b. Four divided by 25 equals 0.16 or 16%.

13. b. $2^5 = 2 \times 2 \times 2 \times 2 \times 2 = 32$.

14. b. $-1\frac{1}{3}$ is a mixed fraction and is equal to the whole number plus the fraction; $-1\frac{1}{3} = -(1 + \frac{1}{3})$. Convert $\frac{1}{3}$ into a decimal by dividing 1 by 3; $1 \div 3 = 0.333$; round this portion of the answer to the nearest hundredth, (two decimal places), to get 0.33; $-(1 + 0.33) = -1.33$.

15. a. The mixed number is equal to the whole number plus the fraction; $1\frac{3}{4} = 1.0 + \frac{3}{4}$. Convert the fraction to a decimal by dividing 3 by 4; $3 \div 4 = 0.75$; $1.0 + 0.75 = 1.75$.

16. a. The dimensions of triangle *MNO* are double those of triangle *RST*. Line segment *RT* is 5 cm; therefore line segment *MO* is 10 cm.

17. a. Keep in mind that following a decimal point, the farther to the right the digits go the smaller the number.

18. c. To convert a decimal into a fraction, first note the number of place positions to the right of the decimal point. In 0.4, the 4 is in the tenths place, which is one place to the right of the decimal point. Therefore, the fraction would be $\frac{4}{10}$. Now, the fraction needs to be reduced to its lowest terms. The number 2 is the greatest common factor of 4 and 10, so divide the numerator and denominator by 2. The final fraction is $\frac{2}{5}$.

19. a. In choice **b**, the 9 is in the hundredths place. In choice **c**, it is in the tenths place. In choice **d**, it is in the ten-thousandths place.

20. d. In the decimal 0.75, the 75 is two places to the right of the decimal point. Therefore, the fraction would be $\frac{75}{100}$, which can then be reduced by dividing the top and bottom by 25, the greatest common factor of 75 and 100. $\frac{75 \div 25}{100 \div 25} = \frac{3}{4}$.

21. b. The expression $3x$ means 3 *times x*. The minus sign before the 8 indicates the phrase *less than*.

22. b. Angles 1 and 4 are the only ones NOT adjacent to each other.

23. a. The number 2.25 involves a whole number, which is the 2 to the left of the decimal. This means that the answer will be a mixed number—a whole number plus a fraction. Convert the 0.25 into a fraction; $\frac{25 \div 25}{100 \div 25} = \frac{1}{4}$; adding the whole number, 2, to this fraction gives the answer $2\frac{1}{4}$.

24. b. Perform the operation in parentheses first: $16 \times 4 = 64$. Next, add 10 to get 74.

25. c. The perimeter of a square is the total length of all four sides. In a square, all four sides are of equal length, so the perimeter is $8 \times 4 = 32$.

Part 6: Electronics Information

1. b. The larger the wire's size, the smaller the voltage needed to carry current through it.

2. d. The prefix "micro" means multiply by 10^{-6}, so 287 microamps equals 0.000287 A.

3. b. Wire cutters are used to cut wire. A soldering iron and solder are used to join wires. Heat shrink insulation can be added to wires.

4. d. Typical solders are almost equal parts tin and lead.

5. b. An acid flux will corrode the solder joint.

6. a. Fiberglass is used to make most printed circuit boards.

7. a. Ideally, a fuse should have zero resistance when it is operating normally.

8. c. $I = W/V$ where I is the current, W is the wattage, and V is the voltage.

9. c. The total power in a series circuit is the sum of the power used by the two light bulbs.

10. d. An oscilloscope is used primarily to look at complex waveforms.

11. c. The power in circuit A is one half the power in B, so the current through A must be one half the current through B. If either circuit had no current flowing, there would be zero power dissipated.

12. b. A capacitor has the ability to store charge.

13. d. Copper is used more often because it is a much cheaper option than silver.

14. b. The current through the meter is equal to the current through R_1. The current through R_1 is $\frac{45 \text{ V}}{10 \, \Omega} = 4.5$ A.

15. c. AC stands for alternating current.

16. d. Resistances in parallel have the same voltage across them.

17. d. Linear switches do not exist.

18. d. The charge polarity of electrons is negative; the charge polarity of protons is positive.

19. a. Low potential to electricians most closely means 600 watts or lower.

20. c. Electricity produced in the United States has a frequency of 60 Hz. Some foreign countries produce electricity at 50 Hz.

Part 7: Auto and Shop Information

1. d. A faulty thermostat can cause engine overheating. If the thermostat is stuck in the closed position, the coolant cannot circulate and cool the engine.

2. b. The brake system contains two shoes that are forced against a metal drum, which rotates the wheel.

3. c. The fuses are used as links in the electrical system to prevent damage to other key components. The alternator is used to recharge the battery when the car is running.

4. d. The spark plug sends a spark into the cylinder, igniting the fuel.

5. b. The radiator is part of the cooling system. The cooling fluid is stored in the radiator and is then pumped through the cooling system by the water pump. As air passes over the radiator, the fluid is cooled, which prevents engine overheating.

6. a. The water pump pumps the engine coolant (a combination of water and antifreeze) out of the radiator and around the engine block in order to cool the engine.

7. a. A split lock washer prevents a bolt and nut combination from loosening or backing off because of vibration or use over time.

8. c. Steel is most often used to provide additional strength in concrete slabs and walls due to its high strength and relatively low cost.

9. d. Cement, sand, gravel, and water are the four primary ingredients in concrete.

10. d. Tile shingles are expensive but have a long life. Wooden "shake shingles" are also used as roofing material. The most common outer roofing material is asphalt shingles since they are low in cost and provide good protection.

11. c. A screw digs into the wood with its threads, which grab the wood much more securely than the other options.

12. b. Oil's lubricating properties break down over time, and the oil must therefore be replaced. The recommended interval is normally about 3,000 miles.

13. d. The crankshaft has a radius of 1.0 inch, which means that the diameter is 2.0 inches. If the crankshaft rotates one-half revolution (180 degrees) from its starting point, the attachment of the tie rod to the crankshaft will move from the top of the crankshaft down to the bottom. This is equivalent to the diameter of the crankshaft, which is 2.0 inches.

14. a. The shock absorbers are the components in the suspension that dampen the vibrations in the system.

15. c. The clutch is used to engage and disengage the transmission. The drive shaft is used to transfer power from the engine to the wheels. Universal joints are special linkages in the transmission system.

16. c. The indicated danger zone on the gauge is from 160 degrees to 200 degrees Fahrenheit. Thus, it is acceptable to operate up to 160 degrees for this gauge.

17. d. The braking system can be controlled by the driver by pressing the brake pedal. The other systems listed cannot typically be directly controlled while operating the automobile.

18. d. The cooling system in a car should be flushed every few years.

19. a. The cooling system circulates water around the engine to prevent it from overheating. None of the other systems is connected directly to the engine.

20. c. That this gauge measures temperature can be determined by the units of degrees Fahrenheit and degrees Celsius shown on the gauge.

21. c. A plane is a hand tool that has a sharp blade extending slightly below the bottom surface of the tool. The plane is pushed across the surface of a piece of wood and the blade removes a thin layer of wood from the surface.

22. d. The power from the battery of the electrical system is what makes the turn signal indicator blink.

23. a. The tools listed are all used to form, cut, and punch thin sheets of metal.

24. b. When making a circular cut in a piece of metal, the best chisel to use is a round chisel. The butt chisel and the framing chisel are both wood chisels. A socket chisel is a type of framing chisel.

25. c. These are common shop tools that are used to measure the length of various items.

Part 8: Mechanical Comprehension

1. b. The first 500 pounds generated 1,000 psi of stress in the beam; therefore, 500 more pounds will increase the total stress to 2,000 psi. Another 500 pounds will increase the stress to 3,000 psi, which we are told is the maximum strength of the beam. Therefore, the maximum additional load that can be applied to this beam before it breaks is 1,000 pounds.

2. b. The cars both weigh the same, so friction and acceleration would be identical for both. The difference is that a sports car has a low, sleek shape compared to a minivan and therefore has less drag from the wind.

3. d. Acceleration must be considered in designing the maximum rise of the first hill. Momentum must be considered to ensure the train gets back to the starting point, since it has no motor. Friction must be considered in the design of the braking system.

4. c. Tension is a state of stretching or straining, which is what the rope is experiencing.

5. d. When an object is at equilibrium, it has equal forces acting on it. When both people on a seesaw weigh the same, the seesaw is in equilibrium, and it is easier for each person to push off the ground.

6. a. In the equilibrium position, the pendulum hangs straight down. When displaced from this position, the pendulum does not simply return to the equilibrium position, but swings back and forth in a regular, repetitive manner. This is the definition of periodic motion.

7. c. By definition, deceleration means slowing down.

8. b. While all the choices could achieve the goal of pulling a large weight up a hill, the best and easiest device for doing so would be an electric winch, which would not need human energy to do so.

9. c. Multiply 3.5 inches by 100 pounds per inch, which equals 350 pounds.

10. a. A wedge is a triangular-shaped object that has many mechanical functions.

11. d. Pumps are not used to move liquids downhill since they will flow downhill by gravity. Also, pumps do not separate or clarify liquids, since they agitate and mix liquids.

12. a. Tongs are a class 3 lever.

13. b. Valves are placed in piping systems and can be opened or closed in order to control the flow of liquids or gasses.

14. a. The center of gravity of an object is loosely defined as "the middle of its weight" or "the point at which you could balance it on your finger"; in this case, that would be two feet from the left end (or two feet from the right end).

15. d. Elasticity is defined as "stretchiness." It is a measure of how easy it is to deform a material. Paper is the stiffest or least elastic of the material listed.

16. b. Block B is smaller, but we are told it is made of a material that is three times more dense (density is weight per unit volume) than Block A. Therefore, since Block A is only twice as big as Block B, it is actually 50 percent lighter.

17. b. The volume of the block can be calculated by multiplying its length by its width by its height, or 1 times 1 times 2, which equals 2 cubic inches. The weight is the density multiplied by its volume, which is 2 cubic inches multiplied by 0.29 pounds per cubic inch, which equals 0.58 pounds.

18. a. Snowshoes distribute the weight of the person over a larger area than boots alone and reduce the pressure on the snow. This keeps the person from sinking so far into the snow.

19. c. The four aerodynamic forces that affect an aircraft are lift, weight, thrust and drag.

20. c. The distance from the pivot point to the point of application of the force (20 feet) is twice the distance from the pivot point to the box (10 feet). Therefore, in order to lift the box, the required force will be one half of the weight of the box, or 50 pounds.

21. b. The incompressible nature of fluids would not benefit it as a surface sealant or an engine lubricant.

22. b. A valve is used to control the flow of liquids and gases in a piping system. An example is the faucet on a sink.

23. b. The systems listed produce electric power.

24. c. The two blocks are directly connected by a fixed length of steel cable. Therefore, regardless of the number of pulleys between the two blocks, the distance moved by one block will be the same as the other block.

25. d. The items listed that are *not* fasteners are chairs, tables, windows, scissors, and levers.

Part 9 Assembling Objects

1. c.

2. a.

3. d.

4. a.

5. c.

6. b.

7. b.

8. d.

9. b.

10. d.

11. a.

12. d.

13. d.

14. a.

15. a.

16. a.

Scoring

Write your raw score (the number you got right) for each test in the blanks below. Then turn to Chapter 3 to find out how to convert these raw scores into the scores the armed services use.

1. General Science: _____ right out of 25
2. Arithmetic Reasoning: _____ right out of 30
3. Word Knowledge: _____ right out of 35
4. Paragraph Comprehension: _____ right out of 15
5. Mathematics Knowledge: _____ right out of 25
6. Electronics Information: _____ right out of 20
7. Auto and Shop Information: _____ right out of 25
8. Mechanical Comprehension: _____ right out of 25
9. Assembling Objects: _____ right out of 16

15 ▶ ASVAB PRACTICE TEST 2

CHAPTER SUMMARY

Take this test for more practice and additional improvement over your scores on the first two tests.

For this practice exam, again simulate the actual test-taking experience as closely as you can. Work in a quiet place where you won't be interrupted. If you own this book, tear out the answer sheet and use your number 2 pencils to fill in the circles. As you did for the practice exam in Chapter 14, set a timer or stopwatch, and give yourself the appropriate amount of time marked at the beginning of each subtest.

After you take the test, use the detailed answer explanations that follow to review any questions you missed.

Part 1: General Science

1.	ⓐ	ⓑ	ⓒ	ⓓ	10.	ⓐ	ⓑ	ⓒ	ⓓ	19.	ⓐ	ⓑ	ⓒ	ⓓ
2.	ⓐ	ⓑ	ⓒ	ⓓ	11.	ⓐ	ⓑ	ⓒ	ⓓ	20.	ⓐ	ⓑ	ⓒ	ⓓ
3.	ⓐ	ⓑ	ⓒ	ⓓ	12.	ⓐ	ⓑ	ⓒ	ⓓ	21.	ⓐ	ⓑ	ⓒ	ⓓ
4.	ⓐ	ⓑ	ⓒ	ⓓ	13.	ⓐ	ⓑ	ⓒ	ⓓ	22.	ⓐ	ⓑ	ⓒ	ⓓ
5.	ⓐ	ⓑ	ⓒ	ⓓ	14.	ⓐ	ⓑ	ⓒ	ⓓ	23.	ⓐ	ⓑ	ⓒ	ⓓ
6.	ⓐ	ⓑ	ⓒ	ⓓ	15.	ⓐ	ⓑ	ⓒ	ⓓ	24.	ⓐ	ⓑ	ⓒ	ⓓ
7.	ⓐ	ⓑ	ⓒ	ⓓ	16.	ⓐ	ⓑ	ⓒ	ⓓ	25.	ⓐ	ⓑ	ⓒ	ⓓ
8.	ⓐ	ⓑ	ⓒ	ⓓ	17.	ⓐ	ⓑ	ⓒ	ⓓ					
9.	ⓐ	ⓑ	ⓒ	ⓓ	18.	ⓐ	ⓑ	ⓒ	ⓓ					

Part 2: Arithmetic Reasoning

1.	ⓐ	ⓑ	ⓒ	ⓓ	11.	ⓐ	ⓑ	ⓒ	ⓓ	21.	ⓐ	ⓑ	ⓒ	ⓓ
2.	ⓐ	ⓑ	ⓒ	ⓓ	12.	ⓐ	ⓑ	ⓒ	ⓓ	22.	ⓐ	ⓑ	ⓒ	ⓓ
3.	ⓐ	ⓑ	ⓒ	ⓓ	13.	ⓐ	ⓑ	ⓒ	ⓓ	23.	ⓐ	ⓑ	ⓒ	ⓓ
4.	ⓐ	ⓑ	ⓒ	ⓓ	14.	ⓐ	ⓑ	ⓒ	ⓓ	24.	ⓐ	ⓑ	ⓒ	ⓓ
5.	ⓐ	ⓑ	ⓒ	ⓓ	15.	ⓐ	ⓑ	ⓒ	ⓓ	25.	ⓐ	ⓑ	ⓒ	ⓓ
6.	ⓐ	ⓑ	ⓒ	ⓓ	16.	ⓐ	ⓑ	ⓒ	ⓓ	26.	ⓐ	ⓑ	ⓒ	ⓓ
7.	ⓐ	ⓑ	ⓒ	ⓓ	17.	ⓐ	ⓑ	ⓒ	ⓓ	27.	ⓐ	ⓑ	ⓒ	ⓓ
8.	ⓐ	ⓑ	ⓒ	ⓓ	18.	ⓐ	ⓑ	ⓒ	ⓓ	28.	ⓐ	ⓑ	ⓒ	ⓓ
9.	ⓐ	ⓑ	ⓒ	ⓓ	19.	ⓐ	ⓑ	ⓒ	ⓓ	29.	ⓐ	ⓑ	ⓒ	ⓓ
10.	ⓐ	ⓑ	ⓒ	ⓓ	20.	ⓐ	ⓑ	ⓒ	ⓓ	30.	ⓐ	ⓑ	ⓒ	ⓓ

Part 3: Word Knowledge

1.	ⓐ	ⓑ	ⓒ	ⓓ	13.	ⓐ	ⓑ	ⓒ	ⓓ	25.	ⓐ	ⓑ	ⓒ	ⓓ
2.	ⓐ	ⓑ	ⓒ	ⓓ	14.	ⓐ	ⓑ	ⓒ	ⓓ	26.	ⓐ	ⓑ	ⓒ	ⓓ
3.	ⓐ	ⓑ	ⓒ	ⓓ	15.	ⓐ	ⓑ	ⓒ	ⓓ	27.	ⓐ	ⓑ	ⓒ	ⓓ
4.	ⓐ	ⓑ	ⓒ	ⓓ	16.	ⓐ	ⓑ	ⓒ	ⓓ	28.	ⓐ	ⓑ	ⓒ	ⓓ
5.	ⓐ	ⓑ	ⓒ	ⓓ	17.	ⓐ	ⓑ	ⓒ	ⓓ	29.	ⓐ	ⓑ	ⓒ	ⓓ
6.	ⓐ	ⓑ	ⓒ	ⓓ	18.	ⓐ	ⓑ	ⓒ	ⓓ	30.	ⓐ	ⓑ	ⓒ	ⓓ
7.	ⓐ	ⓑ	ⓒ	ⓓ	19.	ⓐ	ⓑ	ⓒ	ⓓ	31.	ⓐ	ⓑ	ⓒ	ⓓ
8.	ⓐ	ⓑ	ⓒ	ⓓ	20.	ⓐ	ⓑ	ⓒ	ⓓ	32.	ⓐ	ⓑ	ⓒ	ⓓ
9.	ⓐ	ⓑ	ⓒ	ⓓ	21.	ⓐ	ⓑ	ⓒ	ⓓ	33.	ⓐ	ⓑ	ⓒ	ⓓ
10.	ⓐ	ⓑ	ⓒ	ⓓ	22.	ⓐ	ⓑ	ⓒ	ⓓ	34.	ⓐ	ⓑ	ⓒ	ⓓ
11.	ⓐ	ⓑ	ⓒ	ⓓ	23.	ⓐ	ⓑ	ⓒ	ⓓ	35.	ⓐ	ⓑ	ⓒ	ⓓ
12.	ⓐ	ⓑ	ⓒ	ⓓ	24.	ⓐ	ⓑ	ⓒ	ⓓ					

Part 4: Paragraph Comprehension

1.	ⓐ	ⓑ	ⓒ	ⓓ	6.	ⓐ	ⓑ	ⓒ	ⓓ	11.	ⓐ	ⓑ	ⓒ	ⓓ
2.	ⓐ	ⓑ	ⓒ	ⓓ	7.	ⓐ	ⓑ	ⓒ	ⓓ	12.	ⓐ	ⓑ	ⓒ	ⓓ
3.	ⓐ	ⓑ	ⓒ	ⓓ	8.	ⓐ	ⓑ	ⓒ	ⓓ	13.	ⓐ	ⓑ	ⓒ	ⓓ
4.	ⓐ	ⓑ	ⓒ	ⓓ	9.	ⓐ	ⓑ	ⓒ	ⓓ	14.	ⓐ	ⓑ	ⓒ	ⓓ
5.	ⓐ	ⓑ	ⓒ	ⓓ	10.	ⓐ	ⓑ	ⓒ	ⓓ	15.	ⓐ	ⓑ	ⓒ	ⓓ

Part 5: Mathematics Knowledge

1.	ⓐ ⓑ ⓒ ⓓ	10.	ⓐ ⓑ ⓒ ⓓ	19.	ⓐ ⓑ ⓒ ⓓ
2.	ⓐ ⓑ ⓒ ⓓ	11.	ⓐ ⓑ ⓒ ⓓ	20.	ⓐ ⓑ ⓒ ⓓ
3.	ⓐ ⓑ ⓒ ⓓ	12.	ⓐ ⓑ ⓒ ⓓ	21.	ⓐ ⓑ ⓒ ⓓ
4.	ⓐ ⓑ ⓒ ⓓ	13.	ⓐ ⓑ ⓒ ⓓ	22.	ⓐ ⓑ ⓒ ⓓ
5.	ⓐ ⓑ ⓒ ⓓ	14.	ⓐ ⓑ ⓒ ⓓ	23.	ⓐ ⓑ ⓒ ⓓ
6.	ⓐ ⓑ ⓒ ⓓ	15.	ⓐ ⓑ ⓒ ⓓ	24.	ⓐ ⓑ ⓒ ⓓ
7.	ⓐ ⓑ ⓒ ⓓ	16.	ⓐ ⓑ ⓒ ⓓ	25.	ⓐ ⓑ ⓒ ⓓ
8.	ⓐ ⓑ ⓒ ⓓ	17.	ⓐ ⓑ ⓒ ⓓ		
9.	ⓐ ⓑ ⓒ ⓓ	18.	ⓐ ⓑ ⓒ ⓓ		

Part 6: Electronics Information

1.	ⓐ ⓑ ⓒ ⓓ	10.	ⓐ ⓑ ⓒ ⓓ	19.	ⓐ ⓑ ⓒ ⓓ
2.	ⓐ ⓑ ⓒ ⓓ	11.	ⓐ ⓑ ⓒ ⓓ	20.	ⓐ ⓑ ⓒ ⓓ
3.	ⓐ ⓑ ⓒ ⓓ	12.	ⓐ ⓑ ⓒ ⓓ		
4.	ⓐ ⓑ ⓒ ⓓ	13.	ⓐ ⓑ ⓒ ⓓ		
5.	ⓐ ⓑ ⓒ ⓓ	14.	ⓐ ⓑ ⓒ ⓓ		
6.	ⓐ ⓑ ⓒ ⓓ	15.	ⓐ ⓑ ⓒ ⓓ		
7.	ⓐ ⓑ ⓒ ⓓ	16.	ⓐ ⓑ ⓒ ⓓ		
8.	ⓐ ⓑ ⓒ ⓓ	17.	ⓐ ⓑ ⓒ ⓓ		
9.	ⓐ ⓑ ⓒ ⓓ	18.	ⓐ ⓑ ⓒ ⓓ		

Part 7: Auto and Shop Information

1.	ⓐ ⓑ ⓒ ⓓ	10.	ⓐ ⓑ ⓒ ⓓ	19.	ⓐ ⓑ ⓒ ⓓ
2.	ⓐ ⓑ ⓒ ⓓ	11.	ⓐ ⓑ ⓒ ⓓ	20.	ⓐ ⓑ ⓒ ⓓ
3.	ⓐ ⓑ ⓒ ⓓ	12.	ⓐ ⓑ ⓒ ⓓ	21.	ⓐ ⓑ ⓒ ⓓ
4.	ⓐ ⓑ ⓒ ⓓ	13.	ⓐ ⓑ ⓒ ⓓ	22.	ⓐ ⓑ ⓒ ⓓ
5.	ⓐ ⓑ ⓒ ⓓ	14.	ⓐ ⓑ ⓒ ⓓ	23.	ⓐ ⓑ ⓒ ⓓ
6.	ⓐ ⓑ ⓒ ⓓ	15.	ⓐ ⓑ ⓒ ⓓ	24.	ⓐ ⓑ ⓒ ⓓ
7.	ⓐ ⓑ ⓒ ⓓ	16.	ⓐ ⓑ ⓒ ⓓ	25.	ⓐ ⓑ ⓒ ⓓ
8.	ⓐ ⓑ ⓒ ⓓ	17.	ⓐ ⓑ ⓒ ⓓ		
9.	ⓐ ⓑ ⓒ ⓓ	18.	ⓐ ⓑ ⓒ ⓓ		

Part 8: Mechanical Comprehension

1.	ⓐ ⓑ ⓒ ⓓ	10.	ⓐ ⓑ ⓒ ⓓ	19.	ⓐ ⓑ ⓒ ⓓ
2.	ⓐ ⓑ ⓒ ⓓ	11.	ⓐ ⓑ ⓒ ⓓ	20.	ⓐ ⓑ ⓒ ⓓ
3.	ⓐ ⓑ ⓒ ⓓ	12.	ⓐ ⓑ ⓒ ⓓ	21.	ⓐ ⓑ ⓒ ⓓ
4.	ⓐ ⓑ ⓒ ⓓ	13.	ⓐ ⓑ ⓒ ⓓ	22.	ⓐ ⓑ ⓒ ⓓ
5.	ⓐ ⓑ ⓒ ⓓ	14.	ⓐ ⓑ ⓒ ⓓ	23.	ⓐ ⓑ ⓒ ⓓ
6.	ⓐ ⓑ ⓒ ⓓ	15.	ⓐ ⓑ ⓒ ⓓ	24.	ⓐ ⓑ ⓒ ⓓ
7.	ⓐ ⓑ ⓒ ⓓ	16.	ⓐ ⓑ ⓒ ⓓ	25.	ⓐ ⓑ ⓒ ⓓ
8.	ⓐ ⓑ ⓒ ⓓ	17.	ⓐ ⓑ ⓒ ⓓ		
9.	ⓐ ⓑ ⓒ ⓓ	18.	ⓐ ⓑ ⓒ ⓓ		

Part 9: Assembling Objects

1. ⓐ ⓑ ⓒ ⓓ
2. ⓐ ⓑ ⓒ ⓓ
3. ⓐ ⓑ ⓒ ⓓ
4. ⓐ ⓑ ⓒ ⓓ
5. ⓐ ⓑ ⓒ ⓓ
6. ⓐ ⓑ ⓒ ⓓ

7. ⓐ ⓑ ⓒ ⓓ
8. ⓐ ⓑ ⓒ ⓓ
9. ⓐ ⓑ ⓒ ⓓ
10. ⓐ ⓑ ⓒ ⓓ
11. ⓐ ⓑ ⓒ ⓓ
12. ⓐ ⓑ ⓒ ⓓ

13. ⓐ ⓑ ⓒ ⓓ
14. ⓐ ⓑ ⓒ ⓓ
15. ⓐ ⓑ ⓒ ⓓ
16. ⓐ ⓑ ⓒ ⓓ

Part 1: General Science

Time: 11 minutes

1. To which scientific class do gorillas belong?
   a. reptile
   b. mammalia
   c. amphibian
   d. avian

2. What is the simplest aromatic compound (C_6H_6)?
   a. benzoic acid
   b. toulene
   c. phenol
   d. benzene

3. How many different elements are present in glucose, $C_6H_{12}O_6$?
   a. 3
   b. 6
   c. 12
   d. 24

4. 1 micrometer equals 1/1000 of a
   a. kilometer.
   b. meter.
   c. centimeter.
   d. millimeter.

5. What is the scientific notation for 617,000?
   a. 6.17×10^{-5}
   b. 0.617×10^2
   c. 0.617×10^3
   d. 6.17×10^5

6. If you throw a baseball forward, it will accelerate downward due to
   a. orbital motion.
   b. terminal velocity.
   c. gravity.
   d. Newton's third law of motion.

7. Which of these simple machines is NOT a lever?
   a. an ax blade
   b. a shovel
   c. a wheelbarrow
   d. a pair of pliers

8. The layer of the Earth that lies directly below the crust is the
   a. mantle.
   b. core.
   c. troposphere.
   d. subsphere.

9. An instrument used to measure the speed of the wind is called
   a. a hydrometer.
   b. a barometer.
   c. a seismograph.
   d. an anemometer.

10. To which class do tigers belong?
   a. Carnivora
   b. Mammalia
   c. *tigris*
   d. Chordata

11. What sort of rock is created by immense heat and pressure?
   a. sedimentary
   b. metamorphic
   c. igneous
   d. breccia

12. What type of rock is formed by the cooling of lava? (An example is granite.)
   a. metamorphic
   b. sedimentary
   c. igneous
   d. salt

13. Which of the following is an organic compound?
  a. calcium (Ca)
  b. water (H_2O)
  c. salt (NaCl)
  d. glucose ($C_6H_{12}O_6$)

14. Which of the following animals are most closely related to crabs?
  a. beetles
  b. salmon
  c. frogs
  d. robins

15. What causes the human disease scarlet fever?
  a. fungus
  b. virus
  c. bacterium
  d. germs

16. What is the hormone that regulates the amount of sugar in the blood?
  a. estrogen
  b. adrenaline
  c. insulin
  d. androgen

17. Unoxygenated blood travels to the heart via which of the following?
  a. arteries
  b. veins
  c. capillaries
  d. aorta

18. What are animals called that feed ONLY on plant matter?
  a. carnivores
  b. omnivores
  c. decomposers
  d. herbivores

19. The exchange of water, oxygen, carbon dioxide, and other nutrients and waste products in the body occurs at which level of the circulatory system?
  a. arterial
  b. venous
  c. capillary
  d. aortic

20. Yawning equalizes the air pressure in what structure?
  a. nasal cavity
  b. Eustachian tube
  c. windpipe
  d. cochlea

21. James Watson and Francis Crick discovered that DNA has which of the following structures?
  a. a helix
  b. a parabola
  c. a double helix
  d. a hexagon

22. Which of the following contains fiber?
  a. chicken breast
  b. raspberries
  c. steak
  d. butter

23. Which of the following ecosystems could be described as having a temperate climate and many leaf-shedding trees?
  a. a deciduous forest
  b. a tropical rain forest
  c. a tundra
  d. a taiga

24. Which of the following represents a chemical change?
  a. burning a piece of toast
  b. dissolving salt in water
  c. cutting an aspirin in half
  d. freezing water to make ice cubes

25. A human embryo will be female if the
    a. mother's egg contributes an X chromosome.
    b. mother's egg contributes a Y chromosome.
    c. father's sperm contributes an X chromosome.
    d. father's sperm contributes a Y chromosome.

Part 2: Arithmetic Reasoning

Time: 36 minutes

1. What is the estimated product when 234 and 579 are rounded to the nearest tens and multiplied?
    a. 160,000
    b. 180,000
    c. 133,400
    d. 180,000

2. On the cardiac ward, there are 7 nursing assistants. NA Basil has 8 patients; NA Hobbes has 5 patients; NA McGuire has 9 patients; NA Hicks has 10 patients; NA Garcia has 10 patients; NA James has 14 patients, and NA Davis has 7 patients. What is the average number of patients per nursing assistant?
    a. 7
    b. 8
    c. 9
    d. 10

3. If a particular woman's resting heartbeat is 72 beats per minute and she is at rest for $6\frac{1}{2}$ hours, about how many times will her heart beat during that period of time?
    a. 4,320
    b. 28,080
    c. 4,680
    d. 43,200

4. A patient's hospice stay cost $\frac{1}{4}$ as much as his visit to the emergency room. His home nursing cost twice as much as his hospice stay. If his total health care bill was $140,000, how much did his home nursing cost?
    a. 10,000
    b. 20,000
    c. 40,000
    d. 80,000

5. Chuck is making a patio using $1\frac{1}{2}$ foot cement squares. The patio will be 10 cement squares by 10 cement squares. If the cement squares are placed right next to each other without any space in between, what will the dimensions of the patio be?
    a. 10 ft by 10 ft
    b. 20 ft by 20 ft
    c. $12\frac{1}{2}$ ft by $12\frac{1}{2}$ ft
    d. 15 ft by 15 ft

6. At a certain school, half the students are female and one-twelfth of the students are from outside the state. What proportion of the students would you expect to be females from outside the state?
    a. $\frac{1}{12}$
    b. $\frac{1}{24}$
    c. $\frac{1}{6}$
    d. $\frac{1}{3}$

7. The state of Alabama will pay one-fifth of the cost of a government building. If the city of Huntsville is building a police station that will cost a total of $22,650,000, how much will the state pay?
    a. $3,100,000
    b. $7,750,000
    c. $6,200,000
    d. $4,530,000

8. Based on the information below, estimate the weight of a person who is 5'5" tall.

HEIGHT	WEIGHT
5'	110 pounds
6'	170 pounds

   a. 125
   b. 130
   c. 135
   d. 140

9. During exercise, a person's heart rate should be between sixty and ninety percent of the difference between 220 and the person's age. According to this guideline, what should a 30-year-old person's maximum heart rate be during exercise?
   a. 114
   b. 132
   c. 171
   d. 198

10. The local firefighters are doing a "fill the boot" fundraiser. Their goal is to raise $3,500. After three hours, they have raised $2,275. Which statement below is accurate?
   a. They have raised 35% of their goal.
   b. They have $\frac{7}{20}$ of their goal left to raise.
   c. They have raised less than $\frac{1}{2}$ of their goal.
   d. They have raised more than $\frac{3}{4}$ of their goal.

11. A certain water pollutant is unsafe at a level of 20 ppm (parts per million). A city's water supply now contains 50 ppm of this pollutant. What percentage improvement will make the water safe?
   a. 30%
   b. 40%
   c. 50%
   d. 60%

12. The basal metabolic rate (BMR) is the rate at which our body uses calories. The BMR for a man in his twenties is about 2,200 calories per day. If 12% of those calories should come from protein, how many total calories should come from protein?
   a. 254
   b. 264
   c. 244
   d. 284

13. Joey, Aaron, Barbara, and Stu have been collecting pennies and putting them in identical containers. Joey's container is $\frac{3}{4}$ full, Aaron's is $\frac{3}{5}$ full, Barbara's is $\frac{2}{3}$ full, and Stu's is $\frac{2}{5}$ full. Whose container has the most pennies?
   a. Joey
   b. Aaron
   c. Barbara
   d. Stu

14. Rosa kept track of how many hours she spent reading during the month of August. The first week she read for $4\frac{1}{2}$ hours, the second week for $3\frac{3}{4}$ hours, the third week for $8\frac{1}{5}$ hours, and the fourth week for $1\frac{1}{3}$ hours. How many hours altogether did she spend reading in the month of August?
   a. $17\frac{47}{60}$
   b. 16
   c. $16\frac{1}{8}$
   d. $18\frac{2}{15}$

15. A study shows that 600,000 women die each year in pregnancy and childbirth, one-fifth more than scientists previously estimated. How many such deaths did the scientists previously estimate?
a. 120,000
b. 300,000
c. 480,000
d. 500,000

16. Jackie went on a 10 mile hike. Two weeks later, she increased the length of her hike by 5 miles. What percentage did she increase her hike by?
a. 25%
b. 40%
c. 50%
d. 60%

17. What is 250 mg in terms of grams?
a. 0.0250 g
b. 0.250 g
c. 2.50 g
d. 250,000 g

18. After three days, a group of hikers discovers that they have used $\frac{2}{5}$ of their supplies. At this rate, how many more days can they go forward before they have to turn around?
a. 0.75 days
b. 3.75 days
c. 4.5 days
d. 7.5 days

19. A supply truck can carry 3 tons. A breakfast ration weighs 12 ounces, and the other two daily meals weigh 18 ounces each. On a ten-day trip, how many troops can be supplied by one truck?
a. 100
b. 150
c. 200
d. 320

20. A clerk can process 26 forms per hour. If 5,600 forms must be processed in an 8-hour day, how many clerks must you hire for that day?
a. 24 clerks
b. 25 clerks
c. 26 clerks
d. 27 clerks

21. On the same latitude, Company E travels east at 35 miles per hour and Company F travels west at 15 miles per hour. If the two companies start out 2,100 miles apart, how long will it take them to meet?
a. 42 hours
b. 60 hours
c. 105 hours
d. 140 hours

22. During the last week of training on an obstacle course, a recruit achieves the following times in seconds: 66, 57, 54, 54, 64, 59, and 59. The recruit's three best times this week are averaged for his final score on the course. What is his final score?
a. 57 seconds
b. 55 seconds
c. 59 seconds
d. 61 seconds

23. A man drives east at 65 miles per hour. After half an hour, his wife starts to follow him. About how fast must she drive to catch up to him after he has driven four hours?
a. 70 miles per hour
b. 74 miles per hour
c. 76 miles per hour
d. 78 miles per hour

24. If you take recyclables to whichever recycler will pay the most, what is the greatest amount of money you could get for 2,200 pounds of aluminum, 1,400 pounds of cardboard, 3,100 pounds of glass, and 900 pounds of plastic?

	ALUM-INUM	CARD-BOARD	GLASS	PLASTIC
Recycler X	6 cents/ pound	3 cents/ pound	8 cents/ pound	2 cents/ pound
Recycler Y	7 cents/ pound	4 cents/ pound	7 cents/ pound	3 cents/ pound

   a. $440
   b. $447
   c. $454
   d. $485

25. Sarah is eight times as old as Zach. In four years, Sarah will be four times Zach's age. How old is Sarah now?
   a. 24 years old
   b. 16 years old
   c. 20 years old
   d. 22 years old

26. A train must travel 3,450 miles in six days. How many miles must it travel each day?
   a. 525
   b. 550
   c. 600
   d. 575

27. A uniform requires 4 square yards of cloth. To produce uniforms for 84,720 troops, how much cloth is required?
   a. 330,880 square yards
   b. 336,880 square yards
   c. 338,880 square yards
   d. 340,880 square yards

28. A dormitory now houses 30 men and allows 42 square feet of space per man. If five more men are put into this dormitory, how much less space will each man have?
   a. 5 square feet
   b. 6 square feet
   c. 7 square feet
   d. 8 square feet

29. Ron is half as old as Sam, who is three times as old as Ted. The sum of their ages is 55. How old is Ron?
   a. 5
   b. 10
   c. 15
   d. 30

30. To lower a fever of 105 degrees, ice packs are applied for 1 minute and then removed for 5 minutes before being applied again. Each application lowers the fever by half a degree. How long will it take to lower the fever to 99 degrees?
   a. 1 hour
   b. 1 hour and 12 minutes
   c. 1 hour and 15 minutes
   d. 1 hour and 30 minutes

Part 3: Word Knowledge

Time: 11 minutes

1. <u>Erroneous</u> most nearly means
   a. digressive.
   b. confused.
   c. impenetrable.
   d. faulty.

2. <u>Grotesque</u> most nearly means
   a. extreme.
   b. frenzied.
   c. bizarre.
   d. typical.

3. The Adamsville Kennel Club's computer system was <u>outmoded</u>.
   a. worthless
   b. unusable
   c. obsolete
   d. unnecessary

4. <u>Garbled</u> most nearly means
   a. lucid.
   b. unintelligible.
   c. devoured.
   d. outrageous.

5. <u>Rigorous</u> most nearly means
   a. demanding.
   b. tolerable.
   c. lenient.
   d. disorderly.

6. <u>Flagrant</u> most nearly means
   a. secret.
   b. worthless.
   c. noble.
   d. glaring.

7. <u>Oration</u> most nearly means
   a. nuisance.
   b. independence.
   c. address.
   d. length.

8. Although the police might be able to help Mr. Chen recover his stolen property, he <u>obstinately</u> refuses to file a complaint.
   a. repeatedly
   b. reluctantly
   c. foolishly
   d. stubbornly

9. The student's <u>glib</u> remarks irritated the teacher.
   a. angry
   b. superficial
   c. insulting
   d. dishonest

10. <u>Composure</u> most nearly means
   a. agitation.
   b. poise.
   c. liveliness.
   d. stimulation.

11. <u>Eccentric</u> most nearly means
   a. normal.
   b. frugal.
   c. peculiar.
   d. selective.

12. <u>Commendable</u> most nearly means
   a. admirable.
   b. accountable.
   c. irresponsible.
   d. noticeable.

13. <u>Oblivious</u> most nearly means
   a. visible.
   b. sinister.
   c. aware.
   d. ignorant.

14. Philanthropy most nearly means
   a. selfishness.
   b. fascination.
   c. disrespect.
   d. generosity.

15. Most members of the community thought the Neighborhood Guards' red hats were ostentatious.
   a. hilarious
   b. pretentious
   c. outrageous
   d. obnoxious

16. Passive most nearly means
   a. resigned.
   b. emotional.
   c. lively.
   d. woeful.

17. Proximity most nearly means
   a. distance.
   b. agreement.
   c. nearness.
   d. intelligence.

18. Negligible most nearly means
   a. insignificant.
   b. delicate.
   c. meaningful.
   d. illegible.

19. Rational most nearly means
   a. deliberate.
   b. invalid.
   c. prompt.
   d. sound.

20. Vigilant most nearly means
   a. nonchalant.
   b. alert.
   c. righteous.
   d. strenuous.

21. Astute most nearly means
   a. perceptive.
   b. inattentive.
   c. stubborn.
   d. elegant.

22. The prerequisite training to belong to this team is a three-hour course in volleyball.
   a. required
   b. optional
   c. preferred
   d. advisable

23. Coerce most nearly means
   a. permit.
   b. waste.
   c. compel.
   d. deny.

24. Collaborate most nearly means
   a. cooperate.
   b. coordinate.
   c. entice.
   d. elaborate.

25. Abrupt most nearly means
   a. interrupt.
   b. brusque.
   c. extended.
   d. corrupt.

26. Umbrage most nearly means
   a. grudge.
   b. unusable.
   c. like.
   d. calmness.

27. Illusive most nearly means
   a. actual.
   b. right.
   c. real.
   d. misleading.

28. Limpid most nearly means
    a. obvious.
    b. obscure.
    c. vague.
    d. dull.

29. Nomadic most nearly means
    a. modern.
    b. normal.
    c. wandering.
    d. logical.

30. Fraught most nearly means
    a. selected.
    b. filled.
    c. battled.
    d. decided.

31. Inept most nearly means
    a. thorough.
    b. able.
    c. incompetent.
    d. opened.

32. Potable most nearly means
    a. usable.
    b. clear.
    c. drinkable.
    d. tasty.

33. Minutiae most nearly means
    a. microcosm.
    b. regiment.
    c. details.
    d. pattern.

34. Penury most nearly means
    a. destitution.
    b. punishment.
    c. judgment.
    d. agony.

35. Verisimilitude most nearly means
    a. deceit.
    b. fanaticism.
    c. similarity.
    d. realism.

Part 4: Paragraph Comprehension

Time: 13 minutes

Police officers must read suspects their Miranda rights upon taking them into custody. When a suspect who is merely being questioned incriminates himself, he might later seek to have the case dismissed on the grounds of not having been apprised of his Miranda rights when arrested. Therefore, officers must take care not to give suspects grounds for later claiming they believed themselves to be in custody.

1. What is the main idea of the passage?
    a. Officers must remember to read suspects their Miranda rights.
    b. Suspects sometimes mistakenly believe they are in custody when in fact they are only being questioned.
    c. Officers who are merely questioning a suspect must not give the suspect the impression that he or she is in custody.
    d. Miranda rights needn't be read to all suspects before questioning.

2. When must police officers read Miranda rights to a suspect?
    a. while questioning the suspect
    b. while placing the suspect under arrest
    c. before taking the suspect to the police station
    d. before releasing the suspect

Dilly's Deli provides a dining experience like no other! Recently relocated to the old market area, Dilly's is especially popular for lunch. At the counter, you can place your order for one of Dilly's three daily lunch specials or one of several sandwiches, all at reasonable prices. Once you get your food, choose a seat at one of the four charming communal tables. By the time you are ready to carry your paper plate to the trash bin, you have experienced some of the best food and most charming company our city has to offer.

3. According to the passage, if you eat lunch at Dilly's Deli, you should expect to
   a. be surrounded by antiques.
   b. place your order with the waiter who comes to your table.
   c. carry your own food to your table.
   d. be asked out on a date by someone charming.

4. The main purpose of the passage is to
   a. profile the owner of Dilly's Deli.
   b. describe the kind of food served at Dilly's Deli.
   c. encourage people to eat at Dilly's Deli.
   d. explain the historical significance of the Dilly's Deli Building.

There are two types of diabetes, insulin-dependent and non-insulin-dependent. Between 90 and 95 percent of the estimated 13 to 14 million people in the United States with diabetes have non-insulin-dependent, or Type II, diabetes. Its symptoms often develop gradually and are hard to identify at first; therefore, nearly half of all people with diabetes do not know they have it. This can be particularly dangerous because untreated diabetes can cause damage to the heart, blood vessels, eyes, kidneys, and nerves. While the causes, short-term effects, and treatments of Type I and Type II diabetes differ, both types can cause the same long-term health problems.

5. According to the passage, which of the following may be the most dangerous aspect of Type II diabetes?
   a. Insulin shots are needed daily for treatment of Type II diabetes.
   b. In Type II diabetes the pancreas does not produce insulin.
   c. Type II diabetes interferes with digestion.
   d. Persons with Type II diabetes may not know they have it and will therefore not seek treatment.

6. Which of the following are the same for Type I and Type II diabetes?
   a. treatments
   b. long-term health risks
   c. short-term effects
   d. causes

Base Camp Climbing School is a full service, year-round climbing school that's committed to sharing its passion for the mountains throughout the seasons. It offers a complete selection of beginner through advanced rock and ice climbing programs in Daniels State Park, the neighboring Sioux Falls Range, the Whiteface Mountains, and Maxwell State Park. If individuals are looking for more adventure they should consider a climbing, mountaineering, or skiing trip to the western United States, South America, Europe, Canada, or Asia. Whatever an individual's mountain dreams are, Base Camp Climbing School can help make them a reality!

7. What are the main programs offered by the climbing school?
   a. hiking, climbing, and camping
   b. climbing, mountaineering, and ski trips
   c. rock and ice climbing
   d. all the above

8. According to the passage, how many climbing ranges are included in Base Camp Climbing School's home area?
   a. 4
   b. 5
   c. 6
   d. 1

On a barren desert testing ground, code named Trinity, near Alamogordo, New Mexico, the first atomic weapon was tested by the United States on July 16, 1945, ushering in what became to be known as the atomic age. Less than a month later, Colonel Paul Tibbets of the United States Army Air Corp added an exclamation point to this epochal event by piloting his B-29 over Hiroshima, Japan and dropping the first atomic weapon against an enemy. A little over five years later, on August 29, 1949, on a barren testing ground in the steppes of eastern Kazakhstan called Semipalatinsk, the Soviet Union detonated their first atomic weapon, code named Joe 1. Thus began a global competition between these two nations that would last for most of the next 40 years.

9. What is the main idea of the passage?
   a. nuclear power is dangerous.
   b. a brief history of the beginning of the atomic age.
   c. nuclear test sites are barren locations.
   d. the atomic age lasted only 40 years.

10. Based on what's provided in the passage, which is a piece of a larger article, what do you think the rest of the article would most likely discuss?
   a. the nuclear arms race between two super powers
   b. the history of the B-29 Stratofortress
   c. the atmospheric effects of nuclear testing
   d. none of the above

11. Which of the following would be an appropriate title for the article?
   a. Nuclear Test Sites of the U.S. and Russia
   b. The B-29 over Hiroshima
   c. U.S. vs. USSR
   d. The Beginning of the Atomic Age

Some people argue that retribution is the purpose of punishment for a person convicted of a crime, and that therefore the punishment must in some direct way fit the crime. Another view, the deterrence theory, promotes punishment in order to discourage commission of future crimes. In this view, punishment need not relate directly to the crime committed. However, punishment must necessarily be uniform and consistently applied, in order for the members of the public to understand how they would be punished if they committed a crime.

12. The passage suggests that a person who believes that the death penalty results in fewer murders most likely also believes in
   a. the deterrence theory.
   b. the retribution theory.
   c. giving judges considerable discretion in imposing sentences.
   d. the integrity of the criminal justice system.

13. A person who believes in the deterrence theory would probably also support
   a. non-unanimous jury verdicts.
   b. early release of prisoners because of prison overcrowding.
   c. a broad definition of the insanity defense.
   d. allowing television broadcasts of court proceedings.

The city ordinance reads, "Sanitation workers will not collect garbage in containers weighing more than 50 pounds." Workers are expected to use their best judgment in determining when a container weighs more than 50 pounds. If a container is too heavy, workers should attach one of the pre-printed warning messages (which are carried in all trucks) to the container, informing the household that the container weighs more than 50 pounds and cannot be collected.

14. According to the passage, in order to determine if a container is too heavy, sanitation workers should
   a. carry a scale in their truck to weigh containers.
   b. practice lifting 50 pounds at home to know what it feels like.
   c. assume any container he or she can lift weighs less than 50 pounds.
   d. use her or his best guess whether a container weighs more than 50 pounds.

15. According to the passage, if a sanitation worker believes that a container weighs more than 50 pounds, he or she should
   a. attach a pre-printed warning to the container and leave it where it is.
   b. write a note to the household, informing them of the weight limit.
   c. collect it anyway as the household probably did not know about the weight limit.
   d. notify a special collections truck to pick up the item.

Part 5: Mathematics Knowledge

Time: 24 minutes

1. Choose the answer to the following problem:
$-\frac{5}{3} - \frac{1}{3} =$
   a. $\frac{4}{3}$
   b. $-\frac{4}{3}$
   c. 2
   d. –2

2. The area of a region is measured in
   a. units.
   b. square units.
   c. cubic units.
   d. quadrants.

3. When calculating the area of a figure, you are finding
   a. the distance around the object.
   b. the length of a side.
   c. the amount of space that the object covers.
   d. the number of sides it has.

4. Choose the answer to the following problem:
$(18 + 12) \times (77 - 46) =$
   a. 900
   b. 930
   c. 810
   d. 880

5. Choose the answer to the following problem:
$12(84 - 5) - (3 \times 54) =$
   a. 54,000
   b. 841
   c. 796
   d. 786

6. Which of the following numbers is the smallest?
  a. $\frac{6}{10}$
  b. $\frac{8}{15}$
  c. $\frac{33}{60}$
  d. $\frac{11}{20}$

7. Which of the following is the equivalent of $\frac{13}{25}$?
  a. 0.38
  b. 0.4
  c. 0.48
  d. 0.52

8. What is another way to write 0.32×10^3?
  a. 3.2
  b. 32
  c. 320
  d. 3,200

9. How does the area of a rectangle change if both the base and the height of the original rectangle are tripled?
  a. The area is tripled.
  b. The area is six times larger.
  c. The area is nine times larger.
  d. The area remains the same.

10. When calculating the area of a typical family garden, you would most likely use which of the following units of measurement?
  a. square inches
  b. square millimeters
  c. square miles
  d. square feet

11. On the number line below, point L is to be located halfway between points M and N. What number will correspond to point L?

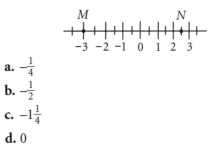

  a. $-\frac{1}{4}$
  b. $-\frac{1}{2}$
  c. $-1\frac{1}{4}$
  d. 0

12. Which of the following statements is true?
  a. Parallel lines intersect at right angles.
  b. Parallel lines never intersect.
  c. Perpendicular lines never intersect.
  d. Intersecting lines have two points in common.

13. What is another way to write 2.75×100^2?
  a. 275
  b. 2,750
  c. 27,500
  d. 270,000

14. $(a^2b)^2(2ab)^3$ is equivalent to which of the following?
  a. $2a^3b^5$
  b. $5ab$
  c. $6a^7b$
  d. $8a^7b^5$

15. What is the next number in the series below?
    3 16 6 12 12 8 _____
  a. 4
  b. 15
  c. 20
  d. 24

16. Which number sentence is true?

   a. $4.3 < 0.43$

   b. $0.43 < 0.043$

   c. $0.043 > 0.0043$

   d. $0.0043 > 0.043$

17. If $x = 3$, $y = -4$, and $z = 6$, what is the value of the following expression?

$$\frac{xz - zy}{x^2}$$

   a. $4\frac{2}{3}$

   b. $-\frac{2}{3}$

   c. 5

   d. $\frac{2}{3}$

18. What is the area of a triangle with a height of 10 inches and a base of 2 inches?

   a. 10 square inches

   b. 12 square inches

   c. 20 square inches

   d. 22 square inches

19. What is 0.473 rounded to the nearest tenth?

   a. 0.3

   b. 0.47

   c. 0.48

   d. 0.5

20. If $\frac{x}{2} + \frac{x}{6} = 4$, what is x?

   a. $\frac{1}{24}$

   b. $\frac{1}{6}$

   c. 3

   d. 6

21. Choose the answer to the following problem:

$$10^5 \div 10^2 =$$

   a. 10

   b. 10^3

   c. 10^7

   d. 10^{10}

22. $-0.05 =$

   a. $\frac{1}{20}$

   b. $-\frac{1}{20}$

   c. $\frac{1}{2}$

   d. $-\frac{1}{2}$

23. Choose the answer to the following problem:

$$\frac{4.24}{0.0848}$$

   a. 50

   b. 5.0

   c. 0.5

   d. 0.05

24. Which of the following is equivalent to $3y^4$?

   a. $3(y + y + y + y)$

   b. $3y(y)(y)(y)$

   c. $y^4 + 3$

   d. $y + y + y + y + 3$

25. If a 25cc dosage of medicine is increased by 30%, what is the new dosage?

   a. 30.5cc

   b. 17.5cc

   c. 32.5cc

   d. 18.5cc

Part 6: Electronics Information

Time: 9 minutes

1. What effect does the type of wiring gauge have on a speaker's sound quality?
   a. Since higher gauge wire is thicker, it produces higher sound quality.
   b. Since lower gauge wire is thicker, it produces lower sound quality.
   c. Since lower gauge wire is thicker, it produces higher sound quality.
   d. Since higher gauge wire is thicker, it produces lower sound quality.

2. A digital multimeter combines an ammeter, an ohmmeter, and a voltmeter into one device. Which parameter CANNOT be directly measured by a multimeter?
   a. voltage
   b. current
   c. capacitance
   d. resistance

3. What is the voltage across the load R and the current through R when the switch is open in the following circuit?

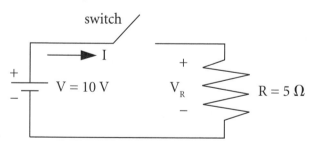

   a. The current is 0 A; the voltage is 10 V.
   b. The current is 2 A; the voltage is 10 V.
   c. The current is 2 A; the voltage is 2 V.
   d. The current is 0 A; the voltage is 0 V.

4. Which of the following is NOT a series resistance circuit?

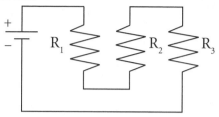

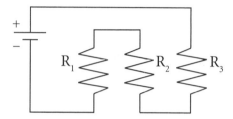

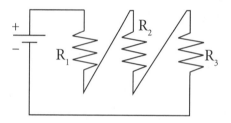

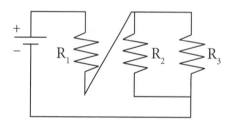

5. A 120 V light bulb is rated for 60 watts. What is the light bulb's rated current?
   a. 0.5 A
   b. 1 A
   c. 2 A
   d. 4 A

6. A toaster has two amperes flowing through it. If the current is doubled and the voltage source does not change, what happens to the power dissipated by the toaster?
  a. It does not change.
  b. It is doubled.
  c. It is reduced by a factor of 2.
  d. It is increased by a factor of 4.

7. Which of the following is another name for a transistor?
  a. a semiconductor
  b. a cathode
  c. a diode
  d. a crystal amplifier

8. Which of the following fossil fuels is NOT heavily used to produce electrical power?
  a. oil
  b. propane
  c. natural gas
  d. coal

9. Which of the following is NOT needed to produce electrical power from fossil fuels?
  a. a dam
  b. a turbine
  c. steam
  d. heat

10. What is the total current for a parallel resistance circuit with three parallel paths that each have four amperes flowing through them?
  a. 2 A
  b. 12 A
  c. 4 A
  d. 8 A

11. Most wires today are manufactured from
  a. gold
  b. copper
  c. aluminum
  d. silver

12. An AC voltmeter is connected across an outlet in your home. Which voltage will it read?
  a. 30 V
  b. 60 V
  c. 110 V
  d. 550 V

13. An AA battery produces a potential difference of 1.5 V. Four AA batteries are placed in series to power a portable FM radio. What is the total voltage of the radio?
  a. 0.75 V
  b. 1.5 V
  c. 3.0 V
  d. 6.0 V

14. A light that can be controlled from two different switches should have which type of switch installed?
  a. two single pole switches
  b. two three way switches
  c. two four way switches
  d. a single pole switch and a three way switch

15. A typical 12 V car battery is made up of eight individual cells, or batteries, connected in series. What is the voltage of each cell in a car battery?
  a. 1.5 V
  b. 12 V
  c. 8 V
  d. 3 V

16. Lightning is a result of the power dissipated when an electrical circuit is established between a charged cloud and the ground. The air provides the circuit path. What is the resistance of the air if 0.1 amperes flow between a cloud and the earth with a potential difference of 100,000 volts?
    a. 10 K Ω
    b. 100 K Ω
    c. 0.1 M Ω
    d. 1 M Ω

17. Which of the following is the symbol for a resistor?

    a.

    b.

    c.

    d.

18. A large speaker at a concert is rated for a maximum of 1,000 watts. What is the maximum voltage that can be applied to the speaker if 10 amperes of current flow through it?
    a. 10 V
    b. 100 V
    c. 1,000 V
    d. 10,000 V

19. Which function does the receiving antenna provide in radio communication?
    a. It broadcasts the signal over the air.
    b. It mixes the signal and the carrier wave.
    c. It catches the signal out of the air.
    d. It separates the carrier wave from the signal.

20. A closed circuit always has which of the following?
    a. one terminal that is positive and one terminal that is negative
    b. two terminals that are positive
    c. two terminals that are negative
    d. no terminals

Part 7: Auto and Shop Information

Time: 11 minutes

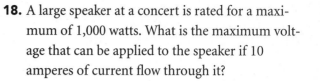

1. The hand tool shown above is a
    a. crescent wrench.
    b. hammer.
    c. screwdriver.
    d. pair of pliers.

2. Which of the following refers to rebuilding an engine according to factory specifications?
   a. spec-ing
   b. reorganizing
   c. blueprinting
   d. redesign

3. In an internal combustion automobile engine, the engine displacement is actually the volume of which of the following components?
   a. the cylinders
   b. the exhaust manifold
   c. the radiator
   d. the oil reservoir

4. A tachometer is a gauge, sometimes found on an automobile, that measures
   a. engine temperature.
   b. road velocity.
   c. engine speed.
   d. oil pressure.

5. Which group of items listed below is essential for proper operation of an automobile's internal combustion engine?
   a. fuel, spark, and oxygen
   b. cooling, shocks, and transmission
   c. heat, fire, and spark
   d. fuel, distributor cap, and muffler

6. Which of the following items is part of the braking system is an automobile?
   a. calipers
   b. drums
   c. master cylinder
   d. all of the above

7. A fire engine has become stuck in a ditch. Which of the following tools would most likely be used to help extract the fire engine from the ditch?
   a. a clamp
   b. an electric winch
   c. a cam
   d. all of the above

8. The purpose of a spark plug in an internal combustion engine is to provide
   a. lubrication of the engine.
   b. rotation of the piston.
   c. cooling of the manifold.
   d. ignition of the fuel.

9. What gauge is used to determine the number of threads per inch on a standard screw?
   a. depth gauge
   b. wire gauge
   c. thickness gauge
   d. thread gauge

10. Which of the following items is used to measure angles?
    a. a lever
    b. a tachometer
    c. a gear
    d. a protractor

11. Which of the following is NOT a type of wrench?
    a. crescent
    b. box end
    c. channel lock
    d. ratchet

12. A wrench with fixed open jaws is called
  a. a box wrench.
  b. an open-end wrench.
  c. an adjustable wrench.
  d. a socket wrench.

13. Which of the following is an electrical, as opposed to a mechanical, device?
  a. a wrench
  b. a clamp
  c. a hydraulic jack
  d. a battery

14. The purpose of a radiator on a car is to
  a. cool the engine.
  b. adjust the tire pressure.
  c. increase the engine horsepower.
  d. reduce engine noise.

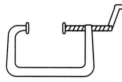

15. The C-clamp shown above would most likely be used to
  a. temporarily hold two boards together.
  b. hold up a car in order to repair a flat tire.
  c. secure a heavy load as it is being transported.
  d. make a straight cut on a board.

16. Which mechanical device is NOT typically found on an automobile?
  a. a valve
  b. a pump
  c. a drill
  d. a fan

17. When working with wood, you should always
  a. sand with the grain.
  b. sand against the grain.
  c. sand in circles.
  d. sand diagonally to the grain.

18. Which of the following best describes the purpose of welding?
  a. cleaning
  b. lifting
  c. joining
  d. moving

19. Which hand tool listed below is used to tighten a nut and bolt?
  a. a crescent wrench
  b. a reamer
  c. calipers
  d. pipe clamps

20. One main purpose of a brace is to
  a. transport water on a construction project.
  b. aid in reading a directional compass.
  c. manually drill holes in wood.
  d. lift heavy loads in a warehouse.

21. If you want to thin paint, which of the following should be used?
  a. varnish
  b. turpentine
  c. mineral spirits
  d. benzene

22. Which of the following woodworking objects would most likely be created with a lathe?
  a. a door
  b. a table leg
  c. a building block
  d. a sign

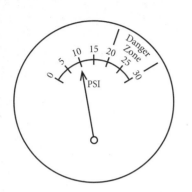

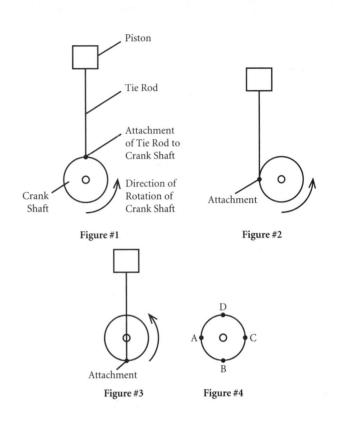

Figure #1   Figure #2

Figure #3   Figure #4

23. On the gauge above, what is the maximum recommended operating pressure in psi, pounds per square inch, for this gauge to remain in a safe zone?

a. 10 psi

b. 20 psi

c. 25 psi

d. 30 psi

24. The function of a catalytic converter is primarily to

a. change pollutants into substances that are less harmful.

b. force air into the engine for better acceleration.

c. improve the starting power of the automobile.

d. control the amount of gasoline that flows into the engine.

25. Figure #1 above shows the initial position of a piston that is connected to a crankshaft by a connecting rod. Figure #2 shows the relative positions after the crankshaft is rotated 90 degrees (one quarter of a revolution) in the direction shown. Figure #3 shows the relative positions after another 90 degrees of rotation. In Figure #4, what will be the position of the connecting rod attachment to the crankshaft after yet another 90 degree rotation?

a. position A

b. position B

c. position C

d. position D

Part 8: Mechanical Comprehension

Time: 19 minutes

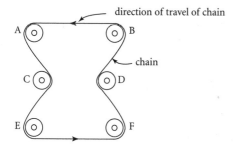

1. In the diagram above, which gears are turning clockwise?
   a. A, C, and E
   b. B, D, and F
   c. C and D
   d. E and F

2. What is the most accurate statement regarding the relationship between weight and density?
   a. Weight equals density divided by volume.
   b. A bathroom scale cannot measure density.
   c. Density can be measured in pounds.
   d. All of the above

3. A fuel tank is receiving fuel at a rate of $\frac{1}{2}$ gallon per minute. It is supplying an engine that uses 6 gallons per hour. How many gallons of fuel will be in the tank after running for 1 hour, assuming the tank was empty at the start?
   a. 12
   b. 30
   c. 18
   d. 24

4. The center of gravity of a baseball bat would be best described as
   a. near the grip.
   b. near the fat end.
   c. near the skinny end.
   d. at the top.

5. Which is heavier, five pounds of feathers or five pounds of lead?
   a. the feathers
   b. the lead
   c. They weigh the same.
   d. It is not possible to compare the two.

6. What mechanical advantage does a set of stairs provide?
   a. the benefits of class 1 lever
   b. the benefits of friction
   c. the benefits of an inclined plane
   d. the benefits of a pulley

7. A submarine would be most likely to use which of the following to aid in decreasing its submergence while under water?
   a. lead
   b. air
   c. steel
   d. none of the above

8. What would happen to a balloon full of air if you moved it from above a water surface to ten feet below the water surface?
   a. The balloon would explode.
   b. The volume of the balloon would stay the same.
   c. The volume of the balloon would increase.
   d. The volume of the balloon would decrease.

9. Which of the following is true regarding mass and weight?

 a. Mass changes with speed and weight remains constant.

 b. Both mass and weight vary with velocity.

 c. Both mass and weight remain the same, regardless of conditions.

 d. Mass remains constant but weight varies with distance from the surface of the Earth.

10. The sprocket on a bicycle is most similar to which of the simple mechanical devices listed below?

 a. a spring

 b. a lever

 c. a gear

 d. all of the above

11. The wheel of a bicycle rotates around which of the following mechanical components?

 a. a pulley

 b. an axle

 c. a cam

 d. a lever

12. Which mechanical components are typically used between a wheel and an axle to reduce friction?

 a. hinges

 b. levers

 c. springs

 d. bearings

13. Chains and belts are used in mechanical systems to do which of the following tasks?

 a. transfer energy

 b. transfer motion

 c. link gears and pulleys

 d. all of the above

14. What mechanical motion principle do the brakes in a car or on a bicycle use?

 a. friction

 b. centrifugal force

 c. acceleration

 d. momentum

15. If one end of each of the following items were to be placed in a pot of boiling water, which would conduct heat the best?

 a. a plastic spoon

 b. a steel utensil

 c. a wooden spoon

 d. none of the above

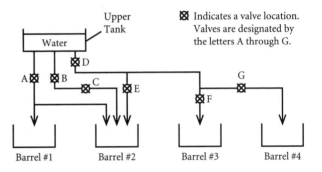

16. In the diagram above, all valves are initially closed. Gravity will cause the water to drain down into the barrels when the valves are opened. Which barrels will be filled if valves A, B, E, F, and G are opened and valves C and D are left closed?

 a. barrels #1 and #2

 b. barrels #3 and #4

 c. barrels #1, #2, #3, and #4

 d. barrels #1, #2, and #3

17. A block of ice is slid across several different surfaces. Which type of surface will provide the least friction?

 a. steel

 b. concrete

 c. wood

 d. ice

18. A hoist is typically used for which of the operations shown below?
- **a.** reducing wind resistance
- **b.** cutting metal objects
- **c.** lifting heavy objects
- **d.** heating water

19. When you add water to a tank, the water pressure at the top will
- **a.** change with the water depth.
- **b.** decrease.
- **c.** stay the same.
- **d.** increase.

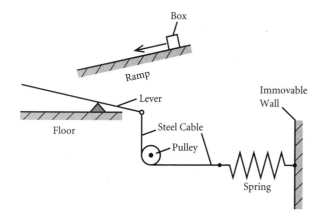

20. In the diagram above, if the box slides down the ramp and drops onto the left side of the lever, what will happen to the spring?
- **a.** It will touch the box.
- **b.** It will remain as it is.
- **c.** It will be compressed, or shortened.
- **d.** It will be stretched, or lengthened.

21. A total of seven columns will be used to support a new bridge. How much of the total bridge weight will each column support?
- **a.** one-half
- **b.** one-fifth
- **c.** one-seventh
- **d.** not enough information

22. Velocity, direction, and acceleration are all topics that fall into which of the following categories?
- **a.** mechanical motion
- **b.** rotary motion
- **c.** torque
- **d.** angular momentum

23. Which of the following mechanical devices is used to open a common soft drink can?
- **a.** a winch
- **b.** a lever
- **c.** a wrench
- **d.** a piston

24. An elevator is most similar to which of the following mechanical devices?
- **a.** a lever
- **b.** a hydraulic jack
- **c.** a crane
- **d.** a spring

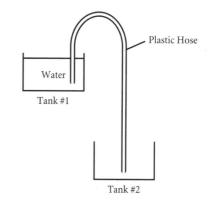

25. What mechanical device could be used to transfer water from tank #1 to tank #2?
- **a.** a pulley
- **b.** a siphon
- **c.** a lever
- **d.** a spring

Part 9: Assembling Objects

Time: 16 minutes

1.

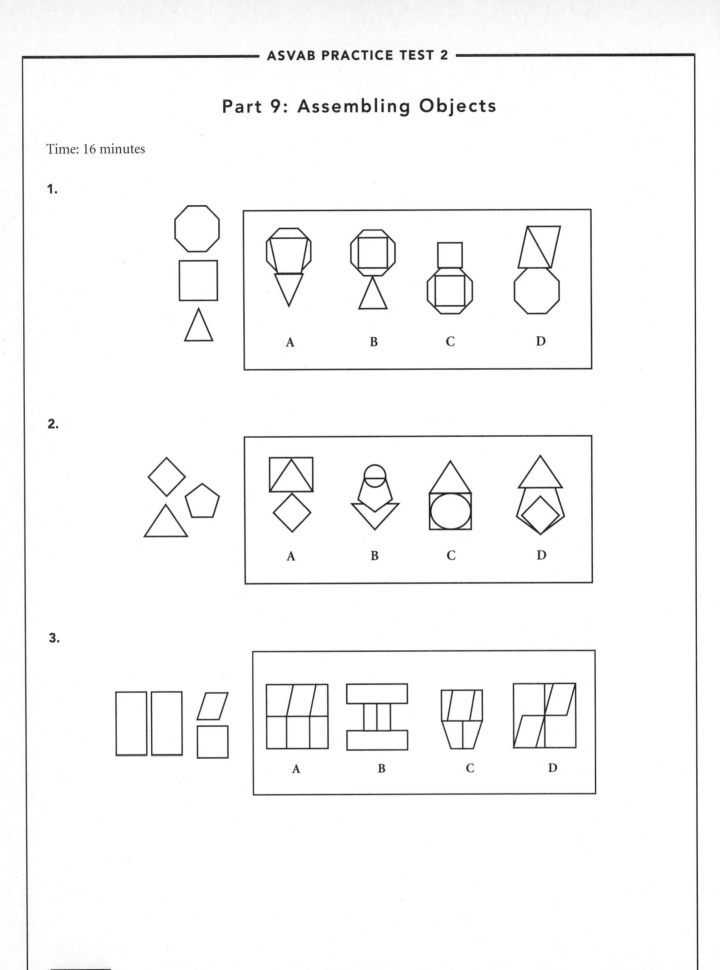

2.

3.

4.

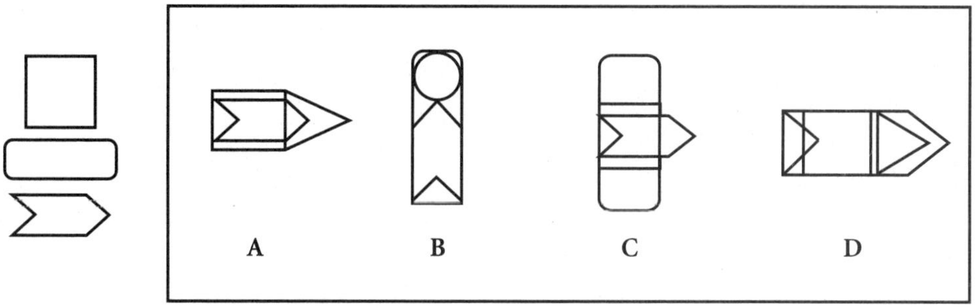

A   B   C   D

5.

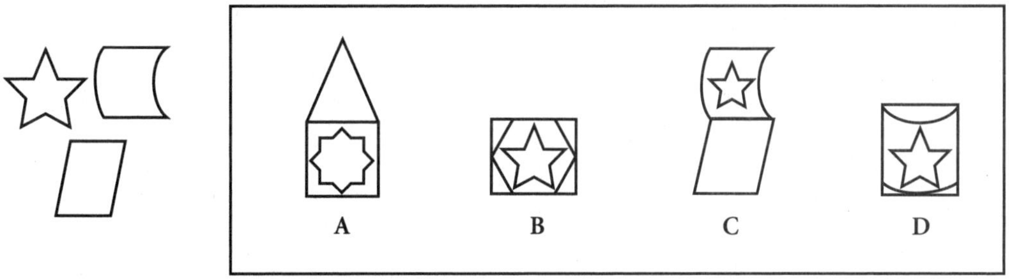

A   B   C   D

6.

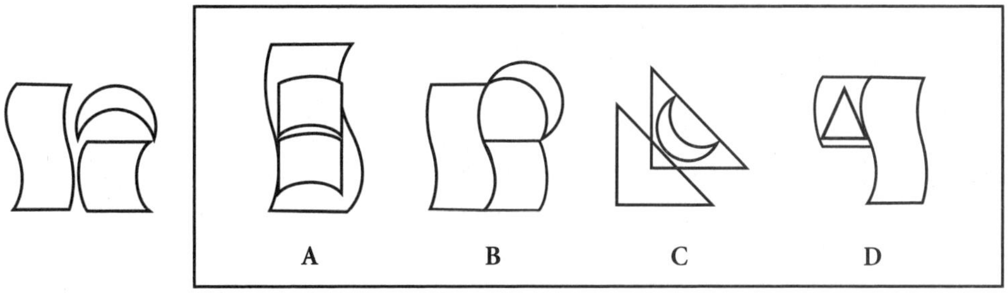

A   B   C   D

7.

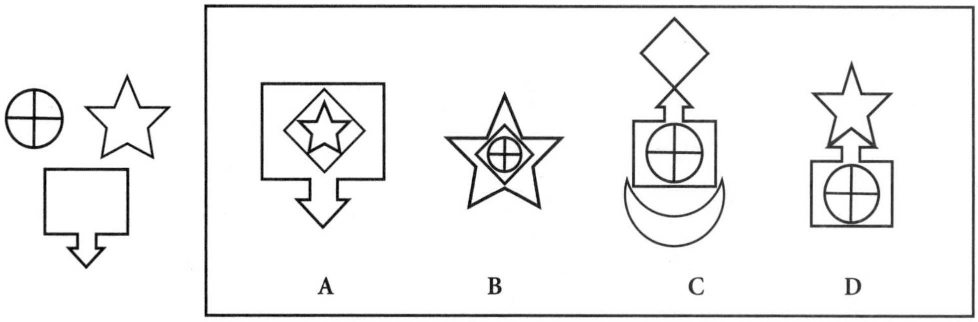

A   B   C   D

8.

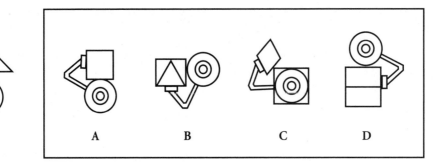

9.

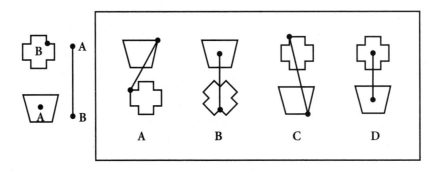

10.

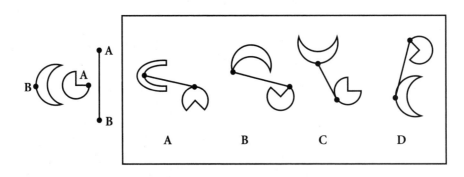

11.

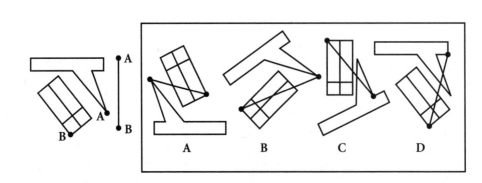

12.

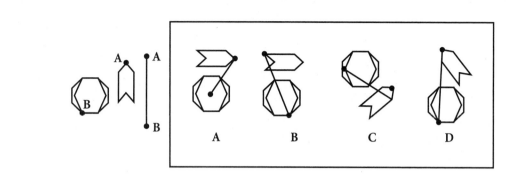

13.

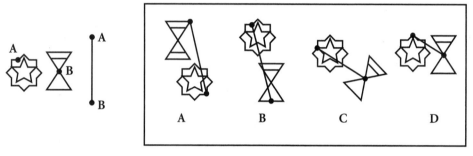

14.

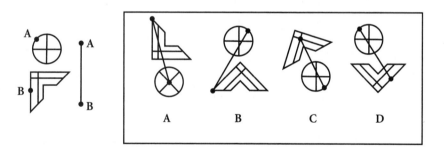

15.

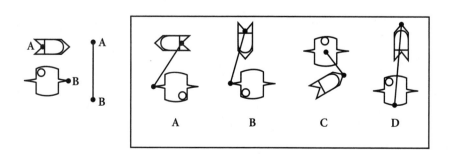

16.

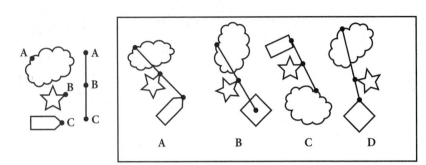

Answers

Part 1: General Science

1. b. Gorillas belong to the mammalia class.

2. d. Benzene consists of a ring of six carbon atoms. This ring is the basis of all aromatic compounds.

3. a. $C_6H_{12}O_6$ contains 3 elements: carbon, hydrogen, and oxygen.

4. d. A micrometer is one-millionth of a meter; it is therefore one-thousandth of a millimeter, because a millimeter is one-thousandth of a meter.

5. d. To express a number in scientific notation, you move the decimal as many places as necessary until there is only one digit to the left of the decimal. For 617,000, you move the decimal to the left by 5 decimal places. The fact that you had to move it to the left means that the 10 should be raised to a positive power, so the result is 6.17×10^5.

6. c. Gravity pulls the ball downward as it moves forward.

7. a. An ax blade is an example of a wedge. A lever is usually a rigid bar used to exert pressure or sustain weight at one point by the application of force at a second point and a turning point at a third.

8. a. The outer surface of the Earth is the crust, followed by the mantle. Next is the core, and finally, the inner core.

9. d. An anemometer measures wind. The other choices are instruments of measure, but they do not measure wind.

10. b. Tigers are in the phylum Chordata, class Mammalia, order Carnivora. Genus and species names are always underlined or in italics, as in the species name *tigris*.

11. b. Metamorphic rocks are formed by the alteration of pre-existing rock, due to heat and pressure caused by burial in the Earth.

12. c. Igneous rocks make up a group of rocks formed from the crystallization of magma (lava). Sedimentary rock is formed by silt or rock fragments.

13. d. All organic compounds contain carbon (C). Calcium (Ca) is only a single element, and it does not contain carbon.

14. a. Beetles and crabs are both in the arthropod phylum. Arthropods are invertebrates characterized by having a hard exoskeleton (outer skeleton), at least six jointed legs, and a segmented body. Salmon, frogs, and robins are all in the chordate phylum; all chordates have a nerve cord (a spine) at some point in their development.

15. c. Scarlet fever, sometimes called *scarlatina*, is a disease caused by a bacteria called group A Streptococcus.

16. c. Insulin promotes the uptake of glucose (a sugar) in the body. Estrogen and androgen control the development of sex characteristics in women and men respectively.

17. b. Veins carry blood devoid of oxygen to the right atrium of the heart. Arteries, capillaries, and the aorta carry oxygenated blood from the heart to blood cells throughout the body.

18. d. Herbivores are animals that subsist on plant matter. Omnivores eat a variety of foodstuff, and carnivores eat other animals.

19. c. The exchange of water, oxygen, carbon dioxide, and other nutrients and waste products in the body occurs at the capillary level of the circulatory system.

20. b. The Eustachian tube connects the middle ear and throat. The cochlea is a fluid-filled structure in the inner ear.

21. c. The Watson-Crick model of DNA is a double-stranded twisted ladder, or double helix.

22. b. Fiber is found only in plants. Raw vegetables, fruit with seeds, whole cereals, and bread are other possible sources of fiber.

23. a. Deciduous forests are characterized by having mild temperatures and many trees that shed leaves periodically. Taigas are characterized by evergreen trees and long, harsh winters.

24. a. Burning a piece of toast changes the composition of the substance, so it is a chemical change. Choices **b**, **c**, and **d** are physical changes.

25. c. A human embryo's sex is always determined by the sperm. The egg always contributes an X chromosome, while the sperm contributes either an X (for a female) or a Y (for a male).

Part 2: Arithmetic Reasoning

1. c. Here, 234 is rounded to 230 and 579 is rounded to 580, giving 230 × 580 = 133,400.

2. c. First, add the number of patients to find the total: 63. Then divide the number of patients by the number of nursing assistants: 63 divided by 7 is 9.

3. b. This is a two-step multiplication problem. To find out how many heartbeats there would be in one hour, you must multiply 72 by 60 (minutes) and then multiply this result, 4,320, by 6.5 hours.

4. c. Let E = emergency room cost; H = hospice cost, which is $(\frac{1}{4})$E; N = home nursing cost, which is 2H, or $2(\frac{1}{4})$E. The total bill is E + H + N, which is E + $(\frac{1}{4})$E + $(\frac{2}{4})$E, = 140,000. Add the left side of the equation to get $\frac{7}{4}$E = 140,000. To solve for E, multiply both sides of the equation by $(\frac{4}{7})$. E = 140,000$(\frac{4}{7})$, or 80,000. H = $(\frac{1}{4})$E, or 20,000, and N = 2H, or 40,000.

5. d. Multiply $1\frac{1}{2}$ by 10. Change $1\frac{1}{2}$ to an improper fraction $(\frac{3}{2})$ and make 10 into a fraction by placing it over 1 $(\frac{10}{1})$; $\frac{3}{2} \times \frac{10}{1} = \frac{30}{2}$ = 15 feet. Each side is 15 feet long, so the dimensions are 15 ft by 15 ft.

6. b. If half the students are female, then you would expect half of the out-of-state students to be female. One half of $\frac{1}{12}$ is $\frac{1}{24}$.

7. d. $22,650,000 × $\frac{1}{5}$ = $4,530,000

8. c. A foot in height makes a difference of 60 pounds, or 5 pounds per inch of height over 5′. A person who is 5′5″ is (5)(5 pounds), or 25 pounds, heavier than the person who is 5′, so add 25 pounds to 110 pounds to get 135 pounds.

9. c. The difference between 220 and this person's age is 190. The maximum heart rate is 90% of this: (0.9)(190) = 171.

10. b. The part of their goal that they have raised is $2,275 and the whole goal is $3,500. The fraction for this is $\frac{2,275}{3,500}$. The numerator and denominator can both be divided by 175 to get a simplified fraction of $\frac{13}{20}$. They have completed $\frac{13}{20}$ of their goal, which means that they have $\frac{7}{20}$ left to go $(\frac{20}{20} - \frac{13}{20} = \frac{7}{20})$.

11. d. Thirty ppm of the pollutant would have to be removed to bring the 50 ppm down to 20 ppm. Thirty ppm represents 60% of 50 ppm.

12. b. This problem is solved by multiplying 2,200 by $\frac{12}{100}$. 2,200 × $\frac{12}{100}$ = 264.

13. a. Compare $\frac{3}{4}$, $\frac{3}{5}$, $\frac{2}{3}$, and $\frac{2}{5}$ by finding a common denominator. The common denominator for 3, 4, and 5 is 60. Multiply the numerator and denominator of a fraction by the same number so that the denominator becomes 60. The fractions then become $\frac{45}{60}$, $\frac{36}{60}$, $\frac{40}{60}$, and $\frac{24}{60}$. The fraction with the largest numerator is the largest fraction; $\frac{45}{60}$ is the largest fraction. It is equivalent to Joey's fraction of $\frac{3}{4}$.

14. a. Add the number of hours together using a common denominator of 60; $4\frac{30}{60}$ + $3\frac{45}{60}$ + $8\frac{12}{60}$ + $1\frac{20}{60}$ = $16\frac{107}{60}$, which is simplified to $17\frac{47}{60}$ hours.

15. d. Let E = the estimate. *One-fifth more than the estimate* means $\frac{6}{5}$ or 120% of E, so 600,000 = (1.20)(E). Dividing both sides by 1.2 leaves E = 500,000.

16. c. Calculate the percentage by dividing 5 miles by 10 miles. 5 ÷ 10 = .50, which is equivalent to 50%.

17. b. Here, 250 milligrams is $\frac{250}{1000}$ gram, or 0.250 g.

18. a. First find out how long the entire hike can be, based on the rate at which the hikers are using their supplies. If 1 = all supplies and x = entire hike, then $\frac{\frac{2}{5}}{3} = \frac{1}{x}$. Cross-multiply to get $\frac{2x}{5} = 3$, so that $x = \frac{(3)(5)}{2}$, or $7\frac{1}{2}$ days for the length of the entire hike. This means that the hikers could go forward for 3.75 days altogether before they would have to turn around. They have already hiked for 3 days, which leaves 0.75 for the amount of time they can now go forward before having to turn around.

19. c. Three tons is 6,000 pounds; 6,000 pounds multiplied by 16 ounces per pound is 96,000 ounces. The total weight of each daily ration is 48 ounces; 96,000 divided by 48 is 2,000 troops supplied; 2,000 divided by 10 days is 200 troops supplied.

20. d. Twenty-six forms multiplied by 8 hours is 208 forms per day per clerk; 5,600 divided by 208 is approximately 26.9, which means you have to hire 27 clerks for the day.

21. a. The companies' combined rate of travel is 50 miles per hour; 2,100 miles divided by 50 miles per hour is 42 hours.

22. b. The recruit's three best times are 54, 54, and 57. To find the average, add the 3 numbers and divide the sum by 3.

23. b. In 4 hours the man would have traveled 260 miles. His wife must drive approximately 74 mph (260 miles ÷ 3.5 hours) to catch up with him.

24. d. 2,200(0.07) = $154; $154 + 1400(0.04) = $210; $210 + 3100(0.08) = $458; $458 + $900(0.03) = $485.

25. a. Let S stand for Sarah and Z stand for Zach. We are told that S = 8Z and S + 4 = 4(Z + 4). Simplify the second equation to 8Z + 4 = 4Z + 16. So Z = 3 and S = 24.

26. d. Here, 3,450 miles divided by 6 days is 575 miles.

27. c. 84,720 troops multiplied by 4 square yards of cloth is 338,880 square yards of cloth required.

28. b. Thirty men multiplied by 42 square feet of space is 1,260 square feet of space; 1,260 square feet divided by 35 men is 36 square feet, so each man will have 6 less square feet of space.

29. c. Let T = Ted's age; S = Sam's age = 3T; R = Ron's age = $\frac{S}{2}$, or $\frac{3T}{2}$. The sum of the ages is 55, which means T + 3T + $\frac{3T}{2}$ = 55. Find the common denominator (2) to add the left side of the equation. T = 10. If Ted is 10, then Sam is 30, and Ron is $\frac{3T}{2}$, which is 15 years old.

30. b. The difference between 105 and 99 is 6 degrees. The temperature is lowered by half a degree every six minutes, or 1 degree every 12 minutes; 6 degrees multiplied by 12 minutes per degree is 72 minutes, or 1 hour and 12 minutes.

Part 3: Word Knowledge

1. d. Something that is *erroneous* is wrong or *faulty*.

2. c. Something that is *grotesque* is distorted, misshapen, or *hideous*.

3. c. To be *outmoded* is to be out-of-date or *obsolete*.

4. b. A statement that is *garbled* is scrambled and confusing, or *unintelligible*.

5. a. Something that is *rigorous* is strict or *demanding*.

6. d. A thing that is *flagrant* is conspicuous or *glaring*.

7. c. An *oration* is a formal speech or an *address*.

8. d. When something is done *obstinately*, it is done in a refractory manner or *stubbornly*.

9. b. A *glib* remark is a quick and insincere, or *superficial*, one.

10. b. When someone has *composure*, that person has self-possession or *poise*.

11. c. To be *eccentric* is to be unconventional or *peculiar*.

12. a. If something is *commendable* it is praiseworthy or *admirable*.

13. d. To be *oblivious* of something is to be unaware or *ignorant* of it.

14. d. An act of *philanthropy* is an act of charity or *generosity*.

15. b. To be *ostentatious* is to be showy or *pretentious*.

16. a. To be *passive* is to be compliant or *resigned*.

17. c. When something is in *proximity* to something else, it is close or in *nearness* to it.

18. a. To be *negligible* is to be unimportant or *insignificant*.

19. d. A *rational* judgment is a logical or *sound* one.

20. b. To be *vigilant* is to be watchful or *alert*.

21. a. To be *astute* is to be keen-minded or *perceptive*.

22. a. A *prerequisite* is something that is necessary or *required*.

23. c. To *coerce* someone to do something is to force, pressure, or *compel* that person to do it.

24. a. To *collaborate* on a project is to work together or *cooperate* on it.

25. b. To be *abrupt* is to be curt or *brusque*.

26. a. *Umbrage* is to be angry or to have a *grudge*.

27. d. *Illusive* means deceptive or *misleading*.

28. a. *Limpid* is clear or *obvious*.

29. b. *Nomadic* refers to *wandering* or roaming about.

30. b. *Fraught* means *filled* or laden.

31. c. *Inept* means *incompetent*.

32. c. *Potable* means to be safe to drink or *drinkable*.

33. c. *Minutiae* refers to very small *details* or trivial matters.

34. a. *Penury* means extreme poverty, or *destitution*.

35. d. *Verisimilitude* is the appearance of being true or real.

Part 4: Paragraph Comprehension

1. a. While choices **b** and **c** are true, they are not the main idea. Choice **d** is contradicted in the last sentence.

2. b. See the first sentence of the passage.

3. c. This is the only one of the choices that is stated in the passage (in the third and fourth sentences). Choices **a** and **d** are not stated in the passage. Choice **b** is contradicted by the passage.

4. c. The whole tone of the passage is complimentary to Dilly's. Choices **a** and **d** are not mentioned in the passage. Although choice **b** is mentioned, it is not the main point.

5. d. The passage mentions that the symptoms of Type II diabetes may occur gradually and thus be attributed to other causes. Left untreated, diabetes can cause damage to several major organs in the body.

6. b. According to the passage, only the long-term health problems are the same for these two different disorders.

7. c. Rock and ice climbing are the only two programs directly referred to in the passage as "main programs."

8. a. According to the passage there are four climbing ranges in Base Camp Climbing School's home area: Daniels State Park, Sioux Falls Range, the Whiteface Mountains, and Maxwell State Park.

9. b. Choices **a** and **c** are not mentioned in the passage. Choice **d** is only mentioned as a description of the locations.

10. a. The whole tone of the passage leaves the reader expecting a discussion of the main idea, that being the nuclear arms race. Choices **b** and **c** might be discussed incidentally, but they will not be the theme of the article.

11. d. Choices **a**, **b**, and **c** are all mentioned tangentially in the passage, but only choice **d** encompasses the idea of the passage, making it the best choice for a title.

12. a. This can be deduced from the second sentence of the passage.

13. d. The last sentence notes that the deterrence theory has the effect of teaching not only criminals but also the public.

14. d. Although the other options are not precluded by the passage, the passage only requires workers to make an educated guess as to the weight of the container.

15. a. See the third sentence of the passage.

Part 5: Mathematics Knowledge

1. d. Subtract to get $-\frac{6}{3}$, which reduces to –2.

2. b. When calculating area, you are finding the number of square units that cover the region.

3. c. The area of a figure is the amount of space the object covers, in square units.

4. b. Perform the operations within the parentheses first, which gives you $30 \times 31 = 930$.

5. d. Perform the operations in the parentheses first: $(12)(79) - 162 = 786$.

6. b. Fractions must be converted to the lowest common denominator, which allows you to compare the amounts: $\frac{36}{60}, \frac{32}{60}, \frac{33}{60}$, and $\frac{33}{60}$.

7. d. The fraction $\frac{13}{25}$ is equal to $\frac{52}{100}$.

8. c. $(0.32)(10^3) = 0.32 \times (10 \times 10 \times 10)$

9. c. Since both dimensions are tripled, there are two additional factors of 3. Therefore, the new area is $3 \times 3 = 9$ times as large as the original.

10. d. A typical family garden is most likely measured in square feet.

11. a. The halfway point on the number line is between 0 and $-\frac{1}{2}$, which is $-\frac{1}{4}$.

12. b. Corresponding points on parallel lines are always the same distance apart, so the lines can never intersect.

13. c. $100^2 = (100)(100)$, or 10,000; $(10,000)(2.75) = 27,500$.

14. d. Multiply the powers of each set of parentheses to get $a^4b^2(8a^3b^3)$. When multiplying the outside of the parentheses by the inside, add the exponents.

15. d. This series actually has two alternating sets of numbers. The first number is doubled, giving the third number. The second number has 4 subtracted from it, giving the fourth number. Therefore, the blank space will be 12 doubled, or 24.

16. c. The farther to the right the digits go, the smaller the number.

17. a. Beginning with the operations in the brackets, you get $\frac{[(3)(6)] - [(6)(-4)]}{9} = \frac{18 - (-24)}{9} = 4\frac{2}{3}$

18. a. The formula for the area of a triangle is $A = \frac{1}{2}bh$; $\frac{1}{2}(10)(2) = 10$.

19. d. 0.473 rounded to the nearest tenth is 0.5.

20. d. To add the left side of the equation, find the common denominator, so that $\frac{3x}{6} + \frac{x}{6} = 4$; $\frac{4x}{6} = 4$; and $4x = 24$.

21. b. In a division problem like this, leave the whole number the same and subtract the exponents.

22. b. You can use trial and error to arrive at a solution to this problem. After the first hour, the number would be 20, after the second hour 40, after the third hour 80, after the fourth hour 160, and after the fifth hour 320. The other answer choices do not have the same outcome.

23. a. Convert the numbers to whole numbers by moving the decimals over 4 places. This gives you $42{,}400 \div 848 = 50$.

24. b. $3y^4 = 3y(y)(y)(y)$.

25. c. Thirty percent of 25cc is $0.30 \times 25 = 7.5$. $25 + 7.5 = 32.5$.

Part 6: Electronics Information

1. c. The thickness or gauge of a wire determines the amount of electronic information that can travel alongside it. A lower gauge wire is thicker; therefore it will produce higher quality sounds.

2. c. An ammeter measures current. An ohmmeter measures resistance, and a voltmeter measures voltage.

3. d. When the switch is open, no current flows. The voltage V_R is I times R, which equals $0(5\ \Omega) = 0$.

4. d. R_2 and R_3 are in parallel; therefore, the circuit is a series parallel resistance circuit.

5. a. $P = VI$. Therefore, $I = \frac{P}{V} = \frac{60\ \text{watts}}{120\ \text{V}}$, or 0.5 A.

6. d. $P = I^2R$. The original current was 2 A, so power $P = 4R$. When the current is doubled to 4 A, the power $P = 16R$. The power is increased by a factor of four.

7. d. A transistor is also known as a crystal amplifier.

8. b. Coal, natural gas, and oil are the primary fossil fuels used to produce electrical power.

9. a. Dams are used to produce power from water.

10. b. The total current is equal to the sum of the currents through each resistance. Therefore, 4 A + 4 A + 4 A = 12 A.

11. b. Most wires are made of copper because it has high conductivity and is relatively inexpensive.

12. c. The voltages most commonly used in the home are 110 V and 220 V.

13. d. Voltages in series are added to determine the total voltage. 1.5 V + 1.5 V + 1.5 V + 1.5 V = 6.0 V.

14. b. Two three way switches will provide the required power control and distribution.

15. a. Voltages in series are added to determine the total voltage, so divide 12 volts by 8 cells to get 1.5 V.

16. d. Ohm's law states V = IR, so $R = \frac{V}{I}$, which is $\frac{100,000\ V}{0.1\ A} = 1,000,000\ \Omega$, which is 1 M Ω.

17. a. Choice **b** is a capacitor; choice **c** is a voltage source, and choice **d** is a switch.

18. b. The power equation states P = VI, so $V = \frac{P}{I}$. $\frac{1000\ W}{10\ A} = 100\ V$.

19. c. The broadcast antenna is used to broadcast the signal over the air. The mixer combines the signal and carrier wave. The de-mixer separates the carrier and the signal.

20. a. A closed circuit always needs one terminal that is positive and one that is negative.

Part 7: Auto and Shop Information

1. b. A hammer is used for driving nails and other general carpentry functions.

2. c. Blueprinting refers to rebuilding an engine to factory specifications.

3. a. The cylinder is the cavity in which the piston moves up and down. An engine with more cylinders (eight versus six or four) or bigger cylinders will have a bigger displacement and will generate more power.

4. c. This gauge measures engine speed in revolutions per minute (RPM).

5. a. The fuel is ignited by the spark from the spark plug. Oxygen is needed for the fuel to burn. The burning of the fuel pushes the piston up and down in the engine's cylinders, and that energy is transferred to the wheels by way of the transmission.

6. d. When the brake pedal is pressed, it operates the master cylinder, which forces the brake fluid through the lines out to each wheel. The pressure in the brake lines causes the calipers to move and press the brake shoes against the brake drum. This causes the automobile to slow down.

7. b. The other devices would not be useful in this situation.

8. d. The spark plug produces a spark inside the cylinder of the engine and causes the fuel to burn.

9. d. A thread gauge is used to determine the thread pitch and diameter of screws.

10. d. A protractor is typically a half-circle made of metal or plastic that has tick marks around the edge spaced at one-degree intervals.

11. c. Channel lock is a type of pliers.

12. b. A wrench with fixed open jaws is called an open-end wrench.

13. d. The other items listed are common mechanical devices.

14. a. The radiator contains fluid (water and antifreeze) that is circulated around the engine block by the water pump. The fluid becomes hot as it passes around the engine and is then cooled as air passes through the radiator.

15. a. The C-clamp would be placed around the two boards and tightened by turning the screw with the handle.

16. c. A drill is a carpenter's hand tool. The other items are common parts of a car.

17. a. When working with wood, you should always sand with the grain.

18. c. Welding is the process of connecting two pieces of material such as metal or plastic.

19. a. A reamer is used to shape or enlarge holes; calipers are used to measure internal and external dimensions. Pipe clamps are used to clamp boards or framing together so they can be bonded by glue.

20. c. A brace can also be used to provide additional torque when driving screws.

21. b. Paint should always be thinned with turpentine. Any of the other compounds will change the chemical makeup of the paint.

22. b. A lathe is a tool which is typically used to carve long, slender pieces of wood. The wood is attached to the lathe and an electric motor spins the piece of wood. A cutting blade is then used to remove parts of the wood, giving a decorative shape. A lathe would not be useful in making the other objects listed.

23. b. The gauge indicates that any pressure greater than 20 psi is in the danger zone.

24. a. The catalytic converter converts pollutants into less harmful substances.

25. c. Figure #3 shows the attachment of the connecting rod to the crankshaft at the bottom of the crankshaft. Another 90-degree counter-clockwise rotation would place the attachment point on the right side of the crankshaft at position C.

Part 8: Mechanical Comprehension

1. c. The other gears are turning counter-clockwise. It helps to follow the direction of the chain, which is connected to all of the gears.

2. b. Choice **a** is not correct, as weight is equal to density multiplied by volume. Choice **c** is not correct, as density is measured in weight (pounds) per unit volume.

3. d. After 1 hour at a rate of $\frac{1}{2}$ gallon per minute, there will be 30 gallons in the tank. The engine burned 6 gallons in that hour, so the fuel remaining is 24 gallons.

4. b. The center of gravity is the place on an object where there is equal weight on either side.

5. c. Weight is measured in pounds, and the question states that both the feathers and the lead weigh five pounds.

6. c. The advantage a set of stairs provides is that it acts as an inclined plane.

7. b. Steel and lead are heavier than water and would therefore not aid in moving upward through the water. Air, which is lighter than water, can be injected into the ballast tanks, which will cause the submarine to rise.

8. d. The volume of the balloon would decrease. The pressure of the water would press inward on the balloon and cause it to shrink in volume.

9. d. Mass never changes, regardless of the location. Regarding weight, the farther an object is away from the Earth's gravitational pull, the more it decreases. Outside of the Earth's gravitational field, an object would be weightless.

10. c. A bicycle sprocket is the classic example of a gear, which is defined as a toothed wheel or cylinder that meshes with a chain or with another toothed element to transfer energy or motion.

11. b. An axle is typically a metal rod located at the center of a wheel around which the wheel rotates. The ends of the axle are then attached to the vehicle.

12. d. A set of bearings is typically a set of small metal balls packed in a groove and lubricated with grease or oil. The wheel rubs against one side of each ball, and the axle rubs against the other side. The net effect is that the wheel rolls much more easily.

13. d. All of the choices are correct.

14. a. When the brakes are applied, the brake pads rub on the wheel and the frictional force of this rubbing slows down the vehicle.

15. b. A steel utensil would conduct heat the best because steel is an ideal conductor of thermal energy. The other selections are poor conductors of heat.

16. a. Since valve D is closed, water will not flow to barrels #3 and #4. Water will flow through valve B but be stopped at valve C. Water will flow through valve A into barrels #1 and #2.

17. d. A low coefficient of friction between two surfaces means that the drag force between the two surfaces is low. A block of ice sliding over an ice surface will slide farther than a block of ice sliding across wood, concrete, or steel.

18. c. A hoist is usually a steel frame with a steel cable running over a pulley with a lifting hook on the end of the cable. The hook is placed around the heavy object to be lifted, and either a hand crank or an electric motor is used to reel in the cable, thus lifting the object.

19. c. Water pressure at the bottom of a tank increases as the weight of water above it increases, but pressure at the top remains the same since it has a finite amount of water above it.

20. d. The box will force the left side of the lever down and the right side of the lever up, which will pull the cable up. The cable will pass across the pulley and apply a pulling force on the spring, which will stretch the spring.

21. d. If we were told that the columns were uniformly spaced along the length of the bridge, then each column would support one-seventh of the total weight. Since this is not specified, there is not enough information to answer the question.

22. a. Velocity, direction, and acceleration are the terms used to describe mechanical motion such as vehicular travel, motion of a clock pendulum, or projectile motion of a bullet.

23. b. The little tab you use to pry open the can is a lever. You lift on one end of the lever, which rotates around a pivot point and forces the other end of the lever downward, so that the can pops open.

24. c. An elevator is simply a crane that raises and lowers people.

25. b. To use a siphon, you would first submerge the entire length of hose in tank #1 in order to completely fill it with water. You would then place one end of the hose in tank #1 and the other end in tank #2, as shown in the diagram. Since the end of the hose in tank #2 is lower than the end in tank #1, the extra weight of the water in the right side of the hose will cause the water to flow into tank #2.

Part 9: Assembling Objects

1. b.

2. d.

3. a.

4. c.

5. c.

6. b.

7. d.

8. b.

9. b.

10. d.

11. b.

12. d.

13. c.

14. d.

15. a.

16. a.

Scoring

Write your raw score (the number you got right) for each test in the blanks below. Then turn to Chapter 3 to find out how to convert these raw scores into the scores the armed services use.

1. General Science: _____ right out of 25
2. Arithmetic Reasoning: _____ right out of 30
3. Word Knowledge: _____ right out of 35
4. Paragraph Comprehension: _____ right out of 15
5. Mathematics Knowledge: _____ right out of 25
6. Electronics Information: _____ right out of 20
7. Auto and Shop Information: _____ right out of 25
8. Mechanical Comprehension: _____ right out of 25
9. Assembling Objects: _____ right out of 16

16 ▶ ASVAB PRACTICE 3

CHAPTER SUMMARY

Here's another sample ASVAB for you to practice with. After working through the review material in the previous chapters, take this test to see how much your score has improved.

For this test, simulate the actual test-taking experience as closely as you can. Find a quiet place to work where you won't be disturbed. If you own this book, tear out the answer sheet on the following pages and find some number 2 pencils to fill in the circles with. Use a timer or stopwatch to time each section. The times are marked at the beginning of each section. After you take the test, use the detailed answer explanations that follow to review any questions you missed.

Part 1: General Science

1.	ⓐ	ⓑ	ⓒ	ⓓ	10.	ⓐ	ⓑ	ⓒ	ⓓ	19.	ⓐ	ⓑ	ⓒ	ⓓ				
2.	ⓐ	ⓑ	ⓒ	ⓓ	11.	ⓐ	ⓑ	ⓒ	ⓓ	20.	ⓐ	ⓑ	ⓒ	ⓓ				
3.	ⓐ	ⓑ	ⓒ	ⓓ	12.	ⓐ	ⓑ	ⓒ	ⓓ	21.	ⓐ	ⓑ	ⓒ	ⓓ				
4.	ⓐ	ⓑ	ⓒ	ⓓ	13.	ⓐ	ⓑ	ⓒ	ⓓ	22.	ⓐ	ⓑ	ⓒ	ⓓ				
5.	ⓐ	ⓑ	ⓒ	ⓓ	14.	ⓐ	ⓑ	ⓒ	ⓓ	23.	ⓐ	ⓑ	ⓒ	ⓓ				
6.	ⓐ	ⓑ	ⓒ	ⓓ	15.	ⓐ	ⓑ	ⓒ	ⓓ	24.	ⓐ	ⓑ	ⓒ	ⓓ				
7.	ⓐ	ⓑ	ⓒ	ⓓ	16.	ⓐ	ⓑ	ⓒ	ⓓ	25.	ⓐ	ⓑ	ⓒ	ⓓ				
8.	ⓐ	ⓑ	ⓒ	ⓓ	17.	ⓐ	ⓑ	ⓒ	ⓓ									
9.	ⓐ	ⓑ	ⓒ	ⓓ	18.	ⓐ	ⓑ	ⓒ	ⓓ									

Part 2: Arithmetic Reasoning

1.	ⓐ	ⓑ	ⓒ	ⓓ	11.	ⓐ	ⓑ	ⓒ	ⓓ	21.	ⓐ	ⓑ	ⓒ	ⓓ
2.	ⓐ	ⓑ	ⓒ	ⓓ	12.	ⓐ	ⓑ	ⓒ	ⓓ	22.	ⓐ	ⓑ	ⓒ	ⓓ
3.	ⓐ	ⓑ	ⓒ	ⓓ	13.	ⓐ	ⓑ	ⓒ	ⓓ	23.	ⓐ	ⓑ	ⓒ	ⓓ
4.	ⓐ	ⓑ	ⓒ	ⓓ	14.	ⓐ	ⓑ	ⓒ	ⓓ	24.	ⓐ	ⓑ	ⓒ	ⓓ
5.	ⓐ	ⓑ	ⓒ	ⓓ	15.	ⓐ	ⓑ	ⓒ	ⓓ	25.	ⓐ	ⓑ	ⓒ	ⓓ
6.	ⓐ	ⓑ	ⓒ	ⓓ	16.	ⓐ	ⓑ	ⓒ	ⓓ	26.	ⓐ	ⓑ	ⓒ	ⓓ
7.	ⓐ	ⓑ	ⓒ	ⓓ	17.	ⓐ	ⓑ	ⓒ	ⓓ	27.	ⓐ	ⓑ	ⓒ	ⓓ
8.	ⓐ	ⓑ	ⓒ	ⓓ	18.	ⓐ	ⓑ	ⓒ	ⓓ	28.	ⓐ	ⓑ	ⓒ	ⓓ
9.	ⓐ	ⓑ	ⓒ	ⓓ	19.	ⓐ	ⓑ	ⓒ	ⓓ	29.	ⓐ	ⓑ	ⓒ	ⓓ
10.	ⓐ	ⓑ	ⓒ	ⓓ	20.	ⓐ	ⓑ	ⓒ	ⓓ	30.	ⓐ	ⓑ	ⓒ	ⓓ

Part 3: Word Knowledge

1.	ⓐ	ⓑ	ⓒ	ⓓ	13.	ⓐ	ⓑ	ⓒ	ⓓ	25.	ⓐ	ⓑ	ⓒ	ⓓ
2.	ⓐ	ⓑ	ⓒ	ⓓ	14.	ⓐ	ⓑ	ⓒ	ⓓ	26.	ⓐ	ⓑ	ⓒ	ⓓ
3.	ⓐ	ⓑ	ⓒ	ⓓ	15.	ⓐ	ⓑ	ⓒ	ⓓ	27.	ⓐ	ⓑ	ⓒ	ⓓ
4.	ⓐ	ⓑ	ⓒ	ⓓ	16.	ⓐ	ⓑ	ⓒ	ⓓ	28.	ⓐ	ⓑ	ⓒ	ⓓ
5.	ⓐ	ⓑ	ⓒ	ⓓ	17.	ⓐ	ⓑ	ⓒ	ⓓ	29.	ⓐ	ⓑ	ⓒ	ⓓ
6.	ⓐ	ⓑ	ⓒ	ⓓ	18.	ⓐ	ⓑ	ⓒ	ⓓ	30.	ⓐ	ⓑ	ⓒ	ⓓ
7.	ⓐ	ⓑ	ⓒ	ⓓ	19.	ⓐ	ⓑ	ⓒ	ⓓ	31.	ⓐ	ⓑ	ⓒ	ⓓ
8.	ⓐ	ⓑ	ⓒ	ⓓ	20.	ⓐ	ⓑ	ⓒ	ⓓ	32.	ⓐ	ⓑ	ⓒ	ⓓ
9.	ⓐ	ⓑ	ⓒ	ⓓ	21.	ⓐ	ⓑ	ⓒ	ⓓ	33.	ⓐ	ⓑ	ⓒ	ⓓ
10.	ⓐ	ⓑ	ⓒ	ⓓ	22.	ⓐ	ⓑ	ⓒ	ⓓ	34.	ⓐ	ⓑ	ⓒ	ⓓ
11.	ⓐ	ⓑ	ⓒ	ⓓ	23.	ⓐ	ⓑ	ⓒ	ⓓ	35.	ⓐ	ⓑ	ⓒ	ⓓ
12.	ⓐ	ⓑ	ⓒ	ⓓ	24.	ⓐ	ⓑ	ⓒ	ⓓ					

Part 4: Paragraph Comprehension

1.	ⓐ	ⓑ	ⓒ	ⓓ	6.	ⓐ	ⓑ	ⓒ	ⓓ	11.	ⓐ	ⓑ	ⓒ	ⓓ
2.	ⓐ	ⓑ	ⓒ	ⓓ	7.	ⓐ	ⓑ	ⓒ	ⓓ	12.	ⓐ	ⓑ	ⓒ	ⓓ
3.	ⓐ	ⓑ	ⓒ	ⓓ	8.	ⓐ	ⓑ	ⓒ	ⓓ	13.	ⓐ	ⓑ	ⓒ	ⓓ
4.	ⓐ	ⓑ	ⓒ	ⓓ	9.	ⓐ	ⓑ	ⓒ	ⓓ	14.	ⓐ	ⓑ	ⓒ	ⓓ
5.	ⓐ	ⓑ	ⓒ	ⓓ	10.	ⓐ	ⓑ	ⓒ	ⓓ	15.	ⓐ	ⓑ	ⓒ	ⓓ

Part 5: Mathematics Knowledge

1. a b c d
2. a b c d
3. a b c d
4. a b c d
5. a b c d
6. a b c d
7. a b c d
8. a b c d
9. a b c d
10. a b c d
11. a b c d
12. a b c d
13. a b c d
14. a b c d
15. a b c d
16. a b c d
17. a b c d
18. a b c d
19. a b c d
20. a b c d
21. a b c d
22. a b c d
23. a b c d
24. a b c d
25. a b c d

Part 6: Electronics Information

1. a b c d
2. a b c d
3. a b c d
4. a b c d
5. a b c d
6. a b c d
7. a b c d
8. a b c d
9. a b c d
10. a b c d
11. a b c d
12. a b c d
13. a b c d
14. a b c d
15. a b c d
16. a b c d
17. a b c d
18. a b c d
19. a b c d
20. a b c d

Part 7: Auto and Shop Information

1. a b c d
2. a b c d
3. a b c d
4. a b c d
5. a b c d
6. a b c d
7. a b c d
8. a b c d
9. a b c d
10. a b c d
11. a b c d
12. a b c d
13. a b c d
14. a b c d
15. a b c d
16. a b c d
17. a b c d
18. a b c d
19. a b c d
20. a b c d
21. a b c d
22. a b c d
23. a b c d
24. a b c d
25. a b c d

Part 8: Mechanical Comprehension

1. a b c d
2. a b c d
3. a b c d
4. a b c d
5. a b c d
6. a b c d
7. a b c d
8. a b c d
9. a b c d
10. a b c d
11. a b c d
12. a b c d
13. a b c d
14. a b c d
15. a b c d
16. a b c d
17. a b c d
18. a b c d
19. a b c d
20. a b c d
21. a b c d
22. a b c d
23. a b c d
24. a b c d
25. a b c d

Part 9: Assembling Objects

1.	ⓐ	ⓑ	ⓒ	ⓓ
2.	ⓐ	ⓑ	ⓒ	ⓓ
3.	ⓐ	ⓑ	ⓒ	ⓓ
4.	ⓐ	ⓑ	ⓒ	ⓓ
5.	ⓐ	ⓑ	ⓒ	ⓓ
6.	ⓐ	ⓑ	ⓒ	ⓓ

7.	ⓐ	ⓑ	ⓒ	ⓓ
8.	ⓐ	ⓑ	ⓒ	ⓓ
9.	ⓐ	ⓑ	ⓒ	ⓓ
10.	ⓐ	ⓑ	ⓒ	ⓓ
11.	ⓐ	ⓑ	ⓒ	ⓓ
12.	ⓐ	ⓑ	ⓒ	ⓓ

13.	ⓐ	ⓑ	ⓒ	ⓓ
14.	ⓐ	ⓑ	ⓒ	ⓓ
15.	ⓐ	ⓑ	ⓒ	ⓓ
16.	ⓐ	ⓑ	ⓒ	ⓓ

Part 1: General Science

Time: 11 minutes

1. How many atoms are there in a molecule of H_2O (water)?
   a. 2
   b. 1
   c. 3
   d. 0

2. Which of the following is an organic compound?
   a. calcium (C)
   b. water (H_2O)
   c. salt (NaCl)
   d. glucose ($C_6H_{12}O_6$)

3. The instrument that allows a simple machine like a lever to work is called
   a. a slant.
   b. an inclined plane.
   c. a wedge.
   d. a fulcrum.

4. All of the following are characteristics of reptiles except
   a. the internal development of eggs.
   b. eggs are laid on land.
   c. adults are land-dwelling creatures.
   d. scaly skin.

5. Diamonds are composed primarily of what element?
   a. iron
   b. carbon
   c. titanium
   d. steel

6. How many cubic feet are in a cubic yard?
   a. 20
   b. 25
   c. 27
   d. 30

7. A life form that lives or grows at or near the open ocean is known as
   a. pelagic.
   b. paludal.
   c. littoral.
   d. tellurian.

8. The outer layer of the Earth is called the
   a. mantle.
   b. core.
   c. crust.
   d. axis.

9. What of the following is the highest level of the Earth's atmosphere?
   a. mesosphere.
   b. stratosphere.
   c. thermosphere.
   d. troposphere.

10. Which of the following is not in the class Insecta?
    a. bees
    b. moths
    c. gnats
    d. spiders

11. The scientific study of plants is called
    a. botany.
    b. entomology.
    c. zoology.
    d. oceanography.

12. In order to focus light rays to a specific point, what sort of lens would you use?
   a. refractive
   b. concave
   c. convex
   d. spectrum

13. The Aurora Borealis is a phenomenon that includes which element of the Earth?
   a. magnetic field
   b. stratosphere
   c. electrical grid
   d. sunspots

14. The mineral in the body that helps transport oxygen in red blood cells is
   a. calcium.
   b. potassium.
   c. sodium.
   d. iron.

15. What type of blood is known as the universal donor type?
   a. O positive
   b. O negative
   c. A positive
   d. AB positive

16. The gas that is most abundant in our atmosphere is
   a. carbon dioxide.
   b. argon.
   c. oxygen.
   d. nitrogen.

17. The area of lowest air pressure in a hurricane is the
   a. leading edge.
   b. trailing edge.
   c. eye.
   d. body.

18. What is the process called when hot water heats up a heating element?
   a. insulation
   b. radiation
   c. convection
   d. conduction

19. The study of earthquakes is known as
   a. ecology.
   b. seismology.
   c. numismatics.
   d. hydrology.

20. Which of the following may cause a tsunami?
   a. a solar storm
   b. an earthquake under the ocean
   c. a very warm ocean current
   d. a flood from a land-based storm

21. How many chromosomes are present in a normal human cell?
   a. 15
   b. 22
   c. 46
   d. 50

22. A nanosecond is
   a. one thousandth of a second.
   b. one millionth of a second.
   c. one billionth of a second.
   d. one trillionth of a second.

23. What is the hormone that regulates the amount of sugar in the blood?
   a. estrogen
   b. adrenaline
   c. insulin
   d. androgen

24. What is the primary purpose of anticoagulants?
  a. to cause amnesia
  b. to paralyze the muscles
  c. to prevent the heart from stopping
  d. to prevent the blood from clotting

25. To which class do tigers belong?
  a. Carnivora
  b. Mammalia
  c. *Tigris*
  d. Chordata

Part 2: Arithmetic Reasoning

Time: 36 minutes

1. Mr. Jack Jones has inherited some books from his father. They are:

   -1 encyclopedia set valued at $1,500
   -2 bibles, each valued at $650
   -2 dictionaries, each valued at $185
   -1 first edition of *Moby Dick* valued at $2,400

In addition, Mr. Jones' father has left him a pair of cufflinks valued at $250, and some hats valued at $76. What is the total value of Mr. Jones inheritance?
  a. $7,050
  b. $5,061
  c. $6,670
  d. $5,896

2. In the third grade, there are 6 teachers. Janet has 22 students in her class, Susan has 18 students, Joyce has 24 students, Anne has 15 students, Cathy has 20 students, and John has 21 students. What is the average number of students per teacher in the third grade?
  a. 15
  b. 18
  c. 20
  d. 21

3. If a man breathes 30 times a minute, how many times will he take a breath in a 5 hour period?
  a. 5,000
  b. 9,000
  c. 6,600
  d. 7,500

4. An artist spent $540 on the following supplies— chalk, oil paint, and canvas. If the canvas costs twice as much as the chalk and oil paint, how much did he spend on canvas?
  a. $135
  b. $270
  c. $405
  d. $500

5. Joe is building a deck using 12 feet × 1 foot planks. If the deck requires 12 planks that are each $\frac{1}{2}$ inch apart, what will the dimensions of the deck be?
  a. 12 ft × 12 ft
  b. 12 ft × 13 ft
  c. 12 ft × 12 ft and $5\frac{1}{2}$ inches
  d. 12 ft × 12 ft 6 inches

6. At a certain university, $\frac{1}{4}$ of the students are female and $\frac{1}{8}$ of the students are from out of state. What portion of the students would you expect to be males from out of state?
  a. $\frac{3}{8}$
  b. $\frac{1}{2}$
  c. $\frac{1}{32}$
  d. $\frac{3}{32}$

7. Which of the following has a 9 in the hundredths place
  a. 6.0092
  b. 6.0902
  c. 6.9002
  d. 6.0029

8. Based on the information in the chart, estimate the average height of a person who is 172 lbs.

Average Height & Weight Chart	
Height	**Weight**
5ft	130 lbs
6ft	202 lbs

a. 5 ft 3 in
b. 5 ft 5 in
c. 5 ft 7 in
d. 5 ft 9 in

9. During exercise, a person's heart rate should be between sixty and ninety percent of the difference between 220 and the person's age. According to this guideline, what should a 40-year-old person's minimum heart rate be during exercise?
a. 108
b. 126
c. 144
d. 162

10. The local high school is sponsoring a rummage sale and car wash to raise money for a local charity. Their goal is to raise $5,000. After 5 hours, they have raised $2,750. Which statement below is accurate?
a. They have 45% of their goal remaining.
b. They have raised 50 % of their goal.
c. They have raised more than $\frac{3}{4}$ of their goal.
d. They have 75% of their goal remaining.

11. A third grade teacher has a box of crayons to use as prizes for her students. If $\frac{1}{8}$ of the crayons are green, $\frac{1}{2}$ of them are white, 25% of them are blue, and the remaining 45 crayons are red. How many crayons are blue?
a. 45
b. 90
c. 135
d. 180

12. If Jack's age is increased by Mike's age, the result is two times Jack's age five years ago. If Mike's age now is M years, what is Jack's present age in terms of M?
a. M + 5
b. M + 10
c. 2M − 10
d. 2M − 5

13. It took eight carpenters nine hours to complete their current job of framing a house. How many additional carpenters would be needed to complete the same job in 3 fewer hours?
a. two
b. four
c. six
d. eight

14 John left a rest stop a 10:00 AM, heading north at 60 miles per hour. Jason left the rest stop an hour later, driving south at 50 miles per hour. What time will it be when they are exactly 225 miles apart?
a. 11:30 AM
b. 12:00 PM
c. 12:30 PM
d. 1:00 PM

15. Bob owes the bank $250 dollars. Last month he paid $\frac{1}{4}$ of the amount owed. This month he paid $\frac{1}{5}$ of the remaining amount, plus $15. How much money does he still owe?
  a. $37.50
  b. $62.50
  c. $122.50
  d. $135.00

16. A gram of fat contains nine calories. A balanced 2,400-calorie diet should include no more than 30% calories from fat. How many grams of fat are allowed in such a diet?
  a. 20 grams
  b. 40 grams
  c. 60 grams
  d. 80 grams

17. Five hockey pucks and three hockey sticks cost $23. Five hockey pucks and one hockey stick cost $20. How much does one hockey puck cost?
  a. $3.20
  b. $3.50
  c. $3.70
  d. $3.90

18. Excavation for a pool is being done in your backyard. It measures 42 ft × 29 ft × 8ft. The dirt is being hauled away in a truck that can hold 4.53 cubic ft of material. How many truckloads of dirt will be hauled away to complete the excavation?
  a. 2,145
  b. 2,151
  c. 2,160
  d. 2,166

19. Sara and Henry brought an equal amount of money for shopping. Sara spent $95 and Henry spent $350. After that, Henry had $\frac{4}{7}$ of what Sara had left. How much money did Sara have left after shopping?
  a. $430
  b. $550
  c. $595
  d. $690

20. 12 crates of oranges were delivered to a local factory. Each crate had 42 oranges. After arriving at the factory it was discovered that four of the oranges were rotten, and they were thrown away. The remaining oranges were packed in boxes of 50. How many boxes of oranges were packed?
  a. 8
  b. 10
  c. 12
  d. 18

21. Bob traveled east at 45 miles an hour and Bill traveled west at 25 miles an hour. If they started out 2,800 miles apart, how long did it take for them to meet?
  a. 30 hours
  b. 35 hours
  c. 40 hours
  d. 45 hours

22. The average test score of a group of 20 students is 70. Two other students, with scores of 95 and 89, were added to the group. What is the new average?
  a. 70
  b. 72
  c. 74
  d. 76

23. Jack can type twice as fast as Max. Together, they type 45 pages per hour. If Max learns to type just as fast as Jack, how many pages will they be able to type in an hour?
   a. 30 pages
   b. 45 pages
   c. 60 pages
   d. 75 pages

24. A triangle has a perimeter of 85. If two of its sides are equal, and the third side is 10 more than either of the other sides, how long is the third side?
   a. 25
   b. 30
   c. 35
   d. 40

25. Apples are being delivered to the factory at a rate that's five times faster than they are being shipped out. If after an hour there are 14,200 apples in the factory, how many are being delivered per hour?
   a. 16,600 apples per hour
   b. 17,750 apples per hour
   c. 18,200 apples per hour
   d. 18,600 apples per hour

26. A bus must cover 5,040 miles in 7 days. If it travels 12 hours a day, what speed must it go to reach its destination in precisely the goal time?
   a. 55 mph
   b. 60 mph
   c. 65 mph
   d. 70 mph

27. A single uniform requires 3 square yards of cloth. How many uniforms can be made from 195,720 square yards of cloth?
   a. 65,240
   b. 65,530
   c. 65,420
   d. 65,650

28. A barracks currently houses 25 people, which allows for an average of 42 square feet of space per person. If the average space per person is reduced by 7 square feet, how many people can be added to the barracks?
   a. 7
   b. 6
   c. 5
   d. 8

29. Sidney is half as old as Mike, who is 4 times as old as Pat. Their ages add up to 56. How old is Pat?
   a. 2
   b. 4
   c. 6
   d. 8

30. Sam can mow a lawn in 40 minutes and Harry can mow the same lawn in 60 minutes. How long will it take them to mow the lawn together?
   a. 20 minutes
   b. 24 minutes
   c. 30 minutes
   d. 36 minutes

Part 3: Word Knowledge

Time: 11 minutes

1. Diurnal most nearly means
   a. daytime.
   b. nighttime.
   c. evening.
   d. morning.

2. Deplorable most nearly means
   a. sorry.
   b. regrettable.
   c. pleasing.
   d. enjoyable.

3. John was recalcitrant about going to the meeting.
   a. agreeable
   b. resistant
   c. enthusiastic
   d. not interested

4. Akin most nearly means
   a. opposite to.
   b. related to.
   c. distant.
   d. thankful.

5. Filch most nearly means
   a. replace.
   b. borrow.
   c. steal.
   d. soiled.

6. Heinous most nearly means
   a. good.
   b. evil.
   c. disputed.
   d. hateful.

7. Dais most nearly means
   a. double.
   b. sidewalk.
   c. ladder.
   d. platform.

8. The instructions did not do much other than obfuscate the goal of the task.
   a. confuse
   b. clarify
   c. simplify
   d. erase

9. The fire gave off noxious fumes.
   a. pleasant
   b. odorless
   c. poisonous
   d. harmless

10. Dissuade most nearly means
   a. agree.
   b. distraction.
   c. deter.
   d. stay neutral.

11. Dominant most nearly means
   a. helpful.
   b. understanding.
   c. overriding.
   d. quiet.

12. Immaculate most nearly means
   a. large.
   b. remote.
   c. spotless.
   d. barren.

13. Panoramic most nearly means
   a. constrained.
   b. artistic.
   c. expansive.
   d. unusual.

14. <u>Prodigious</u> most nearly means
   a. petite.
   b. average.
   c. large.
   d. popular.

15. The school principal thought the student's behavior was <u>reprehensible.</u>
   a. commendable
   b. shameful
   c. brave
   d. responsible

16. <u>Albeit</u> most nearly means
   a. definitive.
   b. except.
   c. although.
   d. all-inclusive.

17. <u>Caustic</u> most nearly means
   a. reason.
   b. soothing.
   c. calming.
   d. corrosive.

18. <u>Frugal</u> most nearly means
   a. rich.
   b. poor.
   c. thrifty.
   d. expansive.

19. <u>Monotonous</u> most nearly means
   a. single-celled.
   b. tedious.
   c. married.
   d. a disease.

20. <u>Sacrilege</u> most nearly means
   a. worship.
   b. irreverence.
   c. sanctuary.
   d. adore.

21. <u>Cleve</u> most nearly means
   a. demand.
   b. deliver.
   c. transfer.
   d. split.

22. The <u>lackluster</u> attitude shown by the team was not encouraging.
   a. excitable
   b. tasteful
   c. static
   d. dull

23. <u>Abstain</u> most nearly means
   a. refrain.
   b. reflex.
   c. diet.
   d. exercise.

24. <u>Obdurate</u> most nearly means
   a. obvious.
   b. duration.
   c. stubborn.
   d. ignorant.

25. <u>Tedium</u> most nearly means
   a. boredom.
   b. excitement.
   c. danger.
   d. threat.

26. Navigate most nearly means
a. search.
b. decide.
c. steer.
d. assist.

27. Tailor most nearly means
a. measure.
b. construct.
c. launder.
d. alter.

28. Yield most nearly means
a. merge.
b. relinquish.
c. destroy.
d. hinder.

29. Eternal most nearly means
a. timeless.
b. heavenly.
c. loving.
d. wealthy.

30. Stow most nearly means
a. pack.
b. curtsy.
c. fool.
d. trample.

31. The hail _____ the cornfield until the entire crop was lost.
a. belittled
b. pummeled
c. rebuked
d. commended

32. The Earth Day committee leader placed large garbage bins in the park to _____ Saturday's cleanup.
a. confound
b. pacify
c. integrate
d. facilitate

33. Her rapport with everyone in the office _____ the kind of interpersonal skills that all of the employees appreciated.
a. prevailed
b. diverged
c. exemplified
d. delegated

34. When you discuss the characters from *The Catcher in the Rye*, please be sure to give a _____ description of the narrator, in order to capture all the details.
a. principled
b. determined
c. comprehensive
d. massive

35. _____ elephants from the wild not only endangers the species but also upsets the balance of nature.
a. Contriving
b. Poaching
c. Promoting
d. Hindering

Part 4: Paragraph Comprehension

Time: 13 minutes

Beginning with the end of World War 1 and continuing through the post-war Europe era, new nations and power centers were created as the empires of the 19th-century world were broken up or realigned. The Austro-Hungarian Empire collapsed, as did the Russian empire. The former was divided into many new nations and the latter resulted in the creation of the Union of Socialist Soviet Republics. This new global paradigm, coupled with an increasingly isolationist United States, the Treaty of Versailles, and the soon-to-arrive Great Depression, set the stage for an international set of conditions that resulted in decades of human rights violations across the globe—largely ignored by the international community until the 1960s.

1. In the paragraph above, which of the following best captures the main idea of the passage?
   a. the rise and fall of Russia
   b. the history behind recent human rights violations
   c. the rise of the Austro-Hungarian Empire
   d. the Treaty of Versailles

2. In this passage, the word <u>paradigm</u> pertains to
   a. history of international events
   b. weather pattern across the globe
   c. model of global events
   d. timing of empire development

Dale's Dairy is your one-stop shopping destination for natural, quality farm products! Their milk comes from a small farm in New York State, where the cows are treated like family. The milk is bottled right on the farm, and they grow their own feed, which never includes artificial hormones or additives—just fresh air, sunshine, grass, and love. Enjoy the freshly bottled milk, farmstead raw-milk cheeses, organic eggs, honey butter, jams, apple cider, organic bread, fresh produce, local, grass-fed beef, and free-range, local chicken!

3. According to the passage, how many different products can one purchase at Dale's Dairy?
   a. 3
   b. 5
   c. 9
   d. 10

4. What does the author say about the use of artificial hormones or additives?
   a. they are used in addition with fresh air and sunshine
   b. they are never used
   c. they are used only on cattle
   d. they are banned by New York State

Any Mars expedition would likely be helped by using resources found on the planet itself for producing return propellant for exploring spacecraft. While most discussions of resource availability on Mars assume that a mission will target an equatorial or mid-latitude site, Mars's polar regions hold significant advantages as an initial landing site. The polar regions provide easy access to frozen water and carbon dioxide. This is important not only for production of rocket fuel for the return to Earth, but also for fuel production for local use. A polar expedition would not have to bring hydrogen from Earth to produce propellant, but could extract hydrogen by simply melting available ice.

5. According to the passage, the ingredients for the production of rocket fuel for a return trip to Earth could best be found where?
   a. a level, flat plain
   b. mid-latitude regions
   c. equatorial regions
   d. the polar regions

6. According to the passage, why does the author discuss the production of rocket fuel on Mars?
   a. Rocket fuel manufacturing techniques are easier performed on Mars.
   b. It would be cheaper to manufacture rocket fuel on Mars.
   c. It would be easier if fuel doesn't have to be brought from Earth.
   d. The fuel can help to melt frozen water and carbon dioxide.

7. What does the author state as proposed uses of rocket fuel?
   a. for return to Earth and local use
   b. for heating and cooling of a Mars base
   c. for food production
   d. for powering Mars exploration vehicles

Venice was founded on and flourished through trade. It owes its phenomenal success to its relatively compact size—confined to such a restricted space, it created in the Venetian citizens a sense of cohesion and cooperation in the handling of day-to-day affairs. Among the Venetian merchant aristocracy, everyone knew one another, and close acquaintances led to a mutual trust of a kind that seldom extended outside the family circle in other cities. Consequently, the Venetians were unique in their capacity for quick and efficient business administration.

8. According to the passage, which is not a factor attributed to Venice's phenomenal success?
   a. a spirit of cohesion
   b. its small size
   c. quick, efficient business administration
   d. its interconnected street design

9. What was the typical relationship amongst members of the Venetian merchant aristocracy like?
   a. argumentative
   b. distant and cool
   c. indifferent
   d. mutually trusting

The black bear (*Ursus americanus*) is the smallest of the three bear species typically found in North America, and it is the only bear found in Vermont. Black bears are members of the order *Carnivora*, which also includes dogs, cats, weasels, and raccoons. Vermont black bears are relatively shy animals and are seldom seen by people. This is an important factor influencing bear distribution, as Vermont bears prefer wild areas with fewer people and are less likely to approach populated areas. However, during times when natural food supplies are low, bears may be attracted to bird feeders and garbage cans, and they can become a nuisance or a potential danger to people.

10. Which of the following is the best title for the passage?
   a. Feeding Habits of the Black Bear
   b. Characteristics of Vermont's Black Bears
   c. Bears and Other Wildlife
   d. Vermont's Carnivores

11. Based on the passage, why are Vermont Black Bears not often seen in populated areas?
   a. Vermont bears dislike dogs, cats, and weasels
   b. Vermont bears prefer wild areas with fewer people
   c. Vermont bears prefer dense urban areas
   d. Vermont bears avoid garbage created by humans

The Durham County Park Authority will provide leadership during the establishment and management of an integrated network of Greenways within the County—to conserve open space; protect sensitive environmental and cultural resources (including wildlife habitat); create riparian corridors; improve water quality; preserve archaeological and historic sites, and aesthetic values; control flooding and erosion; and provide non-motorized access to places where citizens and visitors live, work, and play. Four Civil War era buildings located in the park are scheduled for major maintenance this year, which will result in the closure of the western boundary road. Thus, visitation to these historical sites will be curtailed through June.

12. In this passage, the word <u>riparian</u> refers to
   a. bird sanctuaries.
   b. roads.
   c. waterways.
   d. historical sites.

13. Which of the following best captures the main idea of the passage?
   a. the history of the Durham County Park Authority
   b. park management and leadership for upcoming projects
   c. non-motorized vehicle regulations in the park system
   d. citizen and visitor restrictions in Durham County

In a mixing bowl with an electric mixer, cream four ounces of softened butter with $\frac{1}{4}$ cup of granulated brown sugar. Beat for three to four minutes, slowly adding in two eggs until smooth. Next, add in sour cream, vanilla extract, and almond extract. With mixer on low speed, beat in the flour until just blended and spread across a baking pan. Arrange two thinly sliced peaches evenly over the batter, overlapping where needed.

14. When should you add the sour cream, vanilla extract, and almond extract?
   a. after the eggs
   b. before the softened butter and granulated sugar
   c. after the peaches
   d. as the first step in the recipe

15. According to the passage, how many different ingredients are in this recipe?
   a. 7
   b. 8
   c. 9
   d. 10

Part 5: Mathematic Knowledge

Time: 24 minutes

1. Choose the answer to the following problem:
   $-\frac{3}{4} + \frac{1}{4} =$
   a. $-\frac{1}{2}$
   b. $-\frac{1}{4}$
   c. 1
   d. -1

2. The area of a triangle is measured in
   a. units.
   b. square units.
   c. cubic units.
   d. quadrant units.

3. When calculating the perimeter of a figure, you are looking for
  a. the distance around the object.
  b. the length of a side.
  c. the amount of space that the object covers.
  d. the number of sides it has.

4. Choose the answer to the following problem:
  $(42 + 18) \times (78 - 53) =$
  a. 1,200
  b. 1,500
  c. 1,800
  d. 2,100

5. Choose the answer to the following problem:
  $6 \times (84 - 5) - (3 \times 54) =$
  a. 304
  b. 550
  c. 312
  d. 290

6. Which of the following numbers is the largest?
  a. $\frac{1}{6}$
  b. $\frac{2}{7}$
  c. $\frac{20}{28}$
  d. $\frac{6}{12}$

7. Which of the following is equivalent to $\frac{22}{50}$?
  a. 0.38
  b. 0.44
  c. 0.48
  d. 0.52

8. Which of the following is equivalent to 0.026×100?
  a. .26
  b. 2.6
  c. 26
  d. 260

9. How does the area of a circle change if the radius is doubled?
  a. the area is doubled
  b. the area is eight times larger
  c. the area is four times larger
  d. the area remains the same

10. When measuring the area of a city block, you would most likely use which unit of measurement?
  a. square inches
  b. square millimeters
  c. square miles
  d. square yards

11. What is the relationship between the diameter and radius of a circle?
  a. they are the same thing
  b. the diameter is twice the radius
  c. the diameter is equal to the radius squared
  d. there is no relationship

12. Which of the following statements is true?
  a. Perpendicular lines intersect at right angles.
  b. Parallel lines always intersect.
  c. Perpendicular lines never intersect.
  d. Intersecting lines have multiple points in common.

13. Which of the following is equal to $3.50 \times 10,000$?
  a. 3,500
  b. 3,500,000
  c. 35,000
  d. 350,000

14. $(x^3y^2)2(3xy)$ is equivalent to which of the following?
  a. $2x^3y^2$
  b. $6x^6y^3$
  c. $3x^7y^5$
  d. $9x^5y^3$

15. What is the next number in the series below?

2, 25, 8, 20, 32, 15, _____

a. 64
b. 10
c. 128
d. 24

16. Which number sentence is true?

a. $2.3 < 23$
b. $0.23 < 0.023$
c. $0.0023 > 0.023$
d. $0.023 > 0.23$

17. $\frac{1}{4} + \frac{3}{16} + \frac{7}{8} =$

a. $1\frac{5}{16}$
b. $\frac{11}{28}$
c. $\frac{7}{16}$
d. $1\frac{7}{16}$

18. What is the area of a triangle with a height of eight inches and a base of four inches?

a. 10 square inches
b. 12 square inches
c. 16 square inches
d. 32 square inches

19. What is 0.963 rounded to the nearest tenth?

a. 0.9
b. 0.96
c. 0.97
d. 1.0

20. $4\frac{1}{5}\% =$

a. 420%
b. 0.420%
c. 4.20%
d. 42%

21. $\frac{1}{5}\% =$

a. 0.002%
b. 0.02%
c. 0.20%
d. 20.0%

22. A crowd doubles every hour. If it has 10 people now, how many people will be in the crowd in 4 hours?

a. 160
b. 40
c. 320
d. 240

23. Choose the answer to the following problem:

$5.421 \div .03 =$

a. 18.07
b. 1807
c. 180.7
d. 1.807

24. Choose the answer to the following problem:

$1\frac{1}{2} \div 3\frac{1}{8} =$

a. $4\frac{9}{16}$
b. $\frac{9}{16}$
c. $\frac{12}{25}$
d. $\frac{24}{25}$

25. What is the value of the expression $\frac{xy + yz}{xy}$ when $x = 1$, $y = 3$, and $z = 6$?

a. 3
b. 7
c. 12
d. 21

Part 6: Electronics Information

Time: 9 minutes

1. The following electronic symbol represents what in U.S. circuit diagram language?

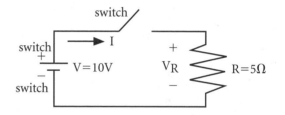

  a. a diode
  b. an inductor
  c. a capacitor
  d. a resistor

2. FM radio broadcasting, amateur radio, broadcast television, and commercial aircraft transmit on what radio frequency?
  a. Low Frequency (LF)
  b. Medium Frequency (MF)
  c. Very High Frequency (VHF)
  d. Ultra High Frequency (UHF)

3. If a vacuum cleaner is rated at 1,200 watts and operates at 120 volts, how much current will it draw?
  a. 10 amps
  b. 100 amps
  c. 120 amps
  d. 144,000 amps

4. A transformer changes which of the following?
  a. power and pressure
  b. voltage and amperage
  c. voltage and current
  d. chemical energy

5. Direct current (DC) is so called because
  a. it provides a steady flow of electricity.
  b. it comes directly from a power station.
  c. it alters the electrical properties of a current.
  d. it has direct applications in an electrical grid.

6. In the following diagram, what is the voltage across the load R and the current through R when the switch is open as shown?

  a. the current is 0 A; the voltage is 10 V
  b. the current is 2 A; the voltage is 10 V
  c. the current is 2 A; the voltage is 2 V
  d. the current is 0 A; the voltage is 0 V

7. A digital Ohmmeter registers a reading of 4.325K ohms. This is equivalent to
  a. 0.4325 ohms
  b. 4.325 ohms
  c. 4,325 ohms
  d. 4.0325 ohms

8. In the United States, which of the following fossil fuels is most heavily used to produce electrical power?
a. oil
b. propane
c. nuclear
d. coal

9. Coulomb's Law describes
a. electromagnetic fields and their association with the electric grid.
b. the relationship between direct current (DC) and alternating current (AC).
c. the electrostatic force between electric charges.
d. the electrical differential between resistors.

10. What symbol is used to represent the unit of electrical impedance called "ohm"?
a. Θ
b. Ω
c. Φ
d. Ψ

11. Two resistors of 20 ohms each are connected in series. What is the total resistance of the circuit?
a. 2 ohms
b. 10 ohms
c. 20 ohms
d. 40 ohms

12. What instrument is used to measure electrical resistance?
a. a voltmeter
b. an anemometer
c. an ohmmeter
d. an ammeter

13. The two most commonly used metals in solder are
a. tin and gold.
b. tin and lead.
c. gold and aluminum.
d. gold and titanium.

14. Most 12V car batteries are made up of eight individual cells connected in series. What is the voltage of each cell in a car battery?
a. 1.5V
b. 3V
c. 6V
d. 12V

15. What is the total resistance in a series circuit with the following six resistors: 60 ohms, 80 ohms, 100 ohms, 120 ohms, 140 ohms, and 160 ohms?
a. 6 ohms
b. 110 ohms
c. 600 ohms
d. 660 ohms

16. An oscilloscope is typically used to measure
a. resistance.
b. power in a circuit.
c. complex waveforms.
d. simple circuits.

17. Printed circuit boards are typically made out of
a. laminated paper.
b. fiberglass.
c. copper.
d. glass.

18. A volt meter is connected to a circuit as shown. What will the meter read?

a. 0 volts
b. 10 volts
c. 20 volts
d. 30 volts

19. A volt is a unit of electric(al)
a. potential
b. energy
c. pressure
d. current

20. Which of the following items would not use a semiconductor device?
a. a telephone
b. a radio
c. a bicycle
d. a computer

Part 7: Auto and Shop Information

Time: 11 minutes

1. This hand tool is known as a
a. screwdriver.
b. hammer.
c. crescent wrench.
d. pair of pliers.

2. Calipers are used for what function?
a. mortaring
b. measuring
c. cutting
d. drilling

3. The turn signal of an automobile is connected to which of the following automotive systems?
a. the braking system
b. the transmission system
c. the suspension system
d. the electrical system

4. The following item is used for what purpose?

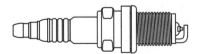

a. to determine gap settings on spark plug electrodes
b. to test air pressure in a tire
c. to create a spark in an internal-combustion engine
d. to regulate oil pressure in an engine

5. Blue smoke coming from an exhaust pipe generally means what?
 a. a lean mixture in the carburetor
 b. a blocked manifold
 c. worn piston rings
 d. an improper setting on the fuel pump

6. The role of an alternator in an automobile's electrical system is to
 a. meter fuel into the carburetor.
 b. measure the amount of oil in the engine.
 c. convert mechanical energy into electrical energy.
 d. store energy in the form of direct current.

7. Which of the following tools are most likely be used together?
 a. a lathe and a claw hammer
 b. an electric winch and a center punch
 c. a ball-peen hammer and a Phillips-head screwdriver
 d. a table saw and a fence guide

8. The purpose of an oil system in an internal combustion engine is to provide
 a. lubrication for the engine.
 b. rotation of the piston.
 c. cooling of the manifold.
 d. ignition of the fuel.

9. The braking system of a typical automobile utilizes what physics-based principle?
 a. force = mass × acceleration
 b. potential energy production
 c. kinetic energy absorption
 d. particle wave theory

10. Which of the following tools is best for making a baseball bat?
 a. a lever
 b. a drill press
 c. a lathe
 d. a table saw

11. Which of the following is NOT a type of hammer?
 a. ball peen
 b. sledge
 c. claw
 d. box

12. A hybrid automobile typically uses what combination of power sources?
 a. hydrogen and electricity
 b. internal combustion and electricity
 c. diesel fuel
 d. diesel fuel and hydrogen

13. Which of the following is a mechanical, not an electrical, device?
 a. a generator
 b. an air conditioner
 c. an hydraulic jack
 d. a battery

14. The purpose of a catalytic converter in a car is to
 a. ensure the air-to-fuel ratio is correct.
 b. reduce the amount of harmful pollutants.
 c. convert mechanical energy to electrical energy.
 d. reduce engine noise.

15. What is the purpose of a universal joint in a vehicle?
    a. it allows for weight reduction
    b. it allows a standard drive shaft to be used on all types of vehicles
    c. it transfers lateral forces into horizontal forces
    d. it allows the drive shaft to bend when on uneven roads

16. The differential on an automobile is found
    a. in the fuel system.
    b. in the braking system.
    c. in the electrical system.
    d. in the drive axle.

17. A nail set is most likely used to
    a. start driving a nail into hard or dense wood.
    b. drive the head of a finished nail below or flush with a surface.
    c. quickly drive a large quantity of nails.
    d. mark the location of the studs for later sheetrock application.

18. Which of the following would you use to dig a post hole?
    a. an auger
    b. an axe
    c. a tap and die tool
    d. an adz

19. Which hand tool is most commonly used to shape or enlarge holes?
    a. a crescent wrench
    b. a reamer
    c. calipers
    d. pipe clamps

20. When two pieces of wood need to be fastened together as securely as possible, which of the following should be used?
    a. a carriage bolt
    b. a nail
    c. a machine screw
    d. a slotted screw

21. A winch is primarily used to perform which of the following functions?
    a. pushing
    b. pulling
    c. welding
    d. lifting

22. A drill press is best used for
    a. drilling with oversized drill bits.
    b. drilling into hard to reach places.
    c. drilling a number of holes in the shortest amount of time.
    d. drilling precisely spaced holes or holes to exact depths.

23. If a line is <u>plumb</u>, what would be its defining characteristic?
    a. It would be as tightly drawn as possible.
    b. It would form a perfect square.
    c. It would be perfectly vertical.
    d. It would form a precise 45 degree angle.

24. The letter and numbers on a tire—for example P215/75R15—refer to
    a. the maximum air pressure allowable.
    b. the weight bearing capacity and inflation standards.
    c. the type, size, inventory number, and designator code.
    d. type, width, height, construction type, and rim diameter

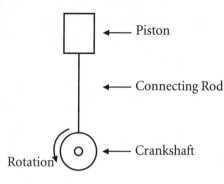

Piston

Connecting Rod

Rotation — Crankshaft

25. The figure above shows a piston that is connected to a crankshaft by a connecting rod. The crankshaft has a radius of 1.0 inch. If the crankshaft rotates 180 degrees (one half of a revolution), how far downward will the piston be pulled?
a. 0.5 inches
b. 1.0 inch
c. 1.33 inches
d. 2.0 inches

Part 8: Mechanical Comprehension

Time: 19 minutes

1. Which of the following should be used to prevent a nut from moving on a bolt?
a. a wire fastener
b. a lock washer
c. a lock nut
d. choices b and c

2. An elevator is an example of which of the following mechanical devices?
a. a fulcrum
b. a lever
c. a spring
d. a crane

3. Which principle of mechanical motion is used in the design of a roller coaster?
a. acceleration
b. friction
c. momentum
d. All the above.

4. The center of gravity of a basketball
a. is near the inflation notch.
b. is in the center.
c. does not exist.
d. is at the top.

5. Which is heavier, ten pounds of feathers or ten pounds of lead?
a. the feathers
b. the lead
c. they weigh the same
d. it is not possible to compare the two

6. Why do large steel ships float?
a. Because steel is lighter than water.
b. The ship's propellers keep it afloat.
c. Ships displace more water than their weight.
d. Because steel is heavier than water.

7. If an object is at equilibrium, it is said to be
a. at rest.
b. moving.
c. moving or at rest.
d. in a state where its mass equals its weight.

8. You are in Baltimore, MD and it is 1:00 PM. You need to be in Greensboro, NC, by 8:00 PM. Greensboro is 350 miles from Baltimore. Assuming you drive straight with no stops, what must your average speed be in order to arrive in Greensboro by 8:00 PM?
a. 50 miles per hour
b. 56 miles per hour
c. 42 miles per hour
d. 65 miles per hour

9. An airplane's ability to fly can be explained by what principle?
  a. Einstein's Theory of Relativity
  b. Bernoulli's Principle
  c. Pythagoras's Theorem
  d. Newton's Principle

10. When two gears are engaged
  a. they always rotate in opposite directions.
  b. they always rotate at the same speed.
  c. one must rotate faster than the other.
  d. all of the above

11. Which of the following examples does not make use of a mechanical advantage?
  a. using a sledge to break up concrete
  b. sliding a heavy box along a concrete floor
  c. moving a load of wood with a wheelbarrow
  d. using a paint brush

12. In the following diagram, the spring is very stiff and can be stretched precisely 1 inch by a pulling force of 100 pounds. How much force must be applied to the block in order to move it 3.5 inches to the left?

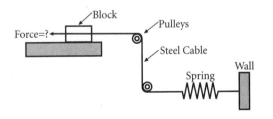

  a. 150 lbs
  b. 250 lbs
  c. 350 lbs
  d. 450 lbs

13. When a load is applied to a structural beam, which of the following does the beam experience?
  a. deflection
  b. stress
  c. strain
  d. all of the above

14. In which direction will gear Z spin if gear X is spinning clockwise?

  a. clockwise
  b. counterclockwise
  c. neither—it will seize
  d. there is not enough information to give an answer

15. Hydrostatic pressure refers to
  a. the pressure created by blood flow.
  b. the pressure exerted by a liquid when it is at rest.
  c. the pressure exerted by a hydroelectric dam.
  d. another word for atmospheric pressure.

16. A block of wood rests on a level surface. What mechanical principle makes it more difficult to push this block sideways if the surface is made of sandpaper than if it is made of glass?
  a. centrifugal force
  b. gravity
  c. wind resistance
  d. friction

17. Based on the following diagram of three pulleys, which pulley would turn the fastest?

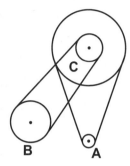

   a. pulley A
   b. pulley C
   c. pulleys B and A would turn equally
   d. pulleys A and C would turn equally

18. A ramp is typically used to assist in which of the following operations?
   a. transferring fluids
   b. cutting metal objects
   c. moving objects
   d. reducing wind resistance

19. Water flows into a tank at a rate of 120 gallons per hour. The tank has a leak that allows water to escape at the rate of 2 gallon per minute. What will happen to the water in the tank?
   a. it will freeze
   b. it will block any water from escaping it
   c. its level will stay the same
   d. it will block any water from entering it

20. A valve is used to perform which of the following functions?
   a. to increase the temperature of a liquid or gas
   b. to control the flow of a liquid or gas
   c. to aid in the evaporation of a liquid or gas
   d. to decrease the density of a liquid or gas

21. A scuba diver has to overcome what natural force in order to sink?
   a. friction
   b. floating
   c. buoyancy
   d. gravity

22. Which physical property can be attributed to the ocean's tides?
   a. sunspots
   b. solar friction
   c. moon gravity
   d. tectonic plates

23. A fuel tank is receiving fuel at the rate of 1 gallon per minute. It is supplying an engine that burns 3 gallons of fuel per hour. How many gallons of fuel will be in the tank after $\frac{1}{2}$ hour, assuming the tank was empty at the start?
   a. 18
   b. 28.5
   c. 31.5
   d. 45

24. Which mechanical components are typically used between a wheel and an axle to reduce friction?
   a. springs
   b. hinges
   c. bearings
   d. levers

25. Which of the following mechanical devices is the best choice to dampen the energy forces produced by earthquakes in a building?
   a. a pulley
   b. a siphon
   c. a lever
   d. a spring

Part 9: Assembling Objects

Time: 16 minutes

1.

2.

3.

4.

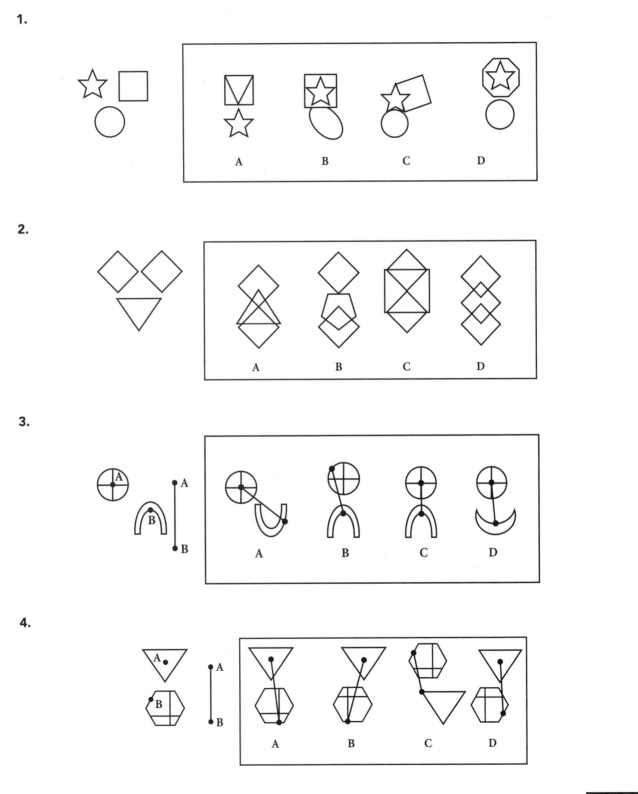

5.

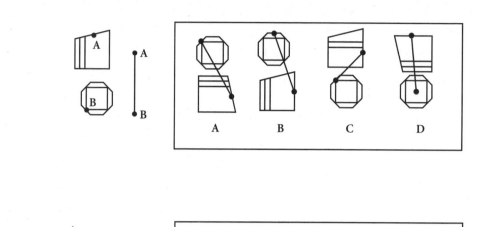

6.

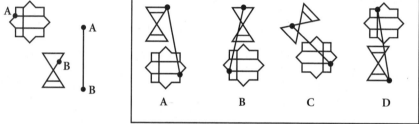

7.

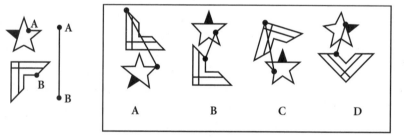

8.

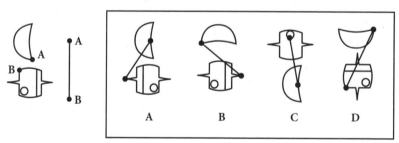

9.

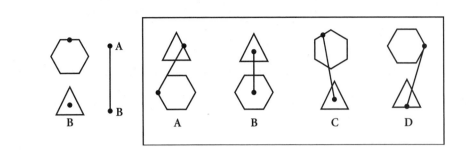

10.

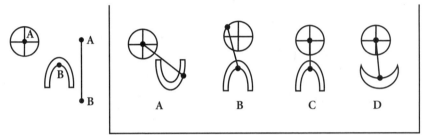

11.

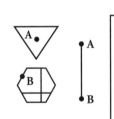
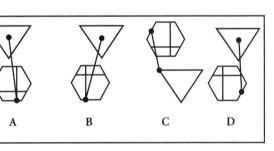

12.

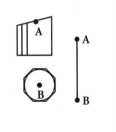
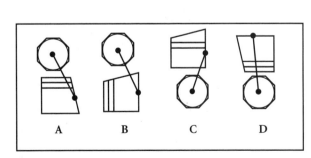

13.

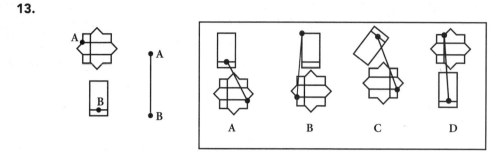

14.

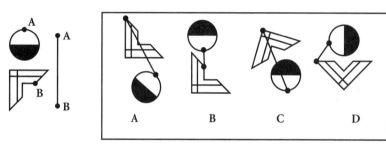
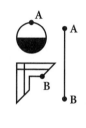

15.

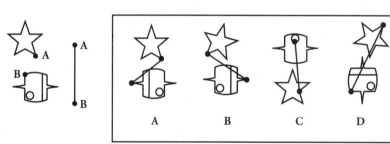

16.

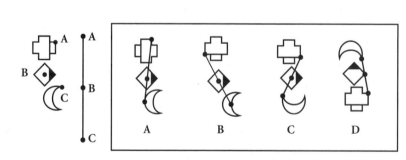

Answers

Part 1: General Science

1. **c.** There are a total of 3 atoms. Two hydrogen (H_2) and one oxygen (O).

2. **d.** Glucose is an organic compound. All organic compounds contain carbon (C). Glucose ($C_6H_{12}O_6$) is the only choice that has carbon.

3. **d.** A fulcrum is the support, or point of rest, on which a lever turns in moving a body.

4. **a.** Reptiles lay their eggs on land, and do not have internal development and incubation of eggs.

5. **b.** Diamonds are composed primarily of carbon.

6. **c.** There are 27 cubic feet in a cubic yard.

7. **a.** *Pelagic* means living or growing at or near the surface of the ocean, far from land.

8. **c.** The layers of the Earth, from outermost to innermost, are crust, upper mantle, lower mantle, outer core and inner core.

9. **c.** Among the choices provided, the highest level of the Earth's atmosphere is the thermosphere.

10. **d.** Spiders belong in the class Arachnida

11. **a.** Botany is the scientific study of plants. Entomology is the study of insects, zoology is the study of animals and oceanography is the study of oceans.

12. **c.** A convex lens will focus light rays to a specific point. A concave lens would spread out the light rays.

13. **a.** The Aurora Borealis occurs when electrically charged particles from the Sun are caught in Earth's magnetic field and interact with atoms and molecule in the upper atmosphere. The aurora borealis takes place approximately 97 to 1,000 kilometers above the Earth, placing it in the thermosphere.

14. **d.** Iron is the main component of the protein hemoglobin, which transports oxygen from the lungs to the body.

15. **b.** O negative blood, because of its lack of A and B antigens, is compatible with any blood type.

16. **d.** Nitrogen makes up approximately 78% of the Earth's atmosphere. Oxygen makes up approximately 20%. The remainder is made up of approximately 14 other gases.

17. **c.** A hurricane's eye is the area of lowest pressure.

18. **c.** Convection is the transfer of heat by the circulation or movement of the heated parts of a liquid or gas.

19. **b.** The study of earthquakes is known as seismology. Ecology is the study of the relations between organisms and their environment, numismatics is the practice of collecting coins, and hydrology is the study of water.

20. **b.** An earthquake under the ocean can shift subocean sediments and cause the wave action that results in a tsunami.

21. **c.** Human cells are diploid and have 22 different types, each present as 2 copies, plus 2 sex chromosomes, totaling 46.

22. **c.** A nanosecond is one billionth of a second. A millisecond is one thousandth of a second, a microsecond is one millionth of a second and a picosecond is one trillionth of a second.

23. **c.** Insulin promotes the uptake of glucose—a sugar—in the body. Estrogen and androgen control the development of sex characteristics in women and men, respectively.

24. **d.** The primary purpose of anticoagulants is to prevent the blood from clotting.

25. **b.** Tigers are in the class Mammalia, phylum Chordata, and order Carnivora. Genus and species names are always underlined or italicized, as in the species name *Tigris*.

Part 2: Arithmetic Reasoning

1. **d.** Don't forget that there are two bibles and two dictionaries, and remember to add the value of the watch and the sheet music. The total value is $5,896.

2. **c.** Add all the students to get a total of 120 students. Then divide 120 by 6 to get an average of 20 students per teacher.

3. b. This is a two-step multiplication problem. To find out how many breaths there would be in one hour, you must multiply 30 by 60 (minutes). Next, multiply this result, 1,800, by 5 hours, which gives you 9,000 breaths in a 5-hour period.

4. b. Let x stand for the cost of the chalk and oil paint. So $2x$ is the cost of the canvas. Therefore, $x + x + 2x = 540$. Then, solve for x: $4x = 540$; $x = 135$. Since we are looking for the cost of the canvas, we need to calculate $2(135) = \$270$.

5. c. First, multiply the 11 spaces between the 12 planks by $\frac{1}{2}$. You get $\frac{11}{2}$ which needs to be converted to a mixed number of $5\frac{1}{2}$. Since the planks are each 12 ft long, one side is 12 ft and the other side is 12×1 ft $+ 5\frac{1}{2}$ inches. Therefore, the dimensions are 12 ft × 12 ft and $5\frac{1}{2}$ inches.

6. d. If $\frac{1}{4}$ of the students are female, then you would expect to learn that $\frac{3}{4}$ of the students are male. Also, you would expect $\frac{3}{4}$ of the out-of-state students to be male. $\frac{3}{4}$ of $\frac{1}{8}$ can be expressed as $\frac{3}{4} \times \frac{1}{8}$, which equals $\frac{3}{32}$, the number of out-of-state students that are male.

7. b. The number 6.0902 has a 9 in the hundredths place.

8. c. According to the chart, 1 foot in height makes a difference of 72 pounds, or 6 pounds per inch of height. For a person who is 172 lbs, they weigh $172 - 130 = 42$ lbs over the 5 ft weight of 130. Divide 6 lbs per inch into 42 lbs and you get 7 inches. Therefore, someone who is 172 lbs, has a height of 5 ft 7 in.

9. a. The difference between 220 and this person's age is $220 - 40 = 180$. The minimum heart rate is 60% of this, so $.6 \times 180 = 108$.

10. a. Thus far, they have raised $2,750 \div 5,000 = .55$ or 55% of their goal. Therefore, they have 45% of their goal remaining.

11. b. If x is the total number of crayons, then $\frac{1}{8}x + \frac{1}{2}x + \frac{1}{4}x + 45 = x$. Multiply each by the lowest common denominator (8) and you get $x + 4x + 2x + 360 = 8x$. Simplify and $x = 360$. $\frac{1}{4} \times 360 = 90$.

12. b. If Jack's age is represented by J and Mike's age is represented by M. $J + M = 2(J - 5)$. Simplify it to get $J + M = 2J - 10$, or $J = M + 10$.

13. b. Let $x =$ the number of carpenters needed to complete the job in $9 - 3 = 6$ hours. The resulting equation would be $6x = 8 \times 9$ or $6x = 72$, so $x = 12$. Therefore, the additional carpenters you'd need to add to the existing 8 carpenters is 4.

14. c. The distance formula is $d = rt$ where d is distance, r is rate (speed) and t is time. We know that John was traveling north at 60 mph so $60t = d$. Jason was traveling south at 50 mph so $50t = d$. But you need to account for the hour difference in their leaving. $60t + 50t + 60 = 225$; $110t = 165$; $t = 1\frac{1}{2}$ hours. So add $1\frac{1}{2}$ hours to 11 when Jason left and you get 12:30 PM.

15. d. Last month, Bob paid back $\$250 \times \frac{1}{4} = \$62.50$, leaving a balance of $\$250 - \$62.50 = \$187.50$. This month he paid back $\frac{1}{5} \times \$187.50 + \$15 = \$37.50 + \$15.00 = \$52.50$. His remaining balance is $\$187.50 - \$52.50 = \$135.00$.

16. d. 30% of 2,400, or $.3 \times 2,400 = 720$ calories are allowed from fat. Since there are nine calories in each gram of fat, divide 720 by 9 to find that $720 \div 9 = 80$ grams of fat are allowed.

17. c. Since the five hockey pucks and three sticks cost $23, and five hockey pucks and one stick costs $20, we can determine that two sticks cost $3 and one stick costs $1.50. Therefore, five pucks + $1.50 = $20, and 5 pucks = $18.50. Divide both sides by 5 and determine that one hockey puck costs $3.70.

18. b. The amount of dirt that will need to be hauled away is $42 \times 29 \times 8$ cubic feet or 9,744 cubic ft. One load holds 4.53 so divide 9,744 by 4.53 to calculate the number of loads: $9,744 \div 4.53 = 2,150.99$. Therefore, it will take 2,151 loads to haul away all the dirt.

19. c. Let H stand for the amount of money Henry has left and S stand for the amount Sara has left. Therefore, $\frac{4}{7}S = H$. If x is the staring amount each had then $H = x - \$350$ and $S = x - 95$. So using substitution, $\frac{4}{7}(x-95) = x-350$. $\frac{4}{7}x - \frac{380}{7}$ = x – 350. Multiply both sides by 7 to eliminate the fraction and you have $4x - 380 = 7x - 2,450$. Combine like terms and you have $3x = 2,070$ or x = \$690. So Sara has \$690 – \$95 = \$595.

20. b. 42 crates, each holding 12 oranges, means a total of 42 × 12 = 504 oranges were delivered. Four were bad and discarded leaving 504 – 4 = 500. If they were boxed at a rate of 50 per box, there would be 500 ÷ 50 = 10 boxes.

21. c. The combined rate of travel is 70 miles per hour. 2,800 miles ÷ 70 miles per hour = 40 hours.

22. b. The total score is the number of students × the average score: 20 × 70 = 1,400. Add 95 and 89 to 1,400 and get 1,584. Divide this by the new total of students: 1,584 ÷ 22 = 72.

23. c. Let J stand for Jack and M for Max. J = 2M; 2M + M = 45, so that M = 15. Since J = 2M, J = 30. If Max catches up to Jack's typing speed, then both J and M will equal 30, and their combined rate will be 60 pages per hour.

24. c. Perimeter is equal to the sum of all three sides so $x + x + (x + 10) = 85$. This means $3x + 10 = 85$, $3x = 75$, and x = 25. The third side is x + 10 = 25 + 10 = 35.

25. b. 5A = rate of apples coming in; A = rate of apples going out; 5A – A = 14,200. Therefore, A = 3,550 and 5A is 17,750.

26. b. Here, 5,040 miles ÷ 7 days = 720 miles, and 720 miles ÷ 12 hours = 60 mph.

27. a Using 195,720 yards of cloth to make uniforms that require 3 yards each, you can make 195,720 ÷ 3 = 65,240 uniforms.

28. c. 25 men × 42 square feet of space = 1,050 square feet of space. 42 square feet – 7 square feet = 35 square feet. 1,050 square feet ÷ 35 square feet = 30 men. Since you started with 25 men, the total has increased by 5.

29. d. Let S = Sidney's age; M = Mike's age = 2S; P = Pat's age = $\frac{1}{4}$M = $\frac{1}{2}$S. The total age of the three is 56, so S + M + P = 56. Substitute and you get S + 2S + $\frac{1}{2}$S = 56. Simplify to get $\frac{7}{2}$S = 56; 7S = 112 and S= 16. Therefore, Pat's age is $\frac{1}{2}$(16) = 8.

30. b. The equation needed is $\frac{1}{40} + \frac{1}{60} = \frac{1}{t}$ where t is the time it takes to mow the lawn together. Simplify by multiplying both sides by 120 and you get $3 + 2 = \frac{120}{t}$. Solve for t: $5 = \frac{120}{t}$; $t = 24$.

Part 3: Word Knowledge

1. a *Diurnal* pertains to a *daytime* occurrence.

2. b. Something that is *deplorable* or regrettable.

3. b. To be *recalcitrant* means to be resistant to something.

4. b. Something that is *akin* means it is *related* to something.

5. c. To *filch* something is to *steal* it.

6. b. A thing that is *heinous* is *evil*.

7. d. A *dais* is a raised *platform*.

8. a To *obfuscate* is to *confuse* an issue.

9. c. Something that is *noxious* is *poisonous*.

10. c. To *dissuade* is to *deter* by advice or persuasion.

11. c. To be *dominant* is to show *overriding* control over something.

12. c. *Immaculate* infers a *spotless* environment.

13. c. *Panoramic* implies an *expansive* view of something.

14. c. *Prodigious* means *large* or extraordinary in size.

15. b. Something that is *reprehensible* is *shameful* in nature.

16. c. *Albeit* means *although* or even if.

17. d. Something that is *caustic* is *corrosive* to many items.

18. c. To be *frugal* is to be *thrifty* in spending habits or matters of usage.

19. b. *Monotonous* means *tedious* or lacking in variety.

20. b. *Sacrilege* means having an *irreverence* to anything sacred.

21. d. To *cleave* something is to *split* it.

22. d. If something is *lackluster* it is *dull* or lacking in excitement.

23. a. To *abstain* from something is to *refrain* from participating or doing it.

24. c. When one is *obdurate* they are *stubborn*.

25. a. *Tedium* means *boredom* or monotony.

26. c. To *navigate* means to direct or *steer* a course.

27. d. To *tailor* means to design or to *alter* to suit a specific need.

28. b. To *yield* means to give up or to *relinquish*.

29. a. *Eternal* means to be *timeless*.

30. a. To *stow* means to store or *pack* away.

31. b. *Pummel* means to pound or beat.

32. d. *Facilitate* means to *make easier* or help to bring about.

33. c. *Exemplify* means to *be an instance of* or serve as an example.

34. c. *Comprehensive* means *covering completely* or broadly.

35. b. To *poach* is to *trespass on another's property* in order to steal, usually fish or game.

Part 4: Paragraph Comprehension

1. b. Choices **a**, **c**, and **d** are all mentioned in the paragraph, but are not discussed as anything more than background information. The passage is mainly about the history behind recent human rights violations.

2. c. *Paradigm* is an example serving as a model. The use of the word in the passage suggests a new global model.

3. d. There are 10 products listed that you could buy at the Dairy. They are: 1) bottled farm fresh milk, 2) farmstead raw-milk cheeses, 3) organic eggs, 4) honey butter, 5) jams, 6) apple cider, 7) organic bread, 8) fresh produce, 9) local, grass-fed beef and 10) free-range, local chicken.

4. b. The passage states that artificial hormones or additives are never used.

5. d. According to the passage, the ingredients for the production of rocket fuel for a return trip to Earth could best be found in the polar regions.

6. c. According to the passage, it would be easier if fuel doesn't have to be brought from Earth.

7. a. Choices **b**, **c**, and **d** are not discussed in the passage. The passage specifically talks about the proposed uses of the rocket fuel, for return to Earth and local use.

8. d. Whether or not interconnected streets are a factor in Venice's development and success, there is no mention of them in the passage.

9. d. According to the passage, the typical relationship amongst members of the Venetian merchant aristocracy is mutually trusting.

10. b. The passage does not delve into the detail required for A to be the answer. Likewise, C and D are not the correct answers because the paragraph does not discuss in detail any other animals or carnivores to warrant a title that broad.

11. b. Based on the passage, Vermont black bears are not often seen in populated areas because they prefer wild areas with fewer people.

12. c. The definition of *riparian* is pertaining to or situated on the bank of a river or other body of water, such as waterways.

13. b. Park management and leadership for upcoming projects is mentioned in the first sentence and sets the theme for the passage.

14. a. The sequence of the recipe has the sour cream, vanilla extract, and almond extract being added after the eggs.

15. c. There are 9 ingredients in the recipe. They are: 1) softened butter, 2) granulated brown sugar, 3) eggs, 4) sour cream, 5) vanilla extract, 6) almond extract, 7) flour, and 8) thinly sliced peaches.

Part 5: Mathematics Knowledge

1. a. $-\frac{3}{4} + \frac{1}{4} = -\frac{2}{4}$, which reduces to $-\frac{1}{2}$.

2. b. When calculating area of a triangle, you are finding the number of square units that cover the region.

3. a. The perimeter of a figure is the distance around the object.

4. b. Perform the operations within the parentheses first, which gives you $(60) \times (25) = 1{,}500$.

5. c. Perform the operations in the parentheses first: $(6) \times (79) - 162 = 312$.

6. c. Find the lowest common denominator of the fractions, which allows you to compare the amounts: $\frac{1}{6} = \frac{14}{84}$; $\frac{2}{7} = \frac{24}{84}$; $\frac{20}{28} = \frac{60}{84}$; $\frac{6}{12} = \frac{42}{84}$. Choice **c** is the largest.

7. b. To answer this question, divide the numerator of the fraction by the denominator: $22 \div 50 = .44$.

8. b. $0.026 \times 100 = 2.6$

9. c. The radius being doubled will make the area 4 times as large.

10. d. A city block would most likely be measured in square yards. Square inches and square millimeters are too small, and square miles is too large.

11. b. The diameter of a circle is twice the radius. This is represented by the formula $d = 2r$.

12. a. Perpendicular lines intersect at right angles.

13. c. $3.50 \times 10,000 = 35,000$.

14. d. Multiply the powers of each set of parentheses to get the powers of each component. When multiplying the outside of the parentheses by the inside, add the exponents. $(x^3 y^2)2(3xy) = 6x^4 y^3$

15. c. This series actually has two alternating sets of numbers. The first number is multiplied by 4 giving the third number. The second number has 5 subtracted from it giving the fourth number. Therefore, the blank space will be 32 multiplied by 4. $32 \times 4 = 128$.

16. a. The number 2.3 is of lesser value than 23, and the symbol < means less than.

17. a. First, find the least common denominator—that is, convert all three fractions to sixteenths, and then add: $\frac{4}{16} + \frac{3}{16} + \frac{14}{16} = \frac{21}{16}$. Now reduce: $1\frac{5}{16}$.

18. c. The formula for the area of a triangle is $A = \frac{1}{2}bh = \frac{1}{2} \times 4 \times 8 = \frac{1}{2} \times 32 = 16$.

19. d. 0.963 rounded to the nearest tenth is 1.0.

20. c. Convert the mixed number to a decimal to get 4.20%.

21. c. Convert the fraction to a decimal and keep the percent sign: $\frac{1}{5}\% = 0.20\%$.

22. a. After the first hour, the number would be 20, after the second hour 40, after the third hour 80, after the fourth hour 160.

23. c. $5.421 \div .03 = 180.7$.

24. c. Convert the mixed numbers to fractions: $\frac{3}{2} \div \frac{25}{8}$, which can be changed to $\frac{3}{2} \times \frac{8}{25} = \frac{12}{25}$.

25. b. Substitute the values of each letter and simplify. The expression becomes $\frac{(1)(3) + (3)(6)}{(1)(3)}$, which simplifies to $\frac{3 + 18}{3}$ after performing multiplication. Add $3 + 18$ in the numerator to get $\frac{21}{3}$, which simplifies to 7.

Part 6: Electronics Information

1. d. This is the component symbol for a resistor.

2. c. FM radio broadcasting, amateur radio, broadcast television, and commercial aircraft transmit on Very High Frequency (VHF). VHF bands utilize the 30-300 MHz frequency band.

3. a. If a vacuum cleaner is rated at 1,200 watts and operates at 120 volts, it will draw 10 amps of current. The Power Law can be applied: $P = I \times E$; $I = P \div E$; $I = 1,200$ watts $\div 120$ volts; $I = 10$ Amperes.

4. b. A transformer changes voltage and amperage.

5. a. Direct current (DC) is so called because it provides a steady flow of electricity.

6. d. When the switch is open, as is the case in the diagram, no current flows. Thus, the current is 0 A and the voltage is 0 V.

7. c. An Ohmmeter reading of 4.325K ohms is equal to 4,325 ohms.

8. d. Coal provides nearly 50% of the electricity-producing power in the United States. The next highest source of energy is nuclear, at nearly 20%.

9. c. Coulomb's Law describes the electrostatic force between electric charges.

10. b. Ω is the symbol used to represent ohms.

11. d. The total resistance of series resistors is the sum of the resistance. $R^T = R^1 + R^2 = 20\Omega + 20\Omega = 40\Omega$.

12. c. An Ohmmeter measures electrical resistance.

13. b. The two most commonly used metals in solder are tin and lead.

14. a. Voltage in a series are added together to determine the total voltage, so divide the total, 12 volts, by 8 cells, resulting in 1.5 volts per cell.

15. d. The total resistance of a circuit is found by adding the resistance values of the individual resistors together: 60 ohms + 80 ohms + 100 ohms, 120 ohms, 140 ohms, and 160 ohms = 660 ohms.

16. c. An oscilloscope is typically used to analyze complex waveforms.

17. b. Printed circuit boards are typically made out of fiberglass.

18. a. In this scenario, the meter will read zero because the meter is not connected across a resistance.

19. c. Electrical pressure results from a difference of electrical force between two points. Hence voltage is what pushes electricity through a circuit.

20. c. A bicycle is a mechanical device that does not use a semiconductor device.

Part 7: Auto and Shop Information

1. c. The hand tool depicted is a crescent wrench.

2. b. Calipers are used to measure thickness of internal or external diameters.

3. d. The power from an automobile's battery and electrical system is what makes the turn signal's indicator blink.

4. c. The spark plug is a device that provides a spark to ignite the fuel/air mixture in an internal combustion engine.

5. c. Worn piston rings allow oil to leak into the cylinders, resulting in it being burned and discharged through the exhaust system as blue smoke.

6. c. The alternator converts mechanical energy from the drive shaft to electrical energy, thus replenishing the battery.

7. d. A fence guide would be used to help guide a piece of wood through a table saw. The other combinations of tools are not usually used together.

8. a. The oil system of an automobile is to lubricate the moving parts of an engine. An internal combustion engine, as is seen in most vehicles on the road today, generates a great deal of heat, not only through the burning of fuel but through friction. An oil system ensures this friction is minimized through lubrication.

9. c. The braking system decreases the speed of or stops a moving or rotating body by absorbing kinetic energy, either mechanically or electrically.

10. c. A lathe is a machine tool that rotates, at an extremely high rate of speed, a block of wood (or other material) to perform various cutting or shaving operations.

11. d. There is no tool known as a box hammer.

12. b. A hybrid automobile is one that uses two or more distinct power sources to move the vehicle. Typically, the two power sources are electricity and an internal combustion engine.

13. c. A hydraulic jack operates under the principle of Pascal's Law, whereby pressure in a close container remains the same at all points. The other choices are all electrical devices.

14. b. Catalytic converters help to reduce the amount of harmful pollutants by converting harmful gases into harmless water vapor or oxygen.

15. d. The universal joint allows the drive shaft to flex as an automobile traverses uneven road surfaces.

16. d. The differential, found in the drive axle, allows each of the rear tires to turn at different speeds as the vehicle turns corners.

17. b. A nail set is used to drive the head of a finish nail flush or just below the surface of the material that is being hammered.

18. a. An auger uses a helical shape to move material as it is rotated about its axis. Similar to a drill bit, an auger attached to an engine would remove dirt from a hole.

19. b. A reamer is used to shape or enlarge holes. Calipers are used to measure internal and external dimensions, pipe clamps are used to clamp boards or framing together so they can be bonded by glue.

20. a. A carriage bolt, with its washer and bolt assembly, pulls the two pieces of wood together and results in a stronger bond than any of the alternative answers.

21. b. A winch is used for pulling tasks.

22. d. A drill press uses a fixed drill unit, usually mounted on a stand and bolted to the floor or workbench, to drill accurate and precise holes at exactly the same depths.

23. c. If a line is plumb, it is perfectly vertical.

24. d. The letter and numbers on a tire refer to type, width, height, construction type, and rim diameter.

25. d. The crankshaft has a radius of 1.0 inch, which means that the diameter is 2.0 inches. If the crankshaft rotates one-half revolution (180 degrees) from its starting point, the attachment of the tie rod to the crankshaft will move from the top of the crankshaft down to the bottom. This is equivalent to the diameter of the crankshaft, which is 2.0 inches.

Part 8: Mechanical Comprehension

1. d. A lock washer and a lock nut would both prevent a nut from backing off or coming loose on a bolt.

2. d. An elevator uses the same principles employed by a crane in the lifting and lowering of objects.

3. d. All the offered mechanical motions are included and used in the design of a roller coaster.

4. b. The center of gravity of an object is determined by the point on any object about which it is in perfect balance, regardless of how it is turned or

rotated about that point. The center of gravity of a basketball is in the center.

5. c. Weight is measured in pounds, and the question states that both the feathers and the lead weigh ten pounds, so they are equally heavy.

6. c. Archimedes's Principle states that the buoyant force on a submerged object is equal to the weight of the fluid that is displaced by the object. In other words, the steel ship displaces more water than its weight.

7. c. An object at equilibrium has a state of balance between opposing forces. Therefore, it can be at rest and staying at rest, or in motion and continuing in motion with the same speed and direction.

8. a. You have 7 hours to reach Greensboro and 350 miles to travel. 350 miles ÷ 7 hours means you have to travel at 50 miles per hour.

9. b. Bernoulli's Principle states that if air speeds up, the pressure is lowered. An aircraft wing generates lift because the air travels faster over the top of the wing, creating a region of lower pressure on the bottom, resulting in the wing lifting up.

10. a. When two gears that are directly connected engage, they always rotate in opposite directions.

11. b. Sliding a heavy box along a concrete floor does not utilize any mechanical advantage.

12. c. 3.5 inches (100 lbs per inch = 350 pounds.

13. d. All of the choices are correct when a load is applied to a structural beam.

14. a. If gear X rotates clockwise, gear Y will rotate counterclockwise, which will cause gear Z to rotate clockwise.

15. b. Hydrostatic pressure refers to the pressure exerted by a liquid when it is at rest and is caused by gravity.

16. d. The friction between the block of wood and the sandpaper will make its movement more difficult.

17. a. Pulley A has the smallest circumference and therefore will turn faster than the larger pulleys.

18. c. A ramp is used to assist in moving objects from a lower area to a higher one.

19. c. The water is flowing in at the same rate as the water flowing out, so the water level will stay the same.

20. b. Valves are placed in piping systems and can be opened or closed to control the flow of liquids or gasses.

21. c. Buoyancy is the natural tendency for objects that displace more water than they weigh to float.

22. c. The moon's gravitational pull, as it orbits the earth, is what is responsible for the motion of the Earth's ocean tides.

23. b. After $\frac{1}{2}$ hour (30 minutes), the tank will have received 30 gallons of fuel. The engine would have used $\frac{1}{2}$ of its hourly burn rate, or 1.5 gallons. 30 gallons – 21.5 gallons = 28.5 gallons.

24. c A set of bearings is typically a set of small metal balls packed in a grooved container and lubricated with grease or oil. The net affect of the wheel rolling against the bearings is that the wheel rolls much easier.

25. d. A spring-building device would help absorb energy and prevent direct impact from horizontal longitudinal movements generated by an earthquake.

Part 9: Assembling Objects

1. c.

2. a.

3. c.

4. d.

5. a.

6. c.

7. b.

8. d.

9. c.

10. c.

11. d.

12. a.

13. c.

14. b.

15. d.

16. c.

Scoring

Write your raw score—the number you got right—for each test in the blanks below. Then turn to Chapter 3 to find out how to convert these raw scores into the scores the armed services use.

1. General Science: _____ right out of 25
2. Arithmetic Reasoning: _____ right out of 30
3. Word Knowledge: _____ right out of 35
4. Paragraph Comprehension: _____ right out of 15
5. Mathematics Knowledge: _____ right out of 25
6. Electronics Information: _____ right out of 20
7. Auto and Shop Information: _____ right out of 25
8. Mechanical Comprehension: _____ right out of 25
9. Assembling Objects: _____ right out of 16

17 ▶ ASVAB PRACTICE 4

CHAPTER SUMMARY

Here's another sample ASVAB for you to practice with. After working through the review material in the previous chapters, take this test to see how much your score has improved.

For this test, simulate the actual test-taking experience as closely as you can. Find a quiet place to work where you won't be disturbed. If you own this book, tear out the answer sheet on the following pages and find some number 2 pencils to fill in the circles with. Use a timer or stopwatch to time each section. The times are marked at the beginning of each section. After you take the test, use the detailed answer explanations that follow to review any questions you missed.

Part 1: General Science

1.	ⓐ	ⓑ	ⓒ	ⓓ
2.	ⓐ	ⓑ	ⓒ	ⓓ
3.	ⓐ	ⓑ	ⓒ	ⓓ
4.	ⓐ	ⓑ	ⓒ	ⓓ
5.	ⓐ	ⓑ	ⓒ	ⓓ
6.	ⓐ	ⓑ	ⓒ	ⓓ
7.	ⓐ	ⓑ	ⓒ	ⓓ
8.	ⓐ	ⓑ	ⓒ	ⓓ
9.	ⓐ	ⓑ	ⓒ	ⓓ

10.	ⓐ	ⓑ	ⓒ	ⓓ
11.	ⓐ	ⓑ	ⓒ	ⓓ
12.	ⓐ	ⓑ	ⓒ	ⓓ
13.	ⓐ	ⓑ	ⓒ	ⓓ
14.	ⓐ	ⓑ	ⓒ	ⓓ
15.	ⓐ	ⓑ	ⓒ	ⓓ
16.	ⓐ	ⓑ	ⓒ	ⓓ
17.	ⓐ	ⓑ	ⓒ	ⓓ
18.	ⓐ	ⓑ	ⓒ	ⓓ

19.	ⓐ	ⓑ	ⓒ	ⓓ
20.	ⓐ	ⓑ	ⓒ	ⓓ
21.	ⓐ	ⓑ	ⓒ	ⓓ
22.	ⓐ	ⓑ	ⓒ	ⓓ
23.	ⓐ	ⓑ	ⓒ	ⓓ
24.	ⓐ	ⓑ	ⓒ	ⓓ
25.	ⓐ	ⓑ	ⓒ	ⓓ

Part 2: Arithmetic Reasoning

1.	ⓐ	ⓑ	ⓒ	ⓓ
2.	ⓐ	ⓑ	ⓒ	ⓓ
3.	ⓐ	ⓑ	ⓒ	ⓓ
4.	ⓐ	ⓑ	ⓒ	ⓓ
5.	ⓐ	ⓑ	ⓒ	ⓓ
6.	ⓐ	ⓑ	ⓒ	ⓓ
7.	ⓐ	ⓑ	ⓒ	ⓓ
8.	ⓐ	ⓑ	ⓒ	ⓓ
9.	ⓐ	ⓑ	ⓒ	ⓓ
10.	ⓐ	ⓑ	ⓒ	ⓓ

11.	ⓐ	ⓑ	ⓒ	ⓓ
12.	ⓐ	ⓑ	ⓒ	ⓓ
13.	ⓐ	ⓑ	ⓒ	ⓓ
14.	ⓐ	ⓑ	ⓒ	ⓓ
15.	ⓐ	ⓑ	ⓒ	ⓓ
16.	ⓐ	ⓑ	ⓒ	ⓓ
17.	ⓐ	ⓑ	ⓒ	ⓓ
18.	ⓐ	ⓑ	ⓒ	ⓓ
19.	ⓐ	ⓑ	ⓒ	ⓓ
20.	ⓐ	ⓑ	ⓒ	ⓓ

21.	ⓐ	ⓑ	ⓒ	ⓓ
22.	ⓐ	ⓑ	ⓒ	ⓓ
23.	ⓐ	ⓑ	ⓒ	ⓓ
24.	ⓐ	ⓑ	ⓒ	ⓓ
25.	ⓐ	ⓑ	ⓒ	ⓓ
26.	ⓐ	ⓑ	ⓒ	ⓓ
27.	ⓐ	ⓑ	ⓒ	ⓓ
28.	ⓐ	ⓑ	ⓒ	ⓓ
29.	ⓐ	ⓑ	ⓒ	ⓓ
30.	ⓐ	ⓑ	ⓒ	ⓓ

Part 3: Word Knowledge

1.	ⓐ	ⓑ	ⓒ	ⓓ
2.	ⓐ	ⓑ	ⓒ	ⓓ
3.	ⓐ	ⓑ	ⓒ	ⓓ
4.	ⓐ	ⓑ	ⓒ	ⓓ
5.	ⓐ	ⓑ	ⓒ	ⓓ
6.	ⓐ	ⓑ	ⓒ	ⓓ
7.	ⓐ	ⓑ	ⓒ	ⓓ
8.	ⓐ	ⓑ	ⓒ	ⓓ
9.	ⓐ	ⓑ	ⓒ	ⓓ
10.	ⓐ	ⓑ	ⓒ	ⓓ
11.	ⓐ	ⓑ	ⓒ	ⓓ
12.	ⓐ	ⓑ	ⓒ	ⓓ

13.	ⓐ	ⓑ	ⓒ	ⓓ
14.	ⓐ	ⓑ	ⓒ	ⓓ
15.	ⓐ	ⓑ	ⓒ	ⓓ
16.	ⓐ	ⓑ	ⓒ	ⓓ
17.	ⓐ	ⓑ	ⓒ	ⓓ
18.	ⓐ	ⓑ	ⓒ	ⓓ
19.	ⓐ	ⓑ	ⓒ	ⓓ
20.	ⓐ	ⓑ	ⓒ	ⓓ
21.	ⓐ	ⓑ	ⓒ	ⓓ
22.	ⓐ	ⓑ	ⓒ	ⓓ
23.	ⓐ	ⓑ	ⓒ	ⓓ
24.	ⓐ	ⓑ	ⓒ	ⓓ

25.	ⓐ	ⓑ	ⓒ	ⓓ
26.	ⓐ	ⓑ	ⓒ	ⓓ
27.	ⓐ	ⓑ	ⓒ	ⓓ
28.	ⓐ	ⓑ	ⓒ	ⓓ
29.	ⓐ	ⓑ	ⓒ	ⓓ
30.	ⓐ	ⓑ	ⓒ	ⓓ
31.	ⓐ	ⓑ	ⓒ	ⓓ
32.	ⓐ	ⓑ	ⓒ	ⓓ
33.	ⓐ	ⓑ	ⓒ	ⓓ
34.	ⓐ	ⓑ	ⓒ	ⓓ
35.	ⓐ	ⓑ	ⓒ	ⓓ

Part 4: Paragraph Comprehension

1.	ⓐ	ⓑ	ⓒ	ⓓ
2.	ⓐ	ⓑ	ⓒ	ⓓ
3.	ⓐ	ⓑ	ⓒ	ⓓ
4.	ⓐ	ⓑ	ⓒ	ⓓ
5.	ⓐ	ⓑ	ⓒ	ⓓ

6.	ⓐ	ⓑ	ⓒ	ⓓ
7.	ⓐ	ⓑ	ⓒ	ⓓ
8.	ⓐ	ⓑ	ⓒ	ⓓ
9.	ⓐ	ⓑ	ⓒ	ⓓ
10.	ⓐ	ⓑ	ⓒ	ⓓ

11.	ⓐ	ⓑ	ⓒ	ⓓ
12.	ⓐ	ⓑ	ⓒ	ⓓ
13.	ⓐ	ⓑ	ⓒ	ⓓ
14.	ⓐ	ⓑ	ⓒ	ⓓ
15.	ⓐ	ⓑ	ⓒ	ⓓ

Part 5: Mathematics Knowledge

1.	ⓐ	ⓑ	ⓒ	ⓓ	10.	ⓐ	ⓑ	ⓒ	ⓓ	19.	ⓐ	ⓑ	ⓒ	ⓓ
2.	ⓐ	ⓑ	ⓒ	ⓓ	11.	ⓐ	ⓑ	ⓒ	ⓓ	20.	ⓐ	ⓑ	ⓒ	ⓓ
3.	ⓐ	ⓑ	ⓒ	ⓓ	12.	ⓐ	ⓑ	ⓒ	ⓓ	21.	ⓐ	ⓑ	ⓒ	ⓓ
4.	ⓐ	ⓑ	ⓒ	ⓓ	13.	ⓐ	ⓑ	ⓒ	ⓓ	22.	ⓐ	ⓑ	ⓒ	ⓓ
5.	ⓐ	ⓑ	ⓒ	ⓓ	14.	ⓐ	ⓑ	ⓒ	ⓓ	23.	ⓐ	ⓑ	ⓒ	ⓓ
6.	ⓐ	ⓑ	ⓒ	ⓓ	15.	ⓐ	ⓑ	ⓒ	ⓓ	24.	ⓐ	ⓑ	ⓒ	ⓓ
7.	ⓐ	ⓑ	ⓒ	ⓓ	16.	ⓐ	ⓑ	ⓒ	ⓓ	25.	ⓐ	ⓑ	ⓒ	ⓓ
8.	ⓐ	ⓑ	ⓒ	ⓓ	17.	ⓐ	ⓑ	ⓒ	ⓓ					
9.	ⓐ	ⓑ	ⓒ	ⓓ	18.	ⓐ	ⓑ	ⓒ	ⓓ					

Part 6: Electronics Information

1.	ⓐ	ⓑ	ⓒ	ⓓ	10.	ⓐ	ⓑ	ⓒ	ⓓ	19.	ⓐ	ⓑ	ⓒ	ⓓ
2.	ⓐ	ⓑ	ⓒ	ⓓ	11.	ⓐ	ⓑ	ⓒ	ⓓ	20.	ⓐ	ⓑ	ⓒ	ⓓ
3.	ⓐ	ⓑ	ⓒ	ⓓ	12.	ⓐ	ⓑ	ⓒ	ⓓ					
4.	ⓐ	ⓑ	ⓒ	ⓓ	13.	ⓐ	ⓑ	ⓒ	ⓓ					
5.	ⓐ	ⓑ	ⓒ	ⓓ	14.	ⓐ	ⓑ	ⓒ	ⓓ					
6.	ⓐ	ⓑ	ⓒ	ⓓ	15.	ⓐ	ⓑ	ⓒ	ⓓ					
7.	ⓐ	ⓑ	ⓒ	ⓓ	16.	ⓐ	ⓑ	ⓒ	ⓓ					
8.	ⓐ	ⓑ	ⓒ	ⓓ	17.	ⓐ	ⓑ	ⓒ	ⓓ					
9.	ⓐ	ⓑ	ⓒ	ⓓ	18.	ⓐ	ⓑ	ⓒ	ⓓ					

Part 7: Auto and Shop Information

1.	ⓐ	ⓑ	ⓒ	ⓓ	10.	ⓐ	ⓑ	ⓒ	ⓓ	19.	ⓐ	ⓑ	ⓒ	ⓓ
2.	ⓐ	ⓑ	ⓒ	ⓓ	11.	ⓐ	ⓑ	ⓒ	ⓓ	20.	ⓐ	ⓑ	ⓒ	ⓓ
3.	ⓐ	ⓑ	ⓒ	ⓓ	12.	ⓐ	ⓑ	ⓒ	ⓓ	21.	ⓐ	ⓑ	ⓒ	ⓓ
4.	ⓐ	ⓑ	ⓒ	ⓓ	13.	ⓐ	ⓑ	ⓒ	ⓓ	22.	ⓐ	ⓑ	ⓒ	ⓓ
5.	ⓐ	ⓑ	ⓒ	ⓓ	14.	ⓐ	ⓑ	ⓒ	ⓓ	23.	ⓐ	ⓑ	ⓒ	ⓓ
6.	ⓐ	ⓑ	ⓒ	ⓓ	15.	ⓐ	ⓑ	ⓒ	ⓓ	24.	ⓐ	ⓑ	ⓒ	ⓓ
7.	ⓐ	ⓑ	ⓒ	ⓓ	16.	ⓐ	ⓑ	ⓒ	ⓓ	25.	ⓐ	ⓑ	ⓒ	ⓓ
8.	ⓐ	ⓑ	ⓒ	ⓓ	17.	ⓐ	ⓑ	ⓒ	ⓓ					
9.	ⓐ	ⓑ	ⓒ	ⓓ	18.	ⓐ	ⓑ	ⓒ	ⓓ					

Part 8: Mechanical Comprehension

1.	ⓐ	ⓑ	ⓒ	ⓓ	10.	ⓐ	ⓑ	ⓒ	ⓓ	19.	ⓐ	ⓑ	ⓒ	ⓓ
2.	ⓐ	ⓑ	ⓒ	ⓓ	11.	ⓐ	ⓑ	ⓒ	ⓓ	20.	ⓐ	ⓑ	ⓒ	ⓓ
3.	ⓐ	ⓑ	ⓒ	ⓓ	12.	ⓐ	ⓑ	ⓒ	ⓓ	21.	ⓐ	ⓑ	ⓒ	ⓓ
4.	ⓐ	ⓑ	ⓒ	ⓓ	13.	ⓐ	ⓑ	ⓒ	ⓓ	22.	ⓐ	ⓑ	ⓒ	ⓓ
5.	ⓐ	ⓑ	ⓒ	ⓓ	14.	ⓐ	ⓑ	ⓒ	ⓓ	23.	ⓐ	ⓑ	ⓒ	ⓓ
6.	ⓐ	ⓑ	ⓒ	ⓓ	15.	ⓐ	ⓑ	ⓒ	ⓓ	24.	ⓐ	ⓑ	ⓒ	ⓓ
7.	ⓐ	ⓑ	ⓒ	ⓓ	16.	ⓐ	ⓑ	ⓒ	ⓓ	25.	ⓐ	ⓑ	ⓒ	ⓓ
8.	ⓐ	ⓑ	ⓒ	ⓓ	17.	ⓐ	ⓑ	ⓒ	ⓓ					
9.	ⓐ	ⓑ	ⓒ	ⓓ	18.	ⓐ	ⓑ	ⓒ	ⓓ					

Part 9: Assembling Objects

1. (a) (b) (c) (d)
2. (a) (b) (c) (d)
3. (a) (b) (c) (d)
4. (a) (b) (c) (d)
5. (a) (b) (c) (d)
6. (a) (b) (c) (d)

7. (a) (b) (c) (d)
8. (a) (b) (c) (d)
9. (a) (b) (c) (d)
10. (a) (b) (c) (d)
11. (a) (b) (c) (d)
12. (a) (b) (c) (d)

13. (a) (b) (c) (d)
14. (a) (b) (c) (d)
15. (a) (b) (c) (d)
16. (a) (b) (c) (d)

Part 1: General Science

Time: 11 minutes

1. Frogs belong to which animal group?
   a. reptile
   b. mammal
   c. amphibian
   d. avian

2. The nucleus of an atom consists of?
   a. electrons
   b. laptons
   c. protons and neutrons
   d. protons, neutrons, and electrons

3. How many different elements are present in fructose ($C_6H_{12}O_6$)?
   a. 3
   b. 6
   c. 12
   d. 24

4. In the evolution of Earth, once the amount of oxygen in the atmosphere increased, which adaptation helped organisms evolve to more advanced forms?
   a. photosynthesis
   b. anaerobic respiration
   c. perspiration
   d. aerobic respiration

5. The exchange of water, oxygen, carbon dioxide, and other nutrients and waste products in the body occurs at what level of the circulatory system?
   a. arterial
   b. venous
   c. capillary
   d. aortic

6. The fourth planet from the sun is
   a. Venus.
   b. Earth.
   c. Jupiter.
   d. Mars.

7. Enzymes lower the _____ of a reaction.
   a. temperature
   b. activation energy
   c. free energy
   d. speed

8. Ornithology is the scientific study of
   a. mammals.
   b. birds.
   c. dinosaurs.
   d. horses.

9. An Angstrom is a measurement of
   a. a quantity of liquid.
   b. the length of light waves.
   c. the length of underwater communications cables.
   d. the speed of ships.

10. The ozone layer protects us from excessive amounts of
    a. ultraviolet radiation.
    b. carbon dioxide.
    c. gamma radiation.
    d. temperature variation.

11. In plants, which substance provides the green colored matter essential to photosynthesis?
    a. hemoglobin
    b. melanin
    c. carotene
    d. chlorophyll

12. The Earth's moon is the primary influence on what phenomenon?
    a. sunset
    b. sunrise
    c. ocean tides
    d. tectonic forces

13. Rock formed by layers of dirt and other debris over time are called
    a. volcanic
    b. igneous
    c. sedimentary
    d. metamorphic

14. An instrument used to measure humidity is called a
    a. hydrometer.
    b. barometer.
    c. hygrometer.
    d. seismograph.

15. The fire triangle is made up of what 3 elements?
    a. heat, fuel, and igneous rocks
    b. heat, fuel, and oxygen
    c. heat and oxygen
    d. heat, oxygen, and carbon dioxide

16. What is the hormone that regulates the body's fight or flight response?
    a. estrogen
    b. adrenaline
    c. insulin
    d. androgen

17. Oxygenated blood travels to the body via which of the following?
    a. arteries
    b. veins
    c. capillaries
    d. aorta

18. What are animals that feed primarily on animal matter called?
    a. carnivores
    b. omnivores
    c. decomposers
    d. herbivores

19. A proton has
    a. a positive charge.
    b. a negative charge.
    c. a neutral charge.
    d. no charge.

20. What structure connects the middle ear to the throat?
    a. nasal cavity
    b. Eustachian tube
    c. esophagus
    d. cochlea

21. Jonas Salk discovered the vaccine for what disease?
    a. whooping cough
    b. german measles
    c. polio
    d. rickets

22. The kilometer is a unit of
    a. area.
    b. sound.
    c. volume.
    d. length.

23. Which of the following ecosystems could typically be described as having a dry climate and drought-tolerant vegetation?
    a. a deciduous forest
    b. a tropical rain forest
    c. a tundra
    d. a desert

24. Which of the following is not a measurement of fluid?
    a. litre
    b. gallon
    c. pint
    d. gram

25. A human embryo will be male if the
    a. mother's egg contributes an X chromosome.
    b. mother's egg contributes a Y chromosome.
    c. father's sperm contributes an X chromosome.
    d. father's sperm contributes a Y chromosome.

Part 2: Arithmetic Reasoning

Time: 36 minutes

1. Robert's monthly utility bill is equal to 60% of his monthly rent, which is $500 per month. How much is Robert's utility bill each month?
    a. $560
    b. $440
    c. $300
    d. $200

2. In the emergency room, there are 6 nurses. Janet has 4 patients, Susan has 6 patients, Joyce has 0 patients, Mike has 1 patient, Cathy has 2 patients, and John has 5 patients. What is the average number of patients per nurse?
    a. 1
    b. 2
    c. 3
    d. 4

3. If a baby's heart beats 130 times a minute, how many times will it beat in a 6-hour period?
    a. 45,900
    b. 46,800
    c. 46,600
    d. 47,500

4. A gardener spent $625 on supplies—fertilizer, plants, and dirt. If the fertilizer costs three times as much as the plants and dirt, how much did he spend on fertilizer?
    a. $125
    b. $250
    c. $500
    d. $375

5. John is building a patio using 6 inch × 3 inch bricks. How many bricks will he need to cover an area of 12 feet × 8 feet?
    a. 825
    b. 768
    c. 695
    d. 745

6. A bartender earned a total of $87.00 in tips over six hours. What is the average amount of total tips earned per hour?
    a. $15.50
    b. $14.00
    c. $14.50
    d. $15.00

7. $0.0224 + 0.0569 =$
    a. 0.0793
    b. 0.793
    c. 0.7
    d. 0.739

8. If Katie's cat weighs 8.5 pounds, what is the approximate weight of the cat in kilograms? (1 kilogram = about 2.2 pounds)
    a. 2.9 kilograms
    b. 3.9 kilograms
    c. 8.5 kilograms
    d. 18.7 kilograms

9. During exercise, a person's heart rate should be between 60 and 90 percent of the difference between 220 and the person's age. According to this guideline, what should a 45-year-old person's maximum heart rate be during exercise?
   a. 147.5
   b. 167.5
   c. 157.5
   d. 177.5

10. The school band is sponsoring a bake sale and car wash to raise money for a trip. Their goal is to raise $6,000. After 5 hours, they have raised $2,750. Which statement below is accurate?
   a. they have 40% of their goal remaining
   b. they have raised 50% of their goal
   c. they have raised more than 75% of their goal
   d. they have more than 50% of their goal remaining

11. Edward purchased a house for $70,000. Five years later, he sold it for an 18% profit. What was the selling price?
   a. $82,600
   b. $83,600
   c. $85,500
   d. $88,000

12. If Mary's age is decreased by Cathy's age, the result is two times Mary's age five years ago. If Cathy's age now is C years, what is Mary's present age in terms of C?
   a. $10 - 2C$
   b. $5 - C$
   c. $10 - C$
   d. $5 - 2C$

13. It took eight carpenters six hours to complete framing a house. How many additional carpenters would be needed to complete the job in three less hours?
   a. two
   b. four
   c. six
   d. eight

14. Julio left a rest stop a 9 AM heading west at 65 miles per hour. Consuela left the rest stop an hour earlier, driving east at 70 miles per hour. How far apart will they be at 11:30 AM?
   a. 340 miles
   b. 427.5 miles
   c. 407.5 miles
   d. 470 miles

15. LaKeesha owes Omar $150. Last month she paid $\frac{1}{3}$ of the amount owed. This month she paid $\frac{1}{4}$ of the remaining amount plus $10. How much money does LaKeesha still owe Omar?
   a. $65
   b. $75
   c. $85
   d. $55

16. A gram of fat contains nine calories. A 2,000-calorie diet allows no more than 40 grams from fat. What percentage of calories is allowed in this diet?
   a. 20%
   b. 18%
   c. 22%
   d. 16%

17. Four baseballs and three gloves cost $65. Four baseballs and one glove cost $40. How much does one baseball cost?
   a. $6.98
   b. $6.78
   c. $7.08
   d. $6.88

18. The foundation of a home is being dug. It measures 40 ft × 30 ft × 10 ft. The dirt is being hauled away in a truck that can hold 5 cubic ft of material. How many truckloads of dirt will be hauled away?
   a. 2,300
   b. 2,500
   c. 2,400
   d. 2,200

19. Katie and George brought an equal amount of money for shopping. Katie spent $120 and George spent $250. After shopping, George had $\frac{3}{5}$ of what Katie had left. How much money did Katie have left after shopping?
   a. $325
   b. $225
   c. $425
   d. $525

20. 15 crates of 48 apples were delivered to the applesauce factory. Eight apples in each crate were rotten and thrown away. The remaining apples were packed in boxes that each held 25 apples. How many boxes of apples were there?
   a. 18
   b. 20
   c. 24
   d. 22

21. Jamal travels north at 65 miles an hour and Sam travels south at 55 miles an hour. If they started out 1,200 miles apart, how long will it take for them to meet?
   a. 10 hours
   b. 15 hours
   c. 20 hours
   d. 25 hours

22. The average test score of 18 students is 78. If two other students were added to the group with scores of 96 and 100, what is the new average?
   a. 78
   b. 80
   c. 82
   d. 76

23. Carminuccio can type three times as fast as Jessica. Together they type 60 pages per hour. If Jessica learns to type as fast as Carminuccio, how many pages will they be able to type per hour?
   a. 30 pages
   b. 60 pages
   c. 90 pages
   d. 120 pages

24. A triangle has a perimeter of 125. If two of its sides are equal, and the third side is 20 more than either of the other sides, how long is the third side?
   a. 35
   b. 40
   c. 50
   d. 55

25. Water flows into a barrel three times faster than it flows out. If after an hour there are 142 gallons in the barrel, how many gallons flow in per hour?
   a. 200 gallons per hour
   b. 213 gallons per hour
   c. 224 gallons per hour
   d. 210 gallons per hour

26. A bus must cover 1,548 miles in 3 days. If it travels 10 hours a day, what average speed must it travel to reach its destination?
   a. 52.6 mph
   b. 50.6 mph
   c. 51.6 mph
   d. 49.6 mph

27. A single uniform requires four square yards of cloth. How many square yards of cloth are needed to make 150 uniforms?
   a. 500
   b. 550
   c. 600
   d. 650

28. A barracks currently houses 20 soldiers, which allows for an average of 36 square feet of space per soldier. If four soldiers were added to the barracks, what is the square footage of space per soldier reduced by?
   a. 5
   b. 6
   c. 7
   d. 8

29. Samantha is $\frac{1}{3}$ as old as Elizabeth, who is 5 times as old as Laura. Their ages add up to 115. How old is Laura?
   a. 10
   b. 15
   c. 25
   d. 75

30. Jason can paint a wall in 30 minutes and Jonathan can paint a wall in 45 minutes. How long will it take to paint a wall together?
   a. 18 minutes
   b. 20 minutes
   c. 16 minutes
   d. 22 minutes

Part 3: Word Knowledge

Time: 11 minutes

1. Ambient most nearly means
   a. distant.
   b. surroundings.
   c. noisy.
   d. medicine.

2. Coherent most nearly means
   a. understandable.
   b. separate.
   c. in pieces.
   d. foreign.

3. John was ambivalent about going to the meeting.
   a. agreeable
   b. resistant
   c. enthusiastic
   d. uncertain

4. Foment most nearly means
   a. rabid.
   b. threat.
   c. start.
   d. discover.

5. <u>Gregarious</u> most nearly means
  a. outgoing.
  b. regal.
  c. argue.
  d. agree.

6. <u>Divulge</u> most nearly means
  a. secrete.
  b. hide.
  c. disclose.
  d. distant.

7. <u>Premonition</u> most nearly means
  a. unknowing.
  b. historical.
  c. suspicion.
  d. ancient.

8. The trip through the mountains was <u>arduous</u>.
  a. easy
  b. rural
  c. difficult
  d. scenic

9. <u>Martial</u> most nearly means
  a. sheriff.
  b. military.
  c. wedding.
  d. union.

10. <u>Surfeit</u> most nearly means
  a. shortage.
  b. excess.
  c. absence.
  d. lacking.

11. <u>Pretentious</u> most nearly means
  a. plain.
  b. showy.
  c. average.
  d. poor.

12. <u>Altruistic</u> most nearly means
  a. hungry.
  b. evil.
  c. charitable.
  d. swift.

13. <u>Reiterate</u> most nearly means
  a. decide.
  b. argue.
  c. confuse.
  d. emphasize.

14. <u>Rambunctious</u> most nearly means
  a. sweet.
  b. filling.
  c. confusing.
  d. unruly.

15. The bad weather <u>impeded</u> the investigation.
  a. hastened
  b. slowed
  c. enhanced
  d. encouraged

16. <u>Gratitude</u> most nearly means
  a. variety.
  b. thanks.
  c. quantity.
  d. quality.

17. <u>Heeded</u> most nearly means
  a. demanded.
  b. requested.
  c. desired.
  d. followed.

18. <u>Punctual</u> most nearly means
  a. late.
  b. on time.
  c. tardy.
  d. assisted.

19. Famished most nearly means
   a. hungry.
   b. full.
   c. content.
   d. plentiful.

20. Vocation most nearly means
   a. movement.
   b. time off.
   c. job.
   d. placement.

21. Aboriginal most nearly means
   a. new.
   b. native.
   c. used.
   d. shared.

22. The myriad opportunities were encouraging.
   a. exciting
   b. many
   c. challenging
   d. professional

23. Echo most nearly means
   a. repeat.
   b. silence.
   c. loudness.
   d. noise.

24. Placate most nearly means
   a. poster.
   b. soothe.
   c. anger.
   d. trust.

25. To irk is to
   a. annoy.
   b. please.
   c. bore.
   d. trust.

26. Intimate most nearly means
   a. frightening.
   b. curious.
   c. private.
   d. characteristic.

27. Consider most nearly means
   a. promote.
   b. require.
   c. adjust.
   d. ponder.

28. Humidify most nearly means
   a. moisten.
   b. warm.
   c. gather.
   d. spray.

29. Arouse most nearly means
   a. inform.
   b. abuse.
   c. waken.
   d. deceive.

30. Harass most nearly means
   a. trick.
   b. confuse.
   c. betray.
   d. pester.

31. The two cats could be _____ only by the number of rings on their tails; otherwise, they were exactly alike.
  a. separated
  b. diversified
  c. disconnected
  d. differentiated

32. Despite her _____ dress, she was a simple girl at heart.
  a. sophisticated
  b. casual
  c. shoddy
  d. personable

33. The nonprofit agency bought office supplies using a tax _____ number.
  a. liability
  b. exempt
  c. endurance
  d. increase

34. With great and admirable _____, the renowned orator addressed the crowd gathered in the lecture hall.
  a. toil
  b. ado
  c. finesse
  d. tedium

35. _____, the skilled pediatric nurse fed the premature baby.
  a. Carelessly
  b. Precariously
  c. Gingerly
  d. Wantonly

Part 4: Paragraph Comprehension

Time: 13 minutes

Choosing a sleeping bag is a very important decision for an outdoorsman. Aside from mountain climbing clothes, it is the main thing that keeps one comfortable during an overnight, out-of-doors experience. The sleeping bag needs to be small enough to be kept in a large overnight backpack but big enough to keep warm during the freezing mountain nights. A down sleeping bag, made of feathers, is the ideal selection. Synthetic sleeping bags are sufficient at times, but they do not retain as much heat as natural down bags.

1. What is the main idea of the passage?
  a. The value of a comprehensive outdoor education.
  b. The importance of sleeping bags and how to choose the right one.
  c. A discussion of temperature variance when sleeping outdoors.
  d. The advantages of synthetic fiber sleeping bags.

2. What is one of the negative aspects of a synthetic material sleeping bag?
  a. their scarce quantity
  b. their price
  c. they don't retain enough heat
  d. they retain too much heat

Sailplane soaring is one of the most exciting ways to fly. It offers a sense of freedom that cannot be found in powered aircraft flight. As you become more experienced, you will learn to venture farther away from the airport in a sailplane, thus relying on your own skills and judgment to analyze the terrain and weather. Instead of listening to the drone of an engine keeping you aloft, you will actively look for lift clues in the air, such as birds and clouds, and you will learn to identify those aeronautical and geographic features that can help you conquer the challenge of staying aloft in an unpowered aircraft.

3. According to the passage, when you fly in a sailplane, you will be relying on
   a. powered aircraft flight.
   b. the drone of an engine.
   c. your own skills and judgment.
   d. a sense of freedom.

4. The main purpose of the passage is to
   a. talk about how you can learn to fly.
   b. describe soaring in a sailplane.
   c. talk about powered aircraft flight.
   d. describe the types of sailplanes available.

There are 100 senators and 435 representatives in the U.S. Congress. There are two senators from each state, and the number of representatives varies depending on the population of each state. Every state has at least one representative. Representatives serve for two year terms, and senators serve for six. Both representatives and senators are determined through the election process. Historically, the person in the role is re-elected. The House and the Senate are equal partners in the legislative process but each has its own unique powers.

5. According to the passage
   a. every state has the same number of representatives.
   b. the number of representatives is based on square footage of the state.
   c. every state has at least one representative.
   d. representatives server longer terms than senators.

6. The phrase "equal partners in the legislative process" in this passage suggests that
   a. each group has equal say in the process of making laws.
   b. senators have more power regarding creating laws.
   c. representatives have more power regarding creating laws.
   d. neither group can make laws.

Many people believe baking is an art, although some feel that it is a science. Some cooking does not require a strict recipe, or if there is one, the measurements do not have to be precise. However, this is not the case for baking. As with any science, if you follow the same steps time after time, the same results will occur. For example, if you follow the recipe for cake precisely by assembling the exact ingredients needed with the specified measurements, you will get the same cake every time. But if you change any of the ingredients or measurements, you will not get the same cake.

7. As used in the passage, the word "assembling" means
   a. cooking.
   b. measuring.
   c. combining.
   d. separating.

8. According the passage, a person that produces the same cake every time
   a. should stay out of the kitchen.
   b. is good at chemistry.
   c. follows the recipe exactly.
   d. is a scientist.

Davis Valley Dairy Farm is a small, family operated dairy located on the South Branch of the Frenchman River, right in the heart of wine country. It specializes in hand-crafted, artisanal cheese and a variety of soothing goat milk beauty products. Unlike many of the artificial products on the shelves today, their goat milk moisturizer cream is all natural and contains more than 50 nutrients. It is suggested that you visit them to learn more about the myriad benefits of goat milk products. The farm includes a winery, nearly 200 acres of pasture, several barns, a farmhouse, and an apprentice house. In Spring 2003, they began making cheese from the milk of their 20, mixed-breed, grass-fed goats. They are open from 10:00 AM to 5:00 PM and closed Tuesday and Thursday.

9. According to the passage, you could expect to purchase
   a. wine products at the farm.
   b. milk products at the farm.
   c. beauty products at the farm.
   d. All the above.

10. According to the passage, what is one of the major selling points of their goat milk products?
   a. the fact that they have nearly 200 acres of pasture
   b. their relatively low cost
   c. the fact that they're from a small, family operated farm
   d. the fact that they're all-natural and contain more than 50 nutrients

11. Could you purchase goat milk soap at 11:00 AM on Tuesday morning?
   a. Yes, but it would have to be pre-ordered.
   b. Yes, the farm is open at that time.
   c. No, the farm is closed at that time.
   d. No, the farm does not sell goat milk soap.

To make some of the best chocolate chip cookies you will ever taste, just follow this quick and easy recipe. First, preheat an oven to 375 degrees. Mix sugar, brown sugar, butter, vanilla, and eggs in a large bowl by hand, or use a mixer on a low setting with a batter attachment. Next, stir in flour, baking soda, and salt. At this point, the dough will be very stiff. Be sure that the dough is well mixed before moving on. Then stir in chocolate chips, using a sturdy wooden spoon and a bit of muscle. Keep stirring, and fold the chocolate chips into the dough until they are evenly dispersed.

12. According to the passage, what is the first step in this recipe?
   a. taste the cookies
   b. preheat the oven to 375 degrees
   c. mix the ingredients
   d. buy a mixing bowl

13. How many total ingredients are in this recipe?
   a. 7
   b. 9
   c. 10
   d. 11

Grab your knitting needles and yarn, sit back, and learn how to knit by watching an expert knitter knit! These DVD-based knitting lessons begin by teaching you knitting basics, such as long tail cast-on, knit stitch, and purl stitch. These three techniques make up the majority of any knitting project, and once you learn these skills you are well on your way to knitting. Once you have mastered these basic stitches, you'll want to move on and learn some advanced knitting techniques. In this program, you'll learn about the different types of yarn used for different types of projects, and you will quickly begin to understand why knitting is one of the most popular pastimes in the world.

14. According to the passage, how many techniques make up the majority of any knitting project?
   a. three
   b. four
   c. five
   d. six

15. What does the passage say about wool and different projects?
   a. They are not discussed on the DVD.
   b. Advanced knitting techniques always depend on different types of yarn.
   c. Different types of yarn can be used for different types of projects.
   d. Basic stitches cannot be used with different types of yarn.

Part 5: Mathematic Knowledge

Time: 24 minutes

1. When calculating the area of a figure, you are looking for
   a. the distance around the object.
   b. the length of a side.
   c. the amount of space that the object covers.
   d. the number of sides it has.

2. Choose the answer to the following problem: $(33 + 17) \times (28 - 13) =$
   a. 700
   b. 850
   c. 800
   d. 750

3. Which of the following numbers is the largest?
   a. $\frac{2}{5}$
   b. $\frac{3}{8}$
   c. $\frac{24}{30}$
   d. $\frac{10}{20}$

4. Which of the following is the equivalent of $\frac{36}{50}$
   a. 0.72
   b. 0.66
   c. 0.68
   d. 0.62

5. Choose the answer to the following problem: $0.045 \times 1,000 =$
   a. .45
   b. 4.5
   c. 45
   d. 450

6. When measuring the area of a baseball field, you would most likely use
   a. square inches.
   b. square yards.
   c. square miles.
   d. square millimeters.

7. What is the relationship between a square and a parallelogram?
   a. they are both quadrilaterals
   b. they are the same thing
   c. they both have five sides
   d. there is no relationship

8. Which of the following statements is true?
   a. Perpendicular lines never intersect at right angles.
   b. Parallel lines never intersect.
   c. Perpendicular lines intersect multiple times.
   d. Intersecting lines have multiple points in common.

9. Choose the answer to the following problem:
   $0.027 \times 1,000 =$
   a. 27
   b. 2.7
   c. 0.27
   d. 270

10. What is the next number in the series below?
   2, 12, 8, 48, 40, 240 _____
   a. 238
   b. 224
   c. 232
   d. 228

11. Which number sentence is true?
   a. $3.6 < 36$
   b. $0.36 < 0.036$
   c. $0.0036 > 0.036$
   d. $0.036 > 0.36$

12. What is the area of a triangle with a height of 12 inches and a base of 8 inches?
   a. 32 square inches
   b. 36 square inches
   c. 42 square inches
   d. 48 square inches

13. What is 0.573 rounded to the nearest tenth?
   a. 0.6
   b. 0.57
   c. 0.58
   d. 1.0

14. $\frac{36,000}{1,000} =$
   a. 36
   b. 360
   c. 3,600
   d. 36,000

15. Change $\frac{55}{6}$ to a mixed number.
   a. $8\frac{1}{6}$
   b. $9\frac{1}{6}$
   c. $9\frac{1}{55}$
   d. $9\frac{6}{55}$

16. Which is $4\frac{1}{4}\%$ of 574, rounded to the nearest tenth?
   a. 24.4
   b. 24.3
   c. 20
   d. 30

17. Sixteen less than six times a number is 20. What is the number?

a. 12

b. 10

c. 8

d. 6

18. What is the smallest prime number?

a. 0

b. 1

c. 2

d. 3

19. How many faces does a cube have?

a. 4

b. 6

c. 8

d. 12

20. A triangle has one 30° angle and one 60° angle. Which of the following types of triangles is it?

a. isosceles

b. equilateral

c. right

d. scalene

21. What is the perimeter of the following polygon?

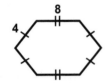

a. 12

b. 16

c. 24

d. 32

22. In the following figure, which pair of angles must be congruent?

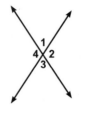

a. 1 and 2

b. 1 and 3

c. 3 and 4

d. 1 and 4

23. Which of the following is an improper fraction?

a. $\frac{22}{60}$

b. $\frac{66}{22}$

c. $\frac{90}{100}$

d. $\frac{1,000}{2,600}$

24. What is the reciprocal of $3\frac{7}{8}$?

a. $\frac{31}{8}$

b. $\frac{8}{31}$

c. $\frac{8}{21}$

d. $-\frac{31}{8}$

25. What is the value of the expression $5(4^0)$?

a. 0

b. 1

c. 5

d. 20

Part 6: Electronics Information

Time: 9 minutes

1. For safety purposes, electrical devices need to be
   a. inspected daily.
   b. limited in volt and amperage.
   c. grounded to prevent electrical shock.
   d. designed under international guidelines.

2. A voltmeter is connected to a circuit as shown. What will the meter read?

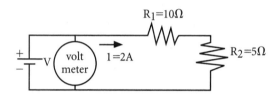

   a. 5 volts
   b. 10 volts
   c. 15 volts
   d. 30 volts

3. A modulator-demodulator is better known as a
   a. modulation resistor
   b. microwave capacitor
   c. gauge to measure impedance
   d. modem

4. What does 25k Ω equal?
   a. 25 Ω
   b. 250 Ω
   c. 25,000 Ω
   d. 250,000 Ω

5. What are Extremely High Frequency (EHF) radio frequencies measured in?
   a. Hz
   b. kHz
   c. MHz
   d. GHz

6. Most wires today are manufactured from
   a. brass.
   b. copper.
   c. aluminum.
   d. titanium.

7. Which of the following is NOT needed to make an electric circuit?
   a. a closed path
   b. resistance
   c. a switch
   d. a potential power source

8. Two hundred kilowatts is equal to how many watts?
   a. 2,000 watts
   b. 20,000 watts
   c. 200,000 watts
   d. 2,000,000 watts

9. Which of the following is NOT needed to produce electrical power from fossil fuels?
   a. a dam
   b. a turbine
   c. steam
   d. heat

10. Which of the following is NOT a good insulator?
  a. a car tire
  b. a wooden dowel
  c. glass
  d. gold

11. What is the frequency of the alternating voltage and current typically used in the United States?
  a. 20 Hz
  b. 40 Hz
  c. 60 Hz
  d. 110 Hz

12. A rheostat is a type of
  a. amplifier.
  b. modulator.
  c. capacitor.
  d. resistor.

13. What is the total current in a parallel resistance circuit with three parallel paths that each have four amperes flowing through them?
  a. 2 A
  b. 12 A
  c. 4 A
  d. 8 A

14. The abbreviation FM stands for
  a. frequency modulation.
  b. frequency multiplier.
  c. feedback multiplex.
  d. farad magnet.

15. In the United States, what color will a ground wire be?
  a. red or black
  b. bare, green, or yellow green
  c. black
  d. red

16. Electrical energy is measured in
  a. volts
  b. farads
  c. watts
  d. coulombs

17. Which of the following is the symbol for a resistor?

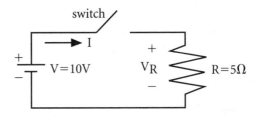

  a.
  b.
  c.
  d.

18. What is the voltage across the load R and the current through R when the switch is open in the following circuit?

  a. The current is 0 A; the voltage is 10 V.
  b. The current is 2 A; the voltage is 10 V.
  c. The current is 2 A; the voltage is 2 V.
  d. The current is 0 A; the voltage is 0 V.

19. What does this electronic circuit symbol depict?

  a. a conversion from AC to DC power
  b. an electrical surge
  c. a wire that does not join another
  d. a wire that intersects another

20. A test tool that is used to display the shape of electrical signals and can be used to measure their voltage and time period is an
a. voltmeter.
b. galvanometer.
c. oscilloscope.
d. ohmmeter.

Part 7: Auto and Shop Information

Time: 11 minutes

1. The tools shown are a set of
a. Phillips wrenches.
b. Allen wrenches.
c. walker wrenches.
d. spanners.

2. Condensation in a fuel line could cause
a. spark plug de-synchronization.
b. fire in the gas tank.
c. a stalled vehicle.
d. increased gas mileage.

3. The braking system in an automobile uses what scientific principle?
a. inertia
b. acceleration
c. gravity
d. friction

4. The fuel filter of an automobile performs what function?
a. it meters fuel to the engine
b. it cleans the fuel prior to it being burned
c. it restricts fuel flow
d. it cools down the manifold

5. A torque converter is made up of what?
a. a turbine, pump, and stator
b. a carburetor, spark plugs, and transmission
c. cylinders and pistons
d. brake pads and disk brakes

6. Antifreeze is used for what purpose?
a. to keep the oil system from freezing
b. to keep the brake fluid from freezing
c. to keep the air conditioning system from freezing
d. to keep the engine coolant from freezing

7. When sanding wood by hand, the best results will be achieved by sanding
a. across the grain
b. against the grain
c. with the grain
d. in small vigorous circles

8. Which of the following is the strongest way to join two pieces of wood together?
a. glue
b. nails
c. screws
d. clamps

9. Which tool would best be used to cut glass?
a. an aluminum-tipped glass cutter
b. a serrated-tooth glass cutter
c. a steel-tipped glass cutter
d. a carbide-tipped glass cutter

10. What function does the distributor perform in an automobile engine?
   a. it reduces wear and tear on the spark plugs
   b. it limits electrical surges
   c. it routes high voltage from the ignition coil to the spark plugs
   d. it controls the electronic ignition system

11. A vise is commonly used to
   a. securely hold a piece of wood.
   b. mark a level line.
   c. find a plumb line.
   d. tighten a drill chuck.

12. A helical fastener used in pre-drilled holes in the assembly of metal parts is
   a. a carriage bolt.
   b. a machine screw.
   c. a cotter key.
   d. an Allen nut.

13. A spark plug is used to
   a. heat the oil in an engine.
   b. create a spark to ignite the fuel mixture in an engine.
   c. create a spark to burn the exhaust gases in an engine.
   d. charge the battery in an engine.

14. The purpose of an exhaust in a car is to
   a. increase gas mileage.
   b. cool the engine.
   c. dispose of burnt gases.
   d. condition the air.

15. The following tool would most likely be used to

   a. temporarily hold two boards together.
   b. hold up a car in order to repair a flat tire.
   c. secure a heavy load as it is being transported.
   d. make a straight cut on a board.

16. Which of the following is NOT a benefit of adding lubricant to a machine?
   a. it serves as a coolant
   b. it improves ignition reliability
   c. it reduces friction
   d. it prevents corrosion

17. The following gauge is reading approximately what RPM?

   a. 175 RPM
   b. 148 RPM
   c. 120 RPM
   d. 105 RPM

18. Which is NOT a type of screwdriver?
   a. slotted
   b. Ball Peen
   c. Phillips
   d. offset

19. The following tool is

   a. a hydraulic clamp
   b. a vise grip
   c. a pair of round-off pliers
   d. a pair of bull-nosed pliers

20. A torque wrench is used to
   a. determine how many turns have been made when tightening a bolt.
   b. determine the strength of a bolt.
   c. determine how tight a bolt is.
   d. All of the above.

21. A crane is primarily used to
   a. provide leverage
   b. provide push
   c. provide reinforcement
   d. provide lift

22. Which of the following woodworking objects would most likely be created with a lathe?
   a. a door jamb
   b. a baseball bat
   c. a decorative box
   d. a bookcase

23. To hide a wood screw head below the surface of wood, what sort of drill bit would you use?
   a. countersink
   b. auger
   c. smooth shank
   d. impact bit

24. What function does the fourth stroke of a four-stroke engine cycle perform?
   a. combustion
   b. compression
   c. ignition
   d. exhaust

25. The amount of energy needed to heat one pound of water one degree Fahrenheit is called
   a. an HVAC.
   b. a Heat Exchange Ratio (HER).
   c. a British Thermal Unit (BTU).
   d. a Newton.

Part 8: Mechanical Comprehension

Time: 19 minutes

1. A chisel is most like
   a. a screwdriver.
   b. a wedge.
   c. an inclined plane.
   d. a hammer.

2. The mechanical action of a doorknob most closely resembles that of a
   a. hinge.
   b. ramp.
   c. wheel and axel.
   d. All of the above.

3. The point upon which a lever acts is called the
   a. centripetal center.
   b. center.
   c. radius.
   d. fulcrum.

4. Joe must lift a 100-pound box using a lever, as per the following diagram. How many pounds of force must Joe apply to the left side of the lever to lift the box?

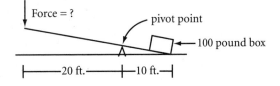

a. 100
b. 200
c. 50
d. 33

5. The type of gear shown in the following image is a

a. straight spur
b. rack and pinion
c. herringbone
d. bevel

6. Which material is best suited for use in a life preserver?
a. metal
b. foam
c. wood
d. glass

7. In the following diagram, which gears are turning clockwise?

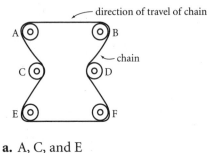

a. A, C, and E
b. B, D, and F
c. C and D
d. E and F

8. If gear A in the following diagram rotates in the clockwise direction, what direction would gear D turn?

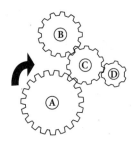

a. clockwise
b. counterclockwise
c. it would seize up
d. it cannot be determined

9. Water is flowing through a piping system. Eventually, due to friction losses and a rise in elevation, the flow rate of the water becomes very slow. Which device can best be used to increase the flow of the water?
a. a gear
b. a winch
c. a pump
d. a compressor

10. The sprocket on a bicycle is most similar to which of the simple mechanical devices listed below?
a. a spring
b. a lever
c. a gear
d. all of the above

11. A playground seesaw uses what mechanical component?
a. a pulley
b. an axle
c. a cam
d. a lever

12. Which mechanical components are typically used between a wheel and an axle to reduce friction?
a. hinges
b. levers
c. springs
d. bearings

13. In the following diagram, what mechanical device could be used to transfer water from Tank #1 to Tank #2?

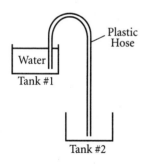

a. a pulley
b. a siphon
c. a lever
d. a spring

14. When a bolt is being tightened, what is the action being applied to the bolt?
a. friction
b. torque
c. kinetic energy
d. none of the above

15. Kinetic energy is
a. energy created from hydroelectric power.
b. energy created from fossil fuels.
c. energy in an object that is at rest.
d. energy in an object that is in motion.

16. Pascal's Law deals with
a. quantum physics.
b. physical entropy.
c. hydrostatic pressure.
d. aerodynamics.

17. What type of pulley is displayed in the following diagram?

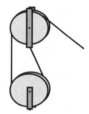

a. a single pulley
b. a double pulley
c. a compound pulley
d. a simple pulley

18. A first class lever would have the fulcrum
   a. on the power end of the tool.
   b. on either end of the tool.
   c. in the middle of the tool.
   d. on both ends of the tool.

19. A shim is a type of
   a. screw.
   b. nail.
   c. ramp.
   d. wedge.

20. A plumb bob uses what force to achieve its results?
   a. gravity
   b. electricity
   c. kinetic energy
   d. relative motion

21. In the following figure, all valves are initially closed. When the valves are opened, gravity will cause the water to drain into the barrels. Which barrels will be filled with water if valves A, B, E, F, and G are opened and valves C and D are left closed?

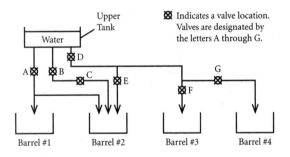

   a. barrels #1 and #2
   b. barrels #3 and #4
   c. barrels #1, #2, #3, and #4
   d. barrels #1, #2, and #3

22. In the following diagram, which pulley will turn the fastest?

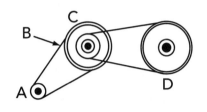

   a. A
   b. B
   c. C
   d. D

23. In the following diagram, the distance from A to B is three feet and the distance from B to C is seven feet. How much force must be applied at A to lift the 50 lbs. at point B?

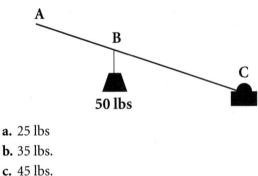

   a. 25 lbs
   b. 35 lbs.
   c. 45 lbs.
   d. 55 lbs.

24. Which mechanical device is used in the normal operation of an elevator?
   a. a lever
   b. a hydraulic jack
   c. a pulley
   d. a spring

25. What device could be used to transfer water between tanks that are at the same level?
   a. a pulley
   b. a siphon
   c. a pump
   d. a spring

Part 9: Assembling Objects

Time: 16 minutes

1.

2.

3.

4.

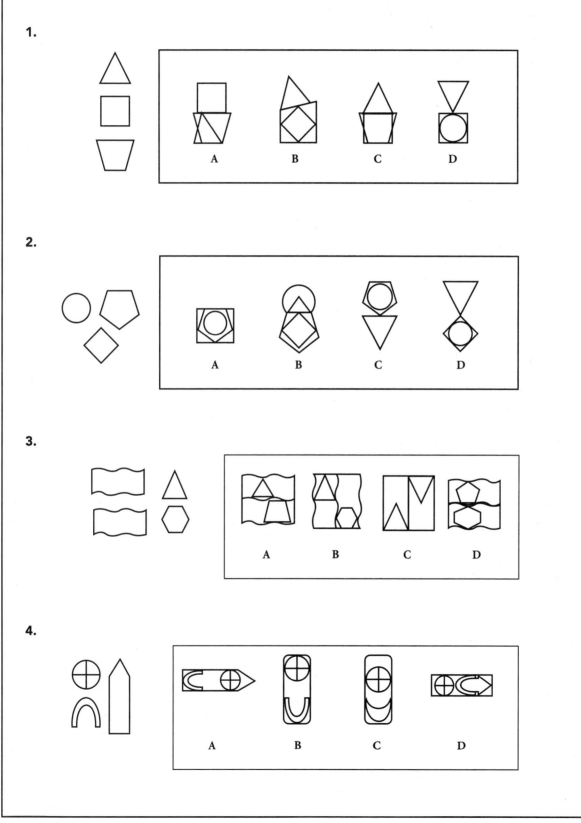

5.

6.

7.

8.

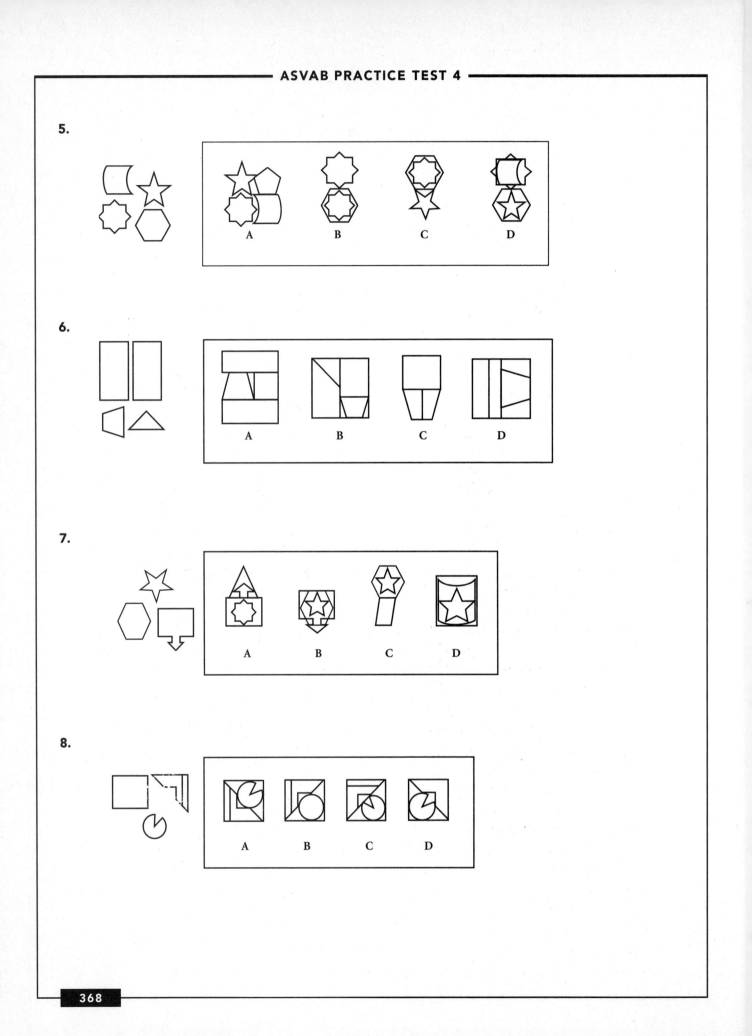

9.

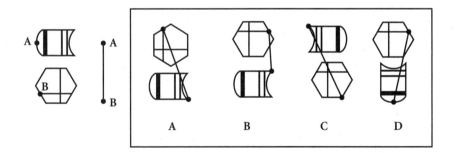

10.

11.

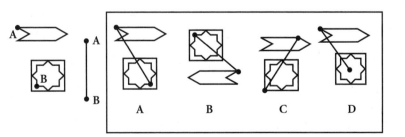

12.

13.

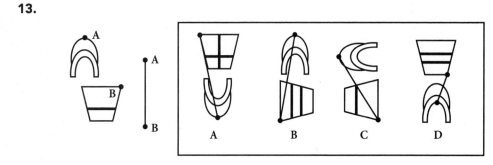

14.

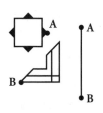
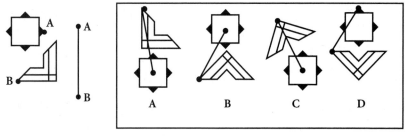

15.

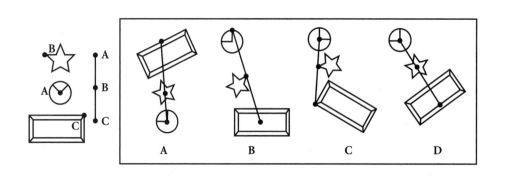

16.

ASVAB PRACTICE TEST 4

Answers

Part 1: General Science

1. **c.** Frogs are amphibians.
2. **c.** The nucleus of an atom consists of nucleons, also called protons and neutrons.
3. **a.** $C_6H_{12}O_6$ contains 3 elements-carbon, hydrogen, and oxygen.
4. **d.** Organisms that adapted to use oxygen through aerobic respiration made energy more efficiently than they did through anaerobic respiration, giving them an evolutionary advantage.
5. **c.** The exchange of water, oxygen, carbon dioxide, and other nutrients and waste products in the body occurs at the capillary level. Arterial blood flow is in the arteries, which is what the aorta is, taking oxygenated blood to the body. Venous blood flow is in veins, taking un-oxygenated blood back to the lungs for replenishment.
6. **d.** The fourth planet from the sun is Mars.
7. **b.** Enzymes lower the activation energy of a reaction, or the energy needed for a reaction to proceed.
8. **b.** Ornithology is the scientific study of birds.
9. **b.** An angstrom is a measurement of the length of light waves.
10. **a.** The ozone layer absorbs 97–99% of the sun's high-frequency, ultraviolet radiation.
11. **d.** Chlorophyll is a green pigment found in most plants and algae.
12. **c.** The Moon's gravitational pull and the slight wobbling of the Earth on its axis contribute to the tidal system of the oceans.
13. **c.** The depositing of layers of sediment over a very long period of time builds up incredible pressure, resulting in rock formations called sedimentary rocks.
14. **c.** A hygrometer is used to measure humidity.
15. **b.** Any fire needs heat, fuel, and oxygen to ignite or burn.
16. **b.** Adrenaline is a hormone produced by the adrenal gland in the body of many animals. It stimulates the heart rate, dilates blood vessels, and widens air passages, preparing the body for either a fight or a flight response.
17. **a.** Arteries carry oxygenated blood through the heart and on to the body.
18. **a.** Carnivores are animals that subsist primarily on other animal matter. Omnivores eat a variety of foodstuff, and herbivores eat only plant matter.
19. **a.** A proton has a positive charge.
20. **b.** The Eustachian tube connects the middle ear and throat. The cochlea is a fluid-filled structure in the inner ear.
21. **c.** Jonas Salk discovered the polio vaccine in 1955.
22. **d.** A kilometer is a measure of length. There are 1,000 meters in a kilometer.
23. **d.** A desert would have a dry climate and drought-tolerant vegetation.
24. **d.** A gram is a measurement of weight, not fluid.
25. **d.** A human embryo's sex is always determined by the sperm. The egg always contributes an X chromosome, while the sperm contributes either an X (for a female) or a Y (for a male).

Part 2: Arithmetic Reasoning

1. **c.** First, change the percent to a decimal and then multiply: 60% = 0.60. The problem becomes $0.60 \times 500 = \$300$.
2. **c.** Use addition to get the total number of patients, 18. Then divide by 6, the total number of nurses: $18 \div 6 = 3$.
3. **b.** This is a two-step multiplication problem. To find out how many heartbeats there would be in one hour, you must multiply 130×60 (minutes) and then multiply this result, 7,800, by 6 hours: $7,800 \times 6 = 46,800$.
4. **d.** Let x be the cost of the plants and dirt. So $3x$ is the cost of the fertilizer. Therefore, $x + x + 3x = 625$. $5x = 625$ and $x = 125$. Since we are looking for the cost of the fertilizer, we need to calculate $3 \times 125 = \$375$.

5. b. It takes 2 bricks set lengthwise to cover one foot and four bricks set widthwise to cover one foot. So, to cover 12 feet, you need 24 bricks lengthwise and you need 32 bricks to cover 8 feet widthwise. The total number of bricks is 24 × 32 = 768.

6. c. To find the average, divide the total by the number of hours: $87 ÷ 6 = $14.50 per hour.

7. a. This is a simple addition problem. 0.0224 + 0.0569 = 0.0793.

8. b. To solve this problem, divide the number of pounds in the weight of the cat (8.5) by the number of pounds in a kilogram (2.2); 8.5 ÷ 2.2 = 3.9 kilograms (approximately).

9. c. The difference between 220 and this person's age is 220 − 45 =175. The minimum heart rate is 90% of this, so 0.9 × 175 = 157.5.

10. d. They have raised 2,750 ÷ 6,000 or about 45.8% of their goal.

11. a. This is a two-step problem. First, find the amount of profit. Convert the percent (18%) to a decimal (0.18) and multiply. 70,000 × 0.18 = 12,600. Next, add the result to the original price: 70,000 + 12,600 = $82,600.

12. c. Let M represent Mary's age. Cathy's age is represented by C. You are told that M − C = 2(M − 5). Simplify it to M − C = 2M − 10 or M = 10 − C

13. d. Let x = the number of men needed to complete the job in 3 hours. The resulting equation would be $3x = (8)(6)$ or $3x = 48$, so $x = 16$. The additional men you need to complete the job is 8.

14. c. The distance formula is $d = rt$ where d is distance, r is rate (speed), and t is time. We know that Bob was traveling north at 65mph, so $65t = d$. Bill was traveling south at 70 mph so $70t = d$. By 11:30 A.M, Bob will have been traveling 2.5 hours and Bill will have been traveling 3.5 hours. Total distance is 65(2.5) + 70(3.5) = 162.5 + 245 = 407.5 miles.

15. a. Last month LaKeesha paid back $150 ÷ 3 = $50 leaving a balance of $100. This month she paid back $\frac{1}{4}$ ($100) + $10 = $25 + $10 = $35. Her remaining balance is $100 − $35 = $65.

16. b. Since there are nine calories in each gram of fat, multiply 40 grams by 9 to get 40 × 9 = 360, the number of calories are allowed in the 2,000 calorie diet. Divide 360 by 2,000 to get: 360 ÷ 2,000 = .18 or 18%.

17. d. Since four baseballs and three gloves cost $65, and four baseballs and one glove costs $40, we can see that two gloves cost $25. Therefore, one glove costs $12.50. Thus, 4 baseballs + $12.50 = $40, and 4 baseballs = $27.50. Therefore, each baseball costs approximately $6.88.

18. c. The amount of dirt that needs to be hauled away is 40 × 30 × 10 = 12,000 cubic ft. One load holds 5 cubic ft, so 12,000 ÷ 5 = 2,400. So it will take 2,400 loads to haul away all the dirt.

19. a. Let G stand for the amount of money George has left and K stand for the amount Katie has left. Thus, $\frac{3}{5}$K = G. If x is the staring amount each had then G = x − $250 and K = x − 120. So using substitution, $\frac{3}{5}$ (x − $120) = x − $250. $\frac{3}{5}x − \frac{360}{5}$ = x − 350. Multiply both sides by 5 to eliminate the fraction and you have 3x − $360 = 5$x$ − $1,250. Combine like terms and you have 2x = $890 or x = $445. So Katie has $445 − $120 = $325 left.

20. c. 15 crates each holding 48 apples means a total of 720 apples were delivered. However, 8 in every box are rotten. Thus, 15 × 8 = 120 were discarded leaving 720 − 120 = 600. If they were boxed at a rate of 25 per box, there would be 600 ÷ 25 = 24 boxes.

21. a. The combined rate of travel is 65 + 55 = 120 miles per hour. 1,200 miles ÷ 120 miles per hour = 10 hours.

22. b. The total score is 18 students' × the average score of 78; 18 × 78 = 1,404. Add 96 and 100 to 1,404 and get 96 + 100 + 1,404 =1,600. Divide this by 20 students to get an average of 80.

23. c. Let C stand for Carminuccio and J for Jessica. Therefore, C = 3J. 3J + J = 60, so J = 15. Since C = 3J, C = 3 × 15 = 45. If Jessica can learn to type as fast as Carminuccio, they can type at a combined rate of 90 pages per hour.

24. d. Perimeter is equal to the sum of all three sides so $x + x + (x + 20) = 125$. This means $3x + 20 = 125$, $3x = 105$, and $x = 35$. The third side is $x + 20 = 35 + 20 = 55$.

25. b. Let 3W = rate of water coming in and W = rate of water going out; $3W - W = 142$, which simplifies to $W = 71$ and $3W = 213$.

26. c. Here, 1,548 miles ÷ 3 days = 516 miles and 516 miles ÷ 10 hours = 51.6 mph.

27. c. One uniform takes 4 square yards to make, so 150 uniforms takes 150 × 4 = 600 square yards.

28. b. 20 men × 36 square feet = 720 square feet of space. Add 4 men to get 20 + 4 = 24 men and 720 ÷ 24 = 30 square feet of space per man. So there is a reduction of 36 − 30 = 6 square feet per man.

29. b. Let S = Samantha's age; E = Elizabeth's age; and L = Laura's age. $S = \frac{1}{3}E = \frac{5}{3}L$ and E = 5L. The total age of the three is 115, so S + E + L = 115. Substitute and you get $L + 5L + \frac{5}{3}L = 115$. Simplify to get $\frac{23}{3}L = 115$; 23L = 345; and L = 15. Therefore, Laura's age is 15.

30. a. The equation needed is $\frac{1}{30} + \frac{1}{45} = \frac{1}{t}$ where t is the time to paint the wall together. Simplify and you get $30t + 45t = 1,350$; $75t = 1,350$; $t = 18$.

Part 3: Word Knowledge

1. b The word *ambient* means *surroundings*, or the immediate environment around you.

2. a. To be *coherent* is to be *understandable*, or clear about something.

3. d. If one is *ambivalent* about something, he or she is *uncertain* about it.

4. c. To *foment* something is to *start* or initiate it.

5. a. If one is *gregarious*, he or she is an *outgoing* person.

6. c. To *divulge* something is to *disclose* it.

7. c. To have a *premonition* is to have a forewarning about something.

8. c Something that is *arduous* is *difficult* to do or accomplish.

9. b. The word *martial* implies *military* connotation.

10. b. A *surfeit* of something means there is an *excess*.

11. b. Something that is *pretentious* is excessively *showy*.

12. c. To be *altruistic* is to be *charitable* to others.

13. d. To *reiterate* something is to *emphasize* it or say again, usually in an important manner.

14. d. *Rambunctious* most nearly means *unruly*.

15. b. Something that is *impeded* is *slowed* down or blocked.

16. b. To express *gratitude* for something is to give *thanks*.

17. d. If you *heeded* someone's advice, then you *followed* it.

18. b. Someone who is *punctual* is *on time*.

19. a. To be *famished* is to be in a state of extreme hunger.

20. c. A *vocation* is a *job* or what you are employed doing.

21. b. Something that is *aboriginal* is *native* to that area or region.

22. b. *Myriad* means *many*.

23. a. To *echo* something is to *repeat* it.

24. b. To *placate* someone is to *soothe* him or her.

25. a. To *irk* someone is to *annoy* him or her.

26. c. *Intimate* means personal or *private*.

27. d. To *consider* means to *ponder*.

28. a. To *humidify* means to dampen or *moisten*.

29. c. To *arouse* means to *waken*.

30. d. To *harass* means to torment or *pester*.

31. d. To *differentiate* between two things is to establish a distinction between them.

32. a. In the context of the sentence, *sophisticated* provides contrast to the girl's simplicity, suggested by the word despite.

33. b. *Exempt* means to be excused from a rule or obligation.

34. c. *Finesse* is skill, tact, and cleverness.

35. c. To handle something *gingerly* means to handle it delicately and with great caution.

Part 4: Paragraph Comprehension

1. b. The first sentence lays out what the paragraph will be about—the importance of sleeping bags—and the rest of the passage talks about choosing the right one.

2. c. The last sentence of the passage mentions that synthetic sleeping bags don't retain enough heat.

3. c. The passage specifically states that you will be relying on your own skills and judgment when you fly in a sailplane.

4. b. Choice **b** talks about specifics covered in the passage, making it the correct answer. Choices **c** and **d** are not discussed in the passage. Choice **a** is not specifically explained in the passage.

5. c. As mentioned in the passage, every state has at least one representative.

6. a. The phrase "equal partners in the legislative process" in this passage suggests that each group has equal say in the process of making laws.

7. c. The word *assembling*, used in the passage in conjunction with the ingredients for baking a cake, implies that you are combining the required ingredients.

8. c. The last sentence implies that if you follow the recipe exactly, you will get the same cake every time you use this recipe.

9. d. According to the passage, all of the products mentioned are available for purchase.

10. d. Choice **d**, the fact that they're all-natural and contain more than 50 nutrients, is why goat's milk products are special.

11. c. The last sentence provides the hours of operation. There is no information given for pre-ordering on a closed day.

12. b. The passage mentions that preheating the oven to 375 degrees is the first step.

13. b. There are a total of nine ingredients in the recipe: sugar, brown sugar, butter, vanilla, eggs, flour, baking soda, salt, and chocolate chips.

14. a. According to the passage, three techniques make up the majority of any knitting project.

15. c. The passage specifically states that different types of yarn can be used for different types of projects.

Part 5: Mathematics Knowledge

1. c. When calculating the area of a figure, you are looking for the amount of space that the figure covers.

2. d. Perform the operations within the parentheses first: $(33 + 17) \times (28 - 13) = (50) \times (15) = 750$.

3. c. Fractions must be converted to the lowest common denominator, which allows you to compare the amounts: $\frac{48}{120}, \frac{45}{120}, \frac{96}{120}, \frac{60}{120}$. The largest number is choice **c**.

4. a. The fraction $\frac{36}{50}$ is equal to $\frac{72}{100}$ or .72.

5. c. $0.045 \times 1,000 = 45$.

6. b. When measuring the area of a baseball field you would most likely use square yards.

7. a. Squares and parallelograms are both quadrilaterals.

8. b. Parallel lines never intersect.

9. a. $0.027 \times 1,000 = 27$.

10. b. This series actually has two alternating sets of numbers. The first number is multiplied by six, which gives the second number. The second number has four subtracted from it, which gives the third number. The third number is multiplied by six, which gives the fourth number. The fourth number has eight subtracted from it, which gives the fifth number. The fifth number is multiplied by six, which gives the sixth number. The fifth number has 16 subtracted from it. Therefore, the blank space will be $240 - 16 = 224$.

11. a. 3.6 is less than 36.

12. d. The formula for the area of triangle is $A = \frac{1}{2}bh$; $\frac{1}{2}(8)(12) = \frac{1}{2}(96) = 48$.

13. a. 0.573 rounded to the nearest tenth is 0.6.

14. a. You can quickly solve this problem by cancelling out the ones in the numerator and denominator to be left with $\frac{36}{1} = 36$.

15. b. Divide the numerator by the denominator to find the whole number of the mixed number. The remainder, if any, becomes the numerator of the fraction. The denominator stays the same: $55 \div 6 = 9$, remainder 1. Therefore, the mixed number is $9\frac{1}{6}$.

16. a. To solve the problem, first change the percent to a decimal: $4\frac{1}{4} = 0.0425; 0.0425 \times 574 = 24.395$. Then, round to the nearest tenth: 24.4.

17. d. Start by adding 16 to 20; $16 + 20 = 36$. Then divide: $36 \div 6 = 6$.

18. c. The smallest prime number is 2.

19. b. A cube has six faces.

20. c. The sum of the angles on a triangle is 180°. The two angles given add to 90°, so the third angle must be a 90° angle. Therefore, it is a right triangle.

21. d. There are four sides measuring four, and two sides measuring eight. Therefore, the perimeter is $(4 \times 4) + (2 \times 8) = 32$.

22. b. Vertical angles are non-adjacent angles formed by two intersecting lines, such as angles 1 and 3 and angles 2 and 4 in the diagram. When two lines intersect, the vertical angles formed are congruent. Therefore, angles 1 and 3 are congruent.

23. b. In an improper fraction, the top number is greater than the bottom number, so $\frac{66}{22}$ is an improper fraction.

24. b. Convert the mixed number $3\frac{7}{8}$ to the improper fraction $\frac{31}{8}$ and then invert to $\frac{8}{31}$.

25. c. Follow the order of operations and evaluate the exponent first. Since any nonzero number raised to the zero power is equal to 1, then $4^0 = 1$. Now multiply $5(1) = 5$.

Part 6: Electronics Information

1. c. Not grounding an electrical device runs the risk of electrocution.

2. d. The voltage across the meter will equal the sum of the voltages across the series resistors R_1 and R_2. Therefore: $V = (I \times R_1) + (I \times R_2) = (2 \text{ A} \times 10\ \Omega) + (2 \text{ A} \times 5\ \Omega) = 20 \text{ V} + 10 \text{ V} = 30 \text{ V}$.

3. d. A modem is a device that modulates an analog signal to encoded digital information, and demodulates a similar carrier signal to decode the transmitted information back into analog.

4. c. The prefix "k" means 1,000. Therefore, 25k would represent 25,000 Ω.

5. d. EHF frequencies are measured in gigahertz, GHz.

6. b. Most wires today are made of copper because it has high conductivity and is relatively inexpensive.

7. c. The three necessary elements of an electric circuit are a potential power source, resistance, and a closed path for current to flow.

8. c. The prefix kilo means 1,000. Therefore, 200 kilowatts is equal to 200,000 watts.

9. a. Dams are used to produce power from water.

10. d. Gold, being a metal, is a good conductor of electricity, not a good insulator.

11. c. 60 Hz is the frequency of the alternating voltage, which is the type of voltage used in the United States.

12. d. A rheostat is a type of resistor, which can adjust the current or vary the resistance in an electrical circuit.

13. b. The total current is equal to the sum of the currents through each resistor. Therefore, 4A + 4A + 4A = 12A

14. a. FM stands for frequency modulation.

15. b. Ground wires in the United States are bare wire, green wire, or yellow-green wire.

16. d. Electrical energy is measured in coulombs.

17. a. This is the symbol for a resistor. Choice **b** is an inductor, choice **c** is a capacitor, and choice **d** is an AC voltage source.

18. d. When the switch is open, no current flows. The voltage V_R is IR, which equals $0(5\ \Omega) = 0$.

19. c. This symbol in a schematic depicts a wire that does not join another.

20. c. An oscilloscope is an electronic test instrument that measures voltage and displays it on a screen for viewing.

Part 7: Auto and Shop Information

1. b. The image shows a set of Allen wrenches.

2. c. Condensation in a fuel line could cause a stalled vehicle by diluting the fuel to the point it will not ignite.

3. d. The braking system in an automobile uses friction to act on the turning tires, to first slow and then eventually stop them.

4. b. The fuel filter removes any impurities and foreign matter from the fuel prior to its being used in the engine.

5. a. A torque converter is made up of a turbine, pump, and stator. It is used in automobile automatic transmissions and converts rotating power from the engine to a rotating load.

6. d. Antifreeze is added to the automobile coolant system to keep the fluid used to cool the engine from freezing in cold weather and cracking the engine block.

7. c. Sanding wood with the grain gives you the best results.

8. c. Screws, with their thread, are designed to bite into the wood and hold tighter than any of the other choices.

9. d. Carbide is an exceptionally strong material and can be sharpened to a precise point to cut into glass.

10. c. The distributor routes voltage to the spark plugs, to provide a spark to ignite the fuel/air mix in an internal combustion engine.

11. a. A vise is used to hold a piece of wood or other material in a secure manner.

12. b. A machine screw is used in the assembly of metal parts.

13. b. A spark plug uses voltage routed by the distributor to generate a spark, which ignites the fuel in an internal combustion engine.

14. c. The purpose of an exhaust in a car is to dispose of burnt gases. The burned gases are ported into the ambient air to prevent them from building up inside the engine.

15. a. This is a C-clamp, which is placed around two boards and tightened by turning the screw with the handle.

16. b. Lubricant in a machine will do nothing to increase the reliability of the ignition process.

17. b. This gauge reading is 148 rpm.

18. b. The Ball Peen is a hammer, not a screwdriver.

19. b. The tool shown is a vise-grip.

20. c. A torque wrench tells you exactly how much pressure is put on a bolt while tightening it.

21. d. A crane is used to raise and lower large items that are typically too heavy or awkward to lift by hand.

22. b. A lathe is a tool that is typically used to carve long, slender pieces of wood such as a baseball bat. The wood is attached to the lathe, and an electric motor spins the piece of wood. A cutting blade is then used to remove parts of the wood, giving a decorative shape. A lathe would not be useful in making the other objects listed.

23. a. A countersink bit would drill out a small bit of the surface wood, allowing the head of a wood screw to fit flush with the surface of the wood.

24. d. The exhaust stroke is the last stroke of the four-stroke cycle.

25. c. The British Thermal Unit (BTU) is the universally recognized standard for heat and cooling units.

Part 8: Mechanical Comprehension

1. b. A chisel is like a wedge.

2. c. The doorknob acts like a wheel and axel in its rotating action.

3. d. The point upon which a lever acts is called the fulcrum.

4. c. The distance from the pivot point (fulcrum) to the point of application of the force (20 feet) is twice the distance from the pivot point to the box (10 feet). Therefore, in order to lift the box, the required force will be one half of the weight of the box, or 50 pounds.

5. b. The image shows a rack and pinion gear.

6. b. Foam and wood both float, but foam has a greater air retention and insulation value, making it a better candidate for use in a life preserver.

7. c. Gears C and D are the only ones that are turning clockwise.

8. a. If gear A rotates clockwise, gear D rotates clockwise.

9. c. A pump would force the water up the increased elevation and increase the flow of the water.

10. c. A bicycle sprocket is a classic example of a gear, which is defined as a toothed wheel or cylinder that meshes with a chain or with another toothed element to transfer energy or motion.

11. d. A playground seesaw pivots on a fulcrum, which is a necessary element for a lever.

12. d. A set of bearings is typically a set of small metal balls packed in a groove and lubricated with grease or oil. The wheel rubs against one side of each ball, and the axle rubs against the other side. The net effect is that the wheel rolls much more easily.

13. b. A siphon takes advantage of the difference in hydrostatic pressure between two locations separated by a height difference.

14. b. Torque is applied in the tightening of a bolt.

15. d. Kinetic energy is in an object that is in motion.

16. c. Pascal's law deals with hydrostatic pressure, and is the principle behind hydraulic systems and the incompressibility of fluids.

17. b. The image shown is a double pulley system.

18. c. A lever that has the fulcrum in the middles is a first-class lever, such as a seesaw.

19. d. A shim is a thin, wedged-shaped piece of material used to fill small gaps or spaces between objects.

20. a. A plumb bob is used to establish an exact vertical reference line, and uses gravity to achieve this result.

21. a. Valves C and D, when closed, prevent water from flowing into barrels #3 and #4, and water will flow into barrels #1 and #2.

22. a. In a system of pulleys, the smallest pulley will have to turn faster, as it has to make up for its smaller surface area when compared to the larger pulleys. Pulley A is the smallest pulley and therefore will turn the fastest.

23. b. The 50-lb weight at B creates a moment about the fulcrum of 350 feet-lbs (50 × 7 feet = 350 feet lbs). If the distance from the fulcrum to the lifting point is 10 feet, then only 35 lbs of force must be used to lift the block (350 feet-lbs ÷ 10 feet = 35 lbs).

24. c. An elevator uses a pulley system as it is raised up and lowered down.

25. c. A pump would be the only answer offered that would force water from one tank to another.

Part 9: Assembling Objects

1. c.
2. a.
3. b.
4. a.
5. d.
6. b.
7. b.
8. a.
9. a.
10. d.
11. d.
12. a.
13. c.
14. d.
15. b.
16. c.

Scoring

Write your raw score (the number you got right) for each test in the blanks below. Then turn to Chapter 3 to find out how to convert these raw scores into the scores the armed services use.

1. General Science: _____ right out of 25
2. Arithmetic Reasoning: _____ right out of 30
3. Word Knowledge: _____ right out of 35
4. Paragraph Comprehension: _____ right out of 15
5. Mathematics Knowledge: _____ right out of 25
6. Electronics Information: _____ right out of 20
7. Auto and Shop Information: _____ right out of 25
8. Mechanical Comprehension: _____ right out of 25
9. Assembling Objects: _____ right out of 16

ADDITIONAL ▶
ONLINE PRACTICE

Whether you need help building basic skills or preparing for an exam, visit the LearningExpress Practice Center! On this site, you can access additional practice materials. Using the code below, you'll be able to log in and take an additional full-length ASVAB practice exam. This online practice exam will also provide you with:

- **Immediate Scoring**
- **Detailed answer explanations**
- **Personalized recommendations for further practice and study**

Log on to the LearningExpress Practice Center by using the URL: **www.learnatest.com/practice**

This is your Access Code: **7410**

Follow the steps online to redeem your access code. After you've used your access code to register with the site, you will be prompted to create a username and password. For easy reference, record them here:

Username: _____ **Password:** _____

With your username and password, you can log in and answer these practice questions as many times as you like. If you have any questions or problems, please contact LearningExpress customer service at 1-800-295-9556 ext. 2, or e-mail us at **customerservice@learningexpressllc.com**

NOTES

NOTES

NOTES

NOTES

NOTES

NOTES

NOTES